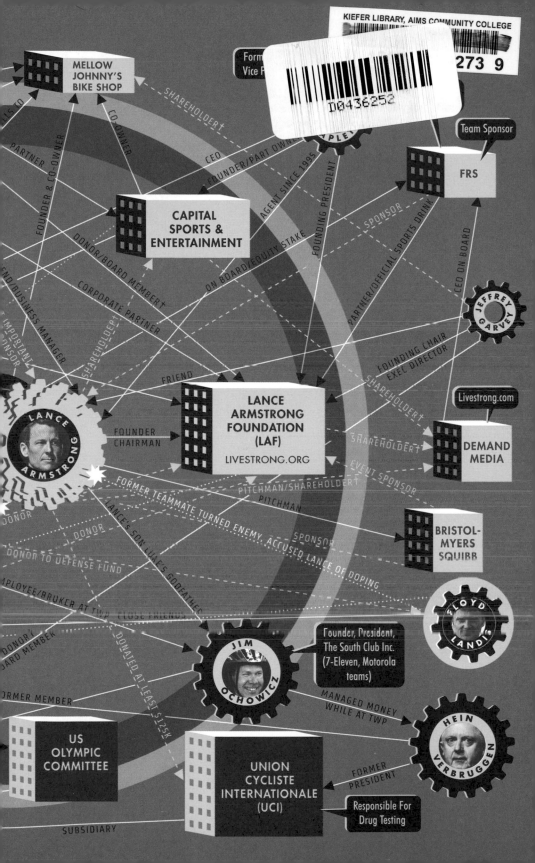

MELLOW JOHNNY'S BIKE SHOP

SHAREHOLDER†

CO-OWNER

PARTNER

FOUNDER & CO-OWNER

CEO

FOUNDER/PART OWNER

AGENT SINCE 1995

FOUNDING PRESIDENT

Form...
Vice P...

Team Sponsor

FRS

CAPITAL SPORTS & ENTERTAINMENT

DONOR/BOARD MEMBER†

ON BOARD/EQUITY STAKE

SPONSOR

PARTNER/OFFICIAL SPORTS DRINK

CEO ON BOARD

CORPORATE PARTNER

SHAREHOLDER†

FRIEND

FOUNDER CHAIRMAN

END/BUSINESS MANAGER

IMPORTANT SPONSOR

LANCE ARMSTRONG

LANCE ARMSTRONG FOUNDATION (LAF)

LIVESTRONG.ORG

JEFFREY GARVEY

FOUNDING CHAIR EXEC DIRECTOR

SHAREHOLDER†

Livestrong.com

DEMAND MEDIA

EVENT SPONSOR

PITCHMAN/SHAREHOLDER†

PITCHMAN

FORMER TEAMMATE TURNED ENEMY, ACCUSED LANCE OF DOPING

LANCE'S SON LUKE'S GODFATHER

DONOR

DONOR

DONOR TO DEFENSE FUND

SPONSOR

BRISTOL-MYERS SQUIBB

FLOYD LANDIS

...PLOYEE/BRUKER AT TWP

CLOSE FRIENDS

Founder, President, The South Club Inc. (7-Eleven, Motorola teams)

JIM OCHOWICZ

...NOR'S ...ARD MEMBER

DONATED AT LEAST $125K

...ORMER MEMBER

US OLYMPIC COMMITTEE

UNION CYCLISTE INTERNATIONALE (UCI)

MANAGED MONEY WHILE AT TWP

HEIN VERBRUGGEN

FORMER PRESIDENT

Responsible For Drug Testing

SUBSIDIARY

WHEELMEN

WHEELMEN

LANCE ARMSTRONG,
THE TOUR DE FRANCE, AND
THE GREATEST SPORTS CONSPIRACY EVER

REED ALBERGOTTI
AND VANESSA O'CONNELL

GOTHAM BOOKS

DUTTON
Published by the Penguin Group
Penguin Group (USA) LLC
375 Hudson Street
New York, New York 10014

USA | Canada | UK | Ireland | Australia | New Zealand | India | South Africa | China
penguin.com
A Penguin Random House Company

LIBRARY OF CONGRESS CATALOGING-IN-PUBLICATION DATA
has been applied for.

ISBN 978-1-592-40848-1

Printed in the United States of America
10   9   8   7   6   5   4   3   2   1

To Sascha, Kathy, Emmett, and Robby—R.A.
To Eric—V.O'C.

Starting in the 1860s, Americans grew enamored with the bicycle. Cyclists and racers began to refer to themselves as wheelmen. Bicycle racing later fell out of favor as Americans began to rally around stick and ball sports, and the automobile became king. But starting in the late 1970s, a new generation of wheelmen set out on a mission to restore American glory to the sport.

Nearly all men can stand adversity,
but if you want to test a man's character, give him power.

—ABRAHAM LINCOLN

CONTENTS

CAST OF CHARACTERS

USADA: United States Anti-Doping Agency—the government-funded non-profit based in Colorado Springs, Colorado, that oversees anti-doping efforts in Olympic sports in the United States.

UCI: Union Cycliste Internationale (or International Cycling Union)—the sport's governing body, in Aigle, Switzerland. It's set up to promote cycling as a sport but also responsible for the sport's anti-doping policy.

Betsy Andreu: Opinionated, feisty wife of Frankie Andreu and a stay-at-home mother to three kids in Dearborn, Michigan.

Frankie Andreu: Michigan-born Motorola cyclist with a lanky build and a cranky disposition. Andreu lived with Lance in Como, Italy, and became road captain on the US Postal team in 1999.

Kristin Richard Armstrong: Career-minded public-relations woman from a wealthy family; met Lance in 1997 in Austin, Texas, shortly after he finished his chemotherapy. After they married in 1998, she quit working to raise their son and twin daughters, living in the French Riviera and Girona, Spain. They divorced in 2003.

Terry Keith Armstrong: Lance's stepfather; Armstrong adopted Lance soon after marrying Linda Mooneyham in 1974.

Dr. Arnie Baker: Floyd Landis's cycling coach and supporter, and a retired San Diego physician.

Michael Ball: Former track cyclist and Los Angeles fashion mogul; founded, owned, and sponsored Rock Racing in 2007. Ball was targeted by FDA special agent Jeff Novitzky in his investigation into the use of performance-enhancing drugs in cycling.

Michael Barry: Lance's teammate from 2002 to 2005; had intimate knowledge of the doping era. Barry wrote a firsthand account of his career with Lance (*Inside the Postal Bus*) without mentioning the doping on the team.

William "Bill" Bock III: USADA's general counsel; a soft-spoken attorney born in Texas and raised in Indiana. Bock represented athletes for years and became the lead attorney for the US Anti-Doping Agency in 2007.

Edward "Eddie B" Borysewicz: Gruff cycling coach who emigrated from Poland to the United States, bringing Eastern Bloc tactics to America and coaching Greg LeMond and Lance Armstrong, among others. Borysewicz convinced eighteen-year-old Lance to join Subaru-Montgomery in 1990, giving Lance his first cycling contract.

Johan Bruyneel: Belgium-born former road racer who became the US Postal Service team boss and oversaw operations, with Lance's input, on Postal, Discovery Channel, Astana, and RadioShack-Nissan teams.

Chris Carmichael: Coach of the US junior national cycling team, who recruited Lance to the team in 1991 and eventually made a name for himself as Lance's cycling coach.

Edward Coyle: University of Texas researcher who studied Lance in a sports lab from 1992 to 1999. His findings that Lance had become a more efficient cyclist post-cancer, with a naturally higher VO_2 max than the average male, were widely reported by the media as fact. He admitted in 2008 to a "minor error" in his calculations.

Rick Crawford: One of Lance's first (unpaid) cycling coaches and a mentor; became a Dallas-based pro triathlete in 1985.

Sheryl Crow: Missouri-born musician and songwriter who began a relationship with Lance in 2003 and became engaged to him in 2005. They broke up before a planned wedding in 2006.

Mark Fabiani: Lance's crisis management consultant and media point man, hired in 2010; a slick-haired Harvard Law grad who became known as the

Master of Disaster when he served as special counsel to President Clinton during the Whitewater investigations in the early 1990s.

Dr. Michele Ferrari: An Italian sports doctor and mathematician; caused a scandal in a 1994 interview by saying erythropoietin (EPO) was no more dangerous than orange juice. Ferrari became Lance's personal trainer in 1995.

Jeffrey C. Garvey: Founding chairman of the Lance Armstrong Foundation and cofounder of Austin Ventures.

Mark Gorski: General manager of the US Postal Service team and one of the owners of Tailwind Sports, which owned and managed Postal. Gorski first achieved fame after winning gold in the 1984 Olympics in track cycling.

Edward "Eddie" Gunderson: Lance's free-spirited biological father, who divorced Linda in 1973, when Lance was two, after a turbulent and abusive relationship.

Tyler Hamilton: Lance's teammate on the US Postal Service team; won a gold medal at the 2004 Olympics but received suspensions and bans from cycling after testing positive for EPO. He admitted to doping before a grand jury in 2010.

Robert "Bob" Hamman: Founder of SCA Promotions, which insured Tailwind Sports against some of Lance's bonuses for winning the Tour de France.

Anna Hansen: Lance's girlfriend since 2008 and the mother of his two youngest children, Olivia Marie and Maxwell Edward.

Timothy Herman: Head of Lance's legal defense team, who started filing lawsuits on Lance's behalf in 2004.

George Hincapie: Lance's New York City–born *domestique* and teammate first on Motorola, then on the US Postal Service, and later on the Discovery Channel Pro Cycling Team. Relocated to Greenville, South Carolina.

Steve Johnson: President and CEO of USA Cycling; a former teammate of Lance's on Subaru-Montgomery and a friend of Thomas Weisel.

Linda Mooneyham Armstrong Kelly: Lance's mother, a New Orleans–born, Dallas-raised, high school dropout who gave birth to Lance at age seventeen.

Bart Knaggs: Lance's business manager and co-owner of Lance's bike store, Mellow Johnny's, and a partner at Capital Sports & Entertainment. Knaggs is also a former cyclist and Lance's friend and riding buddy in Austin.

John Korioth: Cofounder of the Lance Armstrong Foundation and best man at Lance's wedding to Kristin Richard Armstrong.

Floyd Landis: Winner of the 2006 Tour de France; later admitted to doping and was stripped of his title. A thin, ginger-haired pro cyclist; raised as a Mennonite; became Lance's friend and protégé when riding for the US Postal Service team from 2002 to 2004 but moved to the rival Phonak team in 2005.

Levi Leipheimer: Lance's teammate on the US Postal Service team from 2000 to 2001 who rode again with Lance on Astana and Team RadioShack following Lance's second cycling comeback.

Greg LeMond: First American winner of the Tour de France; won the Tour three times before retiring from pro racing in 1994.

Robert Luskin: A veteran white-collar defense lawyer and member of Lance's defense team; a key player in Lance's attack on USADA.

Stephanie McIlvain: Oakley's cycling representative and a longtime friend of Lance's.

John Thomas "J.T." Neal: Eccentric and caring mentor; friend and landlord to Lance in Austin, Texas, and his unpaid personal masseur; tended to Lance's affairs in the United States while Lance competed in Europe.

Jeff Novitzky: A special agent at the Food and Drug Administration; investigated doping in professional sports, including cycling; formerly worked as an IRS special agent.

Jim "Och" Ochowicz: Founder, general manager, and coach of two American teams: 7-Eleven, then Motorola, both managed by the South Club Inc.; godfather to Lance's firstborn child, Luke.

William "Bill" J. Stapleton III: Lance's agent and longtime confidant; a black-haired, broad-faced former Olympic swimmer.

Travis Tygart: Florida-born CEO of USADA, who was previously its director of legal affairs.

Christian Vande Velde: Teammate on Lance's 1999 and 2001 Tour de France teams; also worked with Michele Ferrari.

Jonathan Vaughters: US Postal Service teammate of Lance's who doped while riding with Lance; later became a team manager, most recently for the Garmin-Sharp team.

Hein Verbruggen: Dutchman who was president of the UCI from 1991 until 2005, then became UCI's "honorary president," remaining on its management committee.

David Walsh: Irish sports journalist who is chief sports writer of the British newspaper *The Sunday Times*.

Thomas W. Weisel: Creator of the Subaru-Montgomery team and founder of Tailwind Sports, which managed the Postal Service team; an übercompetitive alpha male with expensive homes in Ross, California, and Maui; headed the San Francisco investment firm Montgomery Securities for nearly two decades.

Paul Willerton: Illinois-born cyclist who rode with Lance as an amateur in the early 1990s during two world championship road races; turned pro in 1991 with Greg LeMond's Team Z.

David "Tiger" Williams: Part owner of Tailwind Sports and friend of Floyd Landis. Williams is an avid cycling enthusiast and founder of Williams Trading, LLC.

Dave Zabriskie: Teammate of Lance's on the US Postal Service team who looked up to team boss Johan Bruyneel.

WHEELMEN

INTRODUCTION

Not long ago, the world witnessed the dramatic downfall of one of America's most celebrated sports heroes: Lance Armstrong.

Millions of viewers were riveted by Lance's confessional interview with Oprah Winfrey in early 2013. Although what he said during that interview was by no means the whole truth, Lance did talk candidly to Oprah about certain subjects. For the first time, he publicly admitted to doping and using blood transfusions for his seven Tour de France victories. He also spoke touchingly about having to ask his thirteen-year-old son, Luke, the oldest of his five children, to stop defending him and telling people that what they were saying about his father wasn't true—because, unfortunately, it was.

But his confession raised more questions than it answered, in part because he failed to put any of it in context, to talk about who had helped him dope, where the drugs came from, and how he managed to cover up his activities for so long, despite the hundreds of drug tests he underwent and the vigorous investigations of journalists who did not believe any of his denials.

This book is an attempt to fill in the gaps he left and tell a much more complete, objective, and nuanced story. It isn't just about Armstrong as an individual, an athlete, or a cancer survivor. It's not solely about doping and cheating—or merely about sports. We view this as a business story—a story about a business that, at least in its participants' eyes, was too big to fail. We will take you behind the scenes, where you will meet many of the cyclists who rode for and against Armstrong, the bureaucrats and businessmen, the sponsors and lawyers who surrounded him during the course of his long career, and finally the investigators who brought him down.

From the clinics and laboratories of shadowy doctors in Spain to the vertiginous mountain roads of the Tour de France, from secret scenes of doping and blood transfusions in hotel rooms and team buses to extravagant victory celebrations at the Musée d'Orsay in Paris, from Armstrong's remarkable comeback from a near-fatal testicular cancer to his final fall from grace, what we have provided here is the first in-depth account of what went into the making—and unmaking—of an American icon. It is also a picture of a multinational conspiracy that yielded its many participants hundreds of millions of dollars over the course of a twenty-four-year sweep of time, as it played out in locations as diverse as Austin, Texas; Washington, DC; Greenwich, Connecticut; Idyllwild, California; Nice, France; St. Moritz, Switzerland; and Girona, Spain.

For most of the past century, Europeans had dominated the sport of cycling, and became its most avid fans. But in Europe cycling was very much a working-class sport. Professional cyclists came from small farm towns or poor urban areas, and their pay reflected it. As recently as the 1970s and 1980s, some of the greatest names in the sport, like Frenchman Bernard Hinault and Belgian Eddy Merckx, made money that would look laughable even to second-tier professionals by the mid-2000s.

For decades few Americans paid any attention to professional cycling at all. But once that began to change, it would be the Americans—the newcomers to the sport—who would change its economics forever, commanding the richest paychecks the sport had ever seen. Cycling's first million-dollar salary went, in 1991, to Greg LeMond, an American who won the Tour de France three times after moving to France at age nineteen. Next came Armstrong, riding on teams with big American sponsors—including the US Postal Service and corporations such as television's Discovery Channel—whose lavish funding helped drive his base pay to $4.5 million and his bonuses to $10 million by 2004. Armstrong's pay was only a tiny fraction of his overall income because of the hugely lucrative endorsement deals he signed, worth about $16.5 million that year alone.

Viewing Armstrong's rise and fall through the prism of business, we see him as both tool and beneficiary of the ambitions of a small group of Americans who wanted the United States to become a major player in what had been a mainly European sport. These men aimed not just to dominate the sport but to commercialize it and make it into a money machine. Armstrong was perfect for their goals—an extraordinary combination of athletic talent, drive, ambition, and ruthlessness. And once he began winning, he became the chairman and CEO of the business of making himself rich and famous. Aided by a vast, interconnected network of supporters, he kept tight control of his image, presenting himself through the media and through his sponsorships as an all-American hero—sports prodigy, cancer survivor who came back from near death to win his first Tour de France, founder of a multimillion-dollar charity that offered hope, help, and support to thousands of people suffering from cancer.

Yet Armstrong's public persona was very different from his private one. The great athlete turned cancer activist and secular saint had a dark side that very few people outside of his inner circle knew about. While he portrays himself as a poor underdog, he came from a reasonably comfortable middle-class home in Plano, Texas, and also was indulged and self-absorbed and arrogant from boyhood. Although Lance seemed to be always searching for a father figure, he struggled to maintain lasting relationships with many of his mentors. He surrounded himself with friends, girlfriends, and business partners, and needed and craved their attention, reassurances, and support. But he had a habit of exploiting those who cared about him.

This book arose from the more than one hundred interviews we conducted and the many articles we wrote in *The Wall Street Journal* about Lance and his take-no-prisoners war with former teammates, federal investigators, and anti-doping officials over accusations that he had doped to win the Tour de France. Our work for the *Journal* was focused on offering the first detailed accounts of the mechanics and culture of the US Postal Service team's doping program and, as such, it ended up playing a role in the events that culminated in his downfall.

The tipping point for Armstrong and his circle came in early 2010, when his former US Postal Service teammate and protégé Floyd Landis sent explosive e-mails to a small handful of men in the top ranks of professional cycling. In these e-mails, Landis admitted to using performance-enhancing drugs and blood transfusions during his years racing alongside Lance, and accused many of his former Postal teammates of taking part in doping as well. Describing Lance as the ringleader of these doping practices, Landis was saying what a few people in the press had suspected for years, but no one had been able to prove. For a month, Landis's e-mails remained a closely guarded secret. Federal agents who had learned of their contents and were looking into whether any crimes had been committed had instructed Landis not to go public with his allegations. Through a source close to US cycling officials, Reed—working with Vanessa—discovered the existence of the e-mails, was able to obtain them, verify their authenticity, and publish what turned out to be an exclusive international scoop, the first of many we had during the years we continued to cover the story.

To interview Landis, Reed spent two weeks in a remote town in Southern California where Landis was living far from the public eye, in a cabin with scenic views of a pine-forested mountainside—and a noticeable array of discarded junk littering the property. It took days for him to persuade Landis to tell his full story—and the cyclist did so despite pressure from many friends and former teammates who beseeched him to remain quiet. Several months later, in August 2010, we broke the news that Landis had filed a whistleblower lawsuit under the federal False Claims Act, alleging that Lance's team had defrauded the US Postal Service, which had spent more than $30 million to sponsor the team. During the course of our investigative work for the *Journal,* we were able to interview at length many of the major figures involved in the story as well as numerous minor ones. We came to know every key player, some of them quite well. But no one, of course, was as mesmerizing as Lance. Lance Armstrong agreed to speak to us several times during the course of our reporting on the investigations against him, although he only very rarely allowed us to quote him or even to attribute what he told us to an anonymous source. The first time came as a surprise. On an August afternoon in 2010, Vanessa had flown to Austin, Texas, to meet with Lance's lawyer, Tim

Herman, at Trio, the restaurant at the Four Seasons Hotel. A few minutes after their lunch began, Lance strolled in and, with his ex-wife seated at a table nearby, joined in a lengthy discussion.

Even though our conversations with him were always on his terms, and carefully designed to influence our opinion of him, they gave us more of an insight into him than he might have realized. As journalists, we found Lance to be an intriguing mixture of open and withholding, controlling and seemingly vulnerable. He reads extensively, including everything written about him, and he likes to get to know some of the writers who are reporting on him. He knows how to turn on the charm when he wants to, but when he's angry about something, he can go negative and rip into people with blistering personal attacks, as he did several times with us.

Thanks to these conversations, as well as interviews conducted with people ranging from his closest friends to his bitterest enemies, this book will allow you to see Lance up close—from his turbulent teenage years to his ascent to the top of his sport, his battle with cancer, and the depths of his disgrace. You will find out what motivated him to take extreme risks and to chase seemingly impossible goals; what fueled his persistent lying and bullying, his contempt for others, and his vendettas against those who spoke the truth.

While Lance Armstrong is its central character, you will also get to know Travis Tygart, a man we've come to see as the idealistic David to Lance's seemingly unconquerable Goliath. Tygart knew the drastically underfunded US Anti-Doping Agency lacked the resources and the subpoena power he would need to build an airtight case. But after federal prosecutors dropped their criminal investigation without bringing charges, Tygart felt he had no other choice than to carry the weight of challenging Lance. He went into battle armed with what might have seemed only a slingshot compared to Lance and his team of high-paid, high-powered lawyers and publicists, but in the end that slingshot proved very powerful. The story of how this all came to pass is what you will read in the following pages.

CHAPTER ONE

TRUE BLUE

At precisely 11:00 A.M. in Lannemezan, a quiet village in Southwest France, nine men in the dark-blue jerseys of the US Postal team—part of a pack of more than 150 cyclists on twenty-one teams—rolled out of town to begin a painful six-hour journey over seven Pyrenean passes. It was Saturday, July 17, 2004. The temperature was already 78 degrees at the start of stage 13 of the 21-day Tour de France.

The Tour de France's brutality is legend. The race lasts for 23 days, including 2 rest days, and is divided into seventeen road "stages," including the flat stages favored by sprinters, mountain stages for climbers, and medium-mountain stage, plus four "time trials" —individually timed races against the clock—beginning with the "prologue," which opens the Tour.

This would be the cruelest day of all. The course ahead stretched 127 miles, winding through the forested Midi-Pyrenees region, where wooded foothills give way to alpine pastures, then to a flat prelude through shaded farmlands, and finally to a series of ever-rising peaks: the gradual Col d'Aspin, the deceptive Col de Latrape, and, finally, the infamous climb to the Plateau de Beille.

Lance Armstrong began the day in second place, meaning that he was second in the so-called overall standings, computed by adding up the stage times thus far and subtracting any time bonuses that had been earned. He was 5 minutes and 24 seconds behind the melancholy Frenchman Thomas Voeckler. Five minutes are substantial by the standards of any normal race, but in the Tour de France, they could easily disappear. Armstrong's main rival, the German Jan Ullrich, the man who had the best chance of emerging from the mountains on his tail, trailed him by just 3 minutes and 36 seconds. Armstrong's aim, and the mission of his US Postal Service team, was to make the time gap between him and the rest of his pursuers insurmountably large.

After they hit the countryside, the Postal squad assumed its typical formation: eight riders forming a spear to pierce the wind, with Armstrong protected in the center. Every team in the Tour de France has a captain, the man who will finish first. While the captain pursues the yellow jersey, awarded to the rider with the lowest overall time, the rest of the team does cycling's grunt work: blocking the wind, putting pressure on rivals with clever tactical moves, even dropping back to the team car and picking up bottles of water for the leader. No team in cycling was more single-mindedly focused on its captain than the US Postal team. And no captain expected more loyalty and hard work from his support riders than Armstrong.

Armstrong's teammates kept him securely in the sweet spot of the pack: right near the front, behind his Postal Service spear, where there's no wind and minimal risk of a crash. Armstrong pedaled in their slipstreams, using the momentum of the group, which enabled him to use 30 to 60 percent less energy than if he were riding alone.

The pack, called a peloton, resembles a graceful amoeba—its perimeter changing shape as it floats down the road. Inside the amoeba, teams elbow each other, jab ribs, and collide wheels in constant combat for the best position. On the twenty-five-mile journey to the base of the day's first climb, the US Postal squad shot to the front of the peloton, accelerating even on the flat roads where riders typically conserve their energy. Driving the pace on the flats—a technique pioneered by the Postal team—neutralized other squads' tiny, elflike climbers, whose smaller size offered no advantage on these relatively flat stretches.

The maneuver came at the direction of team director Johan Bruyneel, a handsome, dark-haired Belgian who trailed the riders in a team car. Watching the broadcast of the race on a television installed on his dashboard, Bruyneel carefully orchestrated every acceleration, attack, or chase. Once the race neared the mountains, Armstrong would rely on the grunts, his four most trusted Postal teammates: José Azevedo, George Hincapie, Floyd Landis, and José Luis Rubiera.

Just forty miles into the stage, the peloton reached the first significant climb—a long, gentle ascent up the eleven-mile Col de Portet d'Aspet. Here, in the climbs, the team faced its most challenging work. Armstrong was big for a cyclist. At 160 pounds, he was about 20 percent heavier than the average climber, weight that had to be carried over the decisive mountain stages.

But the Blue Train, as they were known, proceeded as fast uphill as they had on the flats. Rivals began falling off the back of the pack like loose debris. Dutch, Belgians, Danes, Russians—they were heroes back home, national champions, endurance machines in the 99th percentile of the human race. Yet today they looked like amateurs. Armstrong had shaved Voeckler's lead to less than 4 minutes by the end of the first climb.

It was getting hotter, and empty water bottles shot out of the peloton like popcorn. A bottle an hour for every rider equals about three hundred on the side of the road—free souvenirs for fans. Basque rider Iban Mayo, a top Tour contender, succumbed to the heat and tension on the next climb, the relatively easy four-mile Col de Latrape. Mayo, suffering a deep burning sensation in his legs, simply got off his bike. Orange-clad Basque fans pleaded with him to continue. Slowly, he remounted his bike, his teammates joining onlookers in pushing him up the climb.

At the front of the pack, meanwhile, Armstrong barely seemed to be exerting himself. And he moved at a breathtaking pace. The Postal team hit the climb at roughly twenty miles per hour, a speed cycling teams had never attained in these conditions. The Americans chalked it up to technology and fitness—but the French, and other squads, had their suspicions. So did some members of the press.

On the slopes of the Col d'Agnes, 90 miles into the 127-mile stage, Postal led a pack that had now dwindled to about forty riders. Voeckler couldn't keep up, and Armstrong now trailed him by only 44 seconds in overall time. Sensing the narrowing lead, Voeckler shot down the other side with reckless disregard for the off-camber, hairpin turns, and choppy pavement. Fans winced as he came within inches of launching himself off a thirty-foot cliff. By the start of the final climb, he had regained his advantage over Armstrong: 5 minutes, 24 seconds.

At the base of Plateau de Beille, a ten-mile climb so steep that most people can hardly walk it, Postal took the lead. By then only about thirty or so riders had managed to hang with them. While the others were visibly suffering, the Postal riders looked positively comfortable.

George Hincapie raced to the front of the pack. The lanky, almost simian rider, who grew up racing in New York City, had been Armstrong's most trusted lieutenant through five Tour victories. The two men lived and trained together in Spain, and Armstrong described Hincapie as his best buddy. He executed a technique that was his specialty—the "lead-out"—in which, on the first gentle slopes before the climb, he would accelerate with Armstrong on his tail. Armstrong could rest comfortably in the soft air created by Hincapie's larger silhouette as they tore through the summer heat. Every rider wanted to be at the front at that moment, but Hincapie was the best. He stretched what was left of the peloton like a piece of gum, then peeled off, exhausted, as the real climb began.

As the hill pushed to a 6 percent grade—on its way to an eventual 8 percent—Armstrong had only three teammates still supporting him. The others had dropped out. But Ullrich, the square-jawed German who'd won the Tour in 1997, clung to the wheels of the survivors. The year before, Ullrich had been Armstrong's toughest competitor, his tormentor in the mountains.

As the riders slowed and began to pant in the heat, the Postal team's rising star, Floyd Landis, pushed to the front to do the critical work of keeping pace for Armstrong so that Armstrong would get a smooth ride. Tall for a cyclist but rail thin, Landis was a latecomer to the sport. He had joined the team in 2002 and risen to become Postal's second-best. Landis, who had started out as a mountain biker before switching to road racing, had a cardiovascular capacity that was extremely rare—even more favorable than Armstrong's, according to calculations by team doctors. As he shepherded his team leader up the climb, Landis felt the attention of the cameras, the television commentators touting his talents. Other teams were courting him, and his performance proved he could be a potential rival to Armstrong. Armstrong counted on Landis's extraordinary strength to support him in the mountain stages. But Landis was not supposed to have ambitions of his own.

Slowly, the riders passed one after another of the red-and-white inflatable banners marking the distance to the finish line. With each checkpoint, Armstrong gained ground. Two seconds here, three there. The fans at the top of Plateau de Beille, some of whom had hiked for hours to get a good spot, cheered madly. Some ran alongside the riders, screaming encouragement or, occasionally, epithets. Cries of "doper, doper" could be heard directed at Armstrong from French fans who suspected his performance was drug-fueled. In cycling, whether the fans love you or hate you, the cheers and jeers mostly blend into one savage din—punctuated by cowbells and the occasional air horn.

Landis, exhausted from knifing through the wind, finally pulled off and gave the lead to his Postal teammate José Luis Rubiera, known as Chechu. The Spanish climber screamed up the switchback turns, clearing the way for Armstrong through crowds waving colorful national flags. *"Allez, allez!"* "Go, go!" the fans screamed.

With 6.2 miles still left in the 9.9-mile climb, Ullrich had already lost 40 seconds. Voeckler had lost 1 minute and 41 seconds. The riders passed the 3-mile mark, then the 1-mile mark. Armstrong was alone, far out in front of almost everyone, Ullrich a mere memory at more than 6 minutes behind. The Tour de France was as good as won.

Only one obstacle remained, and Armstrong, ever the assassin, charged after him. The Italian Ivan Basso was already so far down in the standings that he was merely hoping for a strong finish. Armstrong and Basso reached the summit together, and the roads began to flatten out. With less than one mile to go, Armstrong leaned his bike over at frightening angles around every turn. He knew he had gained so much time that he could not lose the Tour de France now, but still he stuck to Basso's wheel. He looked angry, grimacing and pushing the pace. He wanted every second. He wanted not just to beat but to crush his competition.

With 164 yards to go, Armstrong blew past Basso and sprinted across the finish line, raising his arms in the air triumphantly. He was now more than 6 minutes ahead of his closest competition. With a week to go, and only two more mountain stages ahead, it seemed inevitable that—barring some unforeseen disaster—he would win his sixth Tour.

While his teammates boarded a bus, destined for traffic jams down the mountain, Armstrong boarded a helicopter with girlfriend Sheryl Crow. He may well have been, at that moment, the most thoroughly envied man in the world. His performance that day wasn't just miraculous and beautiful—it was a seminal moment in the Armstrong legend. He had stared down cancer. He had a beautiful, famous girlfriend. And now he had once again beaten the Europeans at their own game.

By that point in the 21-day race, Armstrong didn't need to win another stage in order to win the Tour de France. He could have coasted to Paris without breaking a sweat and still sipped champagne on the Champs-Élysées, wearing the victor's yellow jersey. But Lance did not want to simply win the race. He wanted to be sure no other cyclist would dare to dream he had a chance of prevailing.

Over the next several days, Armstrong continued advancing his lead, widening the time gap between himself and his competitors. He won again on the mountain stage from Valréas to Villard-de-Lans. He won the individual time trial—a race against the clock—from the bottom of Alpe d'Huez all the way up the sickeningly steep 9.6 miles of switchbacks. He won the stage from Le Bourg-d'Oisans to Le Grand-Bornand, and he won another time trial—a 34.2-mile flat course around Besançon.

By July 25, the final day of the race, Armstrong was still 6 minutes and 19 seconds ahead of his competition. The peloton took off from the suburban French city of Montereau-Fault-Yonne. The course meandered 101.3 miles to Paris. The ride was largely ceremonial for Armstrong. Someone in the US Postal team car cracked open a bottle of champagne, poured it into a flute, and passed it to Armstrong, who stood out in the bright yellow jersey. In front of cameramen on motorcycles, he toasted his own victory, then put down the glass and rode his bike with no hands on the bars, holding up six fingers, one for each of his six Tour de France victories.

Six years later, Floyd Landis was ten pounds heavier. On the verge of confessing what no American cyclist had ever admitted before, he looked as if he hadn't shaved for a week. A thin, reddish-brown beard sprouted on his pale skin. His eyes were slightly red from lack of sleep, and he wore blue jeans and an old white T-shirt. So much had happened since that day in the 2004 Tour, when the entire world watched him give his all as he shepherded Armstrong over those mountain passes. In those six years, Landis had become a hero, a martyr, a villain—and now he was a broken man. And he was about to tell secrets he knew would tear the sport apart.

He was sitting in a conference room at the Marriott Hotel in Marina del Rey, California, reliving the 2004 race. But the other men in the room had no interest in his heroics on the road. One of the men was a federal agent named Jeff Novitzky—a tall, bald-headed criminal investigator for the Food and Drug Administration. Another was Travis Tygart, the chief executive officer of the US Anti-Doping Agency (USADA), a nonprofit group in charge of policing doping in sport.

What had begun as a cathartic truth-telling exercise for Landis had morphed into a full-blown federal investigation with Landis as the chief witness for the government. The conversation wasn't recorded, but Novitzky and Tygart took careful notes. For the first time in the history of professional bike racing, one of the sport's biggest stars—a true firsthand witness to cycling's most heavily guarded secrets—was going to tell the truth about doping.

Describing the events of that 2004 Tour, Landis told Novitzky and Tygart that one night, after the conclusion of one of the stages—just a few days after Armstrong had climbed into the helicopter with Sheryl Crow—the entire US Postal team, including Armstrong, had been on the team bus, driving along largely deserted mountain roads to a hotel near the start of the following day's stage, when suddenly, the bus came to an abrupt stop. The driver, an old Belgian man, had gotten out carrying orange traffic cones, as if to indicate that there was a mechanical problem. *Great, just what we need. Our legs are aching, our bodies are wasting away, and now we have to sit in a bus on the side of the road and wait for the French equivalent of AAA,* Landis had thought to himself.

But soon everyone on board realized what was happening. The bus was being transformed into a secret blood transfusion unit. As had happened before, someone—sometimes a motorcycle driver who had been hired to do it, sometimes the team chef, sometimes a security worker—had delivered the blood immediately prior to the transfusions. Engine trouble was just a ruse designed to outsmart the journalists and the French police who suspected the Postal team of doping.

As the bus driver pretended to work on the engine, the team doctors began handing out blood bags with code names the riders had chosen for themselves. Some riders used the names of their pets; others used nicknames. Landis used his real name. He was too afraid of accidentally infusing a teammate's blood—a mistake that could end in death—to take the risk.

Landis described to the two investigators what sounded like a well-choreographed, ultrasecret M.A.S.H. unit. As the operation got under way, all the riders, including Armstrong, lay down on the floor of the bus, faceup, while the team doctors, who always rode on the bus, hung the chilled transfusion bags from overhead luggage racks so that gravity could help the blood ease its way into their veins.

The cyclists were gaunt, their faces sunken, the fat burned away by the exertions of the race. Their veins and capillaries had pushed up to the surface of the skin, rising in sinewy, bulging mazes on their arms and legs—the human body's attempt to supercharge itself by maximizing blood flow. Every day during the Tour, the riders burned up red blood cells like kindling, drastically depleting their ability to bring oxygen to their muscles. The extreme physical demands of the race meant they were wasting away from the inside out. The blood transfusions were to counteract those effects. Boosting the number of red blood cells in the cyclists' bodies was like injecting fuel into a car cylinder.

Landis described watching as Armstrong's bag slowly emptied. Normally, he said, Armstrong would squeeze the bag to the last drop, making sure that every possible red blood cell had flowed down the plastic tube and into his veins. This time, though, Armstrong had pulled the needle out of his arm without bothering to squeeze the bag. Landis said he thought it was because Armstrong was in a hurry, or maybe he just didn't care because he was so far ahead in the race by then.

Landis also explained that, during his US Postal years, blood transfusions had come back in vogue in cycling, because they were less easily detected than performance-enhancing drugs—though the practice was banned from the sport and considered as illegitimate as taking those drugs. The US Postal team usually conducted two blood transfusions during the Tour de France—one for each week and a half of racing, he said. Because the US Postal team was under such intense scrutiny at that time, however, trying to arrange for two blood transfusions in a 21-day period was like trying to get away with two bank heists. What made the challenge even more difficult was the fact that blood stays fresh for only three weeks. As soon as it's removed from the body, the red blood cells begin to wither and age and eventually explode. And while it might seem like a good idea to remove blood immediately before the Tour de France to ensure its freshness, that would be a strategic mistake, as it would weaken the body just when it needed to be at its strongest.

So in order for every rider to have two fresh blood bags ready by July, which was when the Tour de France took place, the team had to undergo a secret and complicated process that involved months of advance planning. The first blood draws were done in the spring or early summer. The plastic transfusion bags were stored in refrigerators kept at 1 degree Celsius to preserve the blood as much as possible without freezing it. Then every few weeks during the months leading up to the Tour de France, doctors would draw more fresh blood out of the riders' bodies and re-infuse the old blood into them. The constant swapping ensured the refrigerated blood was always fresh and the red blood cells in the riders' bodies were not depleted by the stress, and the training stayed steady.

Shortly before the beginning of the 2004 Tour, the US Postal team had the bags of blood smuggled into France in an unmarked camper. Then the bags were transported by motorcycles with refrigerated panniers. One of the most trusted motorcycle drivers was Philippe Maire, who later opened a Trek bike dealership in the south of France.

This kind of top secret operation had become something of the norm for the US Postal team, beginning around 2001, by which time Armstrong was well on his way to superstar status. Working out the logistics fell to team chef Geert "Duffy" Duffeleer. Duffy was a good cook—the riders swore by his spaghetti Bolognese—but he also had a dark streak. According to Landis, he was involved in the black market bike trade, along with team mechanic Julien de Vriese. Duffeleer and de Vriese unloaded US Postal bikes, bikes that were supposed to be used by the riders on the team. Instead, they ended up being sold to shops in Belgium. The off-the-books cash helped fund the team's purchases of illicit performance-enhancing drugs.

During the 2004 Tour de France, Landis noticed that Duffy had been intensely paranoid. About a week or so before the bus transfusion, during the race's first rest day, on July 12, Duffy had shown up at the hotel where the team would be staying, to check it out in advance of the arrival of the riders, and he'd gotten a scare when he thought he discovered police reconnaissance equipment in the rooms. Concerned about the possibility of detection, Duffy met the team bus when it arrived at the hotel parking lot, preventing the riders from getting off until he and Bruyneel could discuss what to do. The two men walked out into a nearby field, presumably to avoid any recording equipment that might have been planted by the police, but they remained in full view of the riders on the bus. Though Landis couldn't hear what they said, he could tell Bruyneel and Duffy were worried about something, and he figured it had to do with doping.

Duffy and Bruyneel eventually decided it was okay for the team to enter the hotel that day. Later that evening, the riders were summoned to a hotel room. Every opening in the room had been taped shut to evade any kind of video surveillance, and the riders were told not to speak in case the room had been bugged with audio equipment. All of the riders then got blood transfusions, while security guards stood outside in the hall. Afterward, Bruyneel cut the plastic transfusion bags into tiny shards and flushed them down the toilet. For the second mass blood transfusion of the Tour, a week later, however, it was decided that doing it in the hotel again was too risky, which was why it was done on the bus.

As Landis told his story in the Marriott conference room that day, there was absolute silence. Other than Landis's voice, all that could be heard was the sound of scribbling pens. Novitzky had spent years investigating drug use in Major League Baseball and the National Football League. Tygart had devoted a decade of his life to fighting drug use in sports. The two men thought they had heard everything by that stage of their careers, but this was the most vivid picture ever painted of the secret world of professional sports. They stayed in the room for six hours, pushing for details, for context, and the next morning they met with Landis for another two hours.

By the end of the two interview sessions, Tygart and Novitzky felt they understood just about everything about how doping worked on the US Postal team, and how the riders had gotten away with it. They wanted to believe

Landis, and they knew they had the makings of a good case. But they couldn't rely entirely on Landis's story, because he would be a terribly flawed witness. After all, in the six years since the 2004 Tour de France, Landis had publicly denied doping after failing a drug test, had written a book professing his innocence, and had taken donations from fans who believed he was innocent. In coming clean with Novitzky and Tygart, Landis was completely changing his story.

The investigators also had to wonder about Landis's motivations. Why was he coming clean now? What was in it for him? It was clear that Landis's life was in tatters. After the positive test, he had broken up with his wife and moved to a small cabin in Idyllwild, a remote town in the mountains of Southern California full of hippies, gun-toting survivalists, and people living on the fringes of society. There were reports in the press that Landis had taken to heavy drinking. Perhaps most important, his relationship with Armstrong had ended in a bitter feud that was well documented. Because of Landis's shaky background, Novitzky and Tygart knew that every fact, every detail, every allegation he'd made would have to be corroborated by other sources.

But would anyone else talk?

CHAPTER TWO

A NEW BEGINNING FOR AMERICAN CYCLING

The slender, handsome thirty-eight-year-old Polish man had an athlete's chiseled face and a mustache. He spoke no English and had no clear idea what he was doing in America. He knew only one thing. He was as far away as he could get from his wife, who he believed had been cheating on him during her many business trips out of Poland. He had also left behind his career, and his teenage daughter, with no idea of when he would be able to see her again.

Eddie Borysewicz wasn't so much heartbroken as he was angry that he had allowed his marriage to fall apart. It overshadowed everything he accomplished, and he now looked at his life through the grim tint of failure. He was ready to start his life over, but he did not know how he would reinvent himself. He had originally flown to New York in the summer of 1976 with the intention of attending the Olympics in Montreal, but he never made it to Canada. Now all he knew was that he needed to become someone else.

Borysewicz's life in Poland had revolved around cycling. He joined the Polish national team as a teenager, won national championships, and traveled around Europe competing in bike races. As he moved up through the ranks of cycling in the late 1950s and early 1960s, he thought maybe the life of a professional athlete wasn't so bad. Poland was then a hotbed of cycling, and the sport was fully supported by the Soviet-dominated Communist government. He hoped to make the Polish Olympic team.

His dreams of Olympic glory fell through when he was twenty-one. During a routine chest X-ray, a doctor found a small lesion, and diagnosed tuberculosis. Borysewicz was hospitalized for treatment. When follow-up X-rays showed no sign of improvement, they tripled the dose of his drugs. This went on for weeks before a doctor finally realized that the mark on his chest was simply old scar tissue, and not tuberculosis. When he returned to cycling, he felt weak and was never able to regain his full strength. He had hoped to one day be a world champion; he resigned himself to the fact that he would never achieve that goal.

Borysewicz had a sense of curiosity. He had always been a good student, though he had delayed university education to become a cyclist. Soon after his misdiagnosis, he enrolled in the Academy of Physical Education in Warsaw to study physiology and exercise science, an extremely prestigious field in Communist Poland. He continued to race on the Polish national cycling team, but focused more on his studies. Other riders called him professor. At the university, he took a position coaching the junior national team.

He came up with individual training plans for the cyclists and he kept detailed diaries of their performance and fitness levels and the progress they made in response to his training regimens. He was conducting what was essentially a scientific experiment on some of the finest athletes in Poland to learn the best methods of training. Some of the riders were conducting their own experiments—with drugs. They told him about the various types of amphetamines and hormones they took to be able to compete at a higher level, yet they would always downplay their importance. "Oh, it's just a vitamin," they would say, or "Oh, it's something for my heartburn." Eddie would take mental notes of the names of the drugs and then look them up in an old medical book. He discovered that many of them had dangerous side effects. Sometimes, if the rider was someone he particularly liked, he would show him the book and make him read about the terrible damage the drugs could do.

Soon Borysewicz was one of the top athletic coaches in Poland, in charge of developing young talent to feed the Olympic ranks. But as an employee of the state, he didn't earn much. To bring in some spending money for his family, he also worked as a tour guide. Life was good enough, but after he learned about his wife's affair, he decided he had to leave. The Polish government gave him permission to attend the 1976 Montreal Summer Olympics as a spectator. He flew into JFK and had planned to drive to Montreal. He never did.

As it happened, he arrived in the United States at a moment when recreational cycling clubs—organizations like the Wolverine Sports Club in Royal Oak, Michigan; the Lehigh Wheelmen Association in Trexlertown, Pennsylvania; the Quad Cities Bicycle Club in Davenport, Iowa—were proliferating. Amateur races were popping up everywhere, from the Midwest to California to the eastern seaboard. However, as popular as the sport had become at the amateur level—registrations with the Amateur Bicycle League of America reached 8,621 in 1973, for example, a 70 percent increase from the year before—there was no professional racing scene in the United States. There were no professional cycling teams, no pro races on the calendar, and fewer than a dozen pro cyclists.

While in New York, Borysewicz looked up a former Polish teammate of his who was living in New Jersey. He stayed at his home, earning money doing odd jobs with a Polish work crew, mostly painting bridges and water towers. After Borysewicz had been in the United States for about six months, he stopped by a bike shop in Ridgefield Park, New Jersey.

Unbeknownst to him, the shop was owned by Mike Fraysse, one of the top officials in the United States Cycling Federation. Fraysse had managed the 1976 Olympic cycling events in Montreal, and when he saw Borysewicz standing in his shop, he knew he recognized him from somewhere, though at first he could not place him. Then he remembered: When he had once traveled to Warsaw with a group of American riders to attend a bike race, he'd seen Borysewicz coaching athletes. Now, identifying himself as a fan, he asked Borysewicz—in French, once he realized Borysewicz spoke no English—what he was doing in the United States and what had happened to his cycling career. Borysewicz gave a bit of his story, adding that he didn't even own a bike anymore. In fact, he hadn't yet earned enough money on the odd jobs he was doing to be able to afford one.

Fraysse got excited. "Wait here," he said, and disappeared into his shop's basement. A few minutes later he emerged carrying a lime green, Italian-made

Legnano bicycle with beautiful steel Campagnolo components. "Take this," Fraysse said, and then insisted that Borysewicz join him that weekend for the North Jersey Bicycle Club's weekly Sunday ride.

Borysewicz said he'd love to, but he warned Fraysse that he was out of shape and wouldn't be able to keep up if the pace was too fast. And if Borysewicz got left behind, he'd have no idea where he was or how to get home. He needn't have worried.

The following Sunday, Borysewicz, on his new bike, joined the large crowd of cyclists who had gathered at Fraysse's bike shop. Fraysse and a few of his friends rode at the front of the pack, holding a steady and manageable warm-up pace. As the pack moved down the road, more riders, some from other clubs, joined, until there were about one hundred in all. Their bikes were handcrafted works of art, welded together by specialty bike builders all over the world. The men had shaved legs and wore special shoes with leather soles that gripped the small spikes on their pedals. Their feet were strapped as tightly as possible to the pedals so that they had complete control of the bike and were able to pull up on the pedals for more power. These were serious cyclists, and the ride was competitive—a chance for them to test their mettle against other fanatics from around the region.

Initially, the pack was loud with chatter as cycling buddies caught up on what had happened since their last meet. The din of "How are the kids, how's the wife, how do you like the new car, did you get the job" could be heard as the pack coasted along at about twenty miles per hour. This went on for about half an hour or so, until Fraysse and some pals started to pick up the pace. Soon, the pack was moving at close to thirty miles per hour.

Within an hour, the group of one hundred had dwindled to about twenty-five. Fraysse and his friends were still driving the pace. Borysewicz was still there, too, hanging with the lead group. As the pack went up a long hill just north of Nyack, New York, a steep, grinding climb, most of the remaining cyclists finally dropped off. Now it was just Fraysse, a couple of his friends, and Borysewicz. They had annihilated half the cyclist population in the tristate area. They circled Rockland Lake, taking in the scenery, and then rode back to New Jersey, stopping at a small Italian coffee shop in Fort Lee. As they sipped espressos, Fraysse congratulated Borysewicz on his ability to keep up.

When Borysewicz told him he hadn't ridden a bike in more than two years, everyone at the table was stunned. How was that possible? Borysewicz explained in French, using Fraysse as a translator, that his ability to keep up had nothing to do with his fitness level and everything to do with technique. He knew how to pedal to conserve energy, exactly when to accelerate and when to slow down. "It's about efficiency," he told them.

The truth was that Borysewicz thought these Americans were clueless about bike racing. These macho guys could beat a crowd of New Yorkers, but none of them would be able to keep up in a top-level European race. The problem was, there was nobody in the United States to teach them. He figured it was up to him.

By late 1977, he was schooling the best cyclists in the tri-state area. Before Borysewicz, most of the cyclists in the area rode hard all summer and then got completely out of shape as the weather got cold. Borysewicz explained to them that winter was the best time to lift weights and build up the muscles needed for bike racing. Weight training was anathema. They thought if their muscles got too big, it would weigh them down and make their bodies inflexible. Cycling was about endurance, not strength.

To prove his point, Borysewicz showed Fraysse and some of the other riders the training diaries of some of the top cyclists in Poland, including Ryszard Szurkowski, who had just won the world championship in the road race and the time trial. This would have been the equivalent of opening Lance Armstrong's training diary and showing his secret workout plans—had there been a cyclist of that caliber in the States at the time, which of course there was not. Szurkowski's winter training plan included dozens of weight-lifting sessions and running. The Americans thought it looked more like the training plan for a decathlete than a cyclist. But, convinced by then that Borysewicz knew what he was talking about, they began meeting up with him at a new, state-of-the art gym in Fort Lee, New Jersey. Borysewicz developed individual training plans for the riders, demonstrated weight-training techniques to them, and told them to keep diaries. The regimen worked. Many members of the North Jersey Bicycle Club who trained with Borysewicz had better results in 1977 than they had ever before achieved.

Fraysse thought that if Borysewicz could have such great results with the

North Jersey Bicycle Club in such a short period of time, he might be able to boost the performance of the country's Olympic cyclists, too. Fraysse and Borysewicz came up with an idea: They'd put together a junior training camp for Olympic hopefuls in Squaw Valley, California, which had hosted the 1960 Winter Olympics and whose Olympic training facilities were free for use in the summer months. The camp was advertised largely through word of mouth, at bike shops and cycling clubs.

When Borysewicz showed up in Squaw Valley, he saw very few riders he thought were special. But there was one fourteen-year-old who had been driven up to the camp by his father from his hometown of Reno, about an hour away. The kid was much younger than the others, many of whom had been training for years. His face was plump with extra teenage fat, and his blond hair flowed in the wind. But when he rode, he flew. His bike-handling skills were superb for a novice. His name was Greg LeMond.

LeMond's engine was powerful, but what impressed Borysewicz most was LeMond's face. While he climbed the hills around Lake Tahoe, he grimaced in so much pain that the corners of his mouth nearly reached his ears. Borysewicz knew that a willingness to suffer like that couldn't be taught. It was almost a sickness. A form of masochism. The best bike racers, he knew, usually had deep inner demons that they were running away from. Bike racing was like chemotherapy of the soul, burning and cauterizing the bad thoughts.

LeMond had demons powerful enough for ten cyclists. Since he was eleven or so, he had been molested by a family friend—a pal of his father's, who was seventeen years older than Greg. The abuse had gone on for years. But Greg was so ashamed that he hadn't told anyone. His way of dealing with it was to ride the winding roads that lead to the ski resorts in Lake Tahoe. He would go all out on these rides, rocking back and forth on the bike, pushing against gravity. He'd hit 5,000 feet and the air would get thin. He'd feel lightheaded. He'd breathe hard. So hard he couldn't think anymore—couldn't feel anything. And LeMond liked it that way. He was happiest when he was suffering, when he was in total pain. On the way down, he never hit the brakes. He tasted death at every turn. He was drugging himself with endorphins and adrenaline.

Borysewicz took on LeMond as a special project, keeping in contact after the summer, sending him training plans and updating them as he learned more about LeMond's unique physiology. He acted as another father for LeMond, who desperately needed male role models in his life.

Having seen what Borysewicz could do, Fraysse also wanted to make him the head coach of the US national team. After a few rounds of interviews and approval from cycling's leadership, Eddie got the job in 1978 and was back to doing the work that he loved, full-time. No more painting bridges and water towers to pay the bills. His salary, and the budget of the entire US Olympic Committee, came mostly from corporate sponsorships. Unlike other countries, there was no government funding. The Ted Stevens Olympic and Amateur Sports Act, passed the same year Borysewicz got the job, gave the US Olympic Committee and its member organizations, like the US Cycling Federation, a monopoly on Olympic sports, allowing them to more effectively raise money for the games. The act also specified that only amateur athletes could compete.

As head coach, he spent much of his time in Colorado Springs, headquarters of the US Cycling Federation, where he conducted training camps. He would invite hundreds of young riders to each training camp and put them through the paces to screen them, asking only the top ten or so riders to return for further training. Over time, as he kept refining his choices, narrowing them down to an ever more accomplished group, he assembled a good pool of solid, talented riders.

At each training camp, Borysewicz explained to the young cyclists the core principles of training: The body's fitness level, he said, is constantly peaking and recovering. With periods of intense exercise, the body responds to the stress by increasing its blood volume, lowering its resting heart rate, and priming its cells for a more intense workload. But a body can remain at this peak level only for roughly two or three weeks before it begins to slow down so that it can rebuild itself and recover. The key to training for races, he explained, is to schedule the training so that the rider is peaking at race time.

Borysewicz taught the cyclists about good technique, too, telling them they needed to learn how to ride with smooth, evenly powered pedal strokes. Too often, he said, American riders tended to put all their energy into pressing down on the pedals while neglecting the upstroke. That was what the straps were there for, he explained, so that riders could pull up on the pedals as powerfully as they mashed down on them. Borysewicz adjusted the riders' bikes, taught them proper positioning, and described how to use their abdominal muscles to keep themselves steady on the bike and their hands light on the handlebars. He also taught them about diet. Americans were fat, he said.

It wasn't long before the young American riders learned to trust Borysewicz, despite his broken English and unusual behavior, such as his habit of analyzing every measurable angle of a rider's body, and each component on the bicycle. Unable to properly pronounce Eddie's last name—Bor-eeee-saaayvitz—riders began calling him Eddie B. The nickname stuck so well that new riders had no idea what Eddie B's last name actually was.

Much of what Borysewicz taught the riders was common knowledge in Europe, but in the United States it was revolutionary—and the effects started to be seen. In 1979, when LeMond was eighteen, Borysewicz took him to Argentina for the junior world championships, a race held to determine the best rider in the world under the age of nineteen. Competitors for the title ride on national teams, just as they do in the Olympics. LeMond won the race convincingly, beating the best riders from Russia and from the cycling meccas of Belgium and France. This was arguably the best international racing result any modern American cyclist had ever achieved. LeMond's victory meant he was going to be one of the favorites to win a gold medal in the Moscow Summer Olympics the following year.

But LeMond's gold medal chances were extinguished before he ever got a chance to try. In January 1980, President Jimmy Carter decided to boycott the Moscow games because of the Soviet invasion of Afghanistan. Borysewicz was heartbroken. Everything he had been doing for two years had been aimed at competing in the 1980 Summer Olympics, and with Greg LeMond on the team, he felt he had had a real shot at the gold. Borysewicz tried to convince LeMond to remain an amateur and to train for the 1984 Olympics, but LeMond didn't even consider that as an option. He knew he was good enough to ride professionally in Europe, and immediately turned pro. LeMond's goal in life was not to win a gold medal. It was to win the Tour de France. At the age of twenty, LeMond left the United States to begin his professional racing career in Europe—riding in the European peloton for a French team sponsored by Renault, the French auto company, and Gitane, a French maker of racing bikes.

Looking forward to the 1984 games, which would be held in Los Angeles, Borysewicz worked hard to convince other top American riders not to follow LeMond to Europe. He told them the professional racing scene was a hard slog, filled with grueling travel and low salaries, and that they'd have to leave their families behind and learn other languages. It worked. Borysewicz was able to hold on to a nucleus of good riders. The reality was, for many of Borysewicz's riders, cycling was a hobby, not a profession. For them, winning a medal—in an Olympic Games held on American soil—would be huge. Getting paid to race bicycles in Europe wasn't the goal.

Although he'd been bitterly upset by the 1980 boycott, Borysewicz also knew that there was a silver lining: He would now have a full four years to prepare. Russians and athletes from other Iron Curtain countries won fourteen of the seventeen medals in cycling in the 1980 Olympics—most of them on the track. World records were broken twenty-one times. Borysewicz and the Americans believed the cyclists from the Iron Curtain countries were part of state-sponsored doping efforts, and that was the reason track cyclists were huge and chiseled—like something out of a superhero cartoon.

After the 1980 Olympics, the Americans realized they were behind in the pharmacology department. The general feeling within the US Olympic Committee, which oversees all sports, was that if the Soviets were doping, the Americans needed to do it, too. It was practically a matter of national security. In 1982, the US Olympic Committee funded a laboratory at the University of California, Los Angeles, to develop new tests for detecting steroids and other performance-enhancing drugs. Those tests would be used at the 1984 Olympics. Americans would have the advantage in 1984 because they would know exactly which tests were being used during the games and how they worked. The USOC used the UCLA lab to conduct "informal testing," whereby athletes could voluntarily submit to testing and get the results without facing any consequences. That allowed athletes to see how long the particular drugs stayed in their systems, useful information as well. This was the American version of the state-sponsored doping programs in other countries—the difference being that the US Olympic Committee wasn't part of the government, and no American athlete was forced to use drugs.

Borysewicz trained his team hard during those four years. He brought his team to Europe for international competitions and, for the first time in history, the United States was consistently winning international cycling events. He also began working his connections in East Germany to get top-level cycling equipment smuggled into the United States. Among his scores: He was able to secure carbon fiber wheels and aerodynamic bikes that weren't available in the United States or anywhere else in the West. He also obtained handmade Continental tires, which were made on the other side of the Iron Curtain and could be pumped to higher pressure.

As the coach of the US national team, Borysewicz had thus far been able to count on one thing: His team would be the top choice for America's best cyclists. In fact, it was the only choice for all but the few who could compete in Europe. But that began to change in 1981, when Jim Ochowicz, a stocky twenty-eight-year-old construction worker from Milwaukee who had been an Olympic speed skater, began to put together America's first professional cycling team. Ochowicz had arrived at his interest in professional cycling in a somewhat circuitous fashion—by way of his interest in skating.

Because most ice rinks were outdoors in the 1960s and 1970s, the years when Och—rhymes with *coach*—was building his skating career, he, like many of his fellow skaters, rode bikes in the warmer months to build leg strength. The two sports rely on many of the same leg muscles and are so complementary that competitors like Ochowicz were known colloquially as blades-and-bikes athletes. While riding in a local club called the Milwaukee Wheelmen, Ochowicz was befriended by an older rider who gave him French and British books and magazines about European cyclists, and he became enthralled with the photos of European cycling stars. Och started training as a cyclist and became good enough to make the US Olympic team in 1972 and again in 1976, competing in the 4-kilometer team pursuit, a track cycling event in which two teams, each with up to four riders, start on opposite sides of a velodrome and race for sixteen laps. The United States did not win a medal in cycling in either of those years.

By 1977, Ochowicz was a married man and the father of a child. His wife was Sheila Young, who was also an Olympic speed skater—she'd won a gold medal in the 1976 Winter Olympics—and also someone who had crossed over from speed skating to cycling. Trying to support his family while still competing in cycling events, Ochowicz had been working construction. But he was coming to the realization that his racing days were probably over. Young was offered a job doing promotional work for the 1980 Winter Games in Lake Placid, New York, so the couple and their young daughter pulled up stakes and moved there. Once in Lake Placid, Och got work building the Olympic ski jump.

Through his connections in speed skating, Och befriended the family of a promising young American speed skater, Eric Heiden, and later, while coaching the US speed skating team during the lead-up to the Olympics, became a sort of manager for Heiden. When the speed skating team went to competitions in Europe, Ochowicz's basic role was to look after Heiden, then twenty years old, and to make sure he didn't get into much trouble. It was Och's first foray into sports management.

Heiden performed brilliantly at the Lake Placid Olympics, winning five gold medals in February 1980—a record for a single athlete in the winter games. Heiden was suddenly the most celebrated sports figure in the United States, an instant celebrity who was besieged by agents and corporations chasing him for endorsement deals. A low-key Midwesterner with a humble demeanor, Heiden wasn't interested in most of the endorsement offers, however. He was reluctant to cash in on his Olympic fame, as he believed swimmer Mark Spitz and track star Bruce Jenner had done. And he had other priorities. He planned to return to college, which he had left two years earlier, with the hope of eventually going to medical school to become a doctor like his father, an orthopedic surgeon in Madison, Wisconsin.

Ochowicz, however, had other plans for Heiden. After his Olympic success, Heiden had begun dabbling in bicycle racing as a way of staying fit. That fall, Och traveled to see Heiden at a track cycling event and thought he was good enough to be able to have a second career as a professional cyclist. By this time, Och had begun to dream about building a US team that could eventually compete on the European pro circuit. Heiden, Ochowicz realized, could be his biggest asset. He pitched Heiden on the idea, and Heiden agreed to join the as yet unnamed pro team, with Och as manager. Och then began traveling the racing circuit, attempting to line up other riders, with Heiden's participation as his lure.

If he were really to make a go of it, however, Ochowicz needed a sponsor that could provide funding for equipment, transportation, and riders' salaries. He lined up sponsorships with Schwinn, which had been backing Heiden, and Descente clothing. But he needed a bigger sponsor. With the help of Heiden's agent, the Dutchman George Taylor, he got one. Taylor pitched the Southland Corporation, owner of the 7-Eleven chain of convenience stores, on the idea of a Heiden-led cycling team. Finally, at the end of 1980, the brothers John and Jere Thompson, who owned the company, signed on to a multiyear deal worth millions. The 7-Eleven team was born of Och's desire to develop a professional-level cycling team. But it was also geared toward helping to groom American athletes for the 1984 Olympics. If Och could help some of the 7-Eleven team's riders become good enough to race on the Olympic team, and if some of them were actually able to win medals—which would be the first time the United States had won an Olympics medal in cycling since 1912—it would be both a tremendous personal accomplishment and a marketing coup for 7-Eleven, as well as a great way of helping 7-Eleven reach its marketing and branding objectives. The convenience-store chain had already agreed to shell out $3.5 million to build a new velodrome to help Los Angeles defray the costs of hosting the 1984 Summer Games.

Ochowicz and Borysewicz were now overlapping with each other in their Olympic aspirations, with a number of their riders going back and forth between the two teams. There were bound to be conflicts, especially because Borysewicz and Ochowicz did not see eye to eye on how to get to the goal they both shared. Borysewicz was a cycling coach at heart. Ochowicz was an operations guy who specialized in selecting athletes and raising funds; he saw himself playing a role similar to that of a baseball manager. And the two men had different ideas about how to get their riders ready for the Olympics, which sometimes resulted in scheduling conflicts. Borysewicz wanted his best riders to get ready for the big national and international competitions by working with him at the Olympic training center in Colorado Springs, while Ochowicz felt the good riders didn't need to train as much as they needed to be out there racing, particularly in the big sponsored meets.

The $250,000 7-Eleven spent on its team during the 1981 season was a significant sum, allowing Ochowicz to offer his riders a contract, with expenses, instead of just the promise of prize money. In its first year the team signed up seven riders, including some of the best amateur riders in North America. By the time the 7-Eleven team began racing in the spring of 1981, it was already the highest-caliber cycling team on the domestic circuit.

By the team's second year, Schwinn dropped out, but it didn't matter. 7-Eleven lavished such huge sums of money on the team that Ochowicz was able to hire some of the best riders in the country, luring them away from rival teams, and, in the case of a number of riders, encroaching on Eddie Borysewicz's turf.

While Ochowicz worked on building his commercial enterprise, Eddie B and the US national team knew they would be judged solely on their performance over the course of a week or so the following summer. As the date of the Olympics drew closer, there was an ever greater sense of urgency about winning. On September 30, 1983, US Cycling Federation staff member Ed Burke, PhD, circulated a memo to the rest of the staff saying he wanted to try a method of performance enhancement called blood boosting on the cycling team. The method wasn't technically banned by the International Olympic Committee. It wasn't expressly allowed, either. In essence, blood boosting was a way of increasing the body's supply of red blood cells by way of transfusion.

The staff met in Colorado Springs to discuss the matter. When it came to using drugs, Borysewicz was always concerned about safety. But he made a distinction between doping and blood boosting. Simply adding blood to the body, he thought, wasn't the same as doing something that was both illegal and could cause long-term damage. Borysewicz told Burke that if it was safe, not against the rules, and well supervised, he was fine with it. But he didn't want to be directly involved.

One of the riders on Eddie B's team, twenty-six-year-old Brent Emery of Milwaukee, recalled that one day, just a few months before the 1984 Olympics, an East German coach or support person had come to visit the US national team at its training center in Colorado Springs. The American team was riding at near world-record times in its training. "Why are you guys beating your brains out training at altitudes like this? We're going to get the same boost in fifteen minutes," the East German visitor told Borysewicz—a reference, Emery said, to blood boosting. In other words, why bother training so hard when you could just get an instant hit of energy by injecting fresh blood cells? The remark by the East German triggered a wave of anxiety among some American riders, who felt they were entitled to compete on a level playing field with the Russians.

But the Russian-American rivalry was again thwarted by politics. In early May, less than three months before the start of the Olympics, the Soviets announced they would boycott the games because they feared for their athletes' safety. It was a disappointment for Borysewicz, who believed the real reason for the boycott was retaliation for the United States' 1980 boycott.

The US team, however, went ahead with the blood-boosting effort. Participation in the program was voluntary. If they were interested, they were to arrange for family members with compatible blood types to provide the blood donations. A few days before the Olympic track cycling events, the cyclists and their blood donors lined up in a room at the Ramada hotel in Carson City, and a doctor connected tubes between them, allowing the blood to flow directly from one to the other. There was no screening of the blood for hepatitis or other diseases.

About a third of the team took part in the transfusions. Emery opted to participate, and his mother showed up at the hotel to provide the transfusion. Having her blood flow into his body through a plastic tube was a weird experience, Emery thought, but he felt it was necessary to go into the Olympics as well prepared as he could be. According to him, when the day of the Olympics arrived and he got on his bike and began riding around the track for a warm-up for the 4-kilometer team pursuit, he didn't feel any better or stronger than usual, and his "split times" were in the range of what he would have expected, based on past experience. He wasn't sure the transfusion even helped. He won a silver medal in the event.

Leonard Harvey Nitz, then a twenty-eight-year-old rider from Sacramento, California, also received a transfusion, but he noticed a small difference.

Usually, during multiday competitions, Nitz's fitness level would begin to drop off after about three days of riding. But during the 1984 games, he noticed that after five days, he was still just as strong as he was on the first day. He helped win the United States a silver medal in the team pursuit and a bronze in the individual pursuit.

In all, Borysewicz's US team won nine medals, including five golds, out of a possible fifteen in the 1984 Olympics, including the men's road race. In the six events for which the US riders won medals, 7-Eleven riders had figured in five of them. The United States won more medals in cycling during the 1984 Olympics than the American cycling team has won in all other Olympics combined, before or since those games. Of course, the magnitude of the triumph was somewhat diminished by the fact that the Russians hadn't participated.

After the Olympics, Borysewicz's stature was greater than ever. But he had enemies within the US Olympic Committee. Sheila Young, Ochowicz's wife, who sat on the board of the US Cycling Federation, had repeatedly asked Borysewicz to make her brother a coach on the men's team. Borysewicz stubbornly refused. Sheila wanted Borysewicz out, and less than six months after the Olympics, it looked as though she might get her wish. In February 1985, *Rolling Stone* magazine wrote an exposé on the blood boosting that had taken place on the US cycling team. Borysewicz, who was implicated in the article, suspected that Sheila was behind the leak, and he was furious, but he couldn't prove it.

After the scandal broke, some in cycling's governing body, the very organization that started the program, stepped forth to say publicly that they felt the transfusions were unethical. But Borysewicz, who had had very little to do with them, declined to express contrition. He said the line of morality in sports was a blurry one. "If we pump tires with helium, wear our new [aerodynamic] helmets, use new [disk] wheels, are we immoral because everybody does not have them?" he asked.

He was suspended for thirty days. Although he was able to stay on as an Olympics cycling coach, he was demoted. In the future he would have to operate without the autonomy he had grown accustomed to.

Ochowicz's team sustained little damage from the scandal, despite the fact that some of the riders had participated in the blood transfusions. The team had become iconic by then, so that its "kit"—or uniform—was featured in the movie *American Flyers*, a 1985 Warner Bros. film starring Kevin Costner. In the film, Costner and David Marshall Grant play estranged brothers who become reacquainted in the course of a cross-country, three-day bicycle race modeled after the Coors Classic. Cycling was becoming cool in the eyes of the American public.

Later in 1985, Borysewicz was on his ranch in Ramona, California, just northeast of San Diego, when he got a phone call. It was Mike Fraysse, who wanted to know if Borysewicz would train a masters athlete, a fortysomething banker named Thom Weisel. Borysewicz was livid. "You want me to do what?" he asked. *Masters* was the word used to describe athletes, usually over the age of thirty-five, who competed against athletes in their age bracket. In many sports, it was a polite term for "weekend warrior" or over the hill.

"Listen, Eddie, the thing is, this guy is a big backer of the US Olympic Committee," Fraysse said. "If you help him, it'll help the movement." The argument resonated with Eddie B, who knew funding was always the major issue. He agreed to do it.

Within minutes of Eddie's conversation with Fraysse, Weisel was on the line. "When can I start?" he barked into the phone in his deep, commanding voice.

Weisel was a wealthy Silicon Valley investment banker who, in a power struggle, took control of Montgomery Securities, a firm that had pioneered tech industry investment banking. He'd been an A-student and a speed skater as a boy growing up in Milwaukee but had clashed with his strict father, a prominent surgeon and a disciplinarian who had kept a stick for the purposes of beating Thom and his younger brother. A jock, and the quarterback of his high school football team, young Weisel craved the outdoors and disliked what he viewed to be the parochialism of the Midwest, so he enrolled in Stanford University, with its 8,180-acre campus near Palo Alto, California. He began dreaming of competing in the 1960 Winter Olympics, and shortly after enrolling in Stanford, he took the winter quarter off to prepare. But he didn't spend enough time on the ice and performed dismally in the skate-offs for the US Olympic skating team. He blew it, and he took it hard.

After graduation, Weisel attended Harvard Business School, where he befriended classmate Michael Bloomberg, before returning to the West Coast to become a research analyst working for a firm there. In 1971, he joined the investment bank Robertson, Colman & Siebel, in San Francisco. By the mid-1970s, the firm took several venture-backed tech companies—including Applied Materials—public. With guidance from his friend Bloomberg, then running the Salomon Brothers equity trading desk in New York, Weisel added a profitable trading desk. But when investment banking hit a slump, the firm's trading operation grew bigger, and Weisel, who was the junior partner and the most aggressive, began to battle with his partners over profits. In 1978, Weisel became CEO of the firm, and the partners split up. Weisel changed the name of the firm to Montgomery Securities—after Montgomery Street in downtown San Francisco. Because Montgomery was a relatively young firm, competing with giant New York investment banks, Weisel tried to build a culture that rewarded entrepreneurial drive. He believed in "equity upside" and "huge profit participation." He viewed himself to be a "frustrated athlete," and liked to hire and fraternize with those who were also competitive in sports. After he took up running, for instance, he brought in his running coach as Montgomery's personnel director—and formed a corporate running team that won a series of national championships over the course of a decade. Montgomery placed ads in running magazines, seeking women runners interested in working in financial services—a way to fill out the corporate women's running team for corporate challenge cup races. One of the women who answered the ad wound up as Weisel's second wife. He firmly believed that success in sports would bring success in business and life, too.

By the mid-1980s, Weisel had injured his knee and could no longer run long distances. Inspired by Eric Heiden's success on the 7-Eleven team and his crossover from speed skating to cycling, Weisel wondered about his own potential on the bike. So he bought a bike and began cycling recreationally. But then his fierce competitive drive took over.

For his first meeting with Borysewicz, Weisel flew to San Diego on his twin-engine plane, and then the two drove a few miles to the velodrome at San Diego's Balboa Park. It was a dilapidated wreck, with cracks the size of New York potholes. The view was beautiful, though, with the cycling track perched on a cliff overlooking a desert canyon full of eucalyptus.

By the time he met Eddie B, Weisel had gray hair and a slightly weathered face. His eyes were narrow and overpowered by his bushy gray eyebrows, giving him a blank poker-faced look. He looked fit, but his broad shoulders and pronounced chest kept him from looking like an emaciated cyclist. As Eddie asked Weisel about his athletic history, he learned about his passion for running, and his near miss in qualifying for the Olympic team more than two decades earlier. Weisel also told him about his investment banking success and his passion for skiing. He had bought a condo with Bloomberg near Snowbird, Utah, and later purchased a place near Sun Valley Resort in Idaho and gotten into masters ski racing, where he'd also gotten involved with the US Ski Team. He helped to revamp the organizational structure and bring in new sources of funding. But Weisel's bad knees had forced him to stop racing.

Eddie watched Weisel spin around the track. Like every pupil Eddie had observed, Weisel's form was terrible. He thought to himself that Weisel looked like a mule trying to ride a bicycle. But Eddie had worked with worse. At least he had determination. Eddie gave Weisel a training plan, and after that, the two men met monthly in San Diego.

Eddie also allowed Weisel to join him when he was training Olympic athletes. Weisel got to know Olympic medalists like Steve Hegg and Mark Gorski, who'd won a gold in 1984, and they showed Weisel some of their tricks in track cycling.

One night, Weisel took Eddie out to dinner. He had a proposition: "You make me a national champion and I'll make you a millionaire," he said, in his commanding way. It wasn't a joke. Weisel was offering to invest money for Eddie in the stock market and tech IPOs. He wanted to incentivize Eddie to do everything in his power to turn the middle-aged investment banker into a champion in his age group.

By the end of the 1987 cycling season, Weisel had mastered the technique of track cycling and its strategy. That season, he signed up for the Masters National Championships in Houston, Texas, where he won in the match sprint. Eddie had honored his part of the agreement. Now Weisel had to honor his: make Eddie a millionaire.

Perhaps inspired by his win, Weisel came to Eddie with another proposition. He wanted to start a high-level cycling team with aspirations to race in the Tour de France. It would be an elite team composed of younger riders who hoped to become full-time professionals. But he was also starting a masters team to go alongside it, which would consist of older amateurs like Weisel.

The Montgomery Securities team was a new invention in cycling. Until that point, there were either cycling clubs, with scores of older riders, or professional teams, like 7-Eleven and the many superb European teams, where the average age was somewhere around twenty-five. Nobody had ever thought of combining the two enterprises. It would be like starting a Minor League Baseball team with the stipulation that the team owner and his older friends also got to play. It was fantasy camp.

Weisel also formed Montgomery Sports Inc., based at Montgomery Securities headquarters in San Francisco's Transamerica Pyramid, and became its president. Eddie set up the team headquarters at his ranch in Ramona. The area was a perfect training ground for a cycling team. It was remote, temperate in climate, and the infrequently traveled roads were well maintained. The area also had huge mountains nearby, including Palomar Mountain, and a fourteen-mile winding road that led to the largest mirrored telescope in the world.

Eddie hosted the masters men at his ranch for team rides with the young up-and-coming professional riders. On a hot summer day in 1987, Thom Weisel was driving with Eddie in his old Honda Civic, trailing the pack of riders as they climbed Palomar Mountain. He turned to Eddie and began to talk about his ambitions. "We can build this into something great. One day, this team is going to win the Tour de France," he declared.

Eddie laughed. "That is like a French baseball team trying to win the World Series. You realize that, right?"

"You're damn right I realize that," Weisel said. "That's why I want to do it."

CHAPTER THREE

A RAGE TO WIN

Thirteen-year-old Lance Armstrong hadn't come all the way down to this sprawling Houston theme park to try out the SkyScreamer, a ten-story free-fall ride, or the suspended-swinging coaster. He and his fiery stepfather, Terry, had come for Lance to compete in the IronKids Triathlon that was being conducted on the Six Flags AstroWorld course. The event included 200 yards of swimming, about 6 miles of cycling, and just over 1 mile of running. The top six finishers would get an all-expense paid trip to Orlando for the IronKids Triathlon National Championships at Walt Disney World.

This was Lance's second triathlon. At an IronKids event up in Dallas earlier that summer, Lance had blazed the course, torched his competition. But the organizers hadn't mastered the timing system yet. Because the children were sent off in separate groups rather than competing simultaneously, the race officials couldn't determine who won. Terry was furious. He had witnessed Lance's dominance and was sure he was the winner. He demanded that they be flown to Houston for the next IronKids event so Lance could get another shot at winning—officially. And now, on a hot September day when the temperature was over 90 degrees, here they were.

The IronKids competition divided the field into two groups by age. Lance, who would turn fourteen the following month, was placed in the "senior division" and pitted against rivals age eleven to fourteen. As the race began, Lance splashed into the pool and freestyled his way to a lead. When he popped out of the water, he put on his running shoes and quickly darted out in front of the pack. He hopped on his Mercier bike and sped away. The six miles on the bike vanished in a flash. He sprinted the final mile and crossed the finish line well ahead of all the other adolescents in the competition. He had earned his trip to the IronKids National Championship at Disney World. Terry was ecstatic.

In October, Terry and Lance flew to Orlando to compete for the national championship. Terry was so intensely competitive that he bet another father five hundred dollars that Lance would beat his son. Terry won the bet—Lance torched the other kid—and he was happy. But Lance didn't win the race, coming in second, so Lance was not happy. He was furious with second place. That would never be good enough for him.

Lance wasn't like other athletic kids in his hometown of Plano, Texas. They were into football and baseball. Though Lance played both, agility sports weren't his strength—or his interest. Slender and not particularly tall, he lacked the build of a football player, and wasn't a good ball thrower. Team sports bored him anyway. They forced him to endure something he had learned to hate at a very young age: the mistakes of others. But running and swimming and biking he enjoyed. He'd gotten his first bike when he was five, bought for him by his maternal grandfather. A year later his mother, Linda, spent three hundred dollars to purchase Lance a BMX bike—the small-wheel off-road bikes kids rode on dirt track obstacle courses—and Terry started taking him to youth races.

Lance's mother, Linda Mooneyham, had been raised in the projects near Dallas and was the daughter of an alcoholic father. After she became pregnant at sixteen, she dropped out of high school. Her parents wanted nothing to do with her. At first, she attempted to raise Lance—named for Lance Rentzel, Dallas Cowboys star wide receiver—with his biological father, Eddie Charles Gunderson, a boy from her high school with an imposing physique. They married on her seventeenth birthday and lived in Oak Cliff, a rough Dallas neighborhood, scraping by. Linda worked at Kentucky Fried Chicken, while

Eddie worked as a route manager for *The Dallas Morning News.* They soon split up. After Linda's father sobered up, she moved with Lance into his place and drifted from job to job, including a gig at the dead-letter office. Gunderson fell behind on his $20-a-week child support. When Lance was three, Linda began a relationship with Terry Armstrong, who worked for a meat company that supplied corn dogs and barbecue beef to school cafeterias.

The son of a Christian minister, Terry Keith Armstrong had been sent off to military school at a young age, and his ideas about discipline seem to have been shaped by that experience. When Lance was a young boy, Terry used a wooden college fraternity paddle to punish him. His way of dealing with his stepson's participation in sports was similarly aggressive and outdated. No matter what sport Lance was playing, Terry was determined that he abide by the rules of what it meant to be a real athlete. In one of Lance's first BMX races, Lance wiped out and began to cry. Terry walked over and told him that because of the crying, they would have to go home. So Lance picked himself up and kept at it. Terry was that kind of disciplinarian, the kind who believed in manhood in the strictest, most traditional sense of the word. Terry cared deeply about Lance and wanted him to succeed—especially in sports. But Lance rejected Terry from an early age, often telling him, "You're not my dad!"

Lance's biological father, Eddie, had lost track of Lance after Linda and Terry moved—first to an apartment in suburban Richardson, then to a brick bungalow in Plano, in a neighborhood near the Los Rios Country Club. The last time Eddie saw Lance was when Lance turned three. Over the years, Eddie forgot about Lance, coming to think of him as someone from a chapter in his life that had closed, and Lance had no desire to meet or see Eddie. As far as he was concerned, Eddie had deserted them, after Linda's parents deserted her, until her father managed to quit drinking. People in Dallas thought they were losers. He turned to sports to get out of the house.

Lance wasn't necessarily a naturally gifted athlete, but he worked hard at it. After he quit football in middle school, he and a few of his buddies joined the local swim club. Twelve years old at the time, when he first showed up at the Plano Aquatic Center pool, he flopped into the water and beat his arms and legs down the lane in a manner that made his mother think of a paddle barge. He was grouped with the nine-year-olds. To improve, the swim coach told him, he had to show up for the team's grueling morning workouts every weekday at 6:00 A.M., and then again after school. Within a month or so, his swimming proficiency increased to the point where he was put in a group of mostly thirteen-year-olds. A year later, he took fourth place in the 1,500-meter freestyle at the state swim meet. The swimming helped him to add muscle to his shoulders and to develop a powerful neck.

When Lance was about twelve, Terry flew with him to San Antonio, Texas, for a swim meet, the Texas State Championships. At the time, his mom was in the hospital for a hysterectomy. There were complications and she had to stay there for four days. Lance was angry. He wanted support but not Terry's support. He wouldn't even talk to him. In the airport on the way home, Lance noticed Terry writing notes on a manila legal pad that he had in his briefcase. Terry would scribble a note, rip out the page, crumple it, and throw it out in a trash can nearby. Lance was curious, so, after the boarding announcement, Lance told Terry he had to use the bathroom and would meet him on the plane. When Terry wasn't looking, Lance picked up the wadded-up notes and put them in his bag. He later discovered that they were drafts of Terry's love notes to another woman. He saved them and didn't say anything to his mom.

It was in 1985 that Lance saw the notice at the local bike shop, the Richardson Bike Mart, announcing the IronKids competition—an event that combined swimming, cycling, and running. Terry and Linda wanted to make it possible for him to compete, so they bought him a new bike—the Mercier he would ride to victory in Houston. At that time, the triathlon, which had started in Hawaii as a competition among lifeguards, was just growing into its own sport. Most Americans—especially Texans—had no idea what the word *triathlon* even meant. Participation was minimal. Mostly, it drew fitness nuts—products of the 1980s gym rat and aerobics culture. There was no standardized set of rules, and the techniques and equipment used by competitors were a hodgepodge.

Lance and his two closest friends became a sort of triathlon gang, traveling around Texas, competing in the biggest races they could get into. They trained together—running and swimming but mostly biking—and spent most of their free time together, pulling teenage pranks and getting into trouble. Lance viewed himself as a nonconformist who disliked traditional team sports. But he had essentially created his own kind of team, allowing him to enjoy the camaraderie without having to depend on the performance of anyone else to determine whether he had won or lost. He was able to take all the credit for his victories. He needed it that way.

In June 1986, Lance met Rick Crawford, then a twenty-six-year-old pro triathlete, at a Dallas-area pool. "I want to make money and I want to win. Tell me what I need to know," Lance said. Rick became Lance's coach, an unpaid position. He chaperoned Lance to races and oversaw his training regimen: swimming 10,600 meters, cycling 320 miles, and running 30 miles—the equivalent of roughly twenty-five hours a week. Rick invited Lance to be among less than thirty participants at a "duathlon" swimming-and-running race held at a posh health club on the fourth-story rooftop of the Galleria Dallas shopping mall. Participants swam three hundred yards in a very cold twenty-five-yard hotel pool, and then ran two miles around a synthetic turf track. Lance, then fourteen years old, won the race. The first prize was a pair of running shoes from the Portland, Oregon, athletic company Avia.

Scott Eder, a twenty-eight-year-old promotions rep for Avia who was living in Dallas, showed up at the Armstrong home to deliver the prize—size 10 Avias. As Terry and Linda got to know Eder, who was also a triathlete, they thought he would be a good influence on Lance, who was now interested in going to the next level and participating in some adult triathlon races. They asked Eder to give Lance some tips on training for the sport, and to help keep him out of trouble. Eder was happy to help out. He thought it would be rewarding, for he could see that Lance had potential—that if Lance stuck with it, he could probably turn professional. He took Lance to the pool and to races, and to dinner several times a week. He and Lance talked potential sponsors into giving Lance free running shoes, bikes, and other gear. With Eder's help, Lance was able to secure the sponsorship of the Richardson Bike Mart, which provided his bike as well as a stipend of $400 a month.

That the shop owner, Jim Hoyt, agreed to sponsor the teenager was remarkable. Even then, Lance had a lot of attitude, and his adolescent behavior had so ticked off Hoyt in the past that he had once banned him from even coming into his store.

But Hoyt saw how serious Lance was and invited him on local group rides around Plano, where he became familiar with basic biking terms such as *peloton*, *drafting*, and *domestique*. Lance also began showing up at the so-called Tuesday night crits, racing for Hoyt's Richardson Bike Mart team. Crits, short for criterium races, are multi-lap road races. Usually, the course itself is about a mile long and the races involve anywhere from twenty to fifty laps around the course. The Tuesday night crits in Plano were held in a small industrial park. The track was about 0.8 miles around, with a couple of sharp turns marked by orange cones.

All bike racers who participate in sanctioned races have to be licensed by USA Cycling, the national governing body for the sport. First-time racers start out in the lowest category—at the time, that was category 4—and to move up, they have to participate in a number of races and gather points. The process could take months, if not a full year.

This meant that Lance, technically a novice, would have to begin by racing with the 4s, the slowest and least experienced riders. Hoyt, who organized the races, knew Lance had the ability to ride with the combined 1-2-3 field. So the first time Lance showed up for one of the crits, he allowed him to participate at the higher level on one condition: Lance wasn't allowed to win the race. If he did, the race official, who had been kept in the dark about Lance's "cat 4" status, would find out that he had broken the rules.

Immediately, Lance took off, flying out ahead of the pack of forty or so riders and leaving them behind. Only one rider stuck to Lance's wheel. By the time the final lap approached, Lance was still in the lead. He knew he wasn't supposed to win the race, but something in Lance's DNA wouldn't let him slow down. So he won. As Hoyt had predicted, the race official noticed that he was only a cat 4 and was livid. Hoyt had to smooth everything over. It wouldn't be the last time Lance would hang Hoyt out to dry. But damn, he could fly on a bike.

For the 1986 triathlon season, Crawford and Eder, who had become Lance's informal manager, took him around Texas and Oklahoma, where he competed in small triathlons with relatively short distances, to help him build a résumé. At fourteen, Lance was still too young to race in some of the events. The insurance companies that underwrote the races required the organizers to bar anyone under fifteen. No problem: Linda stopped off for a Wite-Out and a black pen and doctored Lance's birth certificate to say that he was a year older. In at least one instance, for the President's Triathlon in Dallas, Jim Woodman, a race promoter who lived in Miami and published *Florida Sports* magazine, knew the birth certificate was doctored but allowed him to race anyway. All the practice paid off, and Lance kept getting better and better. At one triathlon in Waco, Texas, Lance, clad in a Richardson Bike Mart tank top and swim briefs, came in so far ahead that the second-place finisher hadn't even seen him cross the line, and initially concluded that he himself had won.

Soon, Armstrong was making a name for himself, getting sponsorships and making important business connections that would serve him later in life. Woodman even put him on the cover of *Florida Sports*. But Lance, headstrong and often unwilling to listen to advice, was still working out some kinks in his form and strategy. Twice in the summer of 1986 he had to relinquish leads because he was dehydrated. He hadn't realized the importance of drinking fluids during a competition even when he wasn't thirsty. He suffered an embarrassment at a big race in Dallas when he was penalized for drafting, that is, riding in another racer's slipstream. In professional bike racing, drafting is part of the strategy because it helps a rider conserve valuable energy, but in triathlons, it's generally not allowed. Lance realized he had to become not just a stronger but a smarter athlete, and he was determined to learn from experience.

By the 1987 season, the soon-to-be high school junior, then five feet ten inches and chiseled, at 150 pounds, was emerging as a serious competitor to some of the world's top triathletes, men ten years older and at the top of their games. He was getting stronger by the month, and his endurance was increasing. Later that summer, Lance delivered a standout performance at the President's Triathlon, the race he had participated in the previous year when he was technically too young to have done so. Mark Allen, a twenty-nine-year-old pro, had won the event two years in a row. Allen plunged into Lake Carolyn in the middle of the swanky Las Colinas neighborhood in Irving, Texas, and waited for the countdown to the start. When he emerged from the lake at the end of the 0.6-mile swim, Allen was surprised to discover he was behind Lance, who had finished that leg of the triathlon in third place. Allen didn't know Lance and figured he must be a high-level swimmer who was just dab-bling in triathlon. A few miles into the 21-mile cycling course, however, Allen was shocked to realize that Lance was keeping up with him. He stayed with Allen the whole way. Lance's weakest leg of the triathlon was the run. He ended in sixth place overall—quite an accomplishment for a fifteen-year-old.

After his sixth-place performance, Lance got invited to race all over the country and in more exotic locales, such as St. Croix in the US Virgin Islands and Caracas, Venezuela. He also qualified for the International Triathlon Championships in Bermuda, which offered a $100,000 purse. There he raced alongside professionals from all over the world and finished in an impressive eleventh place.

In all, over Lance's high school years, he participated in more than twenty-five sleepover triathlon races—and typically never paid a single cent for travel, hotels, rental cars, or entry fees. For the trip to Bermuda, for in-stance, the fifteen-year-old talked the owner of the Princess Hotel into flying him in and putting him up for four days. A friend of Eder's worked at Dallas-based advertising agency Moroch & Associates, which managed local adver-tising for the McDonald's corporation. He set Lance up with a McDonald's endorsement of roughly $10,000 a year; Lance wore the golden arches on his helmet and dressed in yellow and red as his racing uniform. McDonald's offset some of his travel costs.

If Lance's athletic ability and talent for self-promotion manifested early, so, too, did his temper. Around this time, Lance received a free Kestrel bike as part of a sponsorship. It was one of the first-ever carbon fiber super-lightweight racing bikes. He rode it in a few triathlons but soon lost his deal with Kestrel after ESPN cameras filmed him throwing the bike across four lanes of traffic into a ditch after getting a flat tire in a South Florida triathlon.

Race promoter Jim Woodman, who became another mentor for Lance, saw how quickly Lance's emotions could change, one minute jubilant, the next fierce. When he took Lance out for training rides around Miami, he observed that whenever a driver honked or cut him off, Lance would completely lose control. He would chase after the driver and catch him at a light, then pound on the car windows and scream obscenities. "Fuck you, you stupid mother-fucker!" Woodman sometimes feared for his life, and counseled Lance to cool down. "You're going to get us killed," he warned him. "A lot of people around here have guns."

Woodman also saw the arrogance in him. On one training ride, Woodman moved his position so that he rode directly behind Lance, with Lance sheltering him from the wind. It was the only way Woodman could keep up with Lance, who was flying in preparation for a big triathlon in Florida. "You think I'm ready, bitch?!" Lance shouted to Woodman behind him.

"Talk with your legs and not your mouth," Woodman advised him that day. "Nobody wants to hear a teenage kid talking a bunch of crap."

Crawford bristled when he overheard Lance's callous teasing of his closest competitors. "What are you doing here? You suck. Go home," Lance said to Chann McRae, a local teen, before the start of one event, according to Crawford's recollection.

Lance's belligerence extended to Terry. "Fuck you!" was Lance's typical snarl when Terry asked him to do anything around the house. Terry worked full-time and provided for the family, buying Lance a used Fiat Spider when he turned fifteen, but Lance thought he was despicable and an insecure, materialistic dork. He also thought Terry was emotionally abusive, and resented his saying, "This is my house and you'll do what I say." Lance felt that had been Terry's way of letting him know he and Linda had been a burden. Crawford understood that Lance had a painful childhood, but he didn't think Terry deserved Lance's abuse.

"Whoa! That's your father. You shouldn't talk to him like that," Crawford said.

"Oh, he's a tool. I hate that guy," Lance told Crawford.

Lance's behavior also strained Linda and Terry's marriage. But Linda figured she couldn't leave Terry because she would be a single parent, with no college education. She was concerned about supporting herself and Lance. But by the time Lance was sixteen, he was supporting himself through pro triathlons, making $1,000 a month, so she finally left Terry—and Lance was inspired by her independence. *God, if she can do that, we can do anything. I can do anything*, he thought. Years later, Terry reached out to Rick to ask: "Why did Lance hate me so much?" Rick didn't have an answer.

Lance meanwhile was developing a healthy interest in the science and psychology of sport. He enjoyed quantifying every aspect of swimming, running, and cycling. Eder heard about a controlled study being conducted at the Cooper Institute, a sports performance lab in Dallas. A researcher there was testing the effects of a cooling vest on athletes, by measuring their core temperatures after wearing the device and running for an hour. In lieu of payment, study participants would get a VO_2 max test, as part of a physical workup. The VO_2 max test was designed to measure how efficiently an athlete consumed oxygen. Each of the athletes got on the treadmill and placed a mask over his face. The mask had a tube protruding from it and connecting it to a large machine that measured the gases coming out of the athlete's body.

About a week after the VO_2 max test, Eder got a call from the director of the research project at the Cooper Institute. "Whoever that kid was that you brought in here, he has the second-highest VO_2 max we've ever tested," he said. The test confirmed what Armstrong was telling everyone with unfiltered confidence: His potential was limitless. Later that month, in a feature on Lance, *Triathlete* magazine cited his 79.5 VO_2 max as world-class.

And then, of course, there was the matter of his ambition. By the summer before his senior year in high school, he was heading to the triathlon mecca of San Diego, where he'd spend the summer months training with professional athletes. Eder had a triathlete friend in Del Mar, north of San Diego, who agreed to let Lance stay with him. The sleepy coastal city attracted endurance athletes from around the world because of its year-round climate, warm and dry with a temperature that always hovered somewhere between 60 and 75 degrees Fahrenheit, and its unique topography. Lance swam at the University of California, San Diego, with a group of competitive weekend warriors and some professional swimmers, and he got his first exposure to riding up climbs similar to those in the Pyrenees or the Alps on the long winding roads that snake up to the top of Palomar Mountain, about 5,500 feet above sea level. Lance was testing his legs daily on terrain that could truly challenge him for the first time.

When he got back to Plano after the summer in San Diego, Lance signed an endorsement agreement with Oakley sunglasses and figured he'd continue making money from his victories in the triathlon. His times during the cycling portions of some triathlons had caught the eye of the US Cycling

Federation coaching staff, which invited him to Colorado Springs in 1989 for tryouts for the junior national team. Although Lance wasn't sold on switching to cycling, he saw an opportunity: a free trip to Russia, where the junior world championships were going to be held the following summer. He ditched school and went to the tryouts, where he was among an elite group of young cyclists chosen to go to Moscow that July.

Lance's teachers at Plano East High didn't take kindly to his truancy. The school informed him that his unexcused absences for the trip would prevent him from receiving his diploma and graduating with the rest of his class. Armstrong had missed a significant amount of school that year, and the school thought of the Colorado trip as the final straw. Linda called every private school in the Dallas-area Yellow Pages until she found one that would let him graduate: Bending Oaks High School. The school had a bad heroin problem, according to Lance's recollection, as well as a large number of suicides, but the teachers were willing to work with Lance to help him get a diploma. His stepfather, Terry, who by this time was divorced from Linda, came up with the tuition, and Lance did graduate.

In Moscow that summer, Lance, now seventeen, ignored the instructions of his coaches about pacing himself. He took off early in the race, leaving the field of some of the best young cyclists in the world far behind. But with only 0.6 miles to go, the pack caught up with him, then surged ahead. Lance finished seventy-third. It was an unremarkable final result, but the time Armstrong spent in the wind, holding off the encroaching pack, was impressive.

When Lance returned home, he felt like Superman. He was done with high school, and his future as a professional triathlete was wide open. He saw women, fame, and fortune ahead. He acted as if he were the star quarterback for the University of Texas and was about to sign a multimillion-dollar contract in the NFL. With the prize money he'd earned from triathlons, and a loan guarantee from bike shop owner Jim Hoyt, he purchased a Chevy Camaro Z/28, which was registered in Hoyt's name, a decision Hoyt would come to regret.

One night in 1989, Lance was partying in Dallas with a group of friends. They had all been drinking, and Lance was speeding down the highway in the Chevy Camaro when he noticed flashing police lights behind him. Rather than pull over and risk losing his license for drunk driving, Lance took off, leading the police officer on a high-speed chase. He pulled off to the side of the road and jumped out of the car, using his endurance skills to run away so fast that the police couldn't catch him. Two of Lance's friends were caught and arrested, but Lance and two others—also fast runners—got away. Because the Camaro was in Hoyt's name, and the police didn't know who had been driving it, they showed up at Hoyt's house that night with their guns drawn. The car was impounded, and when Hoyt later went to pick it up, they arrested him because Lance had racked up so many unpaid speeding tickets. After that, Lance and Hoyt stopped talking, and Lance began riding for a small local team sponsored by Hoyt's fiercest rival, Wheels in Motion, a new bike store on Coit Road, just down the street from Richardson Bike Mart.

Around this time, Mike Fraysse called Eddie B, who was busy working with Thom Weisel to build the professional Montgomery cycling team. "Eddie, there is this young animal in Texas," Fraysse said over the phone in his thick, northern New Jersey accent. "But he doesn't know what he's doing." Fraysse told Eddie about Lance's biking times in the triathlons, and his bizarre performance in Moscow. This is what Eddie B lived for: the diamonds in the rough. He knew how to make them shine. He made arrangements to go to Austin to watch Lance compete in a triathlon.

Eddie B showed up for the event, wearing a cowboy hat to keep the sun out of his eyes. He waited on the side of the road to see Lance go by. He didn't care about the swim or the run. He cared only about watching Lance on the bike.

Lance was the first in the pack. He wore nothing but a skimpy Speedo and cutoff T-shirt, an outfit that Eddie B thought looked silly but which made it possible for him to assess the entire muscular structure of Lance's body, from head to toe. Eddie B saw immediately that Lance had the bulky upper body muscles of a swimmer. A powerful upper back and shoulders are helpful in the water segment of a triathlon, but upper body muscles tend to be a burden in cycling, where any unnecessary body weight will only slow a rider down. Some pro cyclists are so concerned about avoiding bulk in their upper body that they won't even carry heavy bags of groceries.

The race included a gradual climb that forced Lance out of the saddle. Eddie B could see that Lance wasn't comfortable on the bike, that his body rocked from side to side as he pedaled. But he could also see that even though Lance's body wasn't yet fully developed, he could bludgeon the pedals with the power of a linebacker. He was no LeMond. By the time LeMond was Lance's age, he had already won the junior world championship. He knew how to race a bike, and he had the sinewy body type for it.

At lunch after the race, Eddie B told Linda and Lance that he was looking for talent—young athletes he could develop and train to become skilled cyclists—and that he thought Lance had great potential. But before investing his own time and effort in Lance, Eddie B wanted to know how healthy he was. When he asked Lance how often he got sick, the answer was "Never." Eddie B turned to Linda. "Is that true?" he asked. "Yes, he is a very healthy kid," she responded.

Lance was quiet at lunch. He didn't immediately jump at the notion of working with Eddie B, clearly a strict coach who needed to be firmly in control of his riders' training and performance. Lance was also calculating the pros and cons of cycling versus triathlon. Mostly, Lance wanted to know more about Eddie B's team, and whether there were any attractive sponsorship opportunities available in cycling. Did cycling have the potential to deliver the same level of money and fame as the triathlon?

Eddie B described how top pro cyclists competing in Europe could earn a million a year. If they won medals in the track or road racing events at the Olympics, that could bring fame and big endorsements, too. Eddie B's former protégé, Greg LeMond, was proving how far an American could go in the international sport of cycling. And in 1986, LeMond had become the first American to win the Tour de France. The victory made LeMond famous. He earned lucrative endorsements worth millions and, after winning the race for a second time, signed a contract for more than $1 million a year—the highest salary in cycling history.

Lance hadn't thought much about Europe, or the Tour de France. But he had been thinking a lot about the Olympics, and he wondered what winning a gold medal would look like on his résumé. As far as Lance was concerned, it was his ticket to fame and fortune, especially if he could win the gold while still young. By the time the 1992 Olympics took place, he would be just twenty-one years old.

Eddie B invited Lance to come visit him at his ranch in Ramona, where they could train and get to know each other better, and Lance decided to take him up on the offer. He'd join what was then called the Subaru-Montgomery team for the 1990 season, which included a stipend of $12,000 a year. Subaru had recently signed on as the title sponsor, and the team finally had enough cash to compete for some of the best American riders. The stipend would be paid to Lance regardless of how well he did in his races, and while it was high enough to live on, it was low enough to allow Lance to keep his "amateur" status so that he could be eligible to participate in the Olympics if he chose to—which Eddie B was sure he would. Lance would also get team bikes and clothing and have his travel expenses reimbursed.

Soon he was back on a plane to California, headed toward the team's winter training in Escondido, an inland suburb of San Diego near Eddie B's ranch. He was given a Subaru-Montgomery cycling kit—a splashy orange, yellow, and blue pastel uniform that appeared to be inspired by the modern art Weisel collected and displayed on the walls of his large home near the Golden Gate Bridge. The words *Subaru* and *Montgomery*, which were layered over an orange block of color with jagged edges resembling a cartoon explosion, seemed to fly off the front of the team jersey.

There were other benefits to riding for Thom Weisel's team. By the early 1990s, the IPO market was on fire, and Weisel arranged for the Subaru-Montgomery team riders to invest their salaries in a "friends and family" account at Weisel's investment bank, Montgomery Securities. The account made it possible for riders to get small chunks of the IPOs, with small investments of just $2,000 or $3,000 apiece. After the run-ups in stock price, an account manager would automatically sell the holdings for the riders, often doubling their money. Paul Willerton, one ex-Subaru-Montgomery rider, for instance, said he made an extra $6,000 to $12,000 monthly through these accounts.

Willerton recalls Weisel as quiet, but with an explosive temper. He would often yell at his wife, Emily. Willerton was terrified of him. He recalled riding in the passenger seat of Weisel's Bronco, with Weisel behind the wheel, and a slow driver ahead inspired Weisel to explode with the kind of road rage Willerton had only read about.

Lance trained hard. Very hard. In fact, what Eddie B thought was special about Lance, and what he shared with all the greats, was that Lance never wanted to rest. He had to beg Lance to ride easy some days to allow his body to recover. But Lance's single-mindedness had its downside, for it could be impossible to get through to him. Lance refused to take direction from any-one, and thought he could outride everyone through sheer, brute force, with-out regard to finesse and strategy. Moreover, his competitive spirit was so tinged with selfishness and anger that he resisted the kind of teamwork that supporting riders are supposed to offer the leader of the team.

Riding hard at the front of the pack to control the pace of the peloton, riding in front or to the side of the team leader to protect him from the wind or possible crashes, and doing things like hanging back to get fresh water bottles from the team car and delivering them to the leader—all these are part of what is expected of the less experienced riders on a team. But Lance didn't appreciate being put in the role of "helper." In some races, he ignored Eddie B's instructions altogether. Instead of hanging back and playing the role he was expected to fill in the team's tactical agenda, he took off and attempted solo breakaways. Usually, this backfired and the pack would overtake him. But every once in a while, he would be able to stay at the front long enough to win the race.

There was no question that Lance was physically gifted; but by the end of the season, everyone on the team wondered if he had enough strategic smarts to succeed at bike racing. With his earnings from Subaru-Montgomery, Lance could now afford to move from Linda's home in Plano to Austin, Texas, a city that appealed to Lance because of its burgeoning music scene as well as its hilly terrain, ideal for training. Linda had begun rising up the ranks of her company, Ericsson Telecommunications, where she worked as a secretary, and began a new relationship with technical recruiter John Walling in Dallas.

In Austin, Lance rented an apartment from John Thomas Neal, or J.T., a lawyer turned massage therapist and Austin real estate entrepreneur. Lance had originally met him while J.T. was working as a massage therapist for the Subaru-Montgomery team during the 1990 Tour of Texas. Lance had come down from Plano to watch the race. A few months later, when they saw each other at another cycling event, J.T. told Lance about the available apartment in the town house adjoining J.T.'s office. Lance moved in, and they became close friends.

In addition to training with Subaru-Montgomery, Lance was also still keen on the Olympics, a goal Eddie B supported. This meant Lance had to leave Subaru-Montgomery occasionally to train and ride with the US national team in preparation for the 1992 games in Barcelona. In 1990, Armstrong was dressed in the stars-and-stripes jersey at the junior world championships road race in Utsunomiya, Japan. When the race started, Lance broke away alone. Lap after lap around the course, he kept pounding away, solo. Lance's solo split up the race, and he was eventually joined by a handful of other European riders in what would form the winning breakaway. Lance was too tired to propel himself ahead of the others and couldn't outsprint his breakaway mates at the line. He finished eleventh in what the national team coach, Chris Carmichael, viewed as an impressive performance. In fact, it was one of the best for an American in the junior world championships since LeMond's victory in 1979. Still, Carmichael couldn't help but think Armstrong could have come away with the victory if he had done a better job of conserving his energy. Nobody Carmichael coached had the raw power that Armstrong possessed, but Armstrong had some of the worst tactical sense of anyone on the team.

Lance began to improve and hone his riding style under the tutelage of Eddie B, but his big breakthrough came when he was, again, riding for Carmichael on the national team. In April 1991, the US team entered the ten-day Italian stage race called Settimana Bergamasca, which was open to both junior national teams from all over the world and professional teams. Eddie B had also entered Subaru-Montgomery in the race, putting the squad in direct competition with Armstrong and the national team, which created an awkward tug-of-war between the teams that tested Lance's loyalty. Not that this was all that unusual in bike racing. Cyclists went back and forth between their "trade" teams and their national teams all the time, depending on the event, and sometimes the result was that they raced against the very people they had been racing with the week before.

About five days into the Bergamasca, Lance was near the top of the overall standings, just slightly behind Nate Reiss, who was riding for Subaru-Montgomery. Because Reiss was in the lead and had a good shot at winning the event, Eddie B told Lance that he wanted him to play the domestique role, supporting Reiss and giving up his own chances of winning. Armstrong was technically riding for the US national team—not Subaru-Montgomery. Borysewicz expected Armstrong to obey his orders. The idea of sacrificing his own interest in order to help another rider win the race—even one on the team that paid his salary—was a notion so alien to Lance that it rattled the very core of his being. Lance griped to Carmichael, who wanted Lance to go for the win on behalf of the Stars and Stripes, and a battle went on for days. Lance's refusal to work for Reiss caused a rift between Lance and his Subaru-Montgomery teammates, one of whom called Weisel back in the States to complain.

A few days later, Reiss got a flat tire and lost time in the event. Lance took the lead, with just a few seconds' advantage over an Italian pro in second place. Eddie B then decided that Subaru-Montgomery should switch allegiances and work for Lance. Despite their bitterness over Lance's selfish maneuvering earlier in the race, Eddie B's Subaru-Montgomery riders helped guide Lance to victory. Lance, nineteen and still an amateur, became the first American ever to win the event, which became a big story all over Europe. He fell in love with the drama and attention. But he certainly hadn't won a lot of friends in the process.

CHAPTER FOUR

THE FIRST MILLION

On a sunny Friday morning in August 1990, Jim Ochowicz sat in a windowless conference room in the Motorola, Inc. corporate headquarters building in Schaumburg, Illinois, wearing a polo shirt with a red-and-green 7-Eleven logo on his chest. Southland Corporation, which owned 7-Eleven, was hemorrhaging money and it had abruptly canceled its decade-long sponsorship of the team. Soon, Team 7-Eleven would be history, and its twenty-two riders, its team mechanics, and its soigneurs, or assistants, would be jobless.

Anxious and desperate, Ochowicz figured he might as well take a chance at pitching Motorola's head of worldwide advertising to endorse his pro team. Ochowicz knew the tech giant was eager for a way to boost awareness of its brand in countries such as France, Germany, and Britain, and he thought he could make a case for doing so through a title sponsorship.

Sheila Griffin, Motorola's savvy marketer, was skeptical. She knew almost nothing about pro cycling and whatever she did know came to her through conversations at home with her husband, a civil engineer and avid amateur racer who would sometimes ride one hundred miles in one shot as weekend fun.

Griffin had previously considered the idea of sponsoring the Tour de

France itself. For several years, Coca-Cola, a major Tour sponsor, had set up a two-story lounge known as the Coca-Cola pavilion, at the Tour's finish line, which gave Coke major visibility in Europe. But in her eyes, Motorola couldn't justify shelling out millions of dollars just to sponsor a single twenty-one-day event. She had agreed to meet Ochowicz purely as a courtesy to one of her husband's biking buddies, who had known him since childhood. She informed him that he had exactly forty-five minutes to make his pitch.

In his thick Wisconsin accent, Ochowicz began describing himself and his team as American pioneers in Europe, who had successfully brought legitimacy to a sport that for many years had been on the fringes of American athletic culture. Eric Heiden was still riding with the team, drawing crowds of autograph-seeking fans. And in addition to dominating the domestic criterium races, 7-Eleven was also the first US-based team to have a rider who wore the coveted yellow jersey of the overall leader in the Tour de France, and the first to win a stage in a major Tour—an honor in its own right.

Having pillaged competing teams for talented riders such as Andy Hampsten, a thin, curly-haired, bucktoothed kid from North Dakota who was then the team leader, Ochowicz had high hopes for their ability to compete successfully in the European pro peloton. He described in vivid detail the big day earlier that summer, when Hampsten had become the first American to win the Giro d'Italia, cycling's second-biggest race. Undeterred by the heavy snowfall on the 8,600-foot Passo di Gavia in the Italian Alps, Hampsten had descended those snowy roads like a madman, defeating all the other top contenders in the race, none of whom had the guts or the technical skill to keep up on the treacherous downhill.

The forty-five-minute appointment turned into a five-hour discussion. Ochowicz didn't have the most sophisticated argument for why it made financial sense for Motorola to invest in a cycling team. But Griffin was moved by his passion. She began to think that sponsoring a pro cycling team whose riders could compete throughout Europe would be a shrewd, and even inexpensive, way to raise the profile of the Motorola brand. The three million dollars Ochowicz thought he needed to accomplish the big things he had in mind didn't put a big dent in the Motorola marketing budget, and there was plenty of upside: If Ochowicz could use that money to hire a couple of riders strong enough to win stages in cycling's three Grand Tours—the world's only three-week stage races—then the Motorola brand, with its bat-wings logo, would be all over the European newspapers and TV. Back in the States, the brand might get a boost, too, if bike enthusiasts, casual riders such as her husband and his buddies, took to donning Motorola jerseys on their Saturday rides.

Two weeks later, Griffin called Ochowicz to inform him that Motorola had decided to underwrite his team. His American team—managed by his nonstock corporation the South Club Inc., of Waukesha, Wisconsin—would set up European headquarters in Hulste, Belgium, a small West Flanders village near the French border. Ochowicz's bold move had saved his team. What it had done for Motorola was another question.

Team Motorola had a disastrous showing at first, taking 55th place (out of roughly two hundred riders) in its racing debut, the Tour of Lombardy, a one-day Italian "classic" race in Milan, Italy, that fall. But Griffin reassured Motorola executives that its fortunes would turn around soon. And Ochowicz was determined to make sure that happened. Thanks to Motorola's sponsorship, he had the money he needed to buy himself some more promising young riders. The team was already filled with gifted, naturally talented athletes like Frankie Andreu, a solid veteran from Michigan, and great lead-out man, and Ron Kiefel, the first American to win a stage in a Grand Tour. Now he was on a mission to find the next Greg LeMond, who had just won the 1990 Tour riding for the French Z team. Ochowicz was still disappointed over his failure to sign LeMond himself. He and his 7-Eleven squad had made a hefty multimillion-dollar offer to LeMond, but they were outbid by the French team, which had offered LeMond $4.7 million over three years—one of the largest contracts ever signed in cycling. So Ochowicz was on the lookout for a new star.

In the spring of 1991, Lance was in his second season on Subaru-Montgomery, but he was still angry about the feud he'd had with Eddie B and Thom Weisel earlier that year during the Bergamasca race in Italy. Eddie B had been incensed that, after his win, Armstrong had failed to thank his teammates for their support. He saw it as a further sign that Armstrong was immature and self-centered. Armstrong, in turn, felt betrayed by Eddie B and was worried Weisel might fire him. Given the bad feelings, it seemed highly unlikely that Armstrong would stay with their team for much longer. Lance was effectively in play, and Ochowicz wanted to snap him up for the new Motorola team. Although Armstrong was still a junior, and an amateur with little understanding of the European peloton, he was one of the most coveted young riders on the circuit.

When Ochowicz approached Armstrong about joining his team, he offered him a special arrangement: If he signed with Motorola, he could remain an amateur, receiving a stipend, until after the 1992 Barcelona Olympics, at which time he would immediately become a full-time pro racer and join Motorola's European squad. Armstrong was thrilled. In his eyes, Och's team was like the Dallas Cowboys of American cycling. It was one of the top ten or so teams in the world, the kind of team where he wanted to end up.

Now Armstrong had to call Thom Weisel to inform him that, after less than two years with the team, he was quitting Subaru-Montgomery. Weisel was blunt: It was a bad idea. He still had a lot to learn, and if he went over to Europe now, he'd get chewed up and spat out in no time. Weisel also told Armstrong that he could get him to Europe soon but that he'd have to wait until he was ready, and until the team had the budget for it, which it didn't yet. Armstrong, who respected Weisel for his success and his willingness to support the team, at first found it difficult to defend his choice. But by the end of the phone conversation, after Weisel paused for a moment to reflect on everything that had been said, he told Armstrong that he respected his candor and would support his decision to move on.

The Barcelona Olympics would show the world just how much more Armstrong had to learn. His mother, Linda, and new stepfather, John Walling, used rollers to paint an eight-by-four-foot Texas flag on the pavement of the largest hill of the course. Such roadside graffiti is a tradition in bike racing. Alongside it they painted *Texas Flyer*, in honor of Armstrong. But Armstrong got stuck in a pack of riders early on in the race—and was still stuck there when the pack crossed the finish line. He ended up in fourteenth place out of roughly two hundred riders, a most unimpressive performance. Armstrong couldn't explain it. He told reporters he just felt weak that day. Lance was quiet at dinner that night with his mom and stepdad and friends from Plano.

It got worse. About a week after the Olympics road race, Armstrong turned pro, as Ochowicz had promised him he would do, and entered the Clásica San Sebastián, a Spanish one-day road racing "classic," and one of the races that tend to favor bigger riders like him. Armstrong finished dead last.

Armstrong was learning the hard way about the speed of the European cyclist. The peloton in the highest-level European races never slows down. Instead, it hums along at a blistering pace until someone attacks, causing the entire field to accelerate en masse for several minutes until it goes back to the previous, leg-scorching speed. The lack of lulls in the pace means weaker riders have no opportunities to recover. Armstrong may have been good in the junior ranks, but in the top rung of professional racing, he was one of the weaker riders.

Over the course of just a couple of weeks, Armstrong had gone from an extreme high to a depressing low. Despite what he might have believed, he was not superhuman. He had to come to grips with the reality that there were cyclists out there who were faster and tactically smarter. In fact, there were a lot of them. Armstrong had to come back to earth and the reality that he needed to work harder. He spent the off-season in Austin and Florida, riding 500 to 600 miles, 25 to 30 hours a week, preparing for his first full season as a professional on the Motorola squad. To simulate racing, Lance would ride in the slipstream of J.T. Neal's motor scooter, often for hours at a time.

The training paid off. By 1993, Armstrong was starting to realize his potential. He came in second in the Tour DuPont, a prestigious eleven-day stage race in the United States, which attracted many of the sport's top cyclists, and he became a contender for a $1 million prize, available to any rider who could manage to sweep the three races that were held in succession over the course of a couple of weeks. This trio of events, held in Pittsburgh, West Virginia, and Philadelphia, was known as the Thrift Drug Triple Crown. Armstrong easily won the Pittsburgh race, which he had also won in 1992.

During the West Virginia race, a 493-mile, six-stage race in the hills, Armstrong won the opening Morgantown prologue time trial—a race against the clock—by just under 2 seconds. The second day of the race brought a 100-mile mountain course in the Monongahela National Forest near Elkins, a small town. After Armstrong won again, his lead in the overall standings was 14 seconds, with Michael Engleman of the rival Coors Light team in second place.

With the $1 million prize on the line, Armstrong then turned to an age-old tactic to boost his chance of winning. He sent a Motorola teammate to approach Scott McKinley, one of the captains of the Coors Light squad, with a business proposition. Stephen Swart, another Coors team captain, later recalled, under oath during a lawsuit deposition, the following proposition: Would Engleman and his Coors Light teammates be open to a payoff in exchange for agreeing not to challenge Armstrong in what remained of the "Triple Crown"?

Swart, a stocky New Zealander, testified that he met Armstrong in a hotel room to discuss it. In fact, such deals were common in the strange sport of professional cycling, and not seen as entirely unsportsmanlike. The riders quickly came to an agreement, Swart said. If the Coors team riders backed off and didn't challenge Armstrong, and if Armstrong won the $1 million, he would pay the Coors team a total of $50,000. While the payment wasn't a huge amount of money, the Coors riders hadn't won the first leg of the Triple Crown in Pittsburgh, so they weren't in the running for the $1 million anyway. They all agreed to keep it quiet, Swart said in his testimony, knowing that if the insurance company that paid out the $1 million bonus found out, it might refuse to pay up.

Engleman's lead over Armstrong slipped to 45 seconds and he didn't challenge Armstrong for the remainder of the race. Armstrong won the second leg of the Triple Crown. Engleman finished second. Swart testified that even if the Coors team had wanted to challenge Armstrong, doing so may not have been possible because Armstrong was so strong.

The third event in the series, the USPRO National Championships, was one of the few events of that era in American cycling that drew large numbers of fans to the course. Many came to watch the bikers ride up the "Manayunk Wall," a steep climb in Northwest Philadelphia. Fans would pack the sidewalks, cheering, beer in hand. With Armstrong racing for $1 million, the crowds were even larger than usual that year. Newspapers and television stations all over the country were covering Armstrong's potential payday.

Shortly after the start of the race, Armstrong and a group of eight riders—most of them no-names—got out ahead of the rest of the pack. Then, on the final ascent up the Manayunk Wall, Armstrong got out of the saddle and took off, smashing down the pedals, his bike and body swaying from side to side with effort, as he ground his bike uphill. None of the other riders stayed with him, including Roberto Gaggioli, a member of the Coors Light team. By the time Armstrong reached the top, he was far enough ahead that he could coast the final stretch to the finish line. He sat up with no hands on the bars and slowly rolled toward the line, blowing kisses to the tipsy fans.

It was the highlight of his career so far. The sports press ate it up. "Armstrong makes his first million," proclaimed the Agence France-Press. "Armstrong feels like a million bucks," said *The New York Times*. "Just when it seemed the earnings of athletes couldn't go anymore haywire," added the Associated Press.

A few months after the race, the Coors Light team was paid in cash for their lack of effort in the races.

Following his $1 million payday, Armstrong headed back to Europe to start his education in the Tour de France. At twenty-one, he would be the youngest competitor in the race that year. He viewed his first Tour de France sort of like he was Joe Namath arriving in Miami to take on Johnny Unitas and the Colts. Photographers, reporters, the room full of people, the electricity—this was just his style, he decided.

Ochowicz had, since the mid-1980s, set up a training base for his riders at Como, Italy, about forty miles north of Milan, beneath the snowcapped Alps. A town of silk factories, medieval churches, and tourism, Como is considered the spiritual home of cycling and is near the infamous twenty-seven-mile-long Passo del Mortirolo, a climb of nearly 4,400 feet, one of the most difficult mountains a cyclist can face in Italy. It was also the hometown of the 7-Eleven team's first physician and trainer, Massimo Testa, who set up a sports performance lab there, and later became doctor to the Motorola team.

When Lance arrived in Como, he shared an apartment on the fourth floor of a six-story building with Frankie Andreu, a native of Detroit who was five years older. For coaching and fitness testing, Lance relied on the doctor, Testa, who assigned Lance training rides through Passo del Ghisallo, a moderately difficult climb at the tip of the lake's peninsula—with a chapel dedicated to cycling at the summit—and to the Pian del Tivano, with its long, scenic descent.

Far from home, Lance began practicing his Italian, sunbathing on the apartment balcony, and spending hours on the dial-up Internet. Frankie, a lanky cyclist with a sometimes-cranky demeanor, became Lance's mentor. Frankie's girlfriend, Betsy, a petite University of Michigan theater grad with thick brown hair, sometimes snapped at him when he was rude to people.

One night, the three of them went out for pizza at a small restaurant on one of Como's charmingly narrow hillside streets. The waiter at the restaurant was taking forever to bring them their wine and pizzas, and Lance grew impatient. "These fucking Italians!" he shouted. "Can't they bring the fucking wine?!"

"Lance, they understand what you're saying," Betsy said, explaining to Lance that Europeans weren't as quick with the service as Americans.

"I don't fucking care."

"You're not in Texas. If you don't like it, don't go out to eat," she shot back.

Betsy thought Lance had some behavioral problems, but she liked him, and she thought Lance respected her and listened when she tried to steer him in the right direction. But Betsy visited Como only occasionally. She was in the process of leaving her sales job and opening an Italian espresso bar in Detroit.

Considering that Armstrong had not yet won a single major European professional race, his cocky smile and full-of-himself personality was a turnoff to some of the top pros, who viewed him as condescending. In France, Germany, Belgium, and Spain, bike racing was considered a blue-collar vocation. Europeans rode bikes because they didn't want to work in a steel mill or sweat it out on some farm. They kept their heads down, raced their bikes hard, did what they were told, and hoped their meager paychecks would actually arrive. The glitz and glamour of American professional sports were as alien to them as the US tax code.

The man who would probably have been the top contender for that year's Tour de France, three-time winner LeMond, decided to pull out just before the start of the race. He told reporters who were covering the Tour that he was suffering from major fatigue. But privately, LeMond told friends and family that he believed that new, powerful blood-boosting drugs had so dramatically improved the abilities of the riders who used them that it had become impossible for riders who weren't doping to compete.

The Motorola team knew comparatively little about the sport's doping culture, which by then had become quite advanced among the European teams. The new drug that was sweeping the peloton and increasing the speeds of the races by double-digit percentage points—the one that caused LeMond to decide to drop out of the Tour—was recombinant erythropoietin, which the riders called EPO for short. A synthetic version of a natural hormone in the body that causes bone marrow to produce red blood cells, it had been developed in the lab to help patients who had developed anemia because of chronic kidney disease and was prescribed off label for anemic cancer patients. For endurance athletes, whose grueling long-haul exertions turn their bodies into fiery furnaces that burn red blood cells at an astonishing rate, EPO was a godsend—even more powerful than the anabolic steroids that had become commonplace in athletics in the 1970s and 1980s. As LeMond knew, any riders going into the Tour without the advantage of EPO would be at a considerable disadvantage.

The first seven race days of the 1993 Tour de France were uneventful for Armstrong. But on the eighth racing day, a short 114-mile jaunt from a quaint French village, Châlons-sur-Marne, to the town of Verdun, he found himself in a small breakaway group—ahead of all the others. Armstrong, who wore a special American-flag-themed Motorola jersey, an honor for winning the US-PRO National Championship, rocked slightly on the bike and worked hard to keep up his pace. As the group of six men approached the finish, huge crowds, kept at bay by red barriers with Coca-Cola logos, lined the sides of the road.

With 200 meters—656 feet—to go, Armstrong seemed to be at a severe disadvantage, with three riders blocking him from moving up ahead of the pack. Frenchman Ronan Pensec of the Novemail team drove his legs into an all-out, point-of-no-return sprint toward the finish line. But suddenly, Pensec swerved slightly to the left, opening a tiny gap between him and the barriers. Armstrong seized the opportunity immediately, sprinting at full power through the gap. Armstrong's handlebars nearly bumped a security official standing against the barriers and he came within inches of hitting an oversize replica of a Coke can. But he made it through the tiny gap without crashing, which was fortunate because he was not wearing a helmet. It's traditional not to do so on stages that involve mountain climbs—and if he had hit the barrier at thirty-five miles per hour, it would have been a horrific crash. As he crossed the finish line, he threw his hands in the air, swerved left, and nearly knocked a rival off his bike. And with that, Armstrong had become the youngest American to win a stage in the Tour de France.

But he dropped out of the Tour shortly after that. He wasn't ready yet for the long and arduous climbs over the Alps and the Pyrenees, and leaving the Tour early was part of the team's plan for him. He wasn't a skilled climber, and it wouldn't do him any good to endure that kind of pain. He was also competing against teams with sophisticated doping programs. Motorola had no organized doping at that time. It was up to the riders to find their own way.

J.T. Neal had arrived at the Tour de France to collect Lance, and drove him back to Como the next day. Armstrong put the time off to good use: He spent the rest of July and early August in Como, near the home of the Italian team physician, who helped Lance map out a training routine. Lance also shed some weight as he began preparing for cycling's World Championships, a one-day event at the end of August. By now, he had begun using low-octane doping products—such as cortisone and testosterone. Cortisone gave a temporary boost of energy during one-day races. Testosterone aided recovery Much like the Olympics, the annual World Championship road race is a competition between nations. Riders ditch their team kits, the uniforms featuring their sponsors, and put on their national colors for the day to become teammates with their countrymen.

The 1993 World Championship was held in Oslo, Norway, on an urban road course 160 miles long, with one medium-size climb and a bunch of sharp turns through city streets and highways. Lance's mother, Linda, traveled to the event from Plano, Texas, and sat in the metal bleachers near the finish with Stephanie McIlvain, a young, earnest Oakley rep assigned to sponsorships for several pro cyclists, including LeMond, and now Armstrong. The late August weather in Oslo was horrific. The cold downpour made the roads slick. After the race began, many riders slipped and fell. Armstrong himself went down twice.

On the last lap, Armstrong accelerated on the climb and broke away from the pack, solo. The crowd began to buzz with surprise. Armstrong had so little experience, he didn't know how long he could stay ahead of the field at his current speed. But that was what made him different. Most young and inexperienced riders would have erred on the side of caution, waiting in the pack and conserving energy. Armstrong just went and didn't think twice about it. There was a chance he'd implode and get caught by some of the world's best riders who were trailing him—men like Claudio Chiappucci and Miguel Indurain. But Armstrong kept his lead. He slowed down in the turns, taking the bends carefully, as he approached the final three miles. On the final straightaway, on a large four-lane highway, Armstrong ducked his head and shot into the driving rain, occasionally peeking behind him to look for the Chiappuccis and the Indurains. They weren't there. With 0.9 miles to go, the riders behind Armstrong had given up any hope of actually catching him and were now just looking at each other, wondering which one of them would finish second.

As he approached the finish line, the onlookers standing in the cold rain—many of whom previously had no idea who Lance Armstrong was—began cheering him on. When he was still about 0.6 miles from the finish line, he lifted his hands off the handlebars to signal his victory. The Texan was champion of the world. After the race, he hugged his mom. They both wept.

A representative for King Harald of Norway soon approached them and invited Armstrong to the royal viewing area so that the king could congratulate him in person. Armstrong grabbed Linda, bringing her along. They were stopped at a security checkpoint and Linda was told to wait while Armstrong went on to see the king. Armstrong looked at the guard and shot back: "I don't check my mother at the door!" They both strolled right in. Lance would later be quoted as saying of the king, "I'm sure he's great and everything, but I just wanted to get out of there and go party with the guys." And that's exactly what he did.

With the victory, Armstrong became the undisputed star of the team. His résumé now included a Tour de France stage and a World Championship. The majority of professional cyclists would have considered those career-defining achievements. Armstrong was only getting started. One benefit of his success was that he began collecting huge appearance fees—typically $20,000 to $25,000 per race—just for showing up at races in France and elsewhere in Europe. Often the payments were made in cash.

Despite Armstrong's growing success, higher-ups at Motorola were scratching their heads. Why, exactly, was Motorola sponsoring the puny sport of cycling? some of them asked. Sheila Griffin, who traveled to Europe to support the team and often rode in the "pace car" during the Tour, vehemently defended the sponsorship and insisted it would pay dividends over time as riders like Armstrong matured and as the team began winning bigger events. While Lance had racked up two big wins, the team still hadn't won any big races. But to ensure that they did, Griffin wanted to be certain the team had every edge. She even began investing in a new technology for the team, which they called the peloton communications system, the first two-way radio connection between cyclists and team directors. A Motorola engineer created a prototype by soldering a tiny radio earpiece into Motorola team helmets. After the Motorola team began using it, other teams quickly followed suit. Eventually, it became standard technology for the sport. Motorola decided to extend its sponsorship for just one more year.

But there was huge pressure on Ochowicz to deliver big results. When Armstrong heard rumors that Motorola might end its sponsorship, he was concerned about what that would mean for him personally. He knew that even the great Greg LeMond had had to spend a year playing the role of a domestique on the La Vie Claire squad, helping the team's lead rider, the Frenchman Bernard Hinault, before being given his own chance to win the Tour de France. If the Motorola team folded and Armstrong signed onto another team, it seemed likely that he'd have to do the same—riding as a domestique to help out a more famous rider. If so, it might take him years to climb up the totem pole to lead rider. Whereas if things kept going well with Motorola, Armstrong felt sure he would soon become its unrivaled leader and a star in the sport. He was not interested in anything less.

As Armstrong's stature in the sport grew, so did his ego. Motorola had earned a top-five world ranking, a first for an American team. It already was paying Armstrong $500,000 a year, plus bonuses. But he was becoming increasingly demanding of the team management and of his teammates. As a world champion, he believed he should be pampered. He griped about the food riders ate and the team's choice of hotels. "Michael Jordan wouldn't stay at a place like this," he complained. Additionally, he was jealous of Andy Hampsten, the team's leader and star. There was room for only one leader on the team and Armstrong wanted to be it. He expected his teammates to be completely subservient, abandoning their own ambitions for the sake of his glory.

When Lance returned to Austin that September, he was a twenty-one-year-old with a lot of money and a narcissistic streak. Had he been an up-and-coming star in baseball or football, the US media would have been all over him. He would have had his pick of groupies and celebrity friends. But Americans weren't particularly aware of his cycling accomplishments. Some US cycling safety activists had even chastised him for riding in the Worlds without a helmet. Back in Austin, Lance began a relationship with Sonni Evans, an old high school friend in Plano who had graduated from Southwest Texas State University. His relationship with Sonni reassured him, because they had met long before he became a world champion. Soon, she was living with him in Como.

He also asked his former coach, Chris Carmichael, to relocate from Colorado Springs, Colorado, to Austin, where he could train him. But Carmichael declined, wary of Lance's potential demands on him.

For support in Austin, Lance turned again to J.T., who had continued serving as Lance's personal masseur while he rode for Motorola, and who had provided Lance with advice on what to do with his growing assets. An eccentric and opinionated man, with a deep empathy for others, J.T. saw himself as a father figure to Lance, keeping in touch with Linda, helping Lance manage his newfound wealth, and looking after his affairs while he was racing in Europe. J.T also volunteered to act as Lance's personal soigneur at no charge and monitored his training, scolding him for drinking too much beer or not drinking enough water on rides, and making sure Lance ate proper meals. J.T. also gave Lance the use of his speedboat on Lake Austin, for Lance's other passion at the time: waterskiing. For Lance, the relationship was more transactional—J.T. gave him some good tips and advice. He was more like a stock broker than a dad.

Eventually, even Linda became concerned by Lance's attitude and sought out advice about how to handle him. Linda knew that Greg LeMond had a lot in common with Armstrong. He was very young when he went to Europe and had won the World Championship at almost exactly the same age. Linda asked LeMond and his wife, Kathy, if she and J.T. Neal could visit them in Minnesota to talk to them about her son. Over coffee, Linda laid out her concerns. But the LeMonds didn't know what to say. Greg certainly had his issues. He could be demanding to the point of being a jerk. He had character flaws, and he knew it. But LeMond felt he was nothing like Armstrong, who sometimes seemed to be mean simply for the sake of being mean. And Greg, at the time, seemed to have an inner stability very different from Armstrong's volatile nature. He had met his wife, Kathy, at a very young age and they (so far) had stayed happily married throughout all the ups and downs of LeMond's career. Linda left with the sympathy of the LeMonds but few answers.

To kick off the 1994 season, Armstrong raced in Mexico and then did some of the minor tune-up races in Europe in February before flying back to the United States. Armstrong was anxious about the coming season. He knew the public now expected more of him. Despite considerable training, Armstrong's season was marked with a major trouncing in March in Milan–San Remo, a 180-mile single-day race that is usually won by cyclists with incredible endurance capacity and the ability to sprint. It was a major blow to Armstrong's ego. In April, he went to Belgium and raced in the famous Liège–Bastogne–Liège, a spring classic that had been around since 1892. He finished second in the 160-mile course, which winds through the hilly Ardennes region of Belgium. It was an impressive show of strength, but a disappointing finish that showed Armstrong's still immature tactical sense. Russian Evgeni Berzin, who was racing for Ferrari's Gewiss team, caught Armstrong by surprise with a late solo attack for the win. In May, Armstrong finished second in the Tour DuPont for the second year in a row. Armstrong needed to win—not finish second—in big races. And if he wanted to be considered one of cycling's greats, he needed to think about training to win the

Tour de France. But endurance riding—the kind needed to win a race like that—still was not his strength.

When Lance returned to Como for the racing season, he brought along Sonni, who had graduated with a degree in fashion merchandising. The couple lived in Lance's two-bedroom apartment there. To build up his endurance on the bike, Lance spent his days doing long training rides through Bergamo with his teammates Frankie Andreu and George Hincapie. But Lance, who was prone to lose his temper during training rides, would often get into heated arguments with Italian drivers. Sonni recalls that Lance struggled that season, even bailing out of a couple of European races and heading back to Como early. Just before the end of the season, Lance informed Sonni that they had to break up. He told her that his team manager, Ochowicz, felt he was slacking and that Ochowicz and Lance's mother, Linda, thought Sonni was too much of a distraction. Heartbroken, she packed her belongings and headed home. Lance moved on quickly, however. Within months, he began a serious romance with beautiful young Dutch cyclist Danielle Overgaag, whom he met at the Interbike trade show in Las Vegas. The daughter of a chrysanthemum grower, Danielle stayed with him in Como, teaching him how to swear in Dutch. When Lance returned to the States, Danielle came along, moving into the apartment Lance rented from J.T. Neal.

The highlight of the 1994 Tour de France was not a race but Motorola's decision to renew its sponsorship, keeping the American team alive for at least another year or two. Shortly after, Armstrong signed a two-year contract that was estimated at a whopping $850,000 a year—the highest of anyone on the team. Despite Armstrong's less than stellar season, Motorola was willing to invest in the rising star.

As Armstrong rose up, Greg LeMond was struggling during the most difficult period of his career. A mysterious weakness was still holding him back and he dropped out of the Tour de France early in the race. LeMond had improved his training and hoped to perform well in the race, and was extremely disappointed at how it turned out.

When LeMond dropped out of the race, Kathy LeMond was at their house in Belgium, where they lived during the cycling season. The day after Greg's withdrawal, the phone rang and Kathy picked up. "Hi, it's Lance."

"Lance who?" Kathy asked, not thinking that it might be the young up-and-coming American star.

"It's Lance Armstrong," he said. "I'd like to rent your house in Belgium."

"What?" Kathy asked, perplexed.

"Well, Greg's done. I'd like to rent your house," he said.

"Well, our house isn't for rent," Kathy said. At the time, the LeMonds had three kids, all of whom were living there. Besides, Greg wasn't even sure he wanted to retire yet. The phone call left the LeMonds feeling insulted and surprised.

At the end of that year, Greg LeMond announced he was retiring from the sport, and the inevitable stories comparing LeMond and Armstrong circulated around the world. The word was that LeMond was "passing the torch" to Armstrong. Armstrong offered the obligatory praise to LeMond but was annoyed by the comparisons. "I'm not the next Greg LeMond," he took to saying during interviews with the press. "I'm the first Lance Armstrong."

Armstrong headed back to Europe for the beginning of the 1995 season. In early March, Armstrong entered Paris–Nice, one of the stage races that Grand Tour contenders often use as spring training. The eight-day stage race is nicknamed the Race to the Sun because it goes from chilly, rainy Paris to warm, sunny Nice in the south. Armstrong nabbed the fifth stage of the race—an uphill finish. The win gave him a good boost for the season. Viatcheslav Ekimov, Armstrong's rival from the Tour DuPont the previous season, was less than a second behind Armstrong, in fourth place.

A week after Paris–Nice, the Motorola team returned to Milan–San Remo, the long, grueling Italian road race. Armstrong and his teammates were again annihilated. On the way home from the race, Armstrong started complaining to his teammates about other teams using EPO. He felt the Motorola team had done so poorly because they were competing with riders who were pumped to the gills with the stuff. George Hincapie understood Armstrong's message clearly. His buddy Armstrong wanted him and the other Motorola riders to start using EPO, too. If they didn't, they wouldn't be strong enough to support him in the big races.

Hincapie, who was living in Como, Italy, found out from Frankie that EPO was available at a pharmacy in Switzerland, not far from the apartment he shared with several other teammates. In fact, Frankie made regular trips to pick up supplies for himself and some of his teammates. And Hincapie rode over to the pharmacy himself, spending $450 or so for a month's supply of the miracle drug. And it was clear that EPO was working.

Armstrong in particular could ride stronger, for longer. He discovered endurance capacity he'd never had. Armstrong was convinced that EPO—sometimes referred to by riders as Edgar Allan Poe—was safe. But he wondered about the health effects of human-growth hormone, or HGH, which sped up his recovery, and helped Armstrong get leaner, more muscular.

By mid-1995, Armstrong ranked fourteenth in the world cycling standings. He had won the Tour DuPont, the highest-profile race in the United States. To capitalize on his achievements and help him raise his profile, he decided he needed an agent, and, after interviewing several candidates, he ultimately settled on Bill Stapleton. A native of St. Louis, Stapleton had been an Olympic swimmer, though he never quite reached the top of his sport. After leaving the world of competitive athletics, he had gotten business and law degrees at the University of Texas at Austin, then taken a job as an associate at the large Austin law firm Brown McCarroll & Oaks Hartline. Bored by corporate law, Stapleton approached the law firm with his plans for a sports-management practice and convinced the partners to allow him to carve out a sports agency within the firm.

Per the agreement he made with Armstrong, his law firm got a 3 to 5 percent fee on Armstrong's employment contract. On top of that, Stapleton himself would take in 15 to 25 percent of any endorsement and marketing deals he made on Armstrong's behalf, and he quickly began lining them up. He negotiated new endorsement deals with Nike, helmet maker Giro, and Milton Bradley, all within his first year of representing Armstrong. He also negotiated a lucrative extension with Oakley and signed an individual deal with Motorola. The endorsement deals with Oakley, Nike, and Giro stipulated that Armstrong would get an immediate $1 million bonus from each of them—plus another $2 million in possible long-term endorsements—if he won a gold medal in the upcoming 1996 Olympics in Atlanta. The Olympics had recently changed its rules to allow professionals into the competitions, meaning Armstrong would get another shot at a gold medal. Flush with endorsement and prize monies on top of his large salary, Armstrong began work on what would be a $1 million, 4,300-square-foot white Mediterranean-style villa on the banks of Lake Austin. J.T. had helped Lance find and purchase the plot of land, and helped to oversee construction of the villa, while Lance was off racing overseas for most of the year. Lance put his mother, Linda, in charge of finding a designer and hiring the movers. Though Linda hadn't gotten a college degree, she had attended night school to get her real estate license while working as a secretary at Ericsson Telecommunications.

Lance named the villa Casa de Linda after her. Even before the lakeside dock was built, Lance had picked out a name for his boat: *Pedal Faster*. J.T. loved palm trees, and so, to honor him, Lance planted twenty-six palm trees along the property.

As the date of the 1995 Tour de France drew closer, Armstrong was feeling good. He was stronger than he had been the previous year, and his team was stronger, thanks to EPO. George Hincapie noticed that most of the riders on the team were now carrying thermoses that made a clinking sound when they moved around, and he knew what was inside the thermoses—vials of EPO. Before the 1995 Tour de France, Motorola team doctor Massimo Testa gave the riders a talk about the dangers of EPO. Testa believed that if riders took too much of it, their blood would become thick and syrupy and could overload the heart, or cause a dangerous blood clot, possibly resulting in death. So, during the Tour, Testa borrowed a blood centrifuge from another team doctor, which he used to test the riders' blood to make sure their hematocrits—a measure of the ratio of red blood cells to overall blood volume—were not dangerously high. Nobody on the team had taken too much EPO, but most of their hematocrits were unnaturally high, though not yet dangerously, considering the amount of exercise they were doing. The percentage of red blood cells to overall blood volume tends to go down with hard training, especially during grueling races like the Tour de France.

The 1995 Tour de France turned tragic for the Motorola team. One of its riders, twenty-four-year-old Italian Fabio Casartelli, crashed on a mountain road and died of head injuries. Casartelli had won the gold medal in the men's road race in the 1992 Olympics—Armstrong's last race as an amateur, in which he finished a disappointing fourteenth. Two days after Casartelli's death, on stage 18 from Montpon-Ménestérol to Limoges, Armstrong attacked alone and crossed the finish line by himself. He pointed skyward in honor of his fallen teammate. Armstrong would later say it was the most meaningful moment of his own career. Two days later, Armstrong finished the Tour de France for the first time, in 36th place.

Two weeks later, Armstrong won his first major professional European bike race, the Clásica San Sebastián, the same race in which he had finished dead last in 1992, shortly after the Olympics. No American had ever won one of cycling's "classics" races, but this year, Armstrong was red hot.

In late 1995, Lance took another major step in his career. He flew to Ferrara, Italy, to meet an Italian sports doctor named Michele Ferrari. Lance was introduced to Ferarri by Eddy Merckx, the retired Belgian cycling legend. Merckx's bike company sponsored the Motorola team, and all of its riders used Merckx bikes. Merckx's son, Axel, was a rider on the Motorola team, and Lance noticed that Axel had improved significantly in the 1995 season. Lance attributed the improvement to Axel's work with Ferrari.

Ferrari lived largely in the shadows of the sport. He never attended races or official team events. He wore thick glasses and drove an old beat-up station wagon or a camper. He apparently needed nothing for happiness but his Excel spreadsheets and a calculator.

Ferrari's one brush with the public spotlight did not go so well. In 1994, he had served as team doctor for Gewiss-Ballan, an Italian-based cycling team that debuted in 1993. After three Gewiss-Ballan riders took the top three places in one of the major spring classics—a bit like one country winning every Olympic medal in a single sport—one journalist directly questioned Ferrari about the use of EPO. Ferrari proceeded to wax eloquent about EPO's safety. "EPO is no more dangerous than orange juice," he said. Ferrari seemed to be justifying, even advocating, the use of a powerful hormone for performance-enhancing benefit. After the statements, Ferrari was fired from the team.

Of course, when Ferrari made his comments, he and everyone else in the sport knew that EPO was banned in cycling. But there was no test for it. The International Olympic Committee, which at the time oversaw the anti-doping effort in sports, had commissioned a respected sports doctor to develop a test to detect it in urine. Their choice was Francesco Conconi, who had been one of Ferrari's university professors in Italy and had himself been involved in the doping of Italian Olympic athletes. The irony that Conconi, the proverbial fox, was now charged with guarding the henhouse wasn't lost on some of the European press at the time, which pointed out his connection to Ferrari.

But the controversy, which was not covered in a single major newspaper in the United States, might as well have been an advertisement for Ferrari. He was about to become the most coveted secret doctor in professional sports. Armstrong always liked to be on the cutting edge—of music, fashion, technology, and, most of all, sports science. Lance quickly came to regard Ferrari as a genius.

Lance didn't tell his Motorola teammates, such as Frankie Andreu, about the meeting with Ferrari, as he wasn't ready to share that information. Not every rider on the team could afford to work with Ferrari, whose fees were often based on a percentage of a rider's salary and ranged from $15,000 to more than $375,000, including bonuses. Motorola certainly wasn't going to foot the bill.

Armstrong's cycling prowess was about to get a major boost, but trouble was brewing with the Motorola sponsorship. By the end of 1995, Sheila Griffin was under pressure from her European-based colleagues to move the Motorola sponsorship over to a soccer team, which they believed would give the brand more visibility than cycling. Ochowicz hoped for a last-minute rescue and worked for months to identify a new sponsor, but nothing materialized.

Lance, meanwhile, lived as if he didn't have a care in the world. He dumped Danielle and she returned to the Netherlands, heartbroken. When Betsy asked Armstrong what happened, he just shrugged. He explained that he was now dating a bathing suit model, who Armstrong crassly explained was clean shaven—everywhere. With no serious relationship, Armstrong had plenty of time to hang out at Austin bars, drinking Shiner Bock and meeting girls. Lance began spending his evenings with John Korioth, then the manager of the Cactus Room, one of Austin's most popular bars. He also began a casual relationship with Stephanie McIlvain.

One time, when McIlvain visited Como, Betsy heard one of the guys make a crack about Stephanie. "Lance is going to get his blow job," the teammate said.

"Who is Stephanie?" Betsy asked Frankie, who explained.

"But he has another girlfriend," Betsy said. Frankie told her this was more casual than that.

"So is that what's going on here? Women just come here and service you guys?" Betsy asked angrily.

"No, that's not what's going on here. That's just what's going on with Lance," Frankie said.

The beginning of Armstrong's 1996 season was marked by the biggest win in his professional career—a victory in Belgium's prestigious Flèche Wallonne, a one-day race through the hilly Ardennes region of Belgium known for its constant up-and-down climbs and technical curves. He followed that victory with another second place in Liège–Bastogne–Liège. He had just missed first in a close sprint to the line. Back in the United States in May, he won five stages of the Tour DuPont and snagged his second victory in a row.

Michele Ferrari's training seemed to be paying off big-time for Armstrong. The program he devised was perhaps the most carefully monitored, intensive, and unusual training regimen in the history of cycling, if not all sports. And he was well compensated for his efforts. During 1996, Lance paid Ferrari $14,000 in February, $28,500 in May, and $42,000 in July, according to Ferrari's bank records. The July payment came from an account Lance shared with his mother. As Armstrong trained, Ferrari followed his climbs in a battered station wagon, stopping to check how much power Armstrong was putting to the pedals and checking his blood for minute changes in the amount of lactic acid coursing through his veins. He monitored the wattage Armstrong was able to produce per kilogram of his body weight, and the number of vertical feet he ascended per minute, or VAM. And when Ferrari looked down at his spreadsheets through his thick-rimmed glasses, he saw what he considered to be an extraordinarily promising physical specimen. Ferrari had pioneered the use of calculations to predict an athlete's performance potential, and he was convinced that science could transform Armstrong from a bulky and inconsistent athlete into a Tour de France winner.

By early summer, however, Armstrong was showing signs of strain and fatigue. After his Tour DuPont win in May, he took nearly a month off and returned to Austin. It was unusual for Armstrong to take so long a break.

During his training for the Tour of Switzerland in June, Armstrong needed a few days of recovery time after each "hard" day, unusual for a guy who could usually ride hard for several days straight. During the race itself—an eleven-day stage race through the Swiss Alps, which some riders use as a tune-up for the Tour de France—he was clearly struggling. He had started the race as a favorite but finished nowhere near the top of the standings.

Then, Armstrong pulled out of the Tour de France during the sixth stage of the race, complaining of bronchitis and a cold. The kid who never got sick was letting a little flu knock him out of the most important race of the year—one that was supposed to be the key to his preparation for the Atlanta Olympics later that month.

In the Olympics, Armstrong finished twelfth in the road race and sixth in the time trial. Respectable? Sure. But nowhere near his potential. And nowhere near the level of performance he needed to claim the millions of dollars' worth of sponsorship bonuses that Stapleton had negotiated for him.

It was a disappointing end to what began as a spectacular season. Armstrong had won the Tour DuPont, a major stage race. Then, he became the first American to win one of the prestigious spring classics, the Flèche Wallonne. Even more impressive, he had nearly completed the Ardennes double with a second-place finish in Liège–Bastogne–Liège. Even after dropping out of the Tour and missing out on another gold medal, Armstrong considered 1996 the best season of his career.

CHAPTER FIVE

TEAMWORK

I n 1993, Mark Gorski was living with his family in the sleepy town of Newport Beach, commuting to downtown Los Angeles for his cushy job as a vice president of sales at Wells Fargo. Less than a decade earlier, the thirty-three-year-old with a small gap in his front teeth had been the most decorated sprint cyclist in the United States. He was a cutthroat competitor, a killer on a bicycle, a celebrity on the velodrome circuit. Now he wore a business suit and carried a briefcase and commuted to a high-rise office building. It wasn't where he wanted to be.

A powerful sprinter who had been one of the 7-Eleven team's first recruits, Gorksi still longed for the excitement of racing, of traveling around the world, feeling the g-forces on the banked turns of velodromes from San Diego to Stockholm. Winning the match sprint during the 1984 Olympics had been one of the high points of his life. After he put that gold medal around his neck and waved to the crowd, he had wheeled around the track with his eighteen-month-old son, Alex, in one arm, and an American flag in the other, reveling in the moment, probably unaware that it was the last such moment he would enjoy in his athletic career.

After the Games, he landed endorsements from Fuji America, for its

Japanese-made bikes, as well as the city of Indianapolis, which had a new cycling track. He also set out on a mission as a race promoter to try to turn professional track bicycle racing into a spectator sport in the United States. He helped to organize international meets, including one between the Americans and the Soviets, which was broadcast on the cable channel ESPN. But men in spandex and skintight jerseys riding so-called intervals around a banked oval track wasn't something many Americans wanted to watch, and his foray as a race promoter didn't pan out. Gorski also wanted badly to compete in the 1988 Olympics, but there was only one spot on the team and it went to his rival, the younger Ken Carpenter.

When Gorski finally retired from racing in 1989, he thought maybe the macho world of high finance might satisfy his competitive drive. Wells Fargo at the time was snapping up former star athletes, including Bill Ring, the 49ers Super Bowl winning fullback, to handle large-asset investments for groups and individuals. Gorski figured there was unlimited upside potential.

But for Gorski the challenge of selling financial plans to wealthy folks just didn't compare to his passion for track racing. When the strapping six-foot-two 200-pounder was asked by a television station to provide color commentary for cycling events during the 1992 Olympics in Barcelona, he had an epiphany. Cycling was his calling! It helped that he had heard that his buddy, Ring, who had become a top-earning salesman at Wells Fargo, was taking a leave to follow his own dream—to become a running backs coach for Stanford under his old 49ers coach, Bill Walsh. Gorski thought about the off-season internship he had done in sports management after the Olympics. Maybe he could do that again?

Gorski turned to cycling's governing body and was hired by USA Cycling—until 1995, the US Cycling Federation—as national team director, relocating to its headquarters in Colorado Springs. His mandate was to develop young athletes, preparing them for international competition and getting their careers off the ground, but also to use his sales chops to bring in sponsors to help fund the program. For two years, he helped recruit talent, spread the word about the national cycling program, and worked with elite cyclists, often traveling to races.

One of those races was the Santa Rosa Downtown Criterium in 1995. On a cloudy April weekend, about six hundred riders showed up for a series of events including a 40-mile, 57-lap race through city streets around a complex of city, state, and federal buildings. There, Gorski ran into his old friend Thom Weisel, who had come up to Napa to watch his cycling team, Montgomery-Bell (they had lost Subaru as a sponsor and replaced it with helmet maker Bell). The chance encounter in wine country would change both of their lives forever.

Gorski had first met Weisel back in 1987, when Weisel showed up at Eddie B's training camps in Dallas. Gorski provided him with some racing tips. About a year later, when Gorski was living in Indianapolis, he saw Weisel compete in the Masters Track Nationals, for riders age forty-five and older, where Weisel, then forty-seven, placed second.

As the two men watched the bike race in Santa Rosa and caught up on what they were doing, Weisel was direct with Gorski. Funding a cycling team was expensive. "Mark, this thing is bleeding me dry," Weisel told him. "We either need to start pulling in some real sponsorship dollars or it's gonna fold."

Weisel had financed the team pretty much by himself in the late 1980s. But it soon became too expensive and he was fortunate the team landed Subaru as a sponsor. Over the years, Subaru had increased its spending on the team, ultimately giving Eddie B about $2 million to work with toward their long-term goal of gaining entry to the Tour de France.

After Subaru discontinued its sponsorship in 1994, Weisel had to decrease the team's budget, and the team's performance and progress had suffered. Now he wanted back into the big time, so he'd decided to pour more money into the team to reinvigorate it for the 1995 season, spending an amount somewhere in the mid six figures out of his own pocket. But even with the helmet maker Bell stepping in as a sponsor, the total amount of cash supporting the team was only about $800,000—a far cry from the $5 million most Tour de France caliber squads had.

Gorski thought about Weisel's situation—and his own—on the plane ride back to Denver. Working for USA Cycling was not all he'd hoped. He began to scribble on a piece of paper. What if he could get a new sponsor? he thought. A real title sponsor with a big cash infusion? He figured he would need at least $3.5 million but maybe as much as $5 million to make it work. His scribblings on the plane turned into a proposal to find Weisel's team a major title sponsor within three years, big enough to give them the backing and resources they needed to assemble a team of champions capable of winning the Tour de France. He put the proposal in a FedEx envelope and mailed it to Weisel. Two weeks later, Weisel got back to Gorski. "You're hired," he said. Without even so much as a follow-up meeting or a job interview, Gorski left USA Cycling and was hired to bring Weisel's team to the next level of cycling. The way Weisel saw it, it was a no-lose proposition. If Gorski succeeded, Weisel could finally achieve his goal of turning an American cycling team into a Tour de France winner. If he didn't succeed, Gorski's salary was a small amount of money compared to what Weisel was already spending on the team.

Gorski quickly began to think about how he could deliver on his promise. One of the first people Gorski contacted was the sport's biggest hero, Greg LeMond. Now retired from cycling and living in Minneapolis, LeMond had started his own bicycle manufacturing company, which was growing rapidly. He was still a big name in the sports industry, and his name was gold in professional cycling. Gorski flew to Minneapolis. At a meeting at LeMond's house, Gorski asked him to lend his name and persona to the effort to rope in a new sponsor. LeMond agreed to attend meetings with prospective sponsors and to endorse the team's efforts to grow. In return, Gorski promised LeMond a 10 percent cut of whatever sponsorship money he was able to bring in. LeMond knew Weisel through Eddie B, and had already begun investing in Montgomery Securities. Weisel had done well with Eddie B's money, though he fell short of making good on his promise to make a millionaire of him. Weisel's investors got the inside track on big Silicon Valley IPOs and were reaping huge returns. By this point, LeMond had most of his savings with Weisel and was making about 40 percent annual returns.

Gorski also called in a favor with his old agent, Steve Disson, living in Washington, DC, and running a sports marketing outfit with a partner, Allen Furst. Disson had represented several of the top American cyclists after the 1984 Olympics, but these days, he worked as a consultant to companies searching for sports marketing opportunities. And he had a new client: the United States Postal Service, which wanted to grow its brand internationally. While the USPS had taken in more than $50 billion in revenue the previous year, only about $1.5 billion of that came from outside the United States. Disson pitched the Postal Service on the idea that sponsoring a team that would race in Europe and Asia was a good fit for its goal of doubling its overseas revenue in the next five years. To some Americans, it might have seemed odd that a government agency (albeit a somewhat independent one) like the Postal Service would sponsor a sports team. But European countries had done this for years. The Spanish ONCE team was sponsored by the national lottery sales organization whose proceeds go to help the blind; Germany's Telekom team is sponsored by the national telephone company, in which the German government holds a stake; and Banesto, the former team of retired five-time champion Miguel Indurain, was sponsored by Spain's national banking corporation. The Netherlands' national banking corporation, Rabobank, also sponsored a team.

In the fall of 1995, Disson asked Gorski and Weisel to fly to Washington, DC, for a meeting he had set up for them with Loren Smith, the head of marketing for the USPS. One of the team's main selling points was that Eddie B was the coach. Although most people hadn't heard of him, they had seen his work: nine medals in the 1984 Olympics.

Gorski and Weisel convinced Smith that the team would be able to provide the Postal Service with international exposure that it couldn't otherwise get. After the usual series of bureaucratic deliberations, the US Postal Service signed a three-year contract for $4.5 million to take over the Montgomery-Bell team, effective October 1. The sponsorship didn't come without criticism from people inside the US Postal Service, who viewed it as a waste of money. The contract stipulated a payment of $1 million in 1996, increasing to $1.5 million in 1997, then to $2 million in 1998. The escalating payments enabled Eddie B to phase his ambitions for the team. It would spend a year moving up in the international standings, before bringing in powerful cyclists for the team's projected 1998 Tour de France entry.

Loren Smith went into action once the deal was done, featuring the team in an ad campaign for the Postal Service's Priority Mail service. When Smith heard that the team was planning to compete in the 1995 Tour of China, he arranged for the cyclists to wear white jerseys with red-and-blue shoulders, the name of the team, and a huge picture of the $10.75 space launch stamp, since sales of commemorative stamps were exploding in China at the time. By the time the next race came around, the team had changed its uniform and begun wearing the Postal Service's eagle head logo.

Unlike the Motorola team, which spent the bulk of its racing time in Europe, the US Postal Service wanted to have a team in the United States as well as a team in Europe. The best riders would race in Europe, and the farm team would race on the American circuit. By 1996, the team had two main goals: to pick up "points" from the Union Cycliste Internationale (UCI) that might help it get into the Tour de France, and to develop the team's core group of young riders. The Postal team's performance that year was lackluster, however. It didn't even rank among the world's twenty best. Its biggest achievement of the season was when one of its riders, twenty-eight-year-old Eddy Gragus, won the USPRO Championship in Philadelphia—the same race Armstrong had won when he was twenty-one. For Armstrong, it was a stepping-stone. For Gragus, it was a career capper.

In the fall of 1996, the US Postal team got wind that Lance Armstrong's Motorola team was folding. For them this was good news. For the first time in nearly a decade, there would be no American team in the Tour de France, which would pose a problem for Amaury Sport Organisation (ASO), the French parent company of the Tour de France. If the money it got from television contracts were to keep increasing, the ASO needed a sizable audience of American viewers to tune in; but without an American team competing, interest in the Tour in the United States was sure to wane. This essentially meant there was an "open" slot for an American team in the race.

Every January, somewhere between fifteen to eighteen teams automatically qualify for the Tour de France, based on world team rankings and performances in the previous year's three Grand Tours. The remaining teams— sometimes as many as seven—are allowed in as "wild cards," selected by the Société du Tour de France on the basis of performance. The wild card entries give the Tour discretion to invite up-and-coming French teams, preserving the "Frenchness" of the national treasure. But it also enables the organizers to bring in teams from other countries if, for one reason or another, there is a compelling rationale for doing so.

The Tour de France organizers gave the nod to Gorski, indicating that if

USPS had a good season in 1997, the squad would likely be allowed into the Tour as a wild card. Now the team had to bring in some better riders.

Lance Armstrong had just had the season of his life. He had shown his skills fully for the first time since he had turned pro, and was starting to look like a serious threat. He'd left Motorola as soon as it became obvious that the team was about to lose its sponsorship, and he signed with a French team, Cofidis, as did Frankie Andreu, who'd proven to be one of the most consistent American riders for a decade. Armstrong was given a two-year contract through 1998, valued at just over $1 million per year.

Weisel hadn't been planning on signing Armstrong to the US Postal Service team. He had heard from Jim Ochowicz that Armstrong, with his string of successes, was now even harder to handle than he had been when he was on the Subaru-Montgomery team. After speaking with Ochowicz, Weisel worried that Armstrong would become a divisive force on the USPS team bus, the cycling equivalent of the locker room. Although Weisel and Och were former competitors, there was such a tangled web of relationships in this small, incestuous world that they were friendly and willing to share intel with each other. From what Och told him, Weisel didn't think a new team just attempting to establish itself could handle that kind of rider.

While Weisel and his investment bank, Montgomery Securities, were shepherding Yahoo! Inc.'s public offering, Gorski, representing Montgomery Sports, set out to find his own Lance. He flew to France in July, during the first week of the 1996 Tour de France. With money, it wouldn't be hard to sign new riders, several of whom had already expressed interest. Eddie B, then fifty-seven, was left behind to focus on developing the young farm team riders competing on the US circuit. Gorski was beginning to marginalize Borysewicz, his old Olympic coach; he thought Borysewicz's knowledge of cycling was outdated and too narrowly focused on track racing. Tension was brewing between the two men.

The Tour de France, the biggest racing event of the season, also doubles as the biggest signing period of the season. With all the best cyclists in one place, professional cyclists often renew their contracts for the following season, or quietly agree to join new teams. Gorski was especially interested in the man who had been the youngest up-and-comer on the Motorola team, George

Hincapie, who still hadn't signed onto a team for 1997. The six-foot-three-inch, wiry twenty-four-year-old native New Yorker had distinguished himself as a powerful rider who excelled in the classics.

Gorski and Weisel also had their eye on Viatcheslav Ekimov. Ekimov, nicknamed Eki, was the definition of the Soviet-era Russian athlete. He was stoic and tough. He could suffer a horrible crash and keep on going, finishing the race covered in blood and wrapped in bandages. Though he could climb, his body type didn't lend itself to the discipline of steeply ascending mountain roads. But if there was one word to describe Ekimov, it was *solid*. Gorski wanted to lure Eki away from Rabobank, a Dutch squad.

Gorski succeeded in hiring both Hincapie and Ekimov, as well as a slew of European ringers from France, Poland, Denmark, and Italy. It had become an "American" team in name only. But with Hincapie and two other promising American riders, Tyler Hamilton and Marty Jemison, the team was just "American enough" to retain its character and keep the US Postal Service sponsor happy.

Despite Armstrong's illness at the Tour de France, and his poor performance at the Atlanta Olympics, it wasn't obvious to anyone—including him—that he had been slowing down in the summer of 1996. Back in Austin, he was settling into his new home. In the garage: a racing ski boat, a Porsche, a Harley, and a truck. He also began spending time with another new girlfriend, Lisa Shiels, a chemical engineering major at the University of Texas he had met earlier that year.

But that fall, he began suffering pounding headaches, dizziness, and blurred vision. One night, he coughed up blood into his bathroom sink, but figured it was no big deal. Perhaps it was a sinus infection, he thought. He had also noticed some swelling in a testicle, but since one testicle had been larger than the other for three years, the size difference didn't immediately concern him. But now there was some pain there, too. When he was out riding with his buddy John Korioth, Armstrong mentioned the pain in his testicle. John told him it was probably from having too much sex.

Although he was feeling tired, Lance traveled with Lisa to Beaverton,

Oregon, in late September to ride bikes with executives at the headquarters of his biggest sponsor, Nike. The company was making a broader push into the $2 billion cycling market that year. Nike founder and chief executive Phil Knight had been in Paris that June to watch the French Open tennis tournament, and while there, he had signed a sponsorship deal with the organizers of the Tour, calling for Nike to become the supplier of the coveted yellow jersey.

Lance was a key part of Nike's plan to buy legitimacy in a sport its executives knew almost nothing about. Cycling traditionalists scorned Nike as a newcomer because it had replaced the Italian brand Giordana—a name that had lots of heritage and authenticity with cyclists that Nike lacked. As a result of the deal, the yellow jersey, as well as the green jersey worn by the points leader and the polka-dot jersey awarded to the best hill climber, displayed a large black swoosh. Nike even featured Lance on its new website. On Lance's end, he hoped to be able to work with Nike to create his own signature line of pro racing shoes. So despite feeling exhausted, he went to the weekend event.

By the time he got back to Austin, the pain in his testicle had gotten so bad that he could no longer sit on his bike seat to go for a casual ride.

When Lance mentioned the symptoms to a doctor in Austin, the doctor figured he had either a testicular torsion or epididymitis, or some sort of infection, but requested an ultrasound to check for a tumor just to be safe. During the ultrasound, the radiologist confirmed a likely tumor, and the doctor phoned in a request for a chest X-ray. The X-ray revealed metastases to his lungs. Three hours later, Lance called J.T. with the news. Lance was so shaken that he had his neighbor, a plastic surgeon, call his mother at work. The neighbor, Rick Parker, reached Linda just before she left her office for the night. After he informed her, in a doctorly way, that Lance had been diagnosed with cancer, she was in shock. In her mind, Lance had been so invincible and strong. It was hard for her to imagine that he might now face a dramatic fight for his life.

Lance's treatment—surgery to remove the cancerous testicle—was scheduled for the very next day, and shortly after that, he began the first of four three-week chemo cycles. Lying in a recliner at the Southwest Regional

Cancer Center in Austin, he received three intravenous chemotherapy drugs—bleomycin, etoposide, and Platinol—which slowly dripped into his bloodstream over four long hours.

The first day of chemo treatment proved relatively uneventful. He had been given approval to ride up to fifty miles a day to stay in some sort of shape, and he went for a bike ride the following day. Within a week or so, however, there was more bad news: Oncologists at MD Anderson in Houston, brought in for a second opinion, had called Lance's mother with an urgent message. Test results showed it was likely that the cancer had spread to Armstrong's brain. After an MRI confirmed the presence of lesions in his brain, the doctors at Anderson told Linda he needed more aggressive treatment—radiation to the brain—or else he might not make it. His cancer was a particularly virulent form of the disease, with a poor prognosis, and they lowered Lance's odds of survival to less than 50 percent.

About a week after his diagnosis, Lance held a press conference, with Lisa clutching his hand, and his mother at his side. He named himself a spokesperson for cancer awareness and gave his first public service announcement about testicular cancer, urging young men to get checked immediately. The news of Lance's cancer led to an outpouring of letters and e-mails from people around the world who wanted to express support for Lance and share their own experiences. One of the letters was from a doctor who directed Lance to a specialist at the Indiana University Hospital in Indianapolis.

The doctors in Indianapolis discussed the possibility of treating the brain lesions with surgery instead of radiation in order to preserve Lance's coordination and balance. They also suggested eliminating the bleomycin from his chemo treatments, because it damages the patient's lungs. Lance decided that the Indianapolis team would be the team to treat him.

Lance had the brain surgery in Indiana between chemo cycles. The surgery revealed two half-inch cancerous lesions, but one promising sign was that they had been fried by the initial chemo treatment. His primary oncologist, Craig Nichols, informed Lance that this meant he was a "responder."

On October 27, Armstrong was recovering from brain surgery when a group of friends came to visit him. There were so many that Armstrong moved them out of his hospital room and into a room large enough to accommodate everyone. The visitors included Lisa, who had dropped out of college to help; Chris Carmichael and his girlfriend, Paige; Frankie Andreu and Betsy, who was now Frankie's fiancée; and Stephanie McIlvain.

As the friends chatted, two doctors entered the room, introduced themselves to Lance, and began asking questions. Betsy interrupted and suggested that Armstrong's friends leave the room to give him privacy, but Armstrong insisted that they all stay. Among a series of routine questions, one of the doctors asked Armstrong if he had ever taken performance-enhancing drugs. Armstrong responded matter-of-factly, listing EPO, testosterone, growth hormone, cortisone, and steroids.

Betsy was horrified. The thought of Armstrong doing all of those drugs sickened her. But the thought of her soon-to-be husband doing them made her downright angry. "I'm not fucking marrying you if you're doing that shit; that's how he got his cancer!" she later told Frankie. Frankie tried to calm her down with a lie. "I'm not doing that shit," he said.

Armstrong's laundry list of drugs wasn't so much an admission as it was an explicit confirmation of what it was to be a professional cyclist at the time. The drugs were in such common use throughout the peloton that riding without them made it much harder to be competitive, never mind win.

There was no reaction from the doctors, who left the room.

Lance returned to Austin to finish his treatment, and occasionally went for casual rides around Austin with old friends. After one ride with Jim Woodman, the two men ended up in Armstrong's kitchen on Lake Austin when Armstrong, still gaunt and pale from his chemo, pulled out a syringe filled with EPO. He explained that his doctors had prescribed it to boost his red blood cell count, which was depleted by chemotherapy. As Armstrong injected himself with the EPO, he and Woodman began to discuss doping in cycling.

Armstrong told Woodman that he had used EPO and human growth hormone, or HGH, throughout his pro cycling career. Everyone in pro cycling was using these drugs, Armstrong told Woodman, and any pro rider who didn't was at a significant disadvantage.

Woodman was shocked and disappointed. He had watched Armstrong progress from a teenage triathlete to one of the best cyclists in the world. He still thought of him as a kid. Woodman could think of only one thing to ask. "Aren't you afraid of the health effects?"

Armstrong had a quick answer: He said he thought EPO was safe, but that the HGH might have some medical side effects. He also assured Woodman that everything he'd taken during his cycling days had been under the strict supervision of a doctor.

Woodman's mind began racing. Could HGH have contributed to Armstrong's cancer, or made the cancer cells grow faster and larger? He didn't share his thoughts because he didn't want to upset his friend, but Woodman couldn't help wondering whether Armstrong was thinking the same thing.

Certainly others were thinking along those lines. The European press had already begun speculating that Armstrong's cancer was connected to doping. Whether any of the performance enhancers could have caused Armstrong's cancer is unclear. Overall, there is very little research assessing the cancer risk of these substances when they are taken for performance-enhancement purposes. Much of the research that has been carried out was conducted in Europe, and not on healthy athletes but often on patients who already had some type of disease and were taking testosterone or growth hormone for that condition.

What is known about testicular cancer is that it strikes men most commonly in young adulthood, as with Lance, or in middle age. It usually begins in mutations of the cells that make sperm, known as germ cells. The mutant versions of the germ cells tend to originate during the fetal stage, after which they seem to lie dormant until something triggers the cells to start multiplying. Puberty, with the flood of hormones, often triggers the growth. Some doctors have wondered whether the use of anabolic steroids, a synthetic hormone similar to testosterone, may increase testicular cancer risk, since steroids have been linked with some other forms of cancer. But there is no firm evidence linking them to testicular cancer. In fact, the dominant research in the field indicates that an increase in estrogen causes mutant testicular cells to multiply, which implies that an increase in testosterone may even have a protective benefit.

With respect to HGH, however, there's a "reasonably plausible" possibility that it might increase the risk of cancer—though there isn't any known link with testicular cancer—according to Anthony Swerdlow, an epidemiologist at the Institute of Cancer Research in the UK. He and other scientists are currently running an eight-country European study looking at HGH and cancer risk, but the results won't be available until 2014 or later.

As for EPO, biologically, it's difficult to see how it could have an effect on testicular cancer, and in general it's thought to pose few long-term dangers. Katherine McGlynn, deputy chief of the Hormonal and Reproductive Epidemiology Branch of the National Institutes of Health's National Cancer Institute, says cortisone, often used as an anti-inflammatory, also has no obvious mechanism that would link it to testicular cancer. Although Armstrong had directly admitted to using these drugs in front of a handful of friends and physicians, the admissions never got out publicly.

In January 1997, Lance received a clean bill of health. He felt lucky to be alive. All of his ambitions, his cycling career, took a backseat to one very important fact. He wasn't sure if he could ever be a professional cyclist again, or even whether he should try. Armstrong had a disability policy from Lloyd's of London that was worth $20,000 a month for five years, or about $1.5 million tax-free. If he tried to race again, he would forfeit the policy. And he figured there were plenty of other things he could do. At twenty-five, he was confident that if his racing career was over, he could go to college and then get a good job—perhaps in sales, investment banking, or some other industry that favors drive and charisma over pure book smarts. For now he had no money worries. He had money saved up and the tech boom had treated his investments well.

Coincidentally, around the same time Lance had received his cancer diagnosis, J.T. had been diagnosed with myeloma, a cancer of plasma cells. Both men underwent chemo treatments simultaneously, during which time they shared their feelings of fear and dread. As J.T. later told his friends, they truly bonded. One of Lance's most cherished belongings at the time was a photo of himself together with J.T.—both men pale and bald from the chemo.

But whatever Lance's thoughts about insurance money and mortality, by mid-January, the same month he was declared cancer-free, Lance began riding again. In all, he had missed about two and a half months of training. Soon, he was following a training regimen that was roughly on par with what he would have done in November if he hadn't gotten sick.

That same eventful January, Armstrong also went to Europe to meet with his cycling team, Team Cofidis, to test the waters. He was very pale and had absolutely no hair on his head and no eyebrows. He felt the Europeans were looking at him as if he were a sick person about to die, and certainly they had hedged their bets: After his diagnosis, Cofidis had restructured Lance's contract to include an "opt-out clause" after 1997. If Armstrong didn't race in 1997, the team would have the option of terminating their deal with him. He spent a couple of days working out with the team, and hoped he would be able to come back that spring. However, he resented the fact that Cofidis had added the opt-out clause, and Bill Stapleton began searching for a new team. He did not find any takers.

Stapleton was exploring other options for his client, too. He thought an account of Lance's illness and recovery would make a great comeback story—one that would heighten Lance's commercial appeal. He put Lance together with Tom Clynes, a thirty-six-year-old writer then living in Chicago, who had approached him about writing Lance's autobiography. Clynes himself had been treated for testicular cancer, albeit a milder form diagnosed at an earlier stage, and during the course of doing research on it, he had heard about Lance's diagnosis and struggle. Feeling he had a special understanding of what Armstrong was going through, he had his agent reach out to Stapleton with the idea for the book. Stapleton responded that Clynes's timing was good, because Stapleton had imminent plans to travel to New York to meet with publishers about Lance's story. Lance needed a writer to collaborate on the project, and a literary agent to sell it.

Clynes and Lance got together in Indiana while Lance was still getting treatments. Lance was clear from the get-go: his autobiography—the story of a 1993 world cycling champion and 1995 Tour de France stage winner—had to sell for at least $150,000, with Lance taking two-thirds of the sum.

Clynes put together a proposal, and his agent, Peter Sawyer at the Fifi Oscard Agency, began showing it to publishers. Lance's major comment on the proposal, according to Clynes, is that he didn't want to be quoted using "swear words"—the *shits* and *fucks* that are a common feature of Lance's vocabulary were to be weeded out. While some publishers were blown away by the inspiring story of Lance's comeback from cancer, they balked at Lance's asking price, which they considered too high for the autobiography of someone who at the time was not well-known outside of the cycling world. By then, Clynes was beginning to feel ambivalent about Lance's character. Having spent several weekends in Austin with Lance, he had come to think that he was kind of a jerk to many of the people around him, from his girlfriend, Lisa, to the guy who washed his car. Lisa was at Lance's bedside for much of his treatment, and moved into his Austin mansion when he was weak and unsure he would live. But once, after she left the room, Lance made a crude gesture about her. He also revealed that they had had sex a week after his testicle was removed, and Lance had called his friends to brag about it. At one point, when Clynes asked Lance about doping, Lance replied that "everybody does it"—a response that left Clynes with the sense that Lance probably had used performance-enhancing drugs but wasn't about to admit it. Clynes had begun to wonder whether going forward with the book, which was meant to portray Lance in a heroic light, might require him to be patently dishonest about who Lance really was.

In the end, the project never panned out because no one was willing to pay Lance's asking price. Clynes, however, recalls Lance blaming him for the failure, telling him that the proposal didn't properly convey his status as a superstar who had already arrived.

Soon after his recovery, Lance also followed through with his idea of creating a charity for cancer survivors. In early 1997, Lance reached out to a computer specialist in San Antonio, Air Force sergeant Chris Brewer, who had been diagnosed with testicular cancer and had set up an informational website. After Lance suggested they coordinate their efforts, the two men met to plan fund-raisers. Their first event was piggybacked onto a long-standing Austin tradition called the Ride for the Roses, in which Lance had participated in the past. Originally held around Valentine's Day, the bike ride's nickname derived from the practice of awarding a bouquet of roses to the winner, who could bring them home to his significant other.

In January 1997, at a press conference at the Four Seasons Hotel in Austin to announce the Ride for the Roses benefit, Armstrong met Kristin Richard, a slender twenty-five-year-old blonde with green eyes, who worked for a public relations and advertising firm in Austin. She had sold the idea of sponsoring the race to a client, and after that, she had started volunteering for his foundation. Armstrong was still bald from the effects of four courses of chemo, but Kristin thought he was cute, and he seemed to enjoy spending time with her during the benefit and at later foundation meetings at his home and elsewhere. Soon he dumped Lisa and began dating Kristin.

Lance had lined up a stellar list of guests for the benefit, which kicked off on March 23. Eric Heiden, now an orthopedic surgeon, showed up, clad in his old Motorola team kit, and rode in the race along with Lance. Heiden signed autographs as Chris Brewer and Lance handed out informational brochures about testicular cancer. Four bands provided entertainment, including the headliner, the Wallflowers, whose bald-headed guitarist Michael Ward was a passionate cyclist and new friend of Lance's. The Sunday race raised about $20,000.

By the fall of 1997, the foundation had a nest egg of about $300,000, $20,000 of it from Armstrong, another $20,000 from Jeff Garvey, a general partner in a venture-capital firm who became chairman of the foundation that September. Two of Lance's doctors from Indiana, including his oncologist, Craig Nichols, also joined the board. John Korioth quit his job as bar manager to help his friend get the foundation off the ground. Operating on a very small overhead, the foundation was run out of Korioth's 700-square-foot condo in Austin. Its focus was to be on fund-raisers with the potential to generate between $200,000 and $400,000—money that would go to scientists researching better screening methods for testicular and prostate cancer, and to efforts to address lifestyle issues for survivors.

For Thom Weisel's team, 1997 was shaping up to be a major leap forward. Mark Gorski had signed enough new riders to get the team invited to the top races in Europe.

Gorski wanted to be recognized for his work, and Weisel obliged. He named him team manager, promoting him over Borysewicz. Eddie B remained on the team, but he was relegated to coaching the B-level riders—the young cyclists on the Postal Service farm team who weren't yet strong enough to compete in Europe. It was a bitter moment for Borysewicz, who had been a loyal employee of Weisel's for ten years. Borysewicz had coached Weisel when he was shooting for a national masters championship, and he had coached Gorski to his Olympic gold medal in 1984. Now Gorski ranked above him not just on the business side of the team but on the sports side, too—despite the fact that Gorski knew little about the intricate racing tactics of the European circuit.

Borysewicz also felt Gorski was moving the team forward too quickly in the interest of securing big sponsorship dollars and pursuing the glitz and glamour of top-level European racing without really knowing what he was getting himself, or Weisel, into. Eddie B enjoyed the sport of cycling for the intellectual challenge of developing young riders, but he never made any real money doing it, and didn't mind. Though he hated the communist system—after all, the Soviets had sent his father to a prison camp in Siberia—he wasn't a pure capitalist, either. There were things he valued more than money. He thought communism was actually a "nice idea" that could never work. He was beginning to feel his worldview was diametrically opposed to both Gorski's and Weisel's.

With the new riders on the team came a new level of sophistication—and doping. Gorski hired Pedro Celaya, a physician who was well-known in the European professional cycling circuit for his mastery of performance-enhancing drugs. Celaya brought the Postal Service team up to speed with the Europeans by creating individualized training plans and doping schedules for the top riders on the team. Not everyone was on board with the program, however.

In May 1997, during the Tour de Romandie, a bike race in Switzerland, Celaya called team member Scott Mercier into his hotel room. Celaya handed Mercier a calendar with training schedules that told the rider how long and how hard to ride on each day. Mercier noticed that some days on the calendar were marked with symbols, like stars and small dots, and he asked what they meant. Celaya explained that the stars signified the days on which Mercier was to take anabolic steroids, the dots indicated when he was to take testosterone. Then he handed Mercier a bag full of vials. He said the stuff inside the bag would make him "strong like bull." The exchange caught Mercier off guard. "But I don't even know how to inject myself," he said.

Celaya was shocked. "You are a professional cyclist and you really don't know how to inject yourself?" he asked. "Go to a pharmacist or a doctor and get a lesson," he instructed Mercier.

Mercier never took the drugs. He decided to quit cycling and pursue another career immediately after the season ended.

Ekimov was the brightest spot on the team in 1997. He won stages in several big European cycling events, including Paris–Nice and Setmana Catalana, and about a month before the Tour de France, he won the opening stage of the Dauphiné Libéré, a weeklong stage race organized by ASO that takes place on many of the same mountain roads included in the Tour de France. Unlike Mercier, Ekimov seemed to have no qualms with doping.

The Postal team's strategy of hiring these outstanding riders had paid off. It meant that the team delivered performances good enough to be able to meet the ASO's challenge to Gorski, with the result that it received the official invitation to participate in the Tour de France—the lone American representative.

Having gotten in, the Postal squad didn't make much of an impact in 1997. But it did deliver a few respectable finishes on a handful of stages, and the riders got through the race without embarrassing the team. All nine were able to finish and cross the line in Paris. Hincapie finished fifth in the final sprint on the Champs-Élysées.

The 1997 Tour de France had a surprise visitor: Lance Armstrong. He and his new girlfriend, Kristin, had been traveling through France, Monaco, and Spain and stopped by the Tour so Lance could take part in a ceremony honoring his Motorola teammate Fabio Casartelli, who had been killed in the 1995 Tour de France. Soon after, Cofidis announced they were dropping Armstrong. The team had again tried to renegotiate its deal with him for much less money, and he wasn't having any of it. He wasn't just disappointed—he was angry. He had a point to prove, and he fully intended to prove it.

When Bill Stapleton called Thom Weisel to ask him if the US Postal team was interested in signing Lance, Weisel's initial answer was a flat-out no. Still wary of Armstrong and his ability to be a team player, Weisel nonetheless decided it was worth having a conversation with Stapleton.

In September, Weisel and Gorski sat down with Stapleton in San Francisco and they leveled with him about their concerns. Stapleton said that having had cancer, Armstrong was now a changed man—humble, more focused, with a new outlook on life. Stapleton also reassured them that Armstrong could come back from chemotherapy, that Armstrong's doctors had been careful to use drugs that wouldn't cause permanent damage to his lungs, his endurance capacity, or his sense of balance. There were many who thought otherwise, but Weisel believed Stapleton. Weisel and Gorski decided they would bring Armstrong back and build their team around him.

Borysewicz, though, was adamantly against it. Bring him on as a sort of mascot? Fine. As a part-time rider to show up at races? Sure, why not? But as a full-time guy? A team leader like he was before? Borysewicz feared that if Lance got back to bike racing, his cancer might return. This was something he had seen in Europe. Cyclists got over cancer, and then, once they returned to the sport, the cancer came back. Borysewicz believed that training for professional cycling was so draining and debilitating that the body's natural defenses were weakened and could no longer stand up to the disease. And it had crossed Borysewicz's mind that Armstrong's cancer might have been caused or worsened by the "medical program," as he referred to it, on Armstrong's old team. Eddie B tried not to think about what might have been included in that program. To build a team around Armstrong seemed wrong to him. But Borysewicz was outvoted. Weisel and Gorski had made up their minds. Borysewicz had received another offer to run a European cycling team. He already felt marginalized on the US Postal team. The disagreement over Armstrong was the last straw and he resigned.

Armstrong's contract called for eighty "starts"—or races—in the 1998 season. He didn't expect to be a contender for any victories, or a contender for participation in the 1998 Tour de France. But as long as he performed well in some of the minor races, he could rack up nearly as many UCI points as he would have accumulated in the major races. That meant he could still earn as much as $1 million in bonuses.

For his winter training, he and Kristin rented an apartment in Saint-Jean-Cap-Ferrat, the upscale peninsula on the Mediterranean coast, between Nice and Monaco, bringing their cat with them.

Armstrong had already reconnected with Michele Ferrari, who was delighted to have his old client back. On December 2, Armstrong took a blood test in Spain, and Ferrari meticulously scribbled the results into a spreadsheet. Armstrong's hematocrit, or red blood cell percentage, was 41.2. It needed to be much higher for major competitions—preferably in the high 50s. For that, Armstrong needed EPO, which is what Ferrari prescribed.

On February 14, Armstrong took another blood test. This time, his hematocrit had risen to 46.7—perfect for the upcoming Ruta del Sol. The five-day stage race in Spain, held in February 1998, was to be Armstrong's comeback race.

Armstrong finished in fifteenth place, an encouraging result. Armstrong told himself that his comeback was not for him but for cancer survivors all over the world. He had told himself that he wanted to prove to them, and everyone, that you can not only survive cancer, you can come back and perform as well as you did before cancer. And now he thought he had proven that.

Fifteenth place in the Ruta del Sol would show them all. Never mind that nobody outside of Western Europe knew what the race was. Never mind that Americans couldn't even pronounce it. Armstrong, if only for a brief moment, thought he might have proven all he needed to prove. Like Superman giving up his powers, he would go back to Austin, live life as a civilian, walk down the aisle with Kristin. He loved her. They could live a comfortable life even if Lance couldn't ride bikes for a living. Kristin's father was wealthy enough to provide financial help.

She would pop out some kids. He would mow the lawn. Happiness.

CHAPTER SIX

SIT-INS AND SADDLE SORES

Lance's decision to settle down with Kristin Richard shocked some, primarily because he had previously lacked the mind-set of a traditional family man. Before he got sick, he seemed to think of little but sex. Even when he was a teenager and doing the triathlon circuit, there were times when his managers had to pull him off women at hotels. While cycling, he would often chase the "podium girls"—the women who give stage winners and jersey competition leaders awards each day in a multiday race. Lance's pals called him FedEx because the company's slogan, "When it absolutely, positively has to be there overnight," seemed to describe his sex drive.

Richard was the daughter of a kindergarten-teacher mother and a dad who had worked as an IBM executive for three decades. She had a down-home Midwestern accent and a broad smile. When she and Lance met, she was twenty-five, about his age, unlike the women in their thirties whom he had often chased in his late teens. She had a bachelor's degree in marketing from Miami University in Oxford, Ohio, a successful career, and a convertible, and she had recently purchased her first home. She dreamed of becoming a writer.

After dumping Lisa, who had been by Lance's bedside throughout his cancer treatments, he and Kristin dated for only four months before getting engaged in October 1997. They planned a wedding in Santa Barbara, near her parents' summer home, for May 1998.

The woman-chasing Armstrong, the one with the rough edges and unchecked cockiness, seemed to have disappeared along with his cancer. The new Armstrong thought about adult things—family, long-term happiness, the meaning of life. He worked on his golf game, ate tacos, sat on the couch, strummed on his guitar, and played with his kitten, Chemo. He even spent a week on tour in North Carolina with Jakob Dylan and the Wallflowers band. *New York Times* reporter Samuel Abt, who built a career as Armstrong's unofficial post-cancer propagandist, described this period of his life as a soul-searching awakening that included every kind of trope of self-discovery except a pilgrimage to Tibet.

After his fifteenth-place showing in the Ruta del Sol in February, he did consider retiring, but he felt obliged to fulfill his contract to ride for the Postal team. His next big competition was the eight-day stage race Paris–Nice in March. Two years earlier, before Armstrong had been diagnosed with cancer, he had finished second overall. So he knew the course, and was confident going in.

But on day two of the race, a 100-mile stage, Armstrong began to struggle. The weather was wet and windy, with driving rain making the road dangerous and uncomfortable. Things got worse after he was asked to play the role of domestique for George Hincapie, who was now one of the strongest members of the US Postal team. The team's new director, Johnny Weltz, instructed Armstrong to help pace—or lead—Hincapie to a breakaway group that had gotten far ahead of the pack. Armstrong had rarely worked for another cyclist, but he also thought there was something off about Weltz's tactical strategy. Why had he waited so long and allowed the Postal riders to fall so far behind the pack?

Armstrong's mind began to wander and leave the race. He pictured life back in Austin, where the weather was perfect right now, and his sprawling home on the lake. He could fire up the barbecue, invite a few friends over, and drink some beer. Besides, hadn't he already proven himself to the cancer community by his showing in the Ruta del Sol? Hadn't he made his point? What was he going to do—ride around Europe for five years, finishing fifteenth place in every major bike race until people got it through their thick skulls that he had beaten cancer? He'd won. Cancer had lost. Wasn't it time to end this charade?

Ignoring Weltz's instructions, he drifted back, allowing the other riders to pass him until he was the last one in the pack. He pulled over to the right side of the road and raised his arm. The US Postal team car pulled up. Armstrong got off his bike and got in. He was done. He called Kristin in Nice. He was coming back, he told her. He would explain all when he got home.

Back in Nice, Lance told Kristin that he was thinking about retiring and going home to Austin. Kristin had given up her job and settled into a school to learn French. She wasn't happy about leaving. But after all that Armstrong had been through, she felt she couldn't push back.

After they moved back to Austin, they both felt disconnected from the world, without purpose. Armstrong wasn't interested in cycling at all. He didn't even bother to let his new team know his whereabouts. He drafted a retirement statement, and didn't unpack his bike for three weeks. When Kristin asked about his plans for the future, he was evasive. And he played a lot of golf.

Eventually, his informal team of advisers—his mom; his agent, Bill Stapleton; and his former coach, Chris Carmichael—intervened. They persuaded him to try just one more race. In April, he spent ten days off the grid training with Carmichael and Bob Roll, Carmichael's affable thirty-eight-year-old former 7-Eleven teammate, in the college town of Boone, North Carolina, in the Appalachian Mountains.

All day, every day, Lance rode his bike, sometimes through pouring rain. He rode up Beech Mountain, a 5,000-foot climb that had been part of the route of the Tour DuPont. Chris would periodically measure Lance's progress at the Appalachian State University training center, where they could test his wattage using a digital odometer. His VO$_2$ max, which had measured at more than 80, was now at 64.

During those days, Lance also did some soul-searching. He reflected on his childhood and his early career. He thought about what was behind his desire to compete in Europe, and how his victories in cycling had satisfied his inner need.

By the end of the ten days, Armstrong decided that he did want to regain his stature in the sport. If he was going to really go full throttle, he knew it had to be about more than just cancer. Professional cyclists don't ride for causes. They ride because it's their job and they love it. Cancer just wasn't enough of a motivation.

He was going to have to feel the old passion again, to rediscover his motivational fuel. For Armstrong, that was his bitter anger, the burning rage he felt toward those who he believed had treated him unfairly. It was indignation toward a biological father who ditched him, resentment toward his adopted father, Terry, for cheating on his mother and for insinuating that he and Linda had been a burden. It was fury over the way Eddie B expected him to give up his own chance at winning in order to help another rider take first place. It was his hatred of the Cofidis team for dropping him because they didn't believe in him.

He empathized with his mother. He believed that since she was seventeen, people had told her she was a loser who couldn't raise a kid alone, who would never make it.

On May 8, 1998, Lance and Kristin married at a Catholic church in Santa Barbara. Linda attended the wedding with her third husband, John. Lance had always liked John and felt he brought a welcome feeling of love and humor into Linda's home. But John was battling alcoholism and Linda recalls him becoming visibly drunk at the rehearsal dinner, an elegant affair at a restaurant on the beach, even breaking a glass. "Mom, you gotta take him home," Lance beseeched. She enlisted her father to carry John back to the hotel.

The honeymoon for Kristin and Lance was modest in deference to the cycling season. Armstrong had races to prepare for. They spent a few days in a beach house while Lance trained. Later that month, they returned to Austin for the Ride for the Roses, benefiting his foundation to raise money to fight urological cancers. Miguel Indurain and Greg LeMond showed up at the event to show their support.

For his first race back in Europe with the US Postal team, he selected the Tour de Luxembourg in June. Though the four-day race was a grueling 105-mile-a-day ride, it hadn't drawn a strong field of rivals, and Lance won.

By then, Lance and Kristin had rented a small apartment in Nice. The US

Postal team was putting together its nine-man roster for the Tour, and Gorski asked Armstrong whether he would like to participate. Armstrong hadn't even considered it, and he told Gorski he'd sit it out. In July 1998, as the top nine riders on USPS raced in the Tour, Armstrong went back to the States and raced in the Cascade Cycling Classic, a stage race centered around Bend, Oregon, that included high-level amateurs and some professionals. Armstrong, helped by a handful of teammates, including Jonathan Vaughters, a twenty-five-year-old native of Colorado who had turned pro about four years earlier, won the race handily.

During the race, Armstrong was interviewed by a small newspaper in the area. When the reporter made a comparison to Greg LeMond, Armstrong went on a rant, calling LeMond a fat ass. LeMond had been dabbling in auto racing and generating publicity after some limited success. Armstrong told the reporter that LeMond should get out of his car and give back to cycling. A friend mailed the article to LeMond, who was shocked that Armstrong would take a potshot at him, attacking him unprovoked. Hadn't LeMond made a volunteer appearance at Armstrong's Ride for the Roses just a couple of months earlier? LeMond felt stung, but he quickly put it out of his mind, chalking up Armstrong's comments to some sort of frustration stemming from his cancer recovery.

The 1998 Tour de France began in Dublin, Ireland. Occasionally, the Tour holds legs of the race outside of France in order to increase the international appeal of the event. The US Postal team and all of its equipment, including its team cars, traveled to Ireland on a ferry from Belgium, which was scheduled to arrive late at night. Emma O'Reilly, an Irish masseuse and team assistant, or soigneur, planned to meet the team at the Dublin port.

As O'Reilly was waiting for the boat, she noticed several Irish customs agents patrolling the area, and she asked them what they were looking for. The agents explained that they planned to search the Postal team cars after the ferry arrived from Belgium. O'Reilly was anxious. She knew some of the Postal riders used banned drugs, but she tried to play it cool with the customs agents. A young, effervescent brunette from a Dublin suburb, who had trained as an electrician before becoming a massage therapist, she turned on her charm. The people she worked for were top-level professional athletes, she told them. It was already late—close to 2:00 A.M. If these top riders arrived tired and were forced to have to wait for some silly customs search, they might get angry and the agents "would have a riot on their hands." Playing to their sympathy, she said that she, in particular, didn't want to have to deal with them when they were cranky. The customs agents seemed to buy her story. They obliged O'Reilly and left the Postal riders—and their vehicles—alone.

Soigneurs play a crucial role in cycling. They are like personal assistants, charged with everything from massaging riders' legs after long rides to filling up water bottles to—in some cases—smuggling performance-enhancing drugs across borders. Suddenly, some of these formerly anonymous assistants to cycling teams were about to have their fifteen minutes of fame, caught in the glare of the international spotlight. The day after the ferry arrived, O'Reilly heard from someone on the Postal team that Willy Voet, a Belgian physiotherapist and soigneur from the rival Festina team, had been stopped by customs agents while driving into France from Belgium on his way to the Tour. After they searched his car and found four hundred vials of illegal drugs, including EPO, they arrested him.

At first, Voet insisted that the drugs were for his own use, a ridiculous position to take given the quantity the agents found. A few days later, he changed his story and admitted that he was bringing EPO and other drugs to Festina team riders who were participating in the Tour de France. The French watchmaker Festina had lavished its team with major dollars so they could recruit top talent, and Voet was part of their investment. Now he sat languishing in a jail cell somewhere in France.

The race stayed in Ireland for three days, and when it entered France, about a week after Voet's arrest, police officers there raided the hotel rooms of the Festina team and brought its riders in for questioning. In France, it's a crime to use performance-enhancing drugs to cheat in sports, even if some of the drugs, such as EPO, were not expressly illegal. The riders and team officials weren't just facing disqualification from the event; they were facing the threat of criminal charges. Even the Tour de France organizers were called in for questioning by French police, who wanted to know whether the officials were aware of the doping taking place right under their noses.

The events triggered a wave of fear among riders and staffers on the Postal team. As they were heading back to Europe on a ferry, they decided to dump some of their stash of drugs overboard. Later, the Postal team doctor, Pedro Celaya, and other staff members flushed the remainder of the stockpile down the toilet of the team bus as it sat in the middle of a field somewhere in France.

As the race progressed, tensions flared between the French police and the riders. One morning, before the twelfth stage of the race, the entire field of roughly 150 Tour de France cyclists decided to sit down on the road with their bicycles to protest. French rider Laurent Jalabert announced that the riders were refusing to ride the stage, due to harassment by French police.

But the protest didn't seem to deter the police. Just a few days later, the officers raided the hotel rooms of the Dutch TVM squad. There, they discovered masking agents that could disguise drugs in urine samples. They called several riders in for questioning, interrogating them about their drug use.

The riders again pushed back. The next day, during stage 17, dozens of members of the peloton stopped racing, tore off their race numbers, and rode the rest of the stage together, crossing the finish line in a single pack. The stage was nullified. By stage 18, only fifteen of the twenty-one teams remained in the race. The remainder had either been kicked out or left the Tour de France in protest.

No Postal riders or staffers had been busted or eliminated from the event. But the Tour was a near disaster for the team. Thom Weisel had invited Margot Myers, a media relations executive for the US Postal Service, to join him in the team car to watch the events close-up. He had hoped to give her an education in the beauty of the sport her organization was sponsoring. What she got, instead, was a window into the all-out war between cyclists and French officials over doping. It was like a 1960s-style sit-in, except instead of hippies, the strikers were professional athletes wearing spandex.

The French police investigation may have been the main topic of conversation during that year's race, but Myers still managed to have a good time. She was, after all, in France, being wined and dined by Weisel and others at some of the country's best restaurants. Myers got to meet some of the sport's greatest legends, including Eddy Merckx, the Belgian five-time winner of the Tour de France, and Miguel Indurain, who won the race five times in a row.

Toward the end of the race, shortly after the sit-in, Myers was sitting with Weisel at an outdoor patio of a top-rated French restaurant. They were drinking wine, eating some of the best food in the world. During their meal, Greg LeMond, who happened to be at the same restaurant, spotted them and walked up to the table to say hello. LeMond would later recount the conversation under oath in a deposition. He was in France, leading a cycling tour for wealthy Americans. For Myers, then in her mid-forties and responsible for the Postal Service employee communications program, meeting LeMond at a fancy restaurant in France was certainly more exciting than meeting Merckx or Indurain. LeMond was famous, the only true American cycling celebrity, and he had come over to the table specifically to meet her. As LeMond would later recall under oath, the conversation led to an interesting window into Weisel's views on doping.

"Thank you for your support of the sport," LeMond said.

"Oh, we are just thrilled to be able to sponsor this team," she responded.

"Listen, I am really sorry that you have to see this mess this year. The sport obviously has a lot of work to do, but it is cleaning up," LeMond said.

Weisel interjected. "I think this is bullshit," he said. "Riders should be able to take whatever they want."

Myers didn't flinch, and LeMond assumed this was the kind of thing Weisel had been saying to her as the Festina scandal unfolded. LeMond was taken aback, shocked that a team owner would be so open about his acceptance of doping—an American, no less, and in front of an American sponsor. (In fact Weisel had told Myers that the Postal team was clean, and she had believed him, she later told us.)

LeMond left the table with a sick feeling in his stomach. He worried about the future of the sport, and the health of the riders involved. Like many people in that world, he saw the Festina doping busts as a crossroads for cycling, the point at which the major players would have to make a decision—either cycling had to clean itself up, or the cyclists had to be much more careful about being caught.

After his conversation with Weisel at the restaurant, LeMond felt relieved that he had nothing to do with the US Postal team. He had been close to becoming part of it, but Gorski had reneged on the deal he made with

LeMond in Minnesota. At first, LeMond felt he had been screwed over. Now he felt he had dodged a bullet.

LeMond had also pulled all of his money out of Weisel's investment bank, despite the hefty annual returns. He and Kathy had visited Weisel at his bank in the TransAmerica Tower in San Francisco. Weisel had bragged about his multimillion-dollar art collection that covered the office walls. Both Kathy and Greg left with a bad feeling about Weisel, and decided to invest elsewhere.

While Lance was rebuilding his endurance, his training was more important than ever. He'd become obsessive about everything he ate, how long he rested between workouts, and exactly how far and how hard he rode every day. And he really needed to rebuild muscle. Chemo and his lack of exercise had robbed him of much of his muscle mass, which he was working to rebuild.

That loss of muscle had the potential to help Armstrong. It was the equivalent of a forest fire, which clears away all the unnecessary brush and dead trees. Through the training designed by Ferrari, he was now developing only the muscles essential for cycling. By August, he found that he could climb slightly faster at a more sustained pace than he had in the past.

Lance and Kristin felt optimistic enough about his cycling comeback that they purchased a villa situated on a wooded hillside in Nice, France. Armstrong kept his EPO in the butter compartment of his refrigerator, so he code-named it *butter*. If the French police came knocking and wanted to search the house, presumably, Kristin or Lance could warn each other to throw out the "butter."

Though Armstrong and his teammates feared the French police catching them with EPO, they were unconcerned about getting caught via a drug test, since there was still no test that could directly detect it in the body. But the UCI had implemented a new blood test that screened riders for high hematocrits. Since the highest natural hematocrit was about 50 percent, the UCI said that any rider found to have a higher percentage would be suspended from racing for fifteen days. The team had a plan for that, too. As a general practice, riders and staff were given enough advance warning before the tests that the team doctors could inject the riders' veins with a saline solution, which caused their hematocrit levels to drop temporarily. These invaluable advance warnings suggested that the UCI wasn't serious about curbing EPO use—it simply had a public relations problem on its hands and needed to appear to be reacting.

In late August, Ferrari told Armstrong that he was strong enough to race the 1998 Vuelta a España. It would be his first Grand Tour after cancer, and he really just wanted to finish. He had no expectations about how well he'd do. But Armstrong had one thing going for him that set him apart from most of the other participants in the event, who had raced an entire, grueling season: He was relatively well rested.

The Vuelta began in September. By the end of the first week of the race, Armstrong was in twentieth place. But by the end of the second week, he surged ahead, ranking between fourth and sixth. On most stages, he felt good, and his US Postal teammates were mobilized to help him keep his position.

One night, about midway through the race, Lance's teammate Vaughters went to Lance's hotel room to borrow his laptop. While he was there, Lance went into the bathroom to brush his teeth, then emerged, toothbrush still in hand and—in what Vaughters took to be a show of bravado—pulled out a syringe full of EPO and injected it into his stomach. Vaughters had never seen him do this, but it was no secret that both men were on the drug. Celaya kept all the riders' hematocrit levels on his spreadsheet, and Armstrong enjoyed keeping track of his teammates' data so he'd know who was using EPO. Without EPO, a rider's hematocrit could drop by as much as 30 percent during a long race like the Vuelta; with EPO, the hematocrits recorded in Celaya's notebook stayed consistent throughout the race.

Armstrong was holding on to his position in the Vuelta. He was in ninth place on September 25, before the final mountain stage, a 130-mile monster that finished atop the 6,200-foot Alto de Navacerrada. The weather was cold and rainy, with temperatures on the mountain peaks reaching only 34 degrees. Riding a bicycle in 34 degrees is a bit like jumping into a lake in Minnesota in February: It's painful. Armstrong decided that this day—the most painful day—was going to be his day.

He began at the base of the climb with some of the best riders in the world around him—Roberto Heras, José María Jiménez, Fernando Escartín,

Andrei Zintchenko. But Armstrong remained steady, staying on their wheels and alongside them as he crossed the finish line in the cold rain. By the end of the stage, Armstrong had moved up in the standings, to sixth place. After finishing third in the time trial the next day, he was in fourth place overall, where he remained.

Those who had seen Armstrong race before cancer could tell from the way he raced the Vuelta that he was a different rider. He waited for the right moments to attack, and conserved energy whenever he could. He was a more mature rider, more tactical. Though he had lost the explosive power that had helped him to win one-day races, he had gained the mental fortitude that enabled him to keep up on long, steady climbs that went on day after day.

In addition to boosting his confidence, Armstrong's success at the Vuelta and in the other minor stage races in Europe boosted his bottom line. In order to incentivize Armstrong to do more races in Europe, his Postal contract offered him bonus money for gaining UCI points, which he earned by placing well in certain races. In the past, that money would have been paid by Montgomery Securities, Thom Weisel's investment bank. But in 1997, Montgomery Securities was acquired by NationsBank, which had then acquired BankAmerica (which became Bank of America). Weisel had become locked in a power struggle over control of various divisions in what had been his company. In September of 1998, while Armstrong was in the middle of his amazing Vuelta performance, Weisel finally resigned from the company he had once owned and was all too happy to inform Bank of America that they now owed Lance Armstrong, a cyclist they had probably never heard of, more than $1 million. Weisel then bought Montgomery Sports from Bank of America for $1, and promptly merged it with Disson Furst and Partners, the company Steve Disson had founded years earlier.

During the Vuelta, Johan Bruyneel, a former competitor, walked up to Armstrong at the end of one stage and said, "Whew, some result." Armstrong was gracious. The exchange was a short one, but long enough for Bruyneel to see in Armstrong's intensely focused eyes something he had never observed during the years he had raced against him: a desire to win that ran deep, all the way to Armstrong's soul. In the past, Bruyneel thought of Armstrong's competitiveness as shallow—like that of a crazy uncle who wants to beat his nephew at Ping-Pong, or a teenager with his first car who wants to beat his friend in a drag race. But now, Armstrong's eyes revealed an intensity of will that was new.

The next day, Bruyneel's phone rang. It was Lance. Emboldened by his strong finish, he told Bruyneel that he felt the team needed more structure. The Postal team lacked vision, he said. "Can I have Gorski call you?" Armstrong asked. Bruyneel wasn't sure what Armstrong had in mind, but he figured that he might be proposing some sort of consulting gig. Sure, he replied.

Just a few weeks earlier, Bruyneel had been a cyclist like Armstrong. He had been in the Tour de France while the Festina scandal was erupting and had been one of the riders sitting on the pavement, protesting the police raids and the crackdown on doping. Raised in cycling-crazed Belgium, Bruyneel grew up racing. Although nobody ever thought he had superstar potential, he was strong enough to become a known quantity in the junior racing circuit, and later, to Bruyneel's surprise, in 1992, he had been given a spot on Spain's ONCE team.

A day or two later, Bruyneel got a call from Mark Gorski: "So Lance says you're interested in becoming the director of our team?" This was not what Bruyneel was expecting to hear. The job he was being offered was already held by Johnny Weltz, Eddie B's replacement. Armstrong wasn't impressed with Weltz, whom he thought lacked tactical savvy. So Armstrong was determined to give Weltz's job away, insisting to Weisel and Gorski that the team had to hire Bruyneel as *directeur sportif*. The term, translated from French, means simply "sport director" but is the cycling equivalent of a head coach. The sport director decides everything from what the hotels should serve the team for dinner to what tactical role each rider on the team will play.

For Bruyneel to get this job was sort of akin to the second-string quarterback of the New England Patriots retiring, and then a few days later being hired as the head coach of the New York Jets. Astonished by this sudden change of fortune, Bruyneel accepted the offer.

As a rider, Bruyneel was considered a master of strategic thinking. He began competing before cyclists used radios to communicate with a team director. This meant that most of the information he got about the status of a given race came either from witnessing it firsthand or from motorcycles that carried chalkboards with information written on them. If a group of riders was in a breakaway up the road, the motorcycle drivers would drive up ahead, use a stopwatch to record the gap, and then write the number on the chalkboard. In order to assess who the overall leader was at any given moment and make strategic decisions about when to hang back and when to try to sprint forward, riders had to keep track of where each rider stood in the general classification (the GC) and be smart enough to figure out the math in their heads. For instance, if a breakaway contained a rider who was two minutes down in the GC, and the breakaway was three minutes up the road, that rider would be, in effect, winning the race by only one minute, and therefore a target. On the other hand, if all the riders in the breakaway were more than fifteen minutes down in the GC, the top riders in the race wouldn't have any reason to chase them down. This was a lot of thinking and strategizing for riders under extreme physical duress. But Bruyneel had been a master of it.

Bruyneel immediately began talking to Armstrong about his goals for the following season. Armstrong figured he would target the same races he had won before his cancer—the one-day classics and the world championships. But Bruyneel had another thought: If Armstrong could finish fourth in the Vuelta, who was to say he couldn't win the Tour de France? Armstrong had once struggled just to finish the race. "Win it?" he asked incredulously.

Bruyneel explained his reasoning. In the past, Armstrong had won stages in the Tour, which showed that he could compete at that level. He lacked only the endurance capacity to keep up in the mountains. But he had never trained for the Tour in the correct way. He had always tired himself out with a racing schedule focused on the classics and the world championships. Now that he had, quite by accident, discovered his potential by resting during the 1998 season and then racing the Vuelta fresh, imagine: What could he do if he consciously focused all his energies on the Tour de France?

A cancer survivor who had seen death up close coming back to win the Tour de France—the prospect of such an astonishing outcome was worth the gamble. Armstrong had just earned $1 million in bonuses while still building his strength post-cancer. If he won the Tour de France, he would earn multiples of that, including endorsements.

It did not take long for Armstrong to convince himself that winning the Tour de France was a sure thing, even if the rest of the world thought he had long odds. In the late winter of 1998, Armstrong was in Minneapolis visiting Kristin's parents when Greg and Kathy were invited over for dinner at the Richards' house. About midway through dinner, Armstrong announced to the other five people at the table that he planned to win the 1999 Tour de France. "My goal is to win the Tour de France four times," he said.

"Wow," LeMond said, not sure what to say. LeMond had watched Armstrong develop as a bike racer, knew Armstrong's physiology, and thought there was no way Armstrong had a chance at winning the world's biggest race. But he tried to play along, encouraging Armstrong.

On the way home, Greg turned to Kathy. "I feel sorry for him," he said. "He's delusional."

Meanwhile, Lance distanced himself from several of the people who invested the most time and effort in his success—including his mother, whose third marriage was falling apart, and J.T. Neal, who was fighting for his life and undergoing chemo. He also had a significant falling-out with John Korioth, his best friend and cycling buddy, who had put his heart into building the foundation, which by then had three full-time employees and rental space in a downtown Austin house. Korioth had a disagreement with the foundation's board, which was forcing him out. When Lance took the side of the board without first reaching out to him to hear his own version of events, Korioth felt rejected and hurt. He had developed a brotherly love for Lance, particularly when Lance was recovering from cancer. The two men wouldn't speak again for three years.

Armstrong and Bruyneel spent the off-season preparing a plan and training for the race, with Ferrari as part of the team. Ferrari observed Armstrong riding up mountain passes and equipped his bike with a set of sensors that measured the wattage, or power output, he was producing with each pedal stroke. After each climb, he would record the average wattage generated on the climb and divide it by Armstrong's weight, entering the resulting number on his spreadsheets and using it to prescribe the next workout. A typical cyclist might put out 2 or 3 watts per kilogram of body weight. To win the Tour de France, Ferrari calculated that Armstrong needed to generate about 6.5 watts per kilo—a number he arrived at through his intimate knowledge of many of the top riders in the peloton. Aside from his spreadsheet skills, Ferrari was good at his job because he understood what performance-enhancing drugs could and couldn't do. They couldn't turn mediocre endurance athletes into great ones. But what these drugs could do was allow an athlete to keep pushing at his maximum pace for a longer period of time. For instance, Armstrong may have been able to push 400 watts for a half hour up a mountain climb, but could he do it on every climb during the 21-day Tour de France? Probably not. With a steady dose of EPO, or blood transfusions, however, he might be able to maintain that pace.

Armstrong needed to put thousands of difficult training miles in to reach this goal. He needed to get stronger, and to lose weight as the July start date for the Tour de France got closer. So in the months leading up to the race, his life consisted of bike riding and sleep. It was a difficult, solitary life, away from his wife. While Armstrong stayed in Nice, Kristin stayed in Austin, where she was attempting to get pregnant via in vitro fertilization treatments, using sperm that Armstrong had banked before his chemotherapy. She also began keeping a journal of Armstrong's comeback story that she hoped to show their future child.

During the spring months, Armstrong rode many of the same climbs that would be included in the 1999 Tour de France. When riding up a mountain, cyclists learn very quickly that the roads do not go up and up at a constant gradient. The road is steeper in some sections, and flattens out in others. The road twists and turns, and the quality of the pavement also determines the difficulty of the road. Every cyclist has preferences. Some prefer steeper roads, some like more gradual ones. Ferrari and Bruyneel wanted to know which roads Armstrong favored, so they could decide where it would be wise to attack. And Armstrong needed to ride the roads he didn't like over and over again, to train for his weaknesses. Those were the little things that would give Armstrong a mental edge over his competitors, many of whom might be riding the roads for the first time during the race.

On April 24, Armstrong entered Amstel Gold and finished in second place, losing in a sprint to Dutchman Michael Boogerd. The strong finish was a good sign, but at the race, Armstrong's relationship with Frankie Andreu, who was to play a key part in Lance's plan for the Tour, began to fracture.

The row began days earlier when Betsy, who was pregnant, sent an e-mail to Kristin, telling her about an anonymous person on a cycling Internet message board who had written a post questioning what kind of mother Kristin would be and whether she would hire a nanny to look after her new son. Betsy had jumped on the message board to defend her friend, arguing that Kristin would never be one of those moms who practically lets a nanny raise her kids. But when Kristin read Betsy's e-mail, she started to cry and called Lance, who then picked up the phone, steaming mad, and called Frankie. He yelled at Frankie for indirectly making Kristin cry. So Frankie picked up the phone and called Betsy, who tried to explain.

"There's got to be more to it than that," he said to Betsy, who showed him the e-mail exchange.

Now Frankie was pissed off at Lance for overreacting and causing a huge stir over nothing. For days, both men brooded, hashing out the problem.

On April 21, Betsy sent Lance a scathing e-mail.

> Don't even get me started. You can be disrespectful to so many people and so many people put up with it. I won't and don't have to. Kristin and I don't have a problem with what happened; it's cleared up.

> Sorry, Lance, I'm not going to not stand up to you like so many others.

As both men were getting ready for Amstel Gold to start, Lance bumped into Frankie.

"Sorry," he said.

"Fuck you!" Frankie shot back.

"What's your problem?" Lance asked.

"You made such a huge deal out of something so small," Frankie said. "You blew it out of proportion. It's fucking dumb."

"Dumb?" Lance said. "I'll fuck you."

Both men began yelling obscenities. And then Lance crossed a line and began to threaten and taunt Frankie.

"You'll regret messing with me! I'll make you pay!" he shouted. "I'll make sure you're not on the Tour team. I have the power. I can!"

"You don't scare me," Frankie said.

After the race, the two men didn't speak for nearly two months. When Frankie's son was born in Michigan, Frankie sent out a mass e-mail to the entire team announcing the birth but left Armstrong off the distribution list. Lance was pissed off, and thought Frankie was acting unprofessionally. Then, a couple of weeks before the Tour, Armstrong sent Frankie an e-mail.

As we approach the Tour and Johan is trying to decide on the selection I can tell you that you are not, yes I said NOT, currently doing the Tour de France. I have been focusing on the Tour all year and am ready for a big ride so of course my input matters. While I am very pissed about the last few months I realize that I need all the help/support in July and I know that you are one of the strongest guys on the team. Why are you not selected? Because, and this has nothing to do w/ me, others have seen your deteriorating attitude this year and they question you [*sic*] commitment to the team. I can't believe you have all of a sudden become selfish. I know you must have been stressed as hell w/ the baby coming and all but is that the only reason for your unhappiness? Whatever the reason it has showed.

Frankie, I am not willing to scrap a relationship of 7 years because of a couple of bad months and I know you want to be a part of this team for the Tour and for next year but we have to know you are committed.

Armstrong then followed up by forwarding Betsy's April 21 e-mail. "While I was disgusted at the time I realized it wasn't even worth a response however in the future [*sic*] I suggest your wife keep her opinions to herself," Armstrong wrote.

Frankie sent back a long e-mail, ending with, "If the team has a problem with my attitude, commitment, selfishness or whatever and don't [*sic*] want me to help them at the Tour then tell Johan to book me a ticket home. I have a new born [*sic*] baby waiting for me. I've only been getting online every few days. Call if you want or I'll see you in Nice if you want to talk."

Eventually, the two men worked out their differences, and Frankie was added to the Tour team. He was the most experienced veteran Tour rider on the team, and Armstrong needed him. Frankie also needed the extra pay that came with being on the Tour de France team. But the relationship had cooled. Frankie thought he'd gotten a glimpse of the real Lance Armstrong, and he didn't like what he saw. And Lance had begun to wonder whether he could trust Frankie.

In the lead-up to the race, all the teams faced a new dilemma over whether to continue using performance-enhancing drugs while taking ever greater precautions against being caught, or to quit. The already strict French laws had been tightened even further, and stiff penalties awaited anyone caught with EPO or other banned drugs. Some French teams figured they would play it safe and had asked their riders to quit doping cold turkey before the Tour de France.

But Armstrong and Bruyneel had no intention of racing clean. EPO was a central part of their plan to hand Armstrong the team victory. And neither of them believed the other teams were going to race clean, either, despite the propaganda to that effect. For US Postal, the doping arms race was very much on.

Ahead of the 1999 season, the team let go of Pedro Celaya, whom Armstrong felt was too conservative for their approach. Though Celaya had helped the team with doping, he also tried to encourage riders to see how much they could get out of themselves without drugs. "Might as well race clean," Armstrong once remarked to Jonathan Vaughters, referring to Celaya's stinginess with drugs. "He wants to take your temperature to give you even a caffeine pill." Armstrong was so concerned that his teammates weren't getting adequate quantities of drugs from Celaya that during the 1998 World Championships in the Netherlands, he'd enlisted Kristin to do what he considered Celaya's job: She wrapped cortisone tablets in tinfoil and handed them out to Vaughters and others on the team.

For the 1999 season, Bruyneel brought in a new team doctor, Luis Garcia del Moral—whose nickname was El Gato Negro, or the black cat. Every European professional team at that time was required to have a staff doctor, there for the ostensibly legitimate purpose of caring for all the riders on the team, while often playing a role in the increasingly sophisticated doping programs. Only the top riders such as Armstrong could afford their own doctors, although Armstrong paid Ferrari to work with Hamilton, too. The rest of the team had del Moral, who was based in the town of Valencia, not far from where Bruyneel lived when he was racing for ONCE. The doctor ran a small clinic that doubled as a rehab center for sports injuries, and a sort of drug distribution center. After years of working with cyclists, soccer players, and tennis stars, he had become an expert in doping.

Less conservative than Celaya, del Moral was fascinated by the way drugs affected cyclists' bodies. He relished the possibility of taking a cyclist who was struggling to make it in the pro peloton and boosting him to another level with a cocktail of proprietary injections and pills. In his mind, this was the pinnacle of medicine, and it sure beat what he saw as the role of general practitioners and family doctors—handing out antibiotics and placebos to make hypochondriacs feel better.

Del Moral was charged with making sure the US Postal team riders were kept "topped off," or supercharged, throughout the season. When he showed up at the team's preseason training camp, he was armed with spreadsheets detailing each rider's comprehensive season-long doping program. The team devised a system for the administration of the drugs. Every third or fourth day during the Tour, the riders would gather in the camper. Then del Moral or his assistant, Jose "Pepe" Martí would pop into the camper, bringing syringes with EPO. After the injections, the riders stuffed the syringes into soda cans. Del Moral would quickly leave, disposing of the cans. In addition to EPO, del Moral was also injecting the riders with cortisone and Actovegin, an extract made from calf's blood that he believed improved oxygen flow to the muscles.

In case the French police decided to raid team vehicles, Armstrong and some of the other riders on the team, including Americans Tyler Hamilton and Kevin Livingston, took extra measures to ensure the secrecy and safety of their drugs. They hired a Frenchman named Philippe Maire, who had worked as a gardener at Armstrong's villa in Nice, to make secret deliveries of EPO.

The riders called Maire Motoman because he drove around on a motorcycle to deliver the EPO, chilled in refrigerated panniers on the side of the motorcycle.

As the race neared, Armstrong was, for the first time, entering a Grand Tour with a long-range goal. If he wanted an overall victory, he had to think strategically about when he wanted to move and how he wanted to conserve energy throughout the race.

The Tour de France changes every year. In 1999, it began with a 4.2-mile prologue time trial. The first few stages were flat. The eighth stage was a 34.8-mile time trial. Then the mountains began. There were two significant stages in the Alps. The first ended with a climb to Sestriere and the second ended with a climb up Alpe d'Huez, one of the most famous climbs of the Tour. In the third week, there were two stages in the Pyrenees, followed by an individual time trial on the second-to-last day. The good news for Armstrong heading into the race was that the two previous winners, Jan Ullrich and Italian Marco Pantani, weren't racing. Ullrich, who won in 1997, was injured. Pantani, embroiled in controversy for going over the 50 percent hematocrit rule in the Giro d'Italia, had withdrawn.

Armstrong began the Tour with a shocking win of the July 4 prologue time trial in the town of Le Puy du Fou. When Armstrong pulled on the leader's yellow jersey, Bill Stapleton's eyes welled up with tears, while his wife, Laura, cried like a baby. With all Armstrong had endured, it seemed to Stapleton the most life-affirming moment he had ever witnessed. And the drama was just about to begin.

Armstrong lost the yellow jersey the following day, but that was to be expected. The real race for the victory didn't begin for a week.

The time trial in the town of Metz was supposed to be a close one. Even before cancer, Armstrong had never been the strongest time trial rider. But now he turned in an astonishing performance, winning the race by 58 seconds, crushing his closest competitor, Alex Zülle of Switzerland. Armstrong had again slipped into the lead in the Tour by 2 minutes, 20 seconds. Nobody in France could believe what was happening.

Neither could Greg LeMond, who was in France leading a group of mostly American cyclists on rides along the Tour de France route. When

LeMond saw Armstrong dominate the time trial at such high speeds, he began to think that maybe Armstrong wasn't crazy when he said he thought he could win the Tour de France.

LeMond knew that the mountains began two days later, after a rest day, and he began to worry that Armstrong perhaps doubted his ability to climb. LeMond wanted to encourage him, so he traveled to the start of the first mountain stage and found the US Postal team bus, where Gorski told him he could find Lance. LeMond climbed aboard the bus and found Armstrong.

"Man, you are just flying up there. Unbelievable," he said. "I am so happy for you."

"Thanks," Lance responded.

"I've got to tell you, your capability of doing that time trial, that'll translate directly into climbing," LeMond said. "Don't let anybody tell you that you're a time trialist and not a climber. If you can time trial like that, you can win the Tour," LeMond said.

"I know," Lance responded dismissively.

LeMond was taken aback by Armstrong's cockiness and slight air of disrespect. He left the team bus feeling silly for making the effort to encourage Armstrong, who obviously did not need it.

The next day, on the final climb, Armstrong found himself in a small group of elite climbers, including Zülle, who was considered his most dangerous competitor. Suddenly, Armstrong got out of the saddle and began sprinting up the mountain. There was something almost eerie about his ascent on that dark and rainy day, his bright yellow jersey dim in the waning light.

This was the kind of attack that he might have tried up a short climb in Philadelphia, or during one of the classics. But Sestriere is 6,670 feet high. It is a monster. And the next day, the riders would have to do it again up Alpe d'Huez. The attack looked too fast. It looked like Armstrong was being foolish—wasting himself. But he didn't slow down. He kept blasting up the hill, going so fast that when the road bent, Armstrong had to take the turns wide because he was going so fast—uphill. Armstrong crossed the finish line all alone, wearing his yellow jersey and his blue US Postal cap. He was now leading the race by more than 6 minutes.

The shot of Armstrong crossing the line that rain-soaked day ended up in newspapers all over the world, and would remain a lasting image in the sport. It was the day Armstrong became famous around the world.

LeMond was watching the race at a hotel in a nearby town with his group of tourists. As Armstrong conquered Sestriere, everyone in the room, including LeMond, was cheering like mad. Except one man. A former mechanic on the Festina team named Cyrille Perrin tapped LeMond on the shoulder and whispered to LeMond, "*sur le jus*."

LeMond knew what he meant—Armstrong was juicing. But how could the mechanic know this? "What? Why?" LeMond asked, amid the commotion and the cheering.

"No effort," Perrin said. "Look at his eyes, his breathing," he said. Perrin went on to explain that cyclists were now using a powerful cocktail of drugs that propelled them up mountains without effort. "They feel no pain," he said to LeMond.

LeMond continued to cheer. He was truly inspired by Armstrong's comeback and didn't want to think about him doping. He wanted to believe that after Festina, the sport was cleaning itself up. But he felt strange, although he eventually put Perrin's comments out of his mind and forgot about it.

Betsy Andreu had watched the race on television, with her newborn, "Little Frankie." As she watched Frankie pulling up Sestriere, she couldn't believe it. She'd never seen her husband climb like that in any race. Betsy picked up the phone and called Becky Rast, the wife of one of the Tour de France photographers, James Startt.

"Are you watching? Do you see Frankie pulling?" she said.

"Yeah, he's doing great!" Becky said.

"He's not a climber. He shouldn't be pulling." Becky was silent on the other line. Betsy had told Becky about the hospital room scene, and now they both knew what Frankie's superb climbing meant: He was juiced, and Betsy was furious. She called Frankie that night.

"What's that about?" she asked.

"What?"

"You are not a climber. You fucking gave in, didn't you? How long has this been going on?"

"I don't want to talk about it," Frankie said.

"We're going to talk about it!"

"I'm too tired."

"I'm not going to put up with this. I'm not going to do it," Betsy said, and hung up the phone.

The next day, Armstrong extended his lead again by more than a minute. By this time, his lead was so safe that the US Postal team stopped using EPO and other performance-enhancing drugs for the final week of the Tour. They didn't need it, and it wasn't worth the risk.

As Armstrong raced toward victory, the media was eating it up. For a survivor of cancer to prevail in such a grueling race, outperforming not just everyone else in the field but his own past achievements, was extraordinary. The French paper *Le Monde* hailed it as a major achievement in sports history. *The New York Times* described it as the equivalent of putting a "man on the moon," and not simply because Neil and Lance shared the same last name. Armstrong's own cancer doctors proclaimed it to be a scientific miracle.

On July 14, the evening after Armstrong protected his lead on Alpe d'Huez, Armstrong invited Abt to join the team for dinner at the ski resort atop the mountain. Armstrong was "eager," Abt said in an article that ran a couple of days later, to discuss "innuendo" in the European press about his victory. Over two bowls of risotto and blueberry pie, Armstrong explained to Abt that reporters could not accept his performance as legitimate. The Festina affair, Armstrong said, had made everyone suspicious of him. Abt, of course, must have considered Armstrong's paranoia odd. The European press was hailing Armstrong as the symbol of a new, clean era of cycling.

But Abt spun the story the way Armstrong wanted. "How else, some of the European news media are asking, can somebody who underwent chemotherapy for testicular cancer two and a half years ago be so dominant now in the world's toughest bicycle race?" Abt wrote. The truth was, nobody was asking that question. Abt, in his article, offered two examples of this so-called negative coverage. One was a Belgian newspaper headline: ARMSTRONG PUTS A BOMB UNDER THE TOUR. The word *bomb*, Abt wrote, was code for *drugs*. The second example: A French newspaper that compared Armstrong's performance to the 1996 victory of Danish cyclist Bjarne Riis. The comparison made sense. Armstrong and Riis had a similar body type and style and Riis's win was unexpected. But Abt wrote that Riis had come under suspicion for doping, therefore the comparison was a veiled accusation against Armstrong. It was a ridiculous argument.

Abt wrote that Armstrong was drug tested every day as the race leader, and proceeded to tout the meaningfulness of his victory to the cancer community. "My story is a success story in the world of cancer," Armstrong was quoted as saying. "A lot of people relate to my story. In America, in France, in Europe, they relate to this story," he said. Armstrong said he wouldn't be stupid enough to take drugs after cancer. "I've been on my deathbed," he said.

Armstrong's sudden paranoia wasn't delusional. It was tactical. He was using Abt to get out in front of a story that was going to come out at some point. The team had known for about a week that a urine sample from the first day of the Tour had been tested and found to contain traces of banned corticosteroids. The result had stayed quiet for nearly two weeks, but the French newspaper Le Monde had found out and was preparing to go to press. If Armstrong's sample was officially declared "positive," he could potentially be disqualified from the race. No Tour de France leader had ever been disqualified for doping. Not only would it sully Armstrong's reputation and his inspiring message of cancer survivorship, but it would destroy the entire atmosphere of the race. It would be cycling's second major doping scandal in two years. Abt had unwittingly helped Armstrong create a narrative—albeit a fabricated one—that the French were "out to get" him.

In fact, Armstrong had been injected with the steroids before the race. In previous races that season, the UCI had not tested for the drug. But after the Festina affair, the UCI had been under pressure from the International Olympic Committee to begin testing for the substance, and Armstrong had been ensnared by this unexpected turn of events.

The USPS team was more concerned about Le Monde than it was about punishment from UCI. The UCI might quietly let the test go, they thought, since it wasn't in their interest to have the winner test positive only a year after Festina. But if the test results were published, the UCI would have to take some action.

When they learned that Le Monde was going to publish a story, Armstrong, Gorski, and Weisel gathered around the massage table at the team hotel to discuss their plan of action. Emma O'Reilly, the soigneur who was at the massage table, recalled that they wanted to come up with a story—that the corticosteroid came from some kind of medication. According to O'Reilly's sworn testimony, the men concocted a plan. Dr. Garcia del Moral would write a prescription for a saddle-sore drug that contained corticosteroids, backdating it so that it would appear as though the prescription had been written long before the test. Gorski and Weisel deny O'Reilly's account.

The next day, the story broke in *Le Monde*, and the team's public relations guru, Dan Osipow, spent all morning fielding questions from every cycling reporter in the world. He explained that Armstrong had used an ointment that he didn't know contained a drug that was banned. Later that day, the UCI made its announcement: Armstrong would be cleared of the test because he had produced a doctor's prescription for the substance.

Some reporters, including David Walsh of *The Sunday Times* of London, who up until then had been so admiring, were suspicious. But nobody wanted to believe that the hero of the hour, Lance Armstrong, could have cheated. It was too heartbreaking. Too bleak. Abt's piece in *The New York Times* did not question the validity of the "saddle sore" story, and he glossed over the details. The paper ignored the story after that.

By the time Armstrong won the event's final time trial in the French theme park Futuroscope, the positive test result had been forgotten. Armstrong was leading the Tour de France by 7 minutes, 37 seconds. It was a trouncing.

The next day, Armstrong was going to roll into Paris wearing the yellow jersey. An American on an American team. A cancer survivor. This was huge, monumental. It was something to be celebrated, not compromised by some nitpicking concern about a prescription drug. If the official line was that Armstrong had used a simple saddle-sore cream, then the media—and the public—were eager to believe it.

When the moment arrived, Americans waving American and Texan flags lined the cobblestoned roads of the Champs-Élysées. People had flown over from the United States just to watch the finish. As the peloton entered Paris and headed onto the Champs-Élysées, the US Postal team rode at the front of the pack, keeping Armstrong safe and out of the path of any crashes that could dampen the day. The pack did its traditional ten laps at warp speed around the Champs to cap off the race, while the sprinters hammered it for a chance at one final stage win. But all anybody wanted to see was Armstrong, in his yellow jersey, crossing the line.

After the win, the team and their managers, including Weisel and Gorski, celebrated by drinking champagne and riding victory laps around the Champs with Armstrong. Weisel had done what no American team owner had ever done before. He had won the Tour de France with an American team—the equivalent, as Borysewicz had told him twelve years before, of winning the World Series with a French baseball team.

CHAPTER SEVEN

LANCE ARMSTRONG INCORPORATED

A few hours after Armstrong stood atop the Tour winner's podium, it was time to celebrate. The US Postal team and about two hundred of their friends and sponsors gathered at a huge party in Armstrong's honor, which was held in the elegant dining salon on the first floor of the Musée d'Orsay, the vast converted train station that houses the world's greatest collection of Impressionist art.

The crowd milled around a lavish spread of food, champagne, and fine Bordeaux, and each table was set with a bowl of apples, a tribute to Lance's perseverance in the mountains. Why apples? As Lance charged up the seven-mile Sestriere, he had shouted, "How do you like them fuckin' apples?!" into the team radio.

An ice sculpture of a cyclist had been installed in the main room. There, under a ceiling decorated in magnificent rococo style and hung with dazzling crystal chandeliers, Lance signed autographs and posed for photographs with his mom and Kristin, now nearly seven months pregnant with their first child. President Clinton and Texas governor George W. Bush had both called him earlier to congratulate him.

The evening fête was paid for by Thom Weisel, who, as an avid art collector, chose the venue. Over the years, Weisel had spent millions of dollars of his own money to keep the team afloat. Finally, his outlay was paying off—in fame and glory if not in money.

Lance, whose public speaking skills had improved significantly in the year following his cancer treatments, thanks to all the speeches he'd given about his recovery at fund-raisers for his fledgling foundation, stood up to address the team—my team, as he referred to them that night. Lance's speech was a disarmingly modest tribute to the support he had received from his teammates. He told the crowd that his own role in the Tour win was "equal to just about the zipper" of that jersey. "The rest of the body, the sleeves, the collar" of the yellow jersey were there because of "my team."

Johan Bruyneel, in a white button-down shirt, sat at a table near one of the tall, gold-framed windows, grinning broadly as he accepted congratulations from the team's sponsors and other guests. Bill Stapleton and Chris Carmichael sipped wine while standing on a balcony overlooking the Seine. Mark Gorski walked around the main room with an unlit cigar in his mouth, reflecting on how far Lance and his supporting riders had come. Tyler Hamilton had finished in 13th place in the Tour, and twenty-five-year-old Kevin Livingston had finished in 36th place, an amazing result for someone riding in his very first Tour. The two would have had even better finishes if they hadn't spent all of their energy and effort working for Lance.

Dr. Luis Garcia del Moral was there, too. Dressed in a dapper green suit and tie, he was seated at a table with his assistant, Pepe Martí.

Now that Lance was the defending champion and no longer the underdog in the sport, there would be a lot more pressure to win the race again the following year. And the pressure began immediately. In a toast, Steve Disson, Weisel's business partner, called for a second Tour victory in 2000. By the time of the party, the team had already lined up six of the seven US riders for the Postal team's 2000 season, including Armstrong, Hamilton, and Livingston. It also had an agreement in principle with Christian Vande Velde, a goofy twenty-three-year-old from the Chicago suburb of Lemont, whose father, John Vande Velde, a two-time Olympic track cyclist, had played one of the evil Italian cyclists in the 1979 hit movie *Breaking Away*.

Armstrong's victory had earned him a $1 million bonus from the team, plus additional "salary enhancements" of $50,000 for winning the leader's yellow jersey, and $25,000 per day for successfully defending the yellow jersey—thanks to a new deal between Armstrong and Gorski, reached just days before the Tour began. That deal also extended Armstrong's contract for two more years, and offered him as much as $2.5 million annually.

His newfound fame had a trickle-down effect for the team. Once Lance had agreed to sign on to the team for the 2000 and 2001 seasons, Gorski, the master salesman, turned to US Postal Service and pitched it on a two-year extension of its sponsorship, with an outlay of $3.3 million to back the team for the 2000 season. That was more than three times its initial $1 million outlay, back in 1996. Winning the 1999 Tour also made it easier for Gorski to line up more than twenty other companies to sign on as sponsors. The significant expansion of the team budget, in turn, made it possible for the organization to begin scouting for high-performing free agents, riders whose special talents could make a big difference in future races.

After the victory party, Kristin returned to Austin, and Armstrong left Paris for a series of criterium races in the Netherlands and Belgium. As the winner of the Tour, he now automatically earned appearance fees of $25,000 for every criterium he rode in, regardless of how he performed.

From the Netherlands, he flew on a jet chartered by his personal sponsor, Nike, arriving in New York at about 1:00 A.M. Now an internationally acclaimed celebrity, Armstrong was becoming a major media phenomenon. He appeared on all three major network morning shows and *Larry King Live*, taped a David Letterman show appearance, did a Nike satellite media tour, and rang the opening bell at the New York Stock Exchange. He then returned to his home in Austin for a day to see Kristin before heading to Washington, DC, where he presided over a question-and-answer session about his cancer with reporters at the National Press Club.

While in Washington, Lance met with President Clinton in the Oval Office and then appeared in the Roosevelt Room with Vice President Gore, who pledged to make the fight against cancer a part of his upcoming presidential campaign.

After the Tour victory, Bill Stapleton's answering machine was flooded. Everyone wanted a piece of Lance. He appeared in TV ads for Bridge Information Systems, then the largest provider of financial news and information in North America, which purchased a large video screen in New York's Times Square to play its Armstrong commercial. He also appeared in ads for American General Insurance, and of course the US Postal Service. In the week after his victory, he was the star of a "Just Do It" commercial by Nike.

With his astonishing comeback from near death to the top of his field, Lance had the best underdog story in sports since Seabiscuit. And on top of that, the Lance Armstrong Foundation to benefit cancer patients made him seem even more of a hero.

Even before he had in fact won the race, he and Stapleton had turned their attention back to the idea of capitalizing on his victory with inspirational dramas in both book and movie form. They had been talking again about a possible autobiography and even a TV biopic.

As Lance was racing in the three-week Tour, Stapleton began conversations with publishing houses in New York about selling the rights to Lance's memoir. This time a bidding war ensued. The price was up to $300,000 after Lance won the first stage, the race against the clock. But about a dozen days later, after he had gained a 6 minute, 15 second advantage over his rivals, the price shot up to $400,000. After Lance won, he signed a deal with Putnam. In announcing the book, Putnam vice president and senior editor Stacy Creamer said he had "given the world hope by example through this amazing comeback from cancer," adding that his autobiography would convey the inspiring message of his accomplishments, bringing the intimate details of his emotional, spiritual, and physical journey to a wider audience. She noted that Lance himself viewed his 1999 Tour win as "a miracle."

Soon after the book was announced, Stapleton arranged for Sally Jenkins, a native of Fort Worth and the daughter of bestselling author and sportswriting icon Dan Jenkins, to cowrite it. At the time, Sally Jenkins was a little-known writer for *Women's Sports and Fitness*. She and Lance had never previously met. Their collaboration, *It's Not About the Bike: My Journey Back to Life*, eventually sold more than a million copies and became an international bestseller that stayed on the *New York Times* bestseller list for roughly a year.

Stapleton also brokered a $500,000 TV movie deal with legendary sports producer Bud Greenspan, who worked on the Lance biopic with producer

Edward R. Pressman of the movie *Wall Street*. Greenspan hired screenwriter Stanley Weiser (who had cowritten the script for *Wall Street*). Shooting was to begin in the fall of 1999 and the movie—*Second Life*—was scheduled to air on Turner Network Television during the 2000–2001 season. But within months, as the monies and offers coming their way kept snowballing to ever larger numbers, Lance and Stapleton seemed to think Lance's story might be worth more than what they had originally envisioned. By the end of 1999, they decided to hold off on the made-for-television movie, figuring it might merit a big-budget Hollywood production, perhaps starring Matt Damon or another of Lance's new celebrity friends. Stapleton informed Greenspan that Armstrong wouldn't cooperate, which left Greenspan's project inactive.

For Stapleton, controlling Lance's image and story was paramount. When Tom Clynes called Stapleton after the Tour, seeking to be reimbursed for his $8,000 outlay for the first book proposal, Stapleton agreed to pay him—Clynes suspects he did so out of his own pocket—but required Clynes to sign a nondisclosure agreement preventing him from using any of the material he had gathered on Lance. Even the owner of Armstrong's team had only limited access to the use of Lance's name and image. His new contract with Disson Furst mandated that before entering into any agreement with a team sponsor who wished to use Lance's likeness in any of its marketing efforts, Disson Furst would have to negotiate a separate marketing agreement with Lance himself.

Capitalizing on the public's intense interest in Armstrong, Stapleton mobilized quickly and made sure that the price of having a product associated with him went up—way up.

In the ten months following his win, Lance signed new endorsement deals, some going through the year 2004, with a total value of more than $7.5 million. By February 2000, Armstrong had signed a deal worth over $500,000 a year, and a total of several million dollars over the course of the contract, to be the cancer spokesman for the health website WebMD.com, and was appearing in commercials for drugmaker Bristol-Myers Squibb and AIM Mutual Funds, as well as on two Wheaties boxes. In all, about sixteen companies were paying Lance for the use of his image. He was also going on the road to make speeches about his amazing comeback, commanding

$100,000 for a one-hour speech, up from about $30,000 per engagement before he won the Tour.

Here is a rough breakdown of the estimated annual value of the individual deals that were struck during those first ten months after the Tour:

Disson Furst/ US Postal Service team	$2,000,000–$2,500,000
Bristol-Myers Squibb	$700,000
Penguin Putnam Books	$525,000 (including estimated royalties for six months through year-end 2000)
Kickstart.com (Denver-based fund-raising site)	$500,000—new in February 2000
Nike	$500,000
BrainLab (medical products maker)	$500,000 (+ stock)
Bridge (financial website)	$500,000—since August 1999
WebMD (online health content site)	$500,000 (+ stock)—new in January 2000
Trek (bicycle maker)	$500,000
AIM Mutual Funds	$300,000
American General Insurance	$300,000
General Mills/Wheaties	$200,000
Bike.com (e-commerce site)	$150,000 (+ stock)
Giro (bike helmet maker)	$150,000
Oakley (sunglasses maker)	$125,000 (+ stock)
Shimano (bike component maker)	$100,000
Grand Total	**$7,550,000**

Expensive as these deals were, the sponsors felt they got their money's worth. The Postal Service's senior vice president Gail Sonnenberg estimated that it had gotten "millions and millions" of dollars' worth of new business specifically because of its association with Armstrong and sponsorship of his team. In retrospect, the Postal Service's decision in 1996 to put its brand on the start-up US cycling team appeared remarkably prescient—and cost-effective.

Even at the price they had to pay when they renewed, the Postal Service was getting a great deal, spending only about $8 million per year of its $146 million advertising budget to sponsor the team.

The US Postal Service, a brand once completely unknown in Europe, was suddenly becoming recognizable all over the world, and also a newfound source of pride to its own employees. The Topeka, Kansas, postmaster B. Steven Pinkerton raised a unique blue-on-yellow flag featuring a likeness of the Postal team jersey to celebrate National Postal Worker's Day in 2002. Pinkerton said the flag was intended to remind Americans of the "hard work" of the Postal Service Pro Cycling Team riders, who competed in more than fifty-eight races all over the world. (Lance sat out most of those races, conserving energy for the Tour de France.)

In hindsight, marketing was really the least of the Postal Service's worries. The digital age was pushing the agency's core business—delivering letters—into obsolescence, and it had already fallen hopelessly behind private sector competitors like Federal Express in the one area of the parcel industry that was growing—express package deliveries.

Armstrong's victory also had a big impact on Wisconsin-based bike maker Trek. Soon it became widely known as the builder of the bikes on which Lance rode to his Tour victories. Sales of Trek's most expensive bicycle line—bikes that sold for up to $4,000 each—more than doubled from 1998 to 1999; its total sales of road bikes rose 143 percent from 2000 to 2005.

Even Lance's face on a Wheaties box pushed product. Boxes with Armstrong's image sold about 10 percent better than other Wheaties boxes.

Overall, the "Lance effect" was profound. Between the time he began winning the Tour de France and his retirement, companies that made everything from bikes to helmets, cycling shoes to pedals, saw tremendous growth.

And no wonder! "He's the all-American, Norman Rockwell–like embodiment of what people want their heroes to be," marketing expert David Carter proclaimed in May 2000.

Nike in particular backed America's newest hero in a substantial way. With Michael Jordan having retired, Nike had been searching for the next big name in sports to help market its products. Rather than presenting Armstrong as merely a champion cyclist, which would have limited his usefulness to selling biking apparel and gizmos, a very small part of the sports marketplace, Nike launched a campaign that incorporated his image into the very identity of the company. To showcase the qualities that made up the "real Lance Armstrong," Nike dispatched film crews to Nice to show him at his cliffside villa with a panoramic view of the French Riviera, eating his breakfast, receiving an intense chiropractic treatment in his workout room, and changing the diaper of his newborn baby, Luke. Then, two producers for Nike's website spent the next three hours in a convertible filming Armstrong biking up and down the back streets in and around Nice.

Meanwhile, Thom Weisel was enjoying a comeback story of his own. After selling and then getting bought out from the investment bank he had founded, he started a new one. This time, he called it simply Thomas Weisel Partners (TWP). In 1999, the same year Armstrong won his first Tour de France, Weisel's new investment bank was the hottest shop in Silicon Valley for hyping previously unknown tech companies and taking them public. Weisel was making hundreds of millions of dollars handling initial public offerings for companies like Akamai Technologies, Drugstore.com, Fogdog .com, FTD.com, InfoSpace.com, MapQuest.com. And the investing public was eating the stocks up. In 2000, TWP's revenues reached $476 million. In January of that year, the nation's largest and most influential public pension fund, the California Public Employees' Retirement System, or CalPERS (with $136 billion in assets), announced it would invest $100 million for a 10 percent stake in TWP, doubling the firm's valuation to $1 billion. *Investment Dealers' Digest* awarded Weisel its coveted Banker of the Year award.

Weisel brought his business acumen and ingenuity to the Postal team. He and Gorski thought they could parlay Armstrong's success into the creation of a timeless sports franchise like Manchester United or the New York Yankees. And he hoped that the sports marketing company partnership he had entered into with Mark Disson and Allen Furst would continue long after Armstrong had retired. But even after the 1999 win and all the money that came rolling in as a result—the new sponsorships, the Postal Service's renewal of its sponsorship for a total of $30.6 million between 2001 and 2004—the team was operating at a loss. And a few months after Armstrong's second Tour de France victory in 2000, Steve Disson decided he was fed up with the way Gorski and Weisel were running the business as if it were all about Lance. He felt that all the hard-earned cash Disson Furst brought into the business through its other deals was going into the cycling side of the business, paying for Armstrong's salary—as much as $9.5 million over the 2001–2004 period, depending on how many Tours de France he would win—and for all the perks he demanded. Armstrong also demanded that the team hire eight of the world's top cyclists to ride alongside him. The last straw was when Gorski and Weisel wanted to put Armstrong on Disson Furst's board of directors. Disson thought that was just ridiculous. "I'm trying to run a business here!" he told them.

In October 2000, Disson pulled out of his arrangement and parted ways with Gorski and Weisel, who renamed the company Tailwind Sports in January 2001. Gorski became CEO of the new company.

According to notebooks containing team finances that were given to Tailwind investors, which included copies of the team's contracts and financial statements, the company seemed to be heading toward solvency by 2003. Buried in the fine print, however, was one item, hidden in plain sight, that presaged looming trouble. Under the heading EUROPEAN ADMINISTRATIVE STAFF COMPENSATION, the report listed a payment of $185,054 to the Institute de Valencia/Medical in Spain—the sports clinic operated by Dr. Luis Garcia del Moral.

As the expenses of the Postal team approached $10.5 million in 2002, Weisel knew he had little choice but to find some new investors to help cover the budget. He turned to a small group of brash, hard-charging American financiers, venture capitalists, investment bankers, CEOs, and fund managers, nearly all avid amateur cyclists. These CEOs, hedge fund managers, and titans of industry, as well as some of their offspring, flocked to cycling at a critical juncture and helped to prop up the sport.

Investing in cycling would have been laughable prior to the arrival of Armstrong and the Postal team. But Armstrong's string of victories had significantly shifted the demographics of the cycling audience. From the early 1990s to the early 2000s, cycling morphed from a quirky working-class hobby to one of the favorite pastimes of the Masters of the Universe set. Wealthy middle-aged men all over America were ditching their golf courses for the open road, pedaling away on their expensive bicycles while wearing their Euro-chic spandex regalia. Participation in races and group bike rides exploded, especially in corporate America.

By courting some of these highfliers, Tailwind Sports drew about twenty-five wealthy investors, mostly in their forties, fifties, and early sixties. They included General Growth CEO John Bucksbaum and former United States Olympic Committee executive director Harvey Schiller, who at Gorski's urging put $100,000 into Tailwind. Among others who invested in 2002 were two-time Olympic rower Richard Cashin Jr., chairman of a private-equity unit of JPMorgan Chase & Co.; David "Tiger" Williams, founder of Williams Trading LLC, a Connecticut firm; and Ward W. Woods Jr., former chief executive of Bessemer Securities.

Many of these investors started out as donors of sums of $200,000 and up, in support of US cycling in general, through the Champions Club, an organization created by Weisel in 2000 to help raise money for the sport's governing body. Word of the Champions Club spread through cycling circles on group rides in San Francisco, New York, and other cities. Both the investors in the team and the members of the Champions Club got a lot of fancy perks, including close access to the Postal team during the Tour de France. As the race wound through the Alps, the American aficionados pedaled segments of the course, trailed by cars carrying their food and water bottles. The group got massages, haute cuisine, and prime views of the race's mountaintop finishes. There were also invitations to gatherings where they got the chance to pound the pedals for 60 miles with Armstrong and other US Postal Service team members including Floyd Landis and George Hincapie.

"There was a lot of macho that day," recalled one of the riders, Kenneth Barnett, chief executive of a Michigan marketing firm. "These fairly accomplished people were like little boys with big toys."

San Francisco ad executive Rich Silverstein, who donated to US cycling through the Champions Club but didn't invest in the Postal team, looked back on those early days with pleasure. "You don't go to spring training of baseball and throw the ball around with the guys," he said. "We got into the spring training of cycling and were able to ride with the guys. Being on the inside of the sport like that was seductive."

Most of the investors in Weisel's team were wealthy dabblers who viewed the investment as something of a down payment on a lifestyle. But Tiger Williams, who bought a 1.55 percent stake in December 2002, for about $100,000, was different in an important regard: He was a salesman and entrepreneur who viewed his investment not just as a lifestyle thing—though it certainly was that, and he didn't hesitate to capitalize on the glamour of being associated with the team—but as a potential moneymaker as well as a marketing vehicle for Williams Trading, the firm he founded in 1997.

A former ice hockey standout at Yale University, Williams had been a star trader at Julian Robertson Jr.'s Tiger Management before starting his own company. Though headquartered in a nondescript office complex in Stamford, Connecticut, Williams Trading's clients have included Cascade Investment, which managed Microsoft founder Bill Gates's fortune, as well as many major hedge funds including Blue Ridge Capital. By the time Weisel approached Williams to invest in Tailwind Sports, Williams was making more than $20 million a year. On weekends, he flew by private helicopter to a beach home he owned in Montauk, on the Long Island shore.

In their pitch to Williams, Weisel and Gorski said that Tailwind had found a way to produce a return. The idea centered around creating a sort of fan club that would leverage Armstrong's popularity into subscription revenues and merchandise sales. When he invested in the team, Williams agreed to pay extra to secure the right to put a logo for his firm, Williams Trading LLC, on the Postal Service team jerseys. In addition, Williams pledged $100,000 a year to the Lance Armstrong Foundation—and he later also helped the foundation raise money by hosting fund-raisers.

During the course of his ever-growing involvement with the team, Williams also struck up close friendships with several of its cyclists, including George Hincapie, Dave Zabriskie, and Floyd Landis.

While all the investors reveled in the team's success, for Weisel, an ultra-competitive alpha male, the team's Tour de France victories were the most exciting ROI he'd ever seen. He proudly displayed Armstrong's yellow jerseys above his desk at his offices in San Francisco's Financial District. So he stuck with the team despite its losses, which ran between about $200,000 and $1.2 million a year through 2003.

Beyond his involvement in his own team, Weisel was also interested in becoming a player in the international world of cycling. He fantasized about ousting the European bureaucrats from the top of the sport's power structure, the UCI. He felt the UCI was old-fashioned, stodgy, and slow. It governed hundreds of individually owned races, mostly in Europe, and each race negotiated with TV broadcasters and sponsors on its own behalf. Unlike baseball and football, cycling lacked a nerve center, with which potential advertisers, corporate partners, and broadcasters could negotiate lucrative deals. The head of the UCI, Hein Verbruggen, had been attempting to change things in cycling, but progress was slow. The bureaucracy was too firmly entrenched. So Weisel set his sights closer to home, on the American branch of the International Olympic Committee.

USA Cycling, which changed its name from the United States Cycling Federation in 1995, enjoyed a congressionally mandated monopoly as the sole governing body for Olympic cycling in the United States. But it was struggling financially after years of what Weisel called mismanagement. "It was in disarray. There was no planning, no funding, no budgets. Nothing," he said.

Weisel set up a separate organization in the summer of 2000 called the USA Cycling Development Foundation, to help raise money for the sport. It was then that Weisel created the Champions Club, modeled after the charitable foundation that supported the US Ski Team.

Soon, USA Cycling grew dependent on the development foundation. In exchange for the cash infusions, which bailed it out of its financial troubles, the organization agreed to change its bylaws, giving the development foundation voting power on the board. Then, in the nonprofit equivalent of audacious corporate shareholder activism, Weisel engineered the ouster of the organization's top leadership.

Weisel's old masters cycling teammate and friend, Steve Johnson, left his job as an associate sports science professor at the University of Utah to become the chief operating officer of the federation. A few years later, Weisel helped to install Jim Ochowicz as president, and hired him as a broker at his investment banking firm, Thomas Weisel Partners.

When Ochowicz, who'd been working as a broker in the years after Motorola folded, began working for Weisel, he took with him a significant client in the cycling world: Verbruggen. In 1999, while Ochowicz was working for Robert W. Baird in Milwaukee, he had opened a brokerage account for Verbruggen. By then, Ochowicz had become a very close friend of Armstrong's, and that year he also became the godfather of Armstrong's son, Luke.

Through his control of the sport in the United States, and his ability to use his investment bank's resources in the cycling world, Weisel also gained some influence over the UCI, which controlled the business and, significantly, all drug testing during the Tour de France. Ochowicz, in his role as head of the US governing body, made trips to Aigle, Switzerland, to meet with UCI president Hein Verbruggen. Ostensibly, he made the visits for the purpose of coordinating promotion of the sport and for reviewing details of upcoming Olympic events. But Ochowicz had another reason to visit: He often discussed financial transactions in Verbruggen's brokerage account. Weisel, the hottest investment banker in Silicon Valley at the time, didn't accept investments from just anybody. USADA and others believe the financial relationship represented a massive conflict of interest for Verbruggen. Armstrong was the sport's biggest star, and Verbruggen, as head of the governing body, was his head disciplinarian. Had the USPS team wanted to transfer funds to Verbruggen, it would have been easy for Thomas Weisel Partners to let Verbruggen in on a hot IPO, which could have been worth hundreds of thousands of dollars, if not millions, depending on the amount of Verbruggen's investment. Weisel had helped other high-profile people in the cycling industry—including LeMond—in this way.

Verbruggen now had several disincentives to police Armstrong's doping, and Armstrong would be thankful for them at various times throughout the remaining years of his career.

CHAPTER EIGHT

HEMATOCRITS AND HYPOCRITES

With Thom Weisel firmly in control of the sport in their home country, and their finances vastly improved, the mood on the US Postal team was more relaxed. The new infusions of money meant that there were more staffers on the team, more mechanics, and extra bikes and other state-of-the-art equipment, much of it custom-made to the riders' specifications. No longer struggling so hard to hold on to its dominance, the Postal team could focus on its strengths: winning bike races. The 1999 Tour de France had proved to the world what Armstrong and his teammates were capable of, and now they had to show the world that it hadn't been an anomaly.

For 2000, the team had set high goals, including a strong showing in the spring classics and, of course, a defense of the yellow jersey by Lance. The team hired five new riders to back their superhuman superstar, including Viatcheslav "Eki" Ekimov, who had left the team in 1998 for a richer offer but would return to become a fixture in all of Armstrong's remaining Tour de France runs.

Before the 2000 Tour de France began, there were rumors in the peloton that a new prototype test for EPO had been discovered and would be used during the race. This was the test that the International Olympic Committee had commissioned Francesco Conconi, the so-called fox in the henhouse, to develop. Concerned about being found out, cyclists were even more afraid of using EPO than they had been in 1999. But that didn't deter the US Postal Service team.

Armstrong bragged to friends that he had inside knowledge of how to get around the test, thanks to the fact that Conconi had been the mentor to his longtime doping doctor, Michele Ferrari. From Ferrari, the US Postal Service team learned that if the riders injected EPO directly into their veins instead of just below the skin—which was the typical method—the drug would leave their system in around twelve hours instead of a few days. Armstrong also knew that the EPO test, still in its infancy, was far from exact. Even if a rider were to be tested a few hours after an EPO injection, the test would likely be inconclusive.

Thanks to its growing budget, the team could also afford to begin to implement a more complicated but less detectable method of doping: blood transfusions. Doctors carried out a blood doping program for all three of its climbers: Lance; Tyler Hamilton, a blue-eyed twenty-nine-year-old prep school graduate who had attended the University of Colorado at Boulder; and Kevin Livingston, a twenty-seven-year-old originally from St. Louis, who was known for his near perfect pedal stroke. About a month before the 2000 Tour, as Johan Bruyneel explained, 500 cc of blood—the equivalent of two cups— would be withdrawn from each of them, then reinfused a few weeks later during the Tour. Since there was no reliable test for blood transfusions, there would be no way for the riders to be caught unless someone witnessed the reinfusion firsthand, or caught them with the blood bags in their possession.

In mid-June, Armstrong, Hamilton, and Livingston stepped aboard a private jet in Nice to fly to Valencia. There, they were driven to a hotel for the extraction. The whole process took about an hour and then the three men went for a training ride down the coast. Fatigued from the loss of blood, they struggled during the training ride to make it up some small hills. But they knew that after the blood was reinfused, they would be able to power up the Tour's climbs.

During that year's Tour, Armstrong was neck and neck with the bald thirty-year-old Italian Marco Pantani, a fan favorite in the late 1990s for his aggressive style, and brown-haired former Tour de France winner and race favorite, twenty-seven-year-old Jan Ullrich of Germany, until the tenth stage—a 127-mile mountain expedition from Dax to Lourdes Hautacam. On the morning before the stage, rain was pouring down and it was cold. These were conditions most cyclists hate, but Armstrong had grown to love them because they brought out the best in him. The course included three major climbs: the Col de Marie-Blanque, the Col d'Aubisque, and the agonizing 8.3-mile Hautacam. Armstrong, Ullrich, and Pantani stayed together until the base of the Hautacam. As the climb began, Pantani jumped up and took off on an attack, opening up a small gap between him and the riders behind him. Armstrong took off after him and, within seconds, caught and passed him. Ullrich was left far behind. By the time he reached the top of the Hautacam, Armstrong had moved into the race lead, with Ullrich in second place, 4 minutes and 14 seconds behind. With such a large lead, Armstrong's second straight victory in the Tour was all but sealed.

Yet the team was taking no chances. On the night of July 11, following the eleventh stage, Lance, Kevin, and Tyler gathered in a Provence hotel room where their blood bags were suspended on picture hooks on the walls. Lying faceup on the bed, the riders were reinfused with their own blood. The next day was a rest day before the twelfth stage, which finished with a climb up Mont Ventoux, where Armstrong's performance would make him a cycling legend.

Ventoux has long been fetishized by cycling fans. Its thirteen-mile road is steep, with grades of up to 10 percent, and it is also extremely windy, making it even more challenging. During the 1967 Tour, British cyclist Tommy Simpson died on Ventoux, pushing himself beyond his limits in a drug-induced daze. But in cycling lore, it wasn't so much the drugs that killed Simpson—it was Ventoux. He's memorialized by a sculpture placed at the very spot where he collapsed—a symbol of the sport's romantic fatalism and the Tour's unparalleled suffering.

A crowd of 300,000 fans lined the cold, blustery road up. The pack of 161 cyclists dwindled to seven of the best climbers, including Armstrong, Pantani, and Ullrich. The crowd roared as they passed. Then, with about three miles to go, Pantani attacked. He was ten minutes down in the GC (the general classification) and was only going for the stage win, so none of the lead riders chased him—except Armstrong. He got up out of the saddle and chased after Pantani, leaving Ullrich behind. In a show of incredible strength, he caught Pantani in seconds. Now Armstrong and Pantani were dueling up the mountain, looking at each other and trading massive accelerations up the slope. Armstrong was happy because Ullrich was far behind, losing more time. As the two men approached the finish line, Armstrong slowed down, and Pantani, exhausted, was able to nudge his bike forward and cross the finish line first. It was clear to anyone that Armstrong—by far the stronger rider—let Pantani win. Armstrong didn't need the stage victory. Pantani had helped him put time into Ullrich, and Armstrong felt he deserved the win that day. Armstrong's gift to Pantani became a topic of debate among cycling fans. Had Armstrong done the gentlemanly thing by letting Pantani win? Or had he disrespected the Tour by not attempting the stage win? Pantani was furious. He didn't want or need gifts. Weisel was also angry that Armstrong had given up a win. For fans, the controversy added delicious drama to the cinematic display of athletic talent. The day would live on forever in the collective imagination of cycling fans. Pantani got one more stage win before dropping out of the race. Armstrong's lead was secure and insurmountable by any of his opponents. He held the yellow jersey all the way to Paris.

Armstrong had done the unthinkable: won a second consecutive Tour de France. This second win also set off discussions about his legacy—whether he had eased past three-time Tour winner Greg LeMond to become the top cyclist in US history, and whether he could go on to win the Tour de France three times, or even five times, to equal the records of Miguel Indurain of Spain, Bernard Hinault of France, and Eddy Merckx of Belgium, the men regarded as the world's greatest riders, the crème de la crème of cycling.

In September, Lance went to compete in the 2000 Olympics, which were being held in Sydney. Lance's presence there was a very big story, and he expected—and received—all kinds of deluxe treatment in accordance with his superstar status. He asked USA Cycling for extra bikes, extra mechanics, and special accommodations.

He had hoped for a gold medal in the time trial, but he finished third, taking bronze behind his Postal teammate, Eki, who took the gold, and Ullrich, who took silver (as well as winning a gold medal in the cycling road race).

For Armstrong to have done even as well as he did was impressive, given that he had been racing injured. A few weeks before the Olympics, while on a training ride on a remote, narrow road in the hills above Nice, he had taken a blind left-hand curve and piled into an oncoming car. He was lucky to be alive, but he had fractured one of the vertebrae of his spine, the link between his back and his neck, and the injury hadn't entirely healed by the time he got to Sydney.

Trouble soon followed, however. During the Tour, investigative reporters working for the TV station France 3 had trailed the US Postal's team doctors and filmed them secretly dumping medical waste at a highway rest stop miles from their hotel. The packaging contained bloody bandages, used syringes, and packaging for a drug known as Actovegin, the blood doping drug made from calf's blood. Actovegin had been developed in both an injectable form and a cream for use by stroke patients and diabetics, and it and similar products have been used in the treatment of acne, rashes, burns, ulcers, eye problems, tendinitis, circulatory disorders, and senility. Among cyclists, the common belief was that the injectable form of Actovegin could help speed oxygen to the muscles and improve the metabolism of glucose, enhancing both energy and recovery.

As the French TV station investigated, debating whether the contents of the trash bags were newsworthy, someone sent an anonymous letter to the prosecutor's office in Paris about what the crew had found. The letter convinced the prosecutor's office to conduct an inquiry, and word of the investigation leaked to the press in late fall, with a story airing on television in France as well.

There was some disagreement among the various sporting agencies about whether Actovegin was actually a banned substance. It was not specifically named on anyone's list of forbidden substances, but similar products were banned. A couple of months after news of the investigation surfaced, the International Olympic Committee officially banned it. The UCI, however, did not. To the contrary: Hein Verbruggen and the UCI fully backed Armstrong, saying that the product was not a banned substance.

Though cleared by the UCI, members of the Postal team could still face criminal charges in France if they were found to have used performance-enhancing drugs to cheat, and the French prosecutor's investigation continued.

Armstrong, indignant over what he considered to be harassment, categorically denied that the US Postal team had ever used Actovegin for performance-enhancing purposes, and made an elaborate show of not even knowing how to spell it. "Activ-o-something," he wrote on his website in December 2000. He said he would skip the 2001 Tour de France if the investigation continued.

Mark Gorski, meanwhile, was floating a carefully concocted story in interviews with the press. He admitted the team carried Actovegin but said it was used for two completely legitimate purposes: to treat skin abrasions and to treat the diabetes of Julien de Vriese, the team mechanic. He called the accusations that it was used for performance-enhancing purposes a "preposterous rumor."

Jonathan Vaughters hadn't realized that Actovegin was derived from calf's blood. He immediately began to worry that he may have exposed himself to mad cow disease, which was going around Europe. In a panic, he called Gorski, who assured Vaughters he had nothing to worry about. "Don't worry, you'll be fine," Gorski said.

When LeMond read the reports about the Actovegin, he was stunned. He knew nothing about this oddly named drug, but he believed Gorski was lying. During the 2000 Tour de France, LeMond had dinner with de Vriese, who had also served as the team mechanic on the Z team. It was the ten-year anniversary of LeMond's first victory on the team, and everyone met in France for an informal reunion.

At dinner, surrounded by a handful of old riders as well as Greg and Kathy LeMond, de Vriese began to talk about the doping on the USPS team. De Vriese said he had been at training camp with the team in the Pyrenees and witnessed the use of doping products. It went beyond the occasional pill or injection, de Vriese said. The team bus was like a hospital. "This isn't cycling anymore," de Vriese told LeMond.

De Vriese also told Kathy he had learned that Armstrong arranged for

$500,000 to be wired to the UCI after his positive corticosteroid test in 1999. The money, he believed, came from either Thom Weisel or Nike.

De Vriese said he was so disgusted by the doping that he'd resigned. But soon after his resignation, Armstrong called him personally and asked him to stay, offering him a hefty raise. De Vriese accepted the offer—mainly because he needed the money—on one condition: He didn't have to work on the main Tour de France squad. De Vriese knew the doping program was amplified during the Tour, and he didn't want to be around it.

So when LeMond read that Gorski was using de Vriese as the smoke screen, he knew it was bullshit. De Vriese's diabetes couldn't account for several trash bags full of Actovegin packaging, and it couldn't explain why the team doctor and head masseuse had driven fifty miles away from the race just to dump the trash bags at a random rest stop.

LeMond was beginning to feel convinced that the team was running a sophisticated doping program, and that Armstrong was a cheat. He'd heard the story of Armstrong's hospital room admission about using drugs, but he'd written it off as rumor. But now, he believed it wholeheartedly.

Despite his threats to skip the Tour in the wake of the Actovegin investigation, Armstrong never seriously considered missing it. To prepare for the race, he spent the early part of the 2001 season at a number of smaller races in Spain and, despite the ongoing investigation by French prosecutors, he even raced in the French stage race Circuit de la Sarthe in April.

In June, however, Armstrong skipped the Dauphiné Libéré, the weeklong French stage race that many riders use as a tune-up. Instead, he competed in the Tour de Suisse, which he won. But if Armstrong had avoided the Dauphiné in order to evade French law enforcement, he was out of luck. Testers working for the UCI collected urine samples from many of the riders at the Tour de Suisse, including Armstrong. The samples were sent directly to an anti-doping lab in Lausanne. One of the samples showed signs of synthetic EPO.

The EPO test used was the one developed by Conconi. It involved dropping a small amount of urine onto a gel that separated synthetic EPO from the natural version of the hormone produced by the body. Testers had to determine if there was enough synthetic EPO present to constitute a positive result, but because the test was so new, testers tended to err on the side of caution and give riders the benefit of the doubt. This test, though, was right on the edge.

The samples were identified only by rider numbers, not names, so the lab had no idea whose test they were looking at. But they notified the UCI of the suspicious test and provided the rider number.

Since the UCI had the records to match names to numbers, it soon knew that the urine test was Lance Armstrong's. It would have been the UCI's responsibility as to whether or not to sanction Armstrong. By this time, UCI President Verbruggen must have been feeling embattled by all the doping problems, and the European press and the French authorities seemed obsessed with it. To Verbruggen, every news story about doping, every police raid on a cyclist's hotel, probably felt like an attack on the sport, and on his livelihood as well.

The UCI notified Armstrong of the suspicious EPO result but informed him that he would not be punished because the test was too close to call. Armstrong's inside information on the EPO test had been right on the money. Had he taken his EPO injections just under the skin, as he had in 1999, instead of directly into his veins, he would surely have registered a more conclusively positive test.

Having gotten away with little more than a slap on the wrist, Armstrong did not hesitate to launch self-righteous attacks on all those other cyclists he said were bringing down his sport. After winning the Tour de Suisse, he chastised those cheaters who "bring shame" on cycling, referring to several riders by name. "These guys must be thrown out of the sport without a backward glance," Armstrong told reporters. "They don't respect the sport, the champions of the past, or the fans."

Just weeks later, Armstrong entered the 2001 Tour de France, seeking his third straight win, a feat only four other cyclists had ever managed. Armstrong's main competition was, again, Jan Ullrich of Germany, who'd won gold and silver medals in the 2000 Olympics. The first day in the mountains came on the tenth day of the race—a 130-mile stage that finished atop the famed Alpe d'Huez. Armstrong blasted up the steep switchbacks to claim his first stage victory of the race. The next day, he won the twenty-mile individual time trial. On stage 13, which finished atop another famous climb, the Pla d'Adet, Armstrong won his third stage and the overall race lead. After the individual time trial on stage 18, Armstrong was ahead of Ullrich by over 6 minutes. It was another decisive victory. Armstrong coasted the rest of the way to Paris in the yellow jersey. That ceremonial victory lap around the cob-blestones of the Champs-Élysées was turning into an annual ritual.

After winning the race, Armstrong was called into a meeting with UCI doctors in Aigle, who, in their thick Swiss accents, informed him that they would watch him more carefully now. If the meeting was meant as a warning, Armstrong didn't see it that way. The very fact that he was being let off with only a warning seemed to be evidence to him that he was indeed invincible. His brand was too strong, too valuable, to be ruined with a positive test result.

Whatever Armstrong may have felt about his invincibility even while he was tackling those precipitous alpine climbs, the suspicions about his doping were being voiced in the press once again—reawakened by the scrutiny now being directed at cycling, and specifically at Michele Ferrari. At the time of the 2001 Tour, Ferrari was facing criminal charges in Italy for allegedly ad-ministering performance-enhancing drugs. The charges against him stemmed from an investigation that went back at least to 1998, when his name was found on prescriptions for performance-enhancing drugs discovered in the possession of professional athletes. Prosecutors in Bologna had opened an inquiry, and Ferrari's home had been raided several times by investigators. Testimony from cyclists who were questioned during the probe led to Ferrari being charged in 2001. Ferrari was eventually convicted by an Italian court of malpractice and sporting fraud for advising riders on the use of performance-enhancing drugs. Two years later, an appeals court threw out the verdict, ac-quitting him of malpractice and ruling that the statute of limitations had expired on the sporting-fraud conviction.

Once the European press linked the two men, Armstrong was forced to admit that he'd worked with Ferrari in the past. The admission came after persistent inquiries from *Sunday Times* reporter David Walsh, who was cover-ing the Tour. Armstrong defended his work with the doctor as legitimate, explaining that Ferrari had been training him to break the one-hour record on the track—a measure of how far a cyclist can travel in exactly sixty minutes. Armstrong denied ever using EPO and, as usual, lashed out at those in the press who expressed suspicion of him.

When LeMond read about Armstrong's links to Ferrari, he no longer had any doubt that Armstrong was doping. In the early 1990s, when LeMond was struggling with health problems and getting weaker on the bike, sports doctors had suggested that he see Ferrari, but he had refused. LeMond knew he'd competed against doped riders. He had no desire to become one.

LeMond sent an e-mail to Walsh. "Great work, David. You're on the right track," he wrote. Soon after the e-mail, Walsh called LeMond and asked for a quote on Ferrari, but LeMond had no desire to get in the middle of the controversy. He didn't want to directly accuse Armstrong, so he settled on what he thought was a less controversial approach. He gave an interview to Walsh, in which he was quoted as saying, "When I heard he was working with Michele Ferrari, I was devastated. . . . If Lance is clean, it is the greatest comeback in the history of sports. If he isn't, it would be the greatest fraud."

Lance responded by telling reporters he was "surprised" and "upset" by LeMond's comments, and then called LeMond, who recalls that Lance threatened to use his clout to ruin his reputation. He reiterated this threat to friends as well. A few weeks after the Tour, Armstrong was having dinner with Frankie and Betsy Andreu and a few other friends when he vowed to take revenge against LeMond. "I'm going to take him down," he said. By making one call to the owner of Trek bicycles, he said, he could "shut him up." He even began to lean on Trek to talk to LeMond.

LeMond also began getting phone calls from Armstrong's supporters. One of the first was from Weisel. "You know, what you're saying about Lance isn't good for you. You better be careful."

John Burke, the president of Trek bikes, got caught in the middle. Burke contacted LeMond and tried to get him to agree to issue a statement retracting his comments. After more than a week of negotiations, an apologetic press release was sent by Trek to *USA Today*. It had been written by Bill Stapleton. Without even calling LeMond for comment, *USA Today* printed the article on August 15. LeMond regretted going along with the idea of a press release. He was furious and clearly in no mood to issue an apology.

In an effort to keep Eddy Merckx from getting roped into the Ferrari scandal, Armstrong concocted a story that he and his coach, Chris Carmichael, had met Ferrari during a training camp in San Diego, California, in 1995 and that Ferrari's role had always been "limited." Ferrari, Lance said, uses only "natural methods of improvement," including altitude tents and diet. "I feel he's honest and innocent," Lance added. For those who might have wondered why Lance would need to work with Ferrari, given that Carmichael was his coach, Lance explained that since Carmichael couldn't be in Europe on an ongoing basis, Ferrari played an important role by doing Lance's physiological tests there, and sending Carmichael his data.

Within days of Lance's defense of Ferrari, the Italian edition of *GQ* magazine printed statements the Italian rider Filippo Simeoni had given to Italian police. Simeoni said Ferrari—nicknamed Il Mito, or "the myth," by Italian cyclists—advised him to use EPO, testosterone, and human growth hormone to improve his performance. Diaries kept by Simeoni recorded the substances he took between 1992 and 1999, the year he was questioned by Italian police, and recounted the advice Ferrari had given him about how to pass the hematocrit blood test used by the UCI. "Dr. Ferrari advised me to use two alternatives: Hemagel [a blood thinning agent] on the morning of the control, albumin [an element contained in white blood cells] on the evening before a possible control."

Responding to the quotes in the *GQ* article, Lance said: "It's a story that is three years old. Anyone can print old articles."

Lance conceded, however, that his association with Ferrari might look suspicious. "People are not stupid," he told reporters at a press conference during the Tour. "They will look at the facts. They will say: 'Here's Lance Armstrong. Here's a relationship. Is it questionable? Perhaps.' But people are smart. They will say: 'Has Lance Armstrong ever tested positive? No. Has Lance Armstrong ever been tested? A lot.' I have a questionable reputation because I'm a cyclist. People love to single out cycling. . . . The [drug] problems are not exclusive to cycling or the Tour de France or Lance Armstrong. I think this is a clean Tour." Armstrong didn't know that LeMond had also told Walsh about the Indiana hospital room. Walsh was now on the hunt to confirm it.

As Armstrong battled his critics in the press, the Lance Armstrong Foundation was getting a new president: Steve Whisnant, a well-respected fund-raiser in the nonprofit world. There was one complicating factor. Whisnant was good friends with Greg LeMond. A recent cancer survivor, Whisnant was inspired by Armstrong's story. He had accepted the job just a couple of months before LeMond's controversial comments about Armstrong.

Whisnant wasn't completely blindsided by the allegations. Before he accepted the job, Whisnant had called people close to the foundation and Armstrong, including John Bucksbaum, and asked them pointed questions.

"But what about the drugs in the sport?" Whisnant had asked Bucksbaum. "There have been allegations about Armstrong and I don't want this to blow up in my face."

"I know about the allegations," Bucksbaum said. "Lance has the potential to do so much good. You just have to give him the benefit of the doubt."

Despite his concerns, Whisnant decided to take the job. He repeated Bucksbaum's advice in his head. "Give him the benefit of the doubt," he told himself.

Just before the Tour de France in 2001, Whisnant called up LeMond and told him he had accepted the job. LeMond was upset.

"Steve, you can't take this job," he said.

"Why?" Whisnant said. "I know there have been questions about drugs."

LeMond was cryptic. He didn't want to tell Whisnant everything he knew. He felt they were, at least at this point, just allegations and he didn't want to repeat them to Whisnant. "Listen, you just have to trust me, Steve. This is a bad idea."

"Look, I've already taken the job, Greg. This thing has so much potential. I have to do this."

"Steve, I understand. But I don't think you're going to last six months there. This guy, he's not someone you want to get involved with."

Before starting in his new job, Whisnant traveled with Lance, Kristin, and Luke to Nike headquarters in Oregon, where the company was naming its fitness center after Lance. The night before the ceremony, Armstrong and Whisnant sat down alone together and had a beer. Whisnant decided it was the right time to ask a tough question.

Looking Armstrong in the eyes, he said, "Lance, I am going to ask you a question, and I need you to look me in the eyes and answer honestly. Is there anything I need to know about that could come out? Anything at all that might embarrass you, me, or harm the mission of the foundation?"

Armstrong knew exactly what Whisnant was getting at.

"No. Absolutely not," Armstrong said, looking straight into Whisnant's eyes. Whisnant replayed Bucksbaum's advice in his head. *Give him the benefit of the doubt.*

Once in Austin, Whisnant went out to lunch with Jeff Garvey at a Chinese restaurant. He casually asked Garvey, "Jeff, do you think Lance was doping before cancer?"

Garvey paused. And then he answered, "Yeah, I think he probably was."

Whisnant left the restaurant shell-shocked. He thought that if Armstrong had taken performance-enhancing drugs, it might have led to his cancer, making the idea behind the foundation a big lie.

Even before LeMond made his public comments about the link between Armstrong and Ferrari at the Tour de France, Whisnant had heard murmurs at the foundation about bad blood between Lance and Greg. At a meeting in early July with top employees of the charity, including Garvey and Doug Ulman, the new director of survivorship, the discussion turned away from cancer and became focused on LeMond. Some staffers began to recite what seemed to Whisnant to be talking points meant to discredit Greg. He was an "alcoholic," they said. He was "emotionally disturbed" and was out to get Armstrong due to some deranged feeling of jealousy.

Finally, Whisnant spoke up. "That's just not true!" he said, defending his friend. Everyone at the meeting turned and looked at him as if were a traitor. Whisnant was confused and had a sinking feeling in his stomach that he might have made a big mistake taking this job. But he stuck with it in the hopes that he could make it work.

After LeMond's comments about Ferrari broke in the press in late July, things became outright hostile at the foundation because of his relationship with LeMond. Whisnant checked his voice mail to discover a message from Lance. "I'm not sure this is going to work out," Lance said.

Soon after, Jeff Garvey burst into Whisnant's office, fuming mad.

You need to make a decision. It's either Lance Armstrong or Greg LeMond," Garvey said.

Garvey stormed out of the office. Whisnant was distraught and worried he had made a huge, career-altering blunder by taking the job. He immediately called Bill Stapleton, who was, to Whisnant's surprise, calm and reassuring. "Listen, it's okay," he said. "We really need you in this job. Jeff was out of control and he owes you an apology," Stapleton said.

The apology took place at Garvey's house in Austin, where Stapleton and Garvey attempted to convince Whisnant to stay. "Sorry that happened," Garvey said. "That isn't what the foundation is about. We want you to stay and Lance is completely behind you," he said.

It was too little, too late. Whisnant called some of his mentors and discussed the situation and came to the conclusion that he needed to resign. He knew it would hurt his career to leave so abruptly. He had just sold the house, and it would cost him a lot of money to undo his real estate transactions. But six weeks after moving to Austin, Whisnant resigned and walked out on Lance and the foundation.

In the spring of 2001, in part because of his problems with French law enforcement, Armstrong moved his European base of operations from Nice to the Spanish town of Girona, where a tight-knit contingent of American bicycle racers had lived for years. He and Kristin still owned their French villa, as well as two homes in Austin, but now they also had the first floor of what had once been a small palace in one of the most historic streets of Girona, a two-thousand-year-old city of about eighty thousand people in northeast Catalonia. Located on a narrow cobblestone footpath, the apartment had a wrought iron terrace and Gothic arches and cornices, as well as small gardens and a small family chapel with a wooden altar. Lance had picked out their new

Girona home on his own while Kristin remained in Austin, trying to become pregnant again through in vitro fertilization. In April she called to tell him she was pregnant with twins.

The Girona location brought him into closer contact with his teammates, including George Hincapie and Tyler Hamilton, who lived in a complex of apartments there during the racing season. The migration of American cyclists to Girona had begun in 1997, when Weisel and Johnny Weltz were putting together a European-style team capable of winning a spot in the Tour de France.

By 2001, following the Postal team's successes, some of the American riders had earned enough in salary and bonuses to be able to afford to bring their wives and girlfriends to Spain, too. "You can't go outside without seeing a wife, a rider, a girlfriend, a soigneur, a director, a team car," Haven Hamilton, then Tyler Hamilton's wife, wrote in an e-mail to Betsy Andreu. "You should see it here in Girona—grand central station," she added.

Girona also had the advantage of being a short train ride to Valencia, where team doctor Luis Garcia del Moral had his sports medicine clinic. That meant that Armstrong and the other riders could go there for treatment without crossing international borders and arousing suspicion.

Girona became a sort of hub for performance-enhancing drugs. Laws against doping in Spain at the time were much more relaxed than they were in France, and there was a pharmacist in town who was more than willing to fulfill practically any prescription for any drug on the market. If a cyclist had been prescribed a round of EPO by a team doctor, all he had to do was stroll down to the pharmacy and order it. If drug testers came to town, the first rider to notice the tester would alert other riders by text message: "The vampires are here." Riders who knew they had drugs in their system would hide, or inject themselves with masking agents and other substances to fool the tests. The US Postal riders, and other Americans riding for other teams, felt emboldened to do whatever they wanted in Spain.

However, the doping began taking a toll on some of the wives and girlfriends. The women talked to each other about the health risks of the drugs. They told each other they wished the men did not have to take these substances, some of them mysterious and with unknown side effects.

Kristin resented the drug testers, or "doping control officers (DCOs)," who would show up at the Armstrong home in Austin during the off-season. The Austin-based testers were typically a husband and wife team, and they were hired by the US Anti-Doping Agency to administer unannounced tests.

In 2000, USADA began these "surprise" out-of-competition visits to cyclists' homes. Cyclists were required to inform USADA of their whereabouts and when they'd be in the States. Lance hated having to fax or e-mail the testers about his movements. He felt he was "under constant surveillance."

The testers in Austin would ring the bell, and when Lance or Kristin opened the door, they'd say, "Random drug control," and hand Lance a piece of paper instructing him of his rights. If he declined the test, it would be considered an automatic positive. The procedure took fifteen or twenty minutes. First, at least one inspector would accompany Lance into the bathroom, where he'd urinate in a container. His pants would have to be down around his knees, and his shirt yanked up to his chest, so the tester could see that no device was being used to somehow switch samples. He would then distribute his pee into two other containers, the A sample and B sample. Generally, the testers would immediately check the pH of the urine. A high pH, for instance, could indicate a cyclist was taking sodium bicarbonate to mask something. These visits often involved paperwork to document the circumstances of the urine sample collection, and then the sample was mailed by the testers to a lab for analysis. Generally, Lance's urine samples were sent to a lab in Los Angeles.

That year, the day before Thanksgiving, Kristin had a routine prenatal checkup, where the obstetrician told her to call Lance, get home to pack a bag, then go immediately to the hospital to prepare to give birth. Lance was standing in the foyer, holding their bags, when the drug testers suddenly arrived at their front door. "My wife is in labor. So it better be fast," Lance told them.

Then, when the twins, Grace and Isabelle, were about a week old, the drug testers showed up again, at about 7:00 A.M. The babies were sleeping and Armstrong's small white Maltese, Boone, started barking. Kristin opened the door. "It's seven in the morning!" she said. The woman tester handed her the paperwork. Lance came to the door. "What are you doing?" he asked. After they tested Lance and completed the paperwork, Kristin, visibly upset, walked the drug testers to the front door. When they reached the doorway, Kristin threw her arm out as a barricade, leaned into the woman's face, and snarled, "I don't want you coming over here early in the morning like this and disrupting this family ever again."

As the allegations about Lance mounted and his stature grew, he built an intricate layer of protection around himself, with a circle of influential friends and associates. The companies that sponsored him, his doctors, and most of his close confidants closed ranks around him. Nike, for example, consistently backed him. In 2000, they began airing commercials in which Armstrong is shown taking a blood test in front of reporters and then saying, "What am I on? I'm on my bike, busting my ass six hours a day."

After having put their friendship on deep freeze, in 2001 during the Tour de France, Lance reached out to his old best friend and biking buddy John Korioth. He'd seen a story in the July *Texas Monthly* magazine in which Korioth was quoted as defending Lance. Korioth said, "Beyond the health reasons for not doing it, Lance has to say, 'What does something like that do to my reputation?' US Postal would drop him. He'd lose his sponsorships. He has everything to lose and nothing to gain." So Lance deputized Stapleton's assistant, then in France, to call his old buddy, reaching him at home in Austin. "Look, Lance is racing in the Tour de France right now, otherwise he would have called you himself," the assistant said. Lance, she told him, would like to fly him to Paris to see the last two days of the Tour. Korioth thought it over. He had been disappointed in how Lance had treated him when he was forced out of the foundation. But he decided to go.

The night he arrived in France, Korioth met Stapleton at a dinner party. "What the fuck am I doing here?" he asked Stapleton, who told him Lance would explain later. The next day, Korioth went to the start of the race and boarded the Postal team bus. He sat down next to Lance, and the two men talked about their feud. "Man, that was a tough time," Lance said, adding that he was confused after listening to the complaints of the foundation board members. "You're listening to people give you advice. You don't know what's right. You don't know what's wrong."

"Well, you could have always called me," Korioth responded.

They agreed to renew their friendship, but Korioth told Lance he wouldn't work for him or his foundation ever again. Years later, Lance invested in a couple of bars Korioth was running in Austin, and another potential enemy was made an ally.

Once the Postal team embarked on an organized, systematic doping program, Lance's most important defenders may have been his own domestiques. They had a vested interest in his success, especially since it was customary for the Tour winner to divide the $400,000 prize money among his teammates. On top of that, Lance would double the amount, using his personal money to add to their winnings.

His domestiques also had a very personal reason for being discreet, since several of them were working with Michele Ferrari. Johan Bruyneel had facilitated this during a meeting at the Postal training camp in late 2000. He told the riders that each of them could meet with Ferrari, but if they decided to hire him, they would be responsible for paying him out of their own salaries.

George Hincapie was among those who hired Ferrari, paying him $15,000 for his services during the 2001 season, and keeping him on for five years after that. Hincapie reached out to Ferrari because he felt Ferrari could help him figure out a training plan incorporating blood transfusions instead of primarily EPO. As far as Ferrari was concerned, Armstrong's close call with testing positive for EPO during the 2001 Tour de Suisse had been the last straw. So he was now pushing transfusions. In fact, Ferrari thought, if transfusions were done in combination with small, undetectable doses of EPO, that combination could be even more effective at delivering oxygen to the muscles than just the EPO. Floyd Landis was another rider on the US Postal team who eventually became involved in doping. At the end of the 2001 season, Hamilton left the Postal team to pursue his own ambitions as a team leader, joining the Danish Team CSC. To replace Hamilton, the team brought in Floyd Landis, who arrived at the team's training camp for new riders in December 2001. Landis had just signed a $60,000-a-year contract to race for the team, and he was thrilled by the chance to be on a team led by such a heroic athlete. But the Lance he got to know in those early days didn't line up with the Lance he'd only read about. Most of what Landis knew about his hero, he had read in Lance's bestselling memoir, *It's Not About the Bike*. He'd devoured the chronicle of Lance's comeback from cancer, and some things in the book stood out to him more than others, like the fact that Armstrong called himself a devoted family man, even going so far as to say he was offended by pornography. Lance had made that remark at a point in his book where he was describing being offered a girlie magazine at a sperm bank when he was storing sperm before chemo. Even to Landis, who had been raised in a Mennonite family in Pennsylvania's Amish country and who used to race mountain bikes in sweat pants because spandex was too risqué, Armstrong's portrayal of himself as such a straight arrow came across as a bit extreme.

And once he got to know him, he realized just how far from the truth that depiction was. One night during the training camp, Landis and a few of the other new riders on the team piled into a black Suburban with Lance behind the wheel. They were headed to the Yellow Rose, a gentleman's club in Austin. Armstrong was driving so fast, running so many stoplights and stop signs, that Dave Zabriskie, another of the new riders, turned to Landis and asked, "Are there no cops in this town?" The US Postal team got its own booth at the strip club, and took turns getting lap dances from the scantily clad women. After leaving the Yellow Rose, Armstrong drove the riders to Bill Stapleton's office. More dancers arrived. As the men partied into the early morning hours, Armstrong retreated to one of the private offices. He sat at a desk with two completely naked women beside him. Landis noticed what looked like cocaine on the desk. When Armstrong looked up and saw Landis staring at him, he shut the door, and that was the last he saw of him that evening.

Landis's eye-opening training camp seemed to him an appropriate time to broach another topic at odds with Armstrong's image in the United States: performance-enhancing drugs. He met Johan Bruyneel in the lobby of the Four Seasons Hotel, where he and most of the rest of the team were staying and, in vaguely worded language, asked what he would be expected to do beyond simply training and racing. Landis had, of course, heard stories about the use of drugs in the pro peloton and assumed he would be asked to use them, too. According to Landis, Bruyneel responded, "Look, just keep training and when the time comes, if it's necessary, we'll figure that out."

"The fact that he didn't totally dismiss it was all I really needed to know," Landis later said.

And within a year, his time would indeed come.

CHAPTER NINE

DOMESTIC DISCORD AND THE DOMESTIQUE

Floyd Landis was wearing bibbed spandex bike shorts over a thin, low-cut undershirt as he rode a stationary bike. His face was covered by a high-tech mask with tubes and wires coming out of it, connecting to a large machine with digital readouts and dozens of buttons. As he pedaled, a sports physiologist looked intently at the numbers. Every few minutes, he told Landis to pedal a little bit harder. Beneath the mask, sweat began to glaze Landis's face, then to roll in rivulets from his forehead down to his nose and onto the floor.

At the physiologist's direction, he gradually built up his pace until he was pedaling madly in an all-out sprint, the stationary bike rocking back and forth, the whir of its tires against the resistance roller sounding like a V-8 engine in the small room. "Go, go, go," the physiologist kept saying as Landis pushed himself to the maximum of his ability. And then finally, "Okay, you're done."

Landis slowed down, slumping over the bike as he recovered from the effort, his chest expanding and contracting as he took massive gulps of air. Meanwhile, the physiologist was punching keys and looking at the computer monitors. After a few minutes of calculations, then double-checking of those calculations, he began to smile. Landis had registered an astonishingly high VO_2 max score—the measure of maximum oxygen intake.

The gist of the computer readouts was that Landis was extremely efficient at processing the air he sucked into his lungs. His body extracted oxygen and delivered it to his muscles at an incredibly high rate. In fact, he consumed more than 90 milliliters of oxygen per kilogram of his body weight, per minute. The average person consumes about 50 milliliters. This meant Landis was a remarkable physical specimen. Cyclists who can consume more oxygen can keep pedaling at a higher pace, for a longer period of time. The best endurance athletes generally average a VO_2 max score in the low to mid 70s. Lance Armstrong's was measured in the low 80s, making him more special than most, but hardly superhuman. Landis's score of 90, significantly higher than Armstrong's, meant he was off the charts in cardiovascular ability. And as the physiologist explained to Landis, it meant that his potential was enormous, limited only by his own desire and determination.

Landis took that test long before he joined the US Postal Service team, and he knew there was more to bike racing than one number, albeit a significant one. But the result had made him feel he was special—destined for great things. On the Postal Service team, though, he'd been slotted to fill the role of one of the lowliest domestiques, whose job was simply to slog it out in races around the world, aiding other riders in their pursuit of glory. From his first day at training camp, when US Postal head coach Johan Bruyneel had given him a training schedule, it was clear that Bruyneel viewed Landis as a lower-level domestique, someone who would ride in support of one of the higher-level domestiques—someone like Roberto Heras.

But thinking back on the test, Landis knew it might not be long before he was riding on the nine-man Tour de France squad, shepherding Armstrong himself over the mountain passes. In fact, his physiology meant he might one day be riding the Tour to win it.

Before Landis could even get invited onto the Tour de France squad, however, he needed to show that he could actually put his genetic gifts to use in the ultracompetitive European racing circuit. Plenty of physically gifted young athletes caved under pressure once they hit the professional ranks of Europe. This was such a common occurrence, it had become almost a cliché in American racing. A cycling coach would spot a promising young rider, bring him in to a lab for testing, and discover that he was amazingly gifted. "This kid could be the next Greg LeMond," he would proclaim. The young rider would think, "Great, if I'm the next Greg LeMond, all I have to do is get on my bike and go." But as the rider rose through the ranks, he'd realize that winning required hard work and sacrifice. Other less gifted but more driven riders wouldn't just roll over. They trained harder, wanted it more. On top of that, cycling doesn't pay well unless a rider rises to the highest echelons. At some point, the gifted rider would quit the sport altogether, go to college, and make more money as some corporate middle manager.

Aware of all the things that could go wrong, the US Postal team coaches chose Landis's races carefully during the 2002 season. They wanted to test out his legs and see how well he could compete in a European peloton.

Floyd shared an apartment in Girona that spring with Dave Zabriskie. Arriving in Spain, Landis had a lot of worries, serious financial problems, credit card debt and medical bills, and he was struggling to support his wife, Amber, and her six-year-old daughter, Ryan. Even so, he was there to focus on riding his bike. The team's deal with Floyd paid him a salary of $60,000, but if he made the nine-man squad that raced in the Tour de France and the team won that event, then Landis would get about $50,000 more in prize money. Plus it was known that Lance sometimes threw in an additional bonus on top of that.

In March, Landis finished third in the 12.7-mile individual time trial on the fourth day of Tirreno–Adriatico, a weeklong stage race that attracts the top talent from all over Europe. That was an impressive finish for a "neopro," the term for a professional cyclist who has just gotten started in Europe. In May, he raced with the US Postal Service's best climbers—including Armstrong—in the Midi Libre Grand Prix, a five-stage race in the south of France with several tough mountain climbs. Armstrong won and Landis finished in 37th place. Helping Armstrong win a stage race was something he could put on his cycling résumé. It meant the team had not wasted their money.

By the early summer, the Postal team was considering Landis a likely possibility for the Tour de France squad, just as he had hoped. The team had experienced men like George Hincapie and Chechu Rubiera, a Spanish climber they had picked up for the 2001 season. But they needed someone with sheer raw speed, and they thought it likely that Landis could fill that role. Johan Bruyneel chose his riders according to the tactical goals he thought each could fulfill. To ensure Armstrong's victory, Bruyneel needed guys who could ride fast into the wind. He needed selfless teammates who could ride in front of Armstrong in the mountains and keep a steady pace for long periods of time. And he needed riders who were good for one or two amazing accelerations up the mountain slopes to break apart the field and make the race more manageable for Lance. That was the role he envisioned for Landis. Bruyneel thought Landis could be the guy who, once given the command through his earpiece to "Attack!" would sail ahead of everyone else, leaving the riders trailing in his wake, gasping for air.

In May, Armstrong rented an apartment for Landis in St. Moritz, the Swiss ski resort town where he was living for the final buildup to the Tour, so they could train together at a high altitude. The town is perched at 6,000 feet and is surrounded by circuitous mountain passes. Nearly every day for weeks, the two men went on punishing rides in the alpine climbs where, as Landis recalled, he often had trouble keeping up with Armstrong. Michele Ferrari followed behind them in an old station wagon stocked with food, water, and warm clothes for the descents. At the top of each climb, Dr. Ferrari would pull over to analyze the "wattage meters" on their bikes. Lance told Floyd that Ferrari was a genius—one of the most brilliant minds in cycling, someone who had a mathematically precise knowledge about technique and physiology—and Landis assumed Lance was right.

Before being awarded a Tour de France spot, however, Landis faced one final test: the Dauphiné Libéré, the early June race in France that follows many of the same mountain roads as the Tour de France. For Landis, the race would be an opportunity, a chance to see if he could handle the mountains and hold his own against many of the same riders who would be competing in the Tour. Bruyneel gave Landis the role of chief domestique so that they could see how he'd perform under the stress and battery of a punishing week-long race. The chief domestique, also called a lieutenant or a super domestique, is the rider who stays with the team leader the longest and has the most responsibility. While other riders on the team could back off the pace early and soft-pedal to the finish line, Landis would have to stick with Armstrong until the final acceleration, when Armstrong pulled away from his rivals and struck out for the finish line alone.

By the start of the fifth day, Armstrong was in second place. Midway through the day, a breakaway of fifteen riders formed. Bruyneel wanted to test Landis's legs and he ordered him to take off and latch himself on to the group, which had zoomed far ahead of the main field. But as they hit the ascent of the final climb, the 9.3-mile Col de Corobin, the group shattered. Landis stayed with the leaders, often pushing the pace up the mountain roads. He finished fourth on that day, nearly 4 minutes ahead of the main contenders, including Armstrong. Armstrong still had his lead, but Landis had moved all the way up to second place overall, trailing Armstrong by only 19 seconds.

The next day was the most difficult of the race. It included a daunting finishing climb called the Col de Joux Plane, a seven-mile stretch with an average gradient of ten pecent, meaning for every one hundred feet of road, the elevation rises ten feet. Armstrong won the stage. But surprisingly, Landis was able to retain his second place in the race. After the finish, the website Cycling News said Landis "may be developing into the best American stage racer since Armstrong." It was a high compliment. And Landis had done it without drugs.

Landis was exhausted after the seven-day race, gaunt and dehydrated from the grueling days of riding for Armstrong in the mountains. But he had loved every minute of it. He savored the pain and the suffering of the race. Still, he wondered how difficult it would be to attempt the same thing over a 21-day period. If he were chosen for the Tour de France team, would he be able to handle it?

Landis was in his room, packing his things for the return trip to St. Moritz, when he heard a knock on the door. It was Johan Bruyneel.

"Congratulations," Bruyneel said. "You're on the Tour de France squad."

Landis was ecstatic. "Thank you!" he exclaimed. "You're going to be happy you made that decision," he said.

"Listen," Bruyneel said. "When you get to St. Moritz, Lance is going to give you something to shorten your recovery time. Just a small testosterone patch. Two out of every three nights, put the patch on before you go to bed, okay?"

"Yeah, got it," Landis said.

"And, Floyd, Ferrari is going to take some blood out. It will be put back in during the Tour," Bruyneel said in a matter-of-fact tone that made everything sound legitimate. Never mind that they were discussing cheating in the biggest cycling event of the year. Never mind that this was the coach of one of the most famous and respected sports teams in the world.

The whole thing felt surreal to Landis, but he had figured this day would come. He knew that if he made the Tour de France squad, nothing would be left to chance. He'd be taken care of. It was kind of exciting, actually. Landis had never done performance-enhancing drugs and he was curious how they would affect him. Would he feel superhuman? Would he start flying up mountains with no pain at all?

Later that day, Landis boarded a helicopter with Armstrong for the flight back to St. Moritz. It was the first time Landis had flown in one and he was in awe, looking out the window at the spectacularly beautiful peaks of the French Alps.

When they landed, the two men were picked up by Armstrong's longtime masseur, Ryszard Kielpinski, and driven to the penthouse near the village center where Armstrong was staying with Kristin, their little boy, Luke, and the twin girls Kristin had given birth to the previous November. As they sat in the kitchen drinking espresso, Armstrong handed him roughly twenty testosterone patches in silvery foil, which Floyd stuffed into his backpack. Armstrong didn't have to say anything. Landis knew what they were for, and Bruyneel had explained how to use them. Landis concluded at that moment that Kristin, who was standing only a few feet away and made no comment about the transaction, knew about the doping. What Landis didn't know was that Kristin was not just aware of the doping, she was complicit in it. Landis hadn't been on the team when Kristin helped pass out cortisone pills. He didn't know about their secret code word for the EPO: *butter.* Back in his own apartment later that night, Landis placed one of the testosterone patches on his stomach as Bruyneel had instructed him. Landis wondered how he'd feel the next day. To his disappointment, he didn't notice anything. The effects of the drugs were subtle. A few days later, Landis went to Armstrong's apartment, where Dr. Ferrari had him lie down on a bed while he stuck a thick needle into his arm and extracted a half liter of blood. "We will put this back in a few days before the Tour. Then, another half liter we take out. That goes back in during the race," Ferrari explained to him.

All of this drawing of blood, and reinfusing it, required considerable resources. During their training rides in the mountains above St. Moritz in the weeks between the Dauphiné and the Tour, Armstrong had explained the complicated logistics, which involved carrying coolers with hidden blood bags across international borders. He also told Landis that this was a change from previous Tours, when cyclists would use EPO. But now that the UCI was testing for EPO, riders had turned to transfusions again. Landis would later tell federal investigators about a dramatic conversation he had with Lance on the subject. Facing the possibility of criminal prosecution if he lied to the feds, Landis said Armstrong told him he'd actually tested positive for the drug during the 2001 Tour de Suisse. He had been too brazen, he told Landis, pushed the EPO use a little too far. Landis told the federal investigators that Armstrong told him cycling authorities at the UCI had let him off the hook because he was the sport's biggest star—and because he had made a financial arrangement with the UCI. Verbruggen and the UCI deny there was any such arrangement. Landis told investigators that he was shocked at the time. He had certainly not found the UCI to be particularly accommodating. Quite the opposite. After his former team, sponsored by car manufacturer Mercury, folded, he waited several months for the UCI to compensate him out of the escrow account it was supposed to maintain for riders in case a team disbanded. In fact, Hein Verbruggen sent Landis a nasty, taunting letter, informing him that the UCI would pay him whenever it felt like it. In the end, Landis got only about half of what he was owed.

In truth, the UCI operated very little like a legitimate governing body. Bribes like the one Armstrong described to Landis had been common in professional cycling for decades. The sport operated with such an undercurrent of corruption that payoffs were almost a given. Not only did governing bodies accept bribes to quash positive drug tests, riders themselves often accepted bribes from other riders. The negotiations for these bribes would take place on the road, during the races. For instance, if a star rider found himself in a breakaway with another, less famous rider, the star might offer to pay the lesser-known rider to allow him to win—just as Armstrong had done in the Triple Crown race that had netted him his first million-dollar payoff a decade earlier. After all, the bigger star could easily afford the bribe because he would be able to capitalize on the win with bonuses and higher endorsement revenues. Partly to grease the wheels for such transactions, riders were paid race winnings and appearance fees in cash. And although the UCI mandated that the teams pay riders a minimum wage, riders were often paid their wages in under-the-table cash, in amounts significantly lower than the minimum. Rather than blow the whistle on the practice, most cyclists were just happy to be on a professional team with a chance to make it big.

When Landis arrived in France for the 2002 Tour de France, his eyes bulged as he took in the surreal, carnival-like atmosphere. The thousands of fans creating a mob scene around the riders, the millions of people who lined the sides of the roads to cheer as the race went by—it was like nothing Landis had ever seen.

During the first half of the race, the Postal team made only a mediocre showing. Armstrong won the opening prologue, but four days later, the USPS lost the team time trial, finishing in second place. On the eighth day of the race, Armstrong took a minor spill and lost 27 seconds. On the tenth day of the race, Armstrong finished second in the individual time trial to Spaniard Santiago Botero. ONCE's Igor González de Galdeano ended up in the race lead, 26 seconds over Armstrong, who was not happy.

On the twelfth day of the Tour—the first day in the mountains—Armstrong pummeled them all. In the final climb up the La Mongie, an eight-mile, 6.8 percent slope, Armstrong sprinted past his opponents for the win. Landis, though, had a bad day. He drifted back and wasn't able to help much in the mountains.

The next day, Landis bounced back to prove his worth. The 123-mile stage included five major climbs, finishing with Plateau de Beille. As the pack began riding up the slopes, Armstrong faced numerous attacks from other teams, but Landis was right there, chasing down the riders and doing the hard work for Armstrong. On the next mountain stage, Landis again proved to be a big help to Armstrong, setting the pace at the bottom of Ventoux for a good 15 minutes before pulling off.

The final opportunity for Armstrong to open an even more decisive lead came on the second-to-last day in the individual time trial. As he had in previous years, Armstrong began the time trial so far ahead—by 5 minutes, 6 seconds over Spaniard Joseba Beloki—that he had absolutely no pressure. But Armstrong wouldn't go easy on his competitors. He won the time trial handily, adding 2 more minutes to his lead. The next day, as he rode into Paris and crossed the finish line, he was more than 7 minutes ahead of Beloki.

For Landis, the win was life-changing. The roughly $40,000 bonus he received for being on the nine-man Tour de France squad, and the multiyear contract he signed with the team afterward, provided him with an income substantial enough that he could afford to buy a home big enough for his family, as well as a nice car. His contract, which had paid him $60,000 for his first year, jumped to $215,000 in 2003, and then increased to $240,000 in 2004.

Landis and his family moved to their new home in Temecula, California, a small town northeast of San Diego with affordable housing, a mild climate, and vineyards surrounded by mountains that had the long steep climbs he needed for training. And the temperate climate—no snow, hardly any rain— meant he could train there even in the winter. Landis had gone from being a vagabond cycling bum maxed out on his credit cards to a man successful enough to support his family comfortably while competing in a professional sport that he enjoyed. It felt like the American dream.

Landis didn't feel as if he'd cheated his way into his new life. The drugs didn't seem to give him any new capabilities on the bike. They did help with recovery. Before he started doping, he'd feel awful after long, hard days of training. Now he felt energetic. But he still had to do the training and it was still challenging. Besides, he thought, everyone is taking the same drugs.

With his fourth Tour de France win, Armstrong had achieved near icon status. *Sports Illustrated* named him Sportsman of the Year, and the Associated Press named him Male Athlete of the Year. His off-season was punctuated with photo shoots, speeches for six-figure honorariums, and celebrity hobnobbing. He developed a close relationship with fellow Texan President George W. Bush, who had added Lance to his cancer advisory panel in September 2002.

Capitalizing on the latest escalation of his fame, he teamed up again with Sally Jenkins, who by then was a *Washington Post* sports columnist, to write his second memoir, *Every Second Counts.* The book glorified cancer survivors, but mostly provided an insider's look at competitive cycling. Although he hadn't yet faced any serious doping allegations in the United States, Lance came across in the memoir as a good guy who'd been victimized—he complained about the incessant drug testing he endured, specifically recounting the indecency of the drug testers who had knocked at his door just as he prepared to take his wife to the hospital to give birth to twins. He mentioned "my friend Robin Williams." Twice.

Fame and fortune were his, but Armstrong's family life was falling apart. His relationship with his mother had deteriorated. Shortly after Lance got married, Linda divorced John and dealt with the emotional distress of their breakup by throwing herself into her work. Lance provided some financial support. He gave her the funds to fix her teeth, and flew her to Paris each year for the Tour de France. But to some of his old friends, it seemed he didn't want much to do with her. He rarely visited her in Plano, and when he and Kristin were living in Nice and Spain, he rarely called her. She continued to work, rising up the ranks at Ericsson, but she missed her young grandson, Luke, and at times felt a profound sense of loneliness.

"Heard from Lance lately?" J.T., Lance's former landlord and close friend in Austin, would ask Linda when they spoke on the phone. "No, not for a while," she would say, explaining that he and Kristin had a lot to handle. "I'm sorry," J.T. would say.

After her third divorce, Linda did meet another man, Ed Kelly, a widower and senior project executive at IBM. They met on a blind date in 2001, eventually fell in love and planned to get married. She badly wanted Lance to be there, and he provided her with a date in June 2002. She went forward with arrangements, but then a month before the event, he called to cancel. She pushed the wedding date back, but that date didn't work out for Lance, either. Eventually, Linda and Ed married in Dallas without Lance there.

J.T. couldn't make it to the wedding that summer, either. He was under-going yet more chemo and radiation, as well as bone marrow transplants. When these treatments were unsuccessful, he turned to alternative medicine. Noth-ing worked. He knew he wouldn't live much longer, and for some reason, he felt profound guilt over how Lance had treated his mom. At times, he blamed himself for not telling Lance directly to call his mother more often, especially after he moved to Austin, but now, it was too late for J.T. to say anything to Lance. After Lance married Kristin he rarely called J.T. to check in, even as J.T. endured the rigors of cancer treatment.

What bothered J.T. was that he wasn't able to point to any arguments or disagreements. He began to wonder if Lance was ashamed of him, and whether Kristin disapproved of him because he was an eccentric older man.

Lance had been a part of J.T.'s family, sharing meals with him and his wife, Frances, and their three young children. J.T. would visit Lance in Como and, during one Tour de France, acted as his soigneur while he was on the Motorola team. He stood by Lance, and truly cared for him.

As his health deteriorated, J.T. was on steroids as well as several medica-tions for pain. He found it difficult to keep the emotional hurt inside. He began telling his close friends that Lance had used him, that he'd become a part of his family and then cut him off. He made plans to write a tell-all book that would expose Lance as a narcissist who lacked empathy for others. His friends talked him out of it, saying nothing good would come of it.

On October 1, 2002, J.T. called Linda to say he was in the hospital. Linda offered to drive to come see him, but he told her his hospital room had not been set up, and to call back later. Linda knew J.T. was saying good-bye to the people he loved, and that he didn't have much time left. She wanted Lance to speak to J.T., so she tried calling him at his house but got his machine. Later, she dialed Lance's home again. Someone picked up. There was a blowout party going on. The person who answered the phone said Lance was unable to come to the phone as he was swinging on a rope with his mother-in-law. The next day would be the sixth anniversary of Lance's cancer diagnosis, his so-called carpe diem day. He had thrown a big party, had invited Kristin's parents, but hadn't told his mom about it. J.T. died the next day. Linda attended the fu-neral and Lance showed up, looking distressed.

"He wanted to tell you good-bye, son. And that he loved you," Linda told Lance. J.T.'s obituary, which appeared October 3, mentioned his volunteer work with many sports programs at the University of Texas, notably as the massage therapist for the swimming and diving teams. It also mentioned that he had "helped cyclists such as Lance Armstrong." Lance wasn't quoted.

The man Kristin had married was a little-known former athlete who was recovering from cancer, happy just to be alive. Now she found herself married to an international celebrity who bore little resemblance to the sensitive, soul-searching cancer survivor who had seemed on the threshold of dedicating his life to giving hope to others struggling with the disease. Having become a superstar, Armstrong, like many of his ilk, slept with other women often. Lots of other women. And as with his doping, Armstrong made few efforts to cover up his philandering.

A few days after J.T. died, Armstrong flew to Las Vegas for the annual Interbike trade show, where he would talk to the press about his Trek bikes, helpfully pointing out that consumers could buy the same bikes in local stores. Walking around the convention center, wearing a navy blue Trek bike mechanic's smock, a baseball cap, and sunglasses, he was mobbed by fans seeking autographs and photos. He called up George Hincapie, who was also at the trade show, and told him he wanted to hang out. Armstrong met up with Hincapie and Bill Stapleton, and others at an upscale club, the Foundation Room, at the top of the Mandalay Bay Hotel. The men were escorted to a private room that was decorated with a Far Eastern aesthetic and accented with dark wood paneling. A number of women showed up and they partied for the rest of the night. The night was nothing out of the ordinary. Lance didn't let his marriage get in the way of cavorting with groupies.

In early 2003, Lance rented a house in Santa Barbara and flew into town to shoot a commercial—that year, he had commercial shoots for Comcast, Subaru, and Nike. Kristin and the three children, as well as Mike Anderson, his personal assistant, came along. Mike, a mountain biker and the former head bike mechanic at an Austin bike shop, had met Armstrong a few years earlier when Armstrong came into the shop to pick up a special Trek bike that he was to ride while carrying the 2002 Winter Olympics torch through Austin. They became casual friends and in late 2001, a mutual acquaintance who worked for Lance approached Mike and explained that Lance needed someone to follow him in the car during his training rides and help him take care of his properties while he was in Europe. So Mike took the job.

Once in Santa Barbara, Lance took Kristin for a walk on the beach and told her the marriage was over, then walked away. Lance later told Anderson that he had read an e-mail between Kristin and the owner of an Austin-area running-shoe store that led him to suspect her of infidelity. But Anderson, who had performed odd jobs around the house for the family and whom Kristin had jokingly called H2—for Husband Two—found it unlikely that Kristin had cheated on Lance.

The split meant that Lance traveled to Girona alone in February, while Kristin and the kids remained behind in Austin. After Lance agreed to enter counseling in an effort to save the marriage, Kristin visited him in April, traveling with him to Nice, where they had lived together before they were married. But the relationship continued to unravel.

Landis, on the other hand, was very happy in his family life. Everything seemed to be going well for him. And then it wasn't.

On a sunny, crisp day in January, Landis went out for a training ride in the small town of De Luz, California. He was going about twenty-five miles per hour, flying through the turns wearing his red, white, and blue US Postal jersey. Landis, who had cut his teeth on mountain biking, was fearless about speed. Unafraid of sharp turns, he was confident in his ability to correct the bike if it skidded or fishtailed. His bike handling ability was one of the things that made him so valuable to Armstrong and the US Postal team. What good is a strong climber if he falls behind on the downhills?

Landis saw an upcoming turn that he had taken a hundred times before. Approaching the apex of the turn, he leaned his bike into it and lightly touched the brakes. But as he hit the corner, he hit a patch of sand on the road and his wheels began to lose traction. He could feel what was happening, but it was too late. He had no choice but to continue into the turn. The wheels completely lost their grip. Because he was leaning to his right, when he hit the asphalt, all his weight came crashing down onto his right hip.

Landis slid across the road, rolling a couple of times before coming to a complete stop on the chalky dirt shoulder. He couldn't get up. *What an idiot,* he thought to himself. It took nearly an hour before someone drove by and offered to help. The driver placed a phone call to Amber, Landis's wife, who came to pick him up. She wanted to take him to the hospital, but he refused. He went home, cleaned off his road rash, and then passed out from the pain. The next day, realizing he was in serious trouble, Landis went to the hospital. X-rays showed that he had severely fractured his hip. He needed emergency surgery, during which three screws were placed in his hip. Landis had a sinking feeling that everything he had just gained might be slipping away.

Later that month, Landis showed up to the team's training camp in Solvang, California, on crutches and was off the bike for most of the early season. Nobody on the team shed any tears for Landis, including Armstrong. The US Postal squad was a business. That business centered around making sure Lance Armstrong won the 2003 Tour de France—for what would be his fifth consecutive win, a record only one other man had achieved. To that end, every rider on the team was disposable, including Landis. Though he had proven himself to be perhaps the most promising young rider on the team, now he was just damaged goods. The only thing that mattered was whether Landis would be ready in time to help Lance win a race that was a little more than six months away. Landis realized he was nothing more than a piece of machinery in the Lance Armstrong factory.

Just as he got back on the bike in the early spring, Landis discovered he would need another surgery to shorten the pins holding his hip together. When Bruyneel heard the news, he urged Landis to have the surgery in Spain, but Landis was wary of the suggestion. A Spanish doctor? Instead, Landis turned to Arnie Baker, a physician and cycling coach whom Landis trusted and viewed almost like a father. Landis was well connected in the medical community in San Diego, and he decided to have his surgery there.

In a normal year, two surgeries inside a period of a few months would have meant Landis was off the Tour de France squad, but US Postal was desperate that season, with a rash of injuries and illnesses among its riders. So Johan Bruyneel asked Landis to fly to Europe the same day as his surgery in order to race just a week or so later in the Tour of Belgium. Landis had to argue with him to explain that it wouldn't be safe, that, in fact, it was insane for Bruyneel to even make the suggestion, and he refused to go that day.

Nonetheless, worried for his job, he flew to Europe the next day. By the time he got off the fifteen-hour flight, so much blood had pooled down from his incision site that the bottom part of his leg had turned completely black. He was also in incredible pain. But a little more than a week later, Landis entered the seven-day Tour of Belgium. Still in intense pain, he was barely able to finish the race.

George Hincapie, Armstrong's trusted lieutenant, was another of the riders who was having health issues that season—in his case, a mysterious illness that left him feeling fatigued for three months. Hincapie was weak and in pain. He confided his problems to Stephanie McIlvain, the rep from Oakley. Hincapie was one of several Postal riders to whom McIlvain had grown close over the years. McIlvain connected Hincapie with a homeopathic doctor in California, who ran tests on Hincapie that showed elevated cortisol levels. He recommended herbal remedies to Hincapie, who thought the doctor was full of crap. Every high-level athlete has elevated cortisol levels, he thought. Hincapie looked around for a doctor who could treat the problem. Various doctors poked, prodded, scanned, x-rayed, and examined every part of his body, but none of them could figure out what was wrong. Finally, Hincapie found a specialist in holistic medicine who said he could help.

The months leading up to the 2003 Tour de France had a different feel for Landis. Instead of training in relative isolation with Armstrong in St. Moritz, he and Armstrong were in Girona with a bunch of other cyclists from the team, though Armstrong was frequently away, dealing with his marital problems.

Since most of the top riders who would be helping Armstrong in the Tour de France were living in Girona for the season, the blood transfusion operation was centralized there. After the blood draws were done, the blood bags were stored in a small refrigerator in Armstrong's closet, each of them labeled with a code name in case they were confiscated by authorities.

The Postal team riders weren't the only ones who were doing transfusions. Jan Ullrich, who would be Armstrong's chief rival in the upcoming Tour, was getting stronger, thanks to a renewed commitment to doping. Ullrich and his trainer had backed off doping after the Festina scandal, on the assumption that everyone else in the field would, too; but they realized, after the 2002 race, that their logic was flawed. Through the gossip in the peloton, they heard that the US Postal team had indeed stopped using EPO but was doing blood transfusions instead. So they began to look for discreet ways to conduct their own blood transfusions. They were playing doping catch-up, but they were confident that they were closing the gap on Armstrong.

By June, Landis's hip was better and Hincapie was on the mend. Both men were now looking well enough to race in the Tour the following month, which was good news for the Postal team.

The news was not all good, however. There were whispers around the team that Kristin was filing for divorce and that lawyers were already involved. Armstrong was racing a lighter schedule than usual in 2003, focusing most of his energies on getting ready for the Tour, but he was having trouble avoiding distractions.

Among those distractions was the book about Armstrong that Irish reporter David Walsh was known to be writing. Armstrong knew Walsh had been gathering sources for his book, and that one of his sources was Emma O'Reilly, the Irish masseuse and his former soigneur. O'Reilly told Walsh that she had transported drugs for Armstrong while working on the team, and that Armstrong had all but confessed to her that he used drugs. "Now you know enough to bring me down," she quoted him as saying to her in 1999, during the Tour de France. Another of Walsh's sources was Steve Swart, the Kiwi on the Coors Light squad who had accepted the $50,000 payment for helping Armstrong win $1 million. Swart later switched to the Motorola team and had raced alongside Armstrong in 1995. Swart, who by then was living a quiet life in New Zealand and had nothing to lose by speaking with Walsh, told him that Armstrong had been an advocate for using EPO. Swart didn't much care for Armstrong and he figured that getting out the truth about cycling would ultimately be good for the sport, helping to reduce the pressure to dope.

Even as Walsh was gathering his evidence, Johan Bruyneel was doing everything he could to hold the team together and keep the riders focused on the Tour de France. Before they got there, however, there was one more critical race: the Dauphiné Libéré.

After a slow start, Armstrong won the time trial on the fourth day of the Dauphiné, taking the race lead. It was a sign that he was coming into form. But on the next day in the mountains, Armstrong was beaten in a sprint finish by Basque Spaniard Iban Mayo, who was looking like another potential rival for Armstrong in the Tour de France. Armstrong and Mayo stayed neck and neck for the rest of the race. Armstrong never shook him, but Mayo never ate into Armstrong's lead. On the final mountain stage, Mayo beat Armstrong up the Galibier, but the race did not finish there. Armstrong chased Mayo down on the descent, carving up the corners of the road at more than fifty miles per hour. It was a harrowing, life-threatening, thrilling performance. Armstrong walked away with the lead, but he was hardly as dominating in the mountains as he had been in the past.

After the June victory, Armstrong got an e-mail from Frankie Andreu. After retiring from racing, Andreu worked for two seasons as director of the Postal's US squad. Now he was doing on-air commentary for the television station Outdoor Life Network, which would be broadcasting every stage of the Tour de France live on cable in the United States. Until then, American viewers had never been able to watch all of the Tour; instead, they were limited to highlights on CBS. But because interest in Armstrong was now running so high in the States, there would be much fuller coverage—which was of direct benefit to Andreu, who loved his role on the network.

In the note, Andreu complimented Armstrong on his descending ability when he caught up with Mayo on the downhill.

Finally!!! a chance to go ballistic on the downhill and show your skills. That must have been fun and Mayo's jaw must have hit the ground when you finally caught him . . . ciao . . . frankie.

Armstrong replied:

yep, it was pretty fun . . . there are some stupid-crazy mofos out there as you well know. bottom line. it was a hard DL to win. much harder than i expected. that mayo(nnaise) was attacking his ass off. and fast too. hope you're well. La.

And then Armstrong expressed his worries about Walsh's book in a note he added at the bottom of the e-mail:

ps. emma o'reilly has gone psycho and decided to spew to david walsh. she's nuts . . . has he called you? surely he has.

Andreu didn't know how Armstrong had gotten the info about O'Reilly. But Armstrong always knew things first. He was the most talented gossip in the professional racing circuit.

Frankie responded:

I was just wondering the other day about Emma and what she is doing. Walsh tried to contact me in April and June through a third party. I told Walsh, through the third party, that I could not talk with him. So, technically, I have not spoken or met the guy yet. I'm sure he will probably try to track me down at the Tour.

On that note, what is Emma talking about and how do you know he talked with Emma?

Armstrong's performance in the four-mile time trial that opened the Tour de France that year was disappointing. He finished more than 7 seconds behind the day's fastest time of 7 minutes, 26 seconds. Ullrich had finished ahead of him by 5 seconds. The results mattered more to him symbolically than in any real way, because Armstrong hated to show weakness on the first day of the Tour. The team time trial a few days later allowed Armstrong to regain momentum, leaving him just a second out of the yellow jersey. But the real tests were yet to come. On day nine, a stage that finished atop Alpe d'Huez, Mayo, who had looked so strong in the Dauphiné, won. Armstrong rolled in third, more than 2 minutes later. Unlike his previous trips up that climb, Alpe d'Huez was no fun for Armstrong that year. But his time was good enough to put him in the overall race lead—if only by 40 seconds—over another Spaniard, Joseba Beloki. Ullrich was still lurking, too, down by only a couple of minutes in eighth place. Armstrong was facing the toughest competition he had ever met in the Tour de France.

Armstrong got a bit of luck the next day, another mountain stage. He was right on Beloki's wheel on a descent. The two men were screaming down the road at close to fifty miles per hour, when Beloki panicked and hit the brakes. The heat caused by the friction between the brake pads and the wheel, in combination with the heat coming off the road, was so intense that it caused the glue on Beloki's tire to melt. The tire slid off the rim and soon Beloki's bike was sliding sideways onto the road. He hit the pavement hard. Armstrong had nowhere to go. To avoid crashing into Beloki, Armstrong veered left, taking his bike off the road and into a field. The course looped around the field, so Armstrong could ride across the field and get back on his bike on the other side. He jumped off his bike to carry it over a ditch and then climbed back on. He had essentially cut the course, but because he was avoiding a crash, this was perfectly legal. He was right back with the lead group of riders, and had averted disaster. Beloki, who was having the race of his life, was seriously injured. The crash ended his Tour.

But by the end of the stage, Armstrong was still nowhere near secure in his lead. Kazakhstani rider Alexander Vinokourov now trailed him by only 21 seconds. Iban Mayo was a minute down and Ullrich was still only about 2 minutes behind. In all of his previous Tour wins, Armstrong had had the race wrapped up by now. Then, on day thirteen: disaster. Armstrong became severely dehydrated during the individual time trial. He finished dry-mouthed and dying of thirst. Ullrich, finally looking like Ullrich again, beat Armstrong by more than a minute. The race was neck and neck. Armstrong lost more time to Ullrich on the next mountain stage, shrinking his lead to a mere 15 seconds. On day sixteen, Armstrong finally had a breakthrough, winning a mountain stage and gaining back 40 seconds on Ullrich. Vinokourov lost more than 2 minutes that day and was now out of the picture, so Lance's lead was now back up to 1 minute and 7 seconds. It was a lead that could completely evaporate if he didn't perform in the individual time trial on the penultimate day of the race before Paris.

The time trial took place on a rainy day in Pornic, France. There were nearly 150 riders who would finish the course that day, but only the last two mattered. Ullrich was the second-to-last rider to be called to the starting gate. Wearing his green Bianchi kit and aerodynamic helmet, he shot out into the rain for his final chance at the yellow jersey. Armstrong was the last out the gate—the honor given to the current leader in the race. As both men pushed themselves to their absolute maximum aerobic capacity, Ullrich was looking stronger. He was chipping away at Armstrong's lead. But then, Ullrich made a fatal mistake, taking a turn too fast. His tires lost traction on the slick roads and Ullrich hit the ground with a thud. Both of Armstrong's toughest opponents in the race had been felled by crashes. When Armstrong crossed the finish line, he pumped his fist in the air. He knew there was no way Ullrich could win now.

Armstrong had won his fifth Tour de France in a row, matching the record of Miguel Indurain, the Spanish champion. The victory was a huge turning point for Armstrong. Even with the team weakened by illnesses and injuries, and with the distractions of the Walsh book and his failing marriage, Armstrong had prevailed.

And now Lance was not just a celebrity, but he was about to be a bachelor celebrity. Although Kristin and their children had joined him at the finish line of the Tour, there was no saving the marriage. By October, he and Kristin finalized their separation, Lance filed for divorce, and they went into mediation to reach a settlement.

That same month, Armstrong flew to Las Vegas to attend Andre Agassi's Grand Slam for Children Benefit Concert. His contribution was to donate a bike ride with himself in Austin, which was auctioned off to the highest bidder for $120,000. The concert had a star lineup that featured Elton John, Billy Joel, Sarah McLachlan, and Sheryl Crow. Armstrong, who considered himself single by then, began flirting with Crow. Within a month, the *Austin*

American-Statesman reported that the two were dating. They were keeping the relationship quiet, the story said, because of Armstrong's pending divorce.

In the spring of 2004, Armstrong flew to Nike headquarters for a meeting. Its sales executives had an idea. Earlier, one of them had seen Kevin Garnett, a basketball player for the Minnesota Timberwolves, wearing an orange-ish thing resembling a hospital bracelet around his wrist, which he snapped, rubber band–style, to give himself a little sting every time he made a mistake. Soon after, Nike developed a similar product called Baller Bands that became popular with street basketball players.

To broaden the appeal of the item, some Nike executives came up with the idea of emblazoning the bands with different messages and using them as promotion items. They pitched Armstrong and his people on the idea and suggested putting the Nike swoosh and a slogan that embodied Armstrong's story on a yellow version of the bracelet. The money would go to his cancer charity, the Lance Armstrong Foundation. They floated a number of possible phrases and finally settled on a single word: *Livestrong*—a play on Armstrong's name as well as a motto that seemed to suggest a lifestyle. The message spoke to the cancer survivors Armstrong advocated for, but it could also appeal to people facing many other kinds of challenges.

Armstrong thought it was a terrible idea that wouldn't go anywhere. But he agreed to give it a try. Sheryl Crow wore one during a *Today* show appearance, and later showed up at the Grammy Awards wearing a yellow Roberto Cavalli gown and a Livestrong bracelet on one arm. Then Lance and Sheryl went on Oprah's TV show to plug the foundation, and 900,000 Oprah viewers bought Livestrong bracelets that same day.

Ordinary people—not just athletes—began wearing the bracelets. Everyone wanted a piece of Lance.

CHAPTER TEN

A NEW GEAR

Armstrong wasted no time moving on after his marriage. He went to Hollywood, partied with Sheryl Crow, attended movie premieres and Lakers games. He was in the limelight as never before. *New York Times* sportswriter George Vecsey described Armstrong's lifestyle as "sybaritic." Producers were working on a feature film about his life, with Matt Damon rumored to be playing his character, according to *Variety* and other Hollywood trade publications.

Lance's relationship with Sheryl Crow was all over the media, and it actually helped soften the blow to his image caused by his shattered nuptials. It was shocking to some fans that Armstrong would leave his wife. He was an almost Jesus-like figure to them, resurrected from the death grip of cancer so that we might all be inspired. But if he were going to leave his wife and run off with a pop singer, he had picked the right one. Crow was down-to-earth, classy, and grown-up, not some twentysomething starlet.

Armstrong's image was further burnished by the role he played as a doting father. After the divorce, Kristin and the children had settled down in Austin, so in order to see his three young children, Armstrong decided to spend more time stateside, training in Texas and California. He told reporters that he would rather lose the Tour de France than be away from his kids. Further reinforcing the idea that he had realigned his priorities, Armstrong called Jan Ullrich the "favorite" in the 2004 Tour de France. Inevitably, the reports got back to Ullrich in Germany, who said Armstrong was using the media to play mind games with him.

Far from being ready to cede the 2004 Tour to Ullrich or anyone else, the truth was that now that Armstrong had catapulted himself into the stratosphere of celebrity life, he wanted his fame to last. He knew the best way—the only way—to make that happen was to win a record sixth Tour de France. Nobody had done it before, and it was a feat not likely to be repeated. Armstrong was as focused as ever. The previous year's race, though, had been too close. Armstrong had nearly lost to Ullrich, and now that Ullrich had sensed a slight weakness in Armstrong and gotten a whiff of the smell of victory, he was sure to dedicate himself more seriously to winning. Armstrong had always been able to count on Ullrich showing up to the early-season races overweight and weakened from an off-season of drinking and eating whatever he wanted; but he wasn't confident he could count on that anymore. So Armstrong had to be proactive and he began with a radical upgrade of his equipment.

Armstrong summoned his sponsors to a meeting at the hippest hotel in Los Angeles: the Standard—a white stucco building on Sunset Boulevard. The sponsors walked past the minimalist, modern bar and the outdoor swimming pool, where models and actresses were showing off their perfect bodies. They entered the hotel conference room and sat around a large table, while Armstrong and his agent, Bill Stapleton, explained that the 2003 Tour win had been too close for comfort. There were problems with nutrition, clothing, and bike components, and all these problems had to be resolved. Armstrong wanted his sponsors to coordinate their efforts in order to make sure that every piece of his equipment was designed to fit perfectly with every other piece and be maximally functional as well as comfortable during racing conditions.

Armstrong instructed Trek, which had become the nation's largest bike maker and which dedicated 30 to 40 percent of its marketing budget to sponsoring Armstrong, and Japanese component maker Shimano, which sponsored the team as well as outfitting it with equipment, to work together on their designs so that the aluminum and titanium chains, cranks, and cogs matched up perfectly with the structure of the carbon fiber bike frame. Armstrong had already pushed Shimano to add an extra gear to its rear cassettes, and Shimano had obliged.

Armstrong told sunglass maker Oakley to work with helmet maker Giro so that his glasses fit snugly within the contours of his helmet. He also wanted the sunglass arms to be sized to fit the small holes on the top of the helmet so that he could remove glasses and place them securely atop his head when he got off the bike. And on top of that, he wanted the glasses to look stylish. Interested as ever in the science of everything to do with racing, Armstrong stipulated that the designs should be tested in wind tunnels, which were mainly used by aerospace companies, to ensure that the sunglasses and helmets created the least amount of drag possible.

Lance wanted something similar to be done with the bikes he rode. He had already spent some time in a wind tunnel at the University of Washington the previous off-season, which had led to the development of a one-piece skin suit designed by Nike for use during time trials. The suit was put together without seams and composed of different types of fabric for specific areas of the body, the aim being to do everything possible to lower Armstrong's drag in the wind. Armstrong's new sponsor, chip maker AMD, also got involved, lending computer processing power to the effort to further improve the Nike skinsuit and the aerodynamics of the bikes and other equipment.

When it came time to test all the newly designed equipment, Johan Bruyneel didn't want to interrupt Lance's training schedule, so the sponsors used a body double for the tests—a Canadian triathlete who had the exact same body dimensions as Lance, even down to the slight hump in his back when he was arched forward over the handlebars.

The attempt to combine all of these technological innovations into one comprehensive, carefully integrated program was dubbed F-One, to reflect Lance's intention for cycling to have access to high-tech equipment that was as outstandingly excellent as that used by a sport like Formula One, the auto racing series featuring the world's fastest circuit-racing cars. The inspiration for doing the wind tunnel testing had come from the top Formula One team, BMW-Williams, which had begun to use computational fluid dynamics technology (a fancy term for wind tunnel tests) to help its race cars become more aerodynamically efficient.

Armstrong's efforts to gain an edge didn't all revolve around high-tech gadgetry. In the interest of shaving minutes and seconds off his race times, he and his team paid equally obsessive attention to some of the basics. For example, even before the debut of F-One, team mechanic Julien de Vriese had been putting Armstrong's tires in storage in a cool, dry cellar, and allowing them to stay there for six or seven years to age, like a fine wine. De Vriese's theory was that the aging process would harden rubber in the tires, making them more resistant to flats.

F-One was also a brilliant business move because it brought more publicity to Lance's sponsors and gave them a chance to speak to the world about what went into the making of their products. The glowing newspaper articles and TV shows describing the futuristic technology gave the sponsors invaluable exposure, which they didn't hesitate to exploit to increase their sales. Thus the extra gear that Shimano added to Lance's bikes was hailed as such a huge success that it was quickly adopted across the cycling industry. This helped Shimano boost its net profit projections by 42 percent after the 2003 Tour de France, which in turn caused its stock to move upward.

The cost of the F-One project exceeded $1 million, counting the team's time and investment. But when Lance took his million-dollar bike out of the wind tunnel and put it on the road . . . well, he didn't like it much. After riding it in a couple of races, he told Bruyneel that his hips hurt, and that he was thinking about going back to his old bike. Ultimately, that's what he did, and Bruyneel had to pick up the phone to inform Trek and the rest of the F-One team that Lance was putting the kibosh on the bike they had devoted such extraordinary resources to developing for him.

F-One was all about the science of Lance's equipment. But, as the title of his autobiography suggests, the story of his success was not simply "about the bike." At a time when the American media were grasping for ways to explain to viewers what made Armstrong so remarkable, there was another story to be told—about the science of Lance himself. At least in the United States the media were willing to give Armstrong the benefit of the doubt about doping because of a growing mythology about him as an extraordinary physiological specimen, a man who had come back from a cancer that had nearly killed him and transformed his body into a machine destined for greatness. And Armstrong and his core group of publicists were happy to provide the measurements and statistics to bring that story to life.

One of their chief weapons was Edward F. Coyle, a professor of sports science at the University of Texas, who had studied Lance in his Austin sports lab over a period of seven years, from 1992 to 1999. Coyle's findings, which were eventually published in the June 2005 issue of the *Journal of Applied Physiology*, included his conclusion that, even if Lance were to become completely sedentary, his oxygen-carrying capacity (VO_2 max) would match the "highest values normal men can achieve with training." He also remarked on the size of Armstrong's heart and its ability to beat fast for an extended period of time, pumping exceptionally high levels of oxygen-rich blood to his muscles.

Coyle's research suggested that between the ages of twenty-one and twenty-eight, a time period that included his being diagnosed and treated for cancer, Lance had improved his muscular efficiency and therefore his cycling power production (the amount of power he generated when consuming a given amount of oxygen) by 8 percent—a remarkable advantage, given that only a 1 to 3 percent difference separates the winner from his competitors in most races. And he had accomplished this even while losing weight prior to each of his Tours de France, so that his power per kilogram of body weight ratio improved by 18 percent.

Another part of the story was that Lance extracted twice as much oxygen from each breath as the average twenty-year-old, while producing less lactic acid—the punishing burn. That meant that when he pushed beyond his aerobic capacity, such as on a sprint, he was able to maintain full power for longer than his competition.

In terms of the "tactics" Lance used to enhance his performance, there was his routine of training and recovery at high altitudes, to increase his oxygen-carrying capacity. When there's less oxygen available to the lungs, as there is at high altitudes, the body creates more red blood cells, and more red blood cells increase a rider's ability to use oxygen.

These statistics—some of them highly questionable—eventually became the underpinning of America's understanding of how Lance had come to dominate the Tour de France, and later a key argument for Lance and his lawyers to use against those who accused him of doping.

Dr. Coyle's research on Armstrong was later questioned by scientists, and he was forced to admit an error in some of his calculations involving Armstrong's muscular efficiency. But Coyle stood by his overall findings, even if his math was off, and accused the scientists of targeting him because of a vendetta against Armstrong himself. Armstrong's heart, it turns out, was not so remarkably large among top athletes, and his VO_2 max was normal for high-level endurance athletes. Armstrong may have been a great athlete, but his dominance over his peers couldn't be explained by one single scientifically measurable thing.

In the off-season leading up to the 2004 Tour, things could not have been going better for Armstrong. He was no longer just the most famous cyclist in the world; he was among the most famous athletes in the world. He was living the life of a globe-trotting celebrity. If all went according to plan and he won a sixth Tour de France, he would become an immortal sports legend by the end of July. Recognizing his economic value to his team, Armstrong approached Weisel with a new demand: He wanted to be given an 11.5 percent ownership stake in Tailwind Sports, the company Weisel had founded and that owned the US Postal Service team. Weisel and his board of directors agreed, voting to transfer shares to Armstrong for a nominal fee, thus diluting their ownership. They also made Lance's agent, Bill Stapleton, CEO of Tailwind and gave his agency, Capital Sports & Entertainment, its own 11.5 percent stake.

But even as Lance seemed to just go from one triumph to the next, trouble was looming. David Walsh was making progress on his book. He had a new source—Betsy Andreu, Frankie's wife. The previous summer, Walsh had called Betsy at her home in Michigan on a tip that she might have some good information. He explained that he was working on a book about Armstrong that was going to prove he had doped to win the Tour de France. Instead of hanging up immediately, as her husband would have wanted her to do, Betsy was intrigued enough to begin speaking with Walsh. She liked him and found his quirky Irish accent engaging. However, she was cautious. She knew that whatever she said about Armstrong could have a ripple effect on her husband. But Walsh had convinced Betsy to allow him to write about the hospital room scene from 1996.

It wasn't long before Armstrong got word of Walsh's conversation with Betsy Andreu. He was furious—and nervous. He and his advisers, namely Bill Stapleton and his business manager, Bart Knaggs, thought they could deflect any allegations from the masseuse, Emma O'Reilly. Armstrong could argue that she had been fired from the team, giving her an apparent motive to make up damning stories about him. Walsh had promised to pay O'Reilly for her many hours spent fact-checking her interview transcripts against her diary. And he told her she would have legal protection, which further compromised her legitimacy as an accuser. Information from Walsh's other main source to date, Steve Swart, hadn't made much of a dent. Walsh had published Swart's allegations in articles in *The Sunday Times*—without naming him—and they had drawn little attention.

But if Betsy Andreu was talking now, that was another matter. After all, she was the wife of someone who knew Armstrong quite well and had been a close friend.

Frankie tried to play the role of peacemaker. When Armstrong asked him about Betsy's conversation with Walsh, he told him that Betsy hadn't meant any harm—she was simply trying to get Walsh off her back, and she had given him the names of other wives to talk to in order to pawn him off on somebody else, an explanation that Armstrong didn't buy.

"[T]he more i think about this though, the harder i find it to understand why your wife did what she did," Armstrong wrote in an e-mail, accusing Betsy of sneaking around behind his back. "i know betsy is not a fan, and that's fine, but by helping to bring me down is not going to help y'alls situation at all," Armstrong wrote. "there is a direct link to all of our success here and i suggest you remind her of that."

Frankie Andreu tried again to fix the situation: "Lance, I gain absolutely nothing from seeing Walsh try to fuck you. If that was my interest I could have talked with him and told you nothing. I didn't do that. When Walsh called, I freaked. I really couldn't believe it because all I ever have heard is how bad this guy [is] and his only point is to take people down. I went off on Betsy to not deal with this guy, she didn't understand what the big deal was," he wrote.

"I don't want to see you get taken down. I also have a lot at stake, besides my livlihood [sic], my reputation. I've always watched your back and it's no different now. . . . frankie."

Frankie may have gone to Betsy's defense, but he, too, was angry at his wife for stirring the pot. He knew Betsy was disgusted by the doping in the sport, and that she hated Armstrong because she viewed him as a ringleader. She told Frankie she supported Walsh's efforts to out Armstrong. But she didn't seem to grasp that the whole thing threatened to bring him down as well.

Andreu felt that what Walsh was doing was bad for the sport, and bad for him personally. He was now a respected television commentator for a sports network, and he liked his job and wanted to keep it. Over the years, he had come to think of Armstrong as something of an asshole. When Frankie refused to take the next step in his doping—to hire Ferrari—Armstrong began saying he wasn't a "team player." Frankie lost his contract and left the team. But Armstrong played nice with Frankie—when he needed something. The team hired Frankie as a coach for its lower-level riders in US races, and Andreu wondered if Armstrong orchestrated this to keep him quiet. But Frankie didn't care, so long as Armstrong kept bringing more money into the sport and more attention.

While Walsh continued to work on his book, Armstrong was looking to another book to counterbalance whatever Walsh would end up writing about him. He had granted access to an amiable journalist named Daniel Coyle, who worked for *Outside* magazine. Coyle would end up spending part of the 2004 season with Armstrong, George Hincapie, and Floyd Landis, as well as Dr. Michele Ferrari. This gave him the closest view of the superstar that any American journalist had ever had. If Walsh's book accused Armstrong of doping, it would have competition on the shelves from a friendlier book. "Coke. Nike. Subaru. If we're fucking lying, we can kiss it all good-bye," Bill

Stapleton told Coyle, referring to three of Lance's premier sponsors. "Does anybody think for a second that a secret that big wouldn't come out?"

Coyle was independent, and had free rein to write anything he wanted about doping. Surely Coyle feared writing the doping story would come with lawsuits and attacks from Armstrong and his followers. But writing an intimate portrait on the hottest athlete on the planet was likely to be a bestseller. To help ensure "openness," Coyle showed Lance and his people drafts of what he wrote, so they might respond and offer corrections. And in order to interview Ferrari, Coyle agreed that he would not ask Ferrari questions about doping. Coyle finished the book, and in it, he explored what factors gave Armstrong the edge over his rivals. But he chose to tread delicately on the doping topic. He gave an airing to Walsh and his investigative work, but focused his story on Armstrong's obsessive training and management style.

In April 2004, Armstrong won the Tour de Georgia, a seven-day race that had become the biggest stage race in the United States. Armstrong's win drew unprecedented attention to the race and millions of dollars in tourism money to the state of Georgia. Soon after, however, there was bad news: The US Postal Service, after years of taking flack for using taxpayer money to sponsor a cycling team, had decided to pull out. Armstrong was in familiar territory—beginning the season knowing there might not be a sponsor the next year.

In May, Armstrong was back in Europe, mostly in Girona, training with George Hincapie and Floyd Landis. Michele Ferrari, who was facing an upcoming trial in Italy over allegations that he was responsible for doping cyclists all over the world, was there with them on most days, seemingly unfazed by the damning testimony. As usual, he followed the riders up and down the slopes of the Pyrenees in his old station wagon. At the tops of the climbs, Ferrari would prick their fingers, take a drop of blood, and analyze their lactate levels on a small, portable machine. Then he would analyze their wattage numbers. The wattage was measured by a tiny stress meter placed inside the bicycle crank, which was made by a Danish company and cost thousands of dollars. Ferrari would compare the lactate in their muscles with the amount of power they were producing to figure out their fitness level, and whether they were on track for Tour de France–level form.

While the group trained in the mountains during the week, Sheryl Crow spent many of her days in Southern France, not far from Girona, sightseeing, shopping, writing music, and seeing Armstrong between training rides.

After one of their training days, Ferrari told Landis that he was impressed with his numbers. In fact, Landis had attained Ferrari's "magic number." He could, for a sustained period of time, produce more than 6.7 watts of energy per kilogram of body weight. This meant, by Ferrari's calculations, that he was potentially good enough to win the Tour de France. Landis's impressive numbers made Armstrong hungrier—and slightly agitated. He couldn't be weaker than one of his domestiques. But Ferrari's data was good news for Landis, who was thinking about leaving the US Postal team. Other teams were courting him. Landis was tempted because, despite all the money that was flowing in, he still felt he deserved more. And he needed it. He spent lavishly on cars, his house, gifts for his family. He wasn't saving and he again had credit card debt.

Also, Landis had begun to resent the system of the US Postal Service team—the way everything was centered on Armstrong, and the rest of the riders were just chattel. Landis had noticed that Armstrong always rode around on newer training bicycles than the rest of the team, and never had any mechanical issues. He was suspicious that USPS was holding back equipment from the rest of the riders.

Landis placed a phone call to Scott Daubert, the Trek employee in charge of the sponsorship, and asked him how many bikes the company supplied to the team. "Dozens" was the reply. Enough to supply every rider on the team with a few frames each season. *So where did they go?* Landis wondered. He called another friend, at Shimano, the component maker that supplied the teams with gears, chains, brakes, cogs, cranks, and every other piece of equipment on the frame. The answer was the same: USPS got enough componently to supply each rider several times over.

After the Paris–Roubaix race in April, Landis was having dinner with a few of the other riders and several staff members, including Geert "Duffy" Duffeleer, who was in charge of the team's equipment. When Landis confronted him about the bikes, Duffy shot back, "Who do you think you are?!"

Later, Landis received a call from Bruyneel, who had gotten wind of the confrontation. Bruyneel explained to Landis that the team sold much of the equipment it received on the secondary market in Belgium. The bikes, which could run more than $5,000 at retail, generated cash for the team to buy performance-enhancing drugs and medications off the books. This explanation did not make Landis feel any better.

Armstrong's patience with Landis's insubordinate attitude was wearing thin. Landis by now realized just how talented he was, and he wanted the team to put more resources into helping him rack up some high-profile wins—and he let Armstrong know it. But Armstrong dismissed Landis. There was no way the team was going to divert resources from its one and only goal: getting Lance his sixth win. Landis felt he was being brushed aside.

Armstrong had bigger problems to deal with at the time than an uppity domestique. David Walsh's book, which now had a title, *L.A. Confidentiel*, was due out in June, just before the 2004 Tour de France. It had become a major worry, and Armstrong turned to litigation to deal with it. He hired lawyers in France and the UK, who promptly sued the authors, the publishers, the sources, as well as a magazine that ran an excerpt of the book and the newspaper Walsh worked for, *The Sunday Times*, which had also run a preview of it. The legal assault began just as the book was hitting the bookstores in France but in time to prevent its publication in the UK. Lance's lawyers also asked the French courts for an "emergency ruling" to insert a statement from Lance into Walsh's book, denying the allegations, but a judge turned down the request. They then sued the publisher in French court, asking that the book be taken off the shelves. Though Lance eventually withdrew his claims before a trial could begin, he later claimed to have won every case. (His claim against *The Sunday Times*, however, was later settled, in his favor.)

June's Dauphiné Libéré was Armstrong's biggest moment to date of the 2004 season. His form there would be a predictor of whether he could produce a record sixth win in next month's Tour de France. Iban Mayo, wearing the bright orange jersey of the Euskaltel-Euskadi team, prevailed in the opening 3.35-mile time trial. Armstrong's former teammate, Tyler Hamilton, finished second. Armstrong was in third, 1.41 seconds off the leading time. The result was not what he'd hoped for, but not dreadful.

The Dauphiné organizers had scheduled another individual time trial up Mont Ventoux. As time trials go, this was one of the more painful ones.

Amateur cyclists could spend the better part of a day climbing Mont Ventoux. By the end of the time trial, Armstrong had finished a disappointing fifth place—nearly 2 minutes behind Mayo's winning time of 55 minutes, 51 seconds, and 1.5 minutes behind Hamilton.

After the ride, Armstrong stormed into his trailer and slammed the door. He was fuming. He picked up his cell phone and dialed the UCI president, Hein Verbruggen. Hamilton and Mayo must be doping, Armstrong told Verbruggen. They couldn't possibly ride that fast. He went on to tell Verbruggen that drug testers needed to keep a closer eye on Mayo and Hamilton and test them more often. Armstrong finished the Dauphiné in fourth place, more than 2 minutes behind Mayo and nearly 1.5 minutes behind Hamilton. His Tour de France hopes were looking grim.

Armstrong also continued his attack on *L.A. Confidentiel*, declaring in a news conference at which Walsh was present that "extraordinary accusations demand extraordinary proof" and that Walsh and his coauthor, Pierre Ballester, had failed to provide such proof. Indeed, they had not revealed all of their sources.

Behind the scenes, Bill Stapleton and Bart Knaggs were doing everything they could think of to undermine Walsh. Besides trying to find out who, exactly, Walsh had talked with, and what, exactly, he had gathered on Armstrong, they were looking for any dirt they could find on Walsh himself. And they were putting so much pressure on Frankie Andreu to help them soil Walsh's reputation that Andreu felt flat-out threatened. When Stapleton and Knaggs tracked him down during the lead-up to the Tour de France, which he was covering for the Outdoor Life Network, he surreptitiously flipped on his tape recorder.

"I ain't got that much time," Andreu said.

"You know your wife is a source for Walsh," Knaggs shot back.

"No, no, no," Andreu said.

Knaggs was insistent that Betsy must have been Walsh's source. "Cuz, see, he's talked to other people about her and said that she's very courageous, and she's willing to take a stand against Lance," Knaggs said. "She knows things about Lance . . . that she's told him."

Knaggs thought Betsy had told Walsh about the hospital room scene in

1996, when Lance admitted to using drugs. But when Frankie denied it, Knaggs and Stapleton pushed him harder.

"Would Betsy be willing to sign an affidavit saying that she wasn't the source for Walsh?" Knaggs asked. "That's very important, cuz it says that he's lying. He lied about sources."

But Betsy *was* the source. She had been actively and enthusiastically helping Walsh.

Andreu was caught in a difficult bind. He was trying to cover for his wife and, at the same time, stay out of the crosshairs of Armstrong, whom he knew to be one of the most powerful and vindictive people in the world of sports. Stapleton said he'd be willing to "draw up something" for her to sign. "She could help," he said.

Andreu tried to change the subject, pull the conversation away from the affidavit idea. "I know Betsy doesn't like Lance, but it's all in our interest not to blow this whole thing up," he said.

Stapleton and Knaggs didn't succeed in getting what they wanted from Andreu. But the public and much of the press seemed to be siding with Armstrong, whose historic effort to win his sixth Tour de France was generating so much excitement that it drowned out the critics. *New York Times* columnist George Vecsey wrote another glowing column defending Armstrong, giving *L.A. Confidentiel* short shrift, and even repeating with approval Armstrong's words about "extraordinary accusations."

Armstrong appeared to have beaten David Walsh. As the Tour de France began, the mainstream press was paying little attention to the book. But if Armstrong was winning the public relations battle against Walsh, Armstrong's team was now worried about a far more formidable foe: the French police. Would they crack down on the team, perhaps with a raid of their hotel rooms or by planting bugs or surveillance cameras? Because the Tour de France required every team to stay at designated hotels, the police had the advantage of always knowing in advance where they would be.

This kind of scrutiny could be disastrous for the team, because even as Stapleton and Knaggs were doing damage control in an attempt to cover up Lance's past doping, the team was engaged in its most brazen acts yet. The doping effort had become more complicated than ever, and more vulnerable to exposure. The riders could no longer just take a train from Girona to Garcia del Moral's clinic in Valencia for their transfusions, because the US Postal team had fired the doctor the year before. Without access to the clinic, the team sometimes had to fly into Belgium, where the new team doctor was based, to have their blood swapped out ahead of the Tour. Then they'd had to arrange for it to be secretly transported to France.

Armstrong let Sheryl Crow accompany him on a private jet to Belgium, where he conducted a blood transfusion. Rather than try to hide the transfusion from her, Armstrong was completely open about it. He trusted that Crow would have no desire to tell the press or anyone else about the team's doping program. He explained that it was simply part of the sport—that all cyclists were doing the same thing.

It was a messy Tour de France for the US Postal team. But on television, it looked beautiful. Armstrong's two biggest competitors in the Dauphiné—Iban Mayo and Tyler Hamilton—dropped out of the race before it was over. And just as he had been unable to do in previous Tours, Jan Ullrich couldn't match Armstrong in the mountains. Armstrong turned the broadcast of the race into a picturesque travelogue through France, as he and his US Postal teammates floated up the narrow mountain roads with the Alps and the Pyrenees in the backdrop. But there were a few strange moments captured by the cameras that no one at the time knew what to make of.

At the start of the seventeenth stage, which was the final climbing day of the Tour, Armstrong was in the lead by almost 4 minutes. He had pummeled Jan Ullrich on the Alpe d'Huez time trial a day earlier, and now Ullrich was almost 8 minutes behind. The long brutal route before them that day was 127 miles long and had five major climbs. Armstrong was shepherded the entire length of that ascent by Floyd Landis, who stayed with him for every pedal stroke. Six hours after they had begun, when Armstrong reached the top of the final climb, Landis was still right beside him, in good form—another indication that Landis was destined for greatness.

Armstrong and Landis had about ten miles to go to the finish line and it was almost all downhill. Armstrong turned to Landis and asked him if he was a good descender. Armstrong, of course, knew that Floyd could descend with the best of them. But Floyd just smiled and said yes. Armstrong told him to go for it: Attack on the descent and win the stage. This was a rare offer. In none of his five winning Tour de France races had Armstrong ever offered a teammate a chance to win a stage.

Landis gunned it down the hill, but Jan Ullrich didn't want to let Landis win, so he took off after him. Armstrong wasn't about to let Ullrich go, and clung to his wheel. At the very end of the descent, it was clear that Landis was not going to win. He was wiped after having spent the whole day pushing the pace for Armstrong on the climbs, and now the other riders, including Ullrich, Ivan Basso, and Andreas Klöden—the top cyclists on the planet—were right on his wheel. Klöden went for the win, but Armstrong wouldn't allow it. If Landis wasn't going to win the stage victory, then Armstrong would. He passed Klöden right at the line and again pumped his fists in the air. It was a bravura show of absolute dominance.

The next day, on stage 18, Armstrong noticed that Filippo Simeoni was attacking the field and attempting to make it into a breakaway group. Breakaway groups were reserved for riders who were so low down in the standings that it didn't really matter if they got far ahead of the field on one stage. But it mattered to them, because doing well in a breakaway could make them look good and keep sponsors happy with their jersey logos plastered all over television. Simeoni fell into that category. But Armstrong would not allow Simeoni to have an ounce of glory. Simeoni was one of the riders who had testified against Michele Ferrari, saying that the doctor had told him how and when to use doping products. After that, Armstrong had blasted Simeoni in the press, calling him a "liar"—to which Simeoni had responded by suing Armstrong for defamation in an Italian court. Now when he saw Simeoni making for the breakaway, Armstrong was so enraged that he left the peloton and chased him down. As he put his hand on Simeoni's back, the television announcers couldn't quite figure out what Armstrong was doing. Speaking in Italian, Lance told Simeoni: "You made a mistake when you testified against Ferrari and you made a mistake when you sued me. I have a lot of time and money and I can destroy you."

Next, the television commentators noticed that he was having discussions with other riders in the breakaway group, but they didn't know what that was about, either. In fact, Armstrong was telling them that as long as Simeoni was in the pack, he would never let the breakaway survive. The men knew that if Armstrong remained with them, the peloton would have no choice but to chase them down. The other riders in the group badgered Simeoni until he agreed to slow down and fall back to the main peloton. Armstrong, satisfied, also fell back. In the middle of the main peloton, Simeoni faced further abuse, this time from the riders in the pack, who were being egged on by Armstrong. Armstrong made a gesture in full view of the television cameras, pretending to zip his mouth shut. It was a clear message to the rest of the peloton: No talk about doping allowed.

A day later, on the final time trial, Armstrong bested Ullrich by more than a minute, winning his fifth stage. He was dominant in every aspect of the tour: The sprints, the climbs, the race against the clock.

The next day would be the relaxing ride to Paris. Champagne toasts while still on the bike, victory laps on the Champs-Élysées. He knew the drill well. Everyone was happy it was about to be over, even Armstrong's competitors—everyone, that is, except Filippo Simeoni. During the early part of the stage on the final day, the US Postal team had planned to pose for some photographs and toast with champagne. The rest of the peloton had agreed to hang back to give them the opportunity to get their media exposure. But before the team could raise a glass, Simeoni decided to attack and race out in front of the field. The Postal team quickly chased Simeoni down, causing a brief delay in the festivities. Once Simeoni was caught, Armstrong celebrated with the traditional toasts and victory laps. The television cameras had largely ignored the interruption, and few viewers would have understood the backstory to Simeoni's attack, even had they witnessed it.

The mood was as jubilant as ever at the team party, which was held, as had come to be their standard practice, at the Musée d'Orsay just hours after the race. Floyd Landis, however, was distracted. His two-year contract was set to expire at the end of the season, and the USPS negotiators were pressing him hard to renew. In fact, one of them had approached him right before the Alpe d'Huez time trial to try to get him to sign, and Landis had blown him off, saying that he had to focus on getting ready for the upcoming race. But the time for a decision was nigh. Among the competitors that had been courting him was Phonak, a team sponsored by a Swiss hearing aid manufacturer, which approached him with a $500,000 offer. The USPS made a counteroffer for significantly less money and now Landis was tormented about the decision he was being forced to make. As he agonized over his dilemma, Tiger Williams, who had come to France along with a number of the team owners and sponsors to watch Armstrong go for his sixth tour win, approached Landis to congratulate him. Williams seemed like a smart guy to Landis. Clearly, he was a successful businessman. And Landis viewed the decision he had to make as a business decision. So he decided to ask him what he thought he should do.

Williams's answer was surprising. Floyd remembers Williams telling him to get out of there. If they weren't willing to pay him what he was worth, just leave, Williams told him. The advice meant a lot to Landis. After all, Williams was part owner of the team. It was against his own interest to tell Landis to leave. But he did it anyway.

Shortly afterward, Landis flew home to California, his contract situation still unresolved. Soon he got a call from Bill Stapleton, who told him that Lance wanted to speak with him about his contract. Lance rarely called Landis—or anyone else, for that matter—so Landis knew it was important. In early August, Armstrong called with "good news"—although the team "never did this for anyone," he said they'd be willing to match his offer from Phonak. Before Landis could say anything, Armstrong followed with a stern warning. "But you better get shit right. You better keep training hard!"

Landis was annoyed. He knew he was supposed to feel special because the great Lance Armstrong had given him a call. But he didn't. "Whatever, man, I'm not really interested," he told Armstrong, who seemed shocked.

Stapleton called Landis again and informed him that there was a clause in his contract that gave US Postal the right to match any offer from a competing team, and Landis had to stay with US Postal. "Well, that's fine," Landis said. "If you want to pay me half a million bucks a year to get fat and eat doughnuts and fuck off for two years. I'll be glad to do that, but I'm not going to train."

"You're being a dick," Stapleton said. "How much do you want?"

At this point, though, Landis was set on leaving. He was fed up with everyone in management, from Armstrong to Bruyneel and Stapleton, and he wanted out. So he picked an outrageously high number—$750,000—which Stapleton promptly declined. And with that, the phone call and, Landis assumed, their negotiations were over.

In the meantime, however, Landis was having a difficult time reaching Phonak, who were not returning his calls. He found out later that someone close to Lance had told Phonak's leadership that Landis had already signed a contract extension with US Postal. That was a lie. In the end, Landis was able to reach Phonak and sort matters out. He would soon be joining former teammate Tyler Hamilton on the Phonak team.

Landis would later recall that Tiger Williams was the only person connected to the Postal team who didn't try to pressure him to stay. And after Landis did decamp to Phonak, the two men stayed in touch, even though Landis was now riding for a rival team.

Landis did one final race for USPS: The 21-day Vuelta a España. Through stage 11, Landis was in the lead. He credited his performance to a pill that Pedro Celaya had given him. Celaya didn't tell Landis what was in it, but it made him feel amazing. He could fly up the mountains without feeling a thing. He was blazing. Landis told his teammates about it, and said that Celaya had given him another one for the next day's stage, but he wasn't going to take it because he was going to bring it back to the United States and have it analyzed in a pharmacy. With the secret formula, Landis was going to "get rich." Landis did save the pill—and promptly lost the lead to Spaniard Roberto Heras, who had left US Postal for Liberty Seguros. Landis had it analyzed, but the lab was unable to find out what was in the pill.

Landis was of course not the only rider doping during the Vuelta. A blood test taken during the race showed that Tyler Hamilton had tested positive for having someone else's blood in him—the same thing he had tested positive for during the Athens Olympics, a month earlier. Hamilton had been lucky that time; the laboratory accidentally froze one of the samples, making the test invalid. Hamilton was puzzled, however. He wasn't transfusing anyone else's blood. He was reinfusing his own. The test result made no sense to him. One explanation was that Hamilton may have accidentally reinfused another rider's blood. This theory was supported by the fact that one of his teammates had also tested positive at the same time for the same thing.

Hamilton denied the positive test, blaming it on a "missing twin" who had died in his mother's womb, causing him to produce two types of blood. Determined to fight back, Hamilton set up a foundation and accepted donations to help him appeal his positive test in an arbitration hearing against USADA, the US Anti-Doping Agency. But Hamilton had chosen to fight an unwinnable war.

By August, Armstrong was on the cover of *Sports Illustrated*, and it seemed few people in the United States had read Walsh's book, since it was published only in French, or cared enough about the allegations it made to talk about it. But one person who had a vested interest in what it said had read it—Bob Hamman, the owner of SCA Promotions, a Dallas-based promotional marketing and insurance company.

Lance Armstrong, according to his contract with Tailwind Sports, was owed $10 million in bonuses for winning his sixth Tour de France in a row. But Tailwind had taken out an insurance policy from SCA Promotions against Armstrong winning the race, thus mitigating some of the risk, specifically, the risk associated with half of the bonus offer. Founded in 1986 by Hamman—the world's top-ranked bridge player for nearly two decades—SCA underwrote long odds events such as hole-in-one competitions. Hamman had paid Armstrong $1.5 million for his 2002 win, and $3 million in 2003. When yet another $5 million was due for winning in 2004, Hamman became suspicious. Nobody else in the world had managed to win the Tour de France six times. *How could this be?* he wondered.

Hamman—whose bridge buddies include Bill Gates and Warren Buffett, and whose bridge team has been called the Gods of Odds—certainly didn't have any firsthand knowledge of performance-enhancing tactics, let alone any inkling of the sophisticated doping program conducted by Lance's team. But by then, American newspapers had begun covering the accusations of covert steroid use by American track-and-field athletes and baseball players, including such stars as Olympic medalist Marion Jones and San Francisco Giants slugger Barry Bonds. If steroids were involved in so many elite-level sports in the United States, Hamman figured they might be in use in European pro cycling, too. So he refused to pay Lance.

He figured he'd do a little research. Based on leads he got in Walsh's book, he began looking for pertinent information that would help him prove that Lance had cheated to attain his victory. Hamman's lawyers got in touch with investigators in France, who had launched an investigation there but had found no proof. So Hamman suggested that they track down Betsy Andreu.

Lance's wealth by then had soared. He had endorsement deals worth $16.5 million a year. But he was incensed that Hamman wouldn't pay him the $5 million bonus and he figured Hamman's refusal to pay was merely a high-stakes bluff.

Lance needed a lawyer.

Bill Stapleton brought in Tim Herman, an Austin lawyer he'd known since 1994. Herman's claim to fame was that he had represented President George W. Bush during the final year of his gubernatorial term, filing a lawsuit against a rental car company in Austin over a fender bender involving Bush's daughter, Jenna. Once Armstrong and Stapleton hired Herman and his partner, Sean Breen, they promptly filed suit in Texas state court to demand an arbitration with SCA.

This was not the only battle on the agenda for Armstrong and his crew. They were also pressuring Trek to punish Greg LeMond over doping allegations he had made to the French paper Le Monde during the 2004 Tour de France: "Lance is ready to do anything to keep his secret. . . . I don't know how he can continue to convince everybody of his innocence." The comments infuriated Armstrong and he leaned hard on Trek to sever ties with him. Trek's lawyers sent LeMond a notice saying that, by speaking out against Armstrong, he had breached his contract. Trek president John Burke sided with Armstrong and drew up plans to cancel its contract with the LeMond bike brand and to start negotiating to acquire Merckx bikes. Cooler heads prevailed, however. Trek's board decided it would be too costly and risky to hastily end their relationship with LeMond. One of Trek's advisers, Andrew K. Morris, wrote in a July 30, 2004, e-mail to Burke:

> I think we should explore every diplomatic avenue to resolve this dilemma rather than to make a judgment as to the accuracy of Greg's claim, go through the legal cost of terminating his contract, lose the profits from the line only to find ourselves back in court with even bigger legal bills, one lost tour winner and one tainted 6 time winner. . . . I'm not so sure I'd "bet the farm" on Lance being completely clean.

Meanwhile, in a laboratory outside Paris, more trouble was brewing for Armstrong. The French anti-doping agency, AFLD (Agence Française de Lutte Contre le Dopage), was conducting tests on urine samples from the 1999 Tour de France. In 1999, there had been no test for EPO, but now that there was one, the lab wanted to get a sense of how many cyclists had used the drug during that year's race. About fifty samples were still in good enough condition to be retested, and out of those fifty, a dozen were positive. Six of those tests shared the same rider identification number, but since the numbers were anonymous, the lab had no idea who the rider was. Someone at the lab leaked the rider number to French journalist Damien Ressiot, who wrote for *L'Équipe*, a French national daily sports newspaper.

Ressiot had an idea how to find out which rider matched the anonymous number.

CHAPTER ELEVEN

ADIEU AND FUCK YOU

Armstrong said the 2005 Tour de France would be his last. He would retire from cycling shortly after the race, whether he won or lost, and then embark on the next phase of his life, which would consist of campaigning for cancer awareness—and, of course, enjoying the good life of a retired athlete with a ton of money in the bank.

But there were people in cycling who thought that for Armstrong to attempt a seventh Tour de France win was greedy, that he was disrespecting the sacred race by dominating it for too long. Armstrong had six victories under his belt. It was a record that might stand forever. Why go for seven? Armstrong himself had considered retiring after his sixth. In fact, he and some partners (including his friend John Korioth) had opened a loft style bar called Six in Austin's downtown district, which seemed to suggest an ending.

Even Armstrong's sponsor thought it was time to call it quits. When the US Postal Service bowed out, Tailwind Sports got the Discovery Channel to sign on as the new sponsor. Tailwind also needed to replace a number of riders. Former teammates such as Bobby Julich, Tyler Hamilton, Levi Leipheimer, Dave Zabriskie, and of course Floyd Landis—all Americans—had all left over the years, having ultimately fallen out with Lance. Tailwind wasn't able to replace those riders with other Americans. There was simply a shortage of talent in a country whose cycling culture was tiny. By the time Armstrong was planning to go for his seventh Tour win, there was only one other American left on the team's Tour de France squad: George Hincapie. The other seven riders were mercenaries from Italy, Spain, Ukraine, and the Czech Republic. Though the team still called itself American, because it was technically based in the United States, it was American in name only, and largely operated out of Belgium and Spain.

The Discovery Channel attempted to market the other cyclists on the team as up-and-coming superstars looking to fill Armstrong's shoes when he retired, and to create suspense around the competition. But the marketing effort was a dud. American fans weren't interested in Armstrong's replacement if that replacement wasn't American; they had been passionate about the Postal team because it was an essentially American team, headed up by an American cyclist—so American that it had counted two US presidents, Bill Clinton and now George W. Bush, among its fans. Bush was such a fan that when a knee injury forced him to give up his jogging routine for a while, he had invited Lance to join him for a mountain bike ride on his Texas ranch.

At the Tour de Georgia in April of that year, the team showcased its newest up-and-comer, American Tom Danielson. The twenty-seven-year-old was known for his physiological gifts—a high VO_2 max and an ability to climb amazingly fast. He had joined the team that year, and Armstrong was riding in support of Danielson in the race. Discovery's biggest competitor was Landis. The rivalry climaxed on the fifth and penultimate stage with a brutal climb up the exceedingly steep Brasstown Bald. Landis was leading the six-day race by one minute. On the final climb, Armstrong played the role of domestique and set a blistering pace, towing a small group of riders behind him. The effort tired out Landis, and Danielson attacked, leaving Landis and Armstrong behind. As Landis lost time to Danielson, Armstrong stayed right on Landis's wheel, marking his former teammate. At the top of the climb, Armstrong sprinted around Landis and pointed at the big clock above the finish line, which showed Landis had lost the lead and now trailed Danielson by 9 seconds. It was an old-fashioned taunt.

After the race, Armstrong commented to reporters that he helped

Danielson out because he was a loyal teammate. Landis got the message. Armstrong was still bitter that Landis had left the team. It confirmed Landis's opinion of Armstrong: that he was a selfish asshole. Landis had given everything he had to Armstrong in the three years he was on the team. His contract was up, and he left for a better opportunity. Armstrong, he felt, had no reason to treat Landis with any disrespect.

As the Tour de France kicked off in 2005, the race took on a different feel. It didn't have the suspense of previous races. It felt more like a victory lap for Lance.

In the race's opening time trial, Armstrong was given the honor of going last—an advantage always extended to the defending champion. By the time he approached the starting gate, the fastest time of the day belonged to another American—shy twenty-six-year-old Dave Zabriskie, now racing for the Danish team CSC (Computer Sciences Corporation).

Zabriskie had bought his first bike after seeing the old 1970s movie *Breaking Away*. He started out riding a mountain bike in junior high in order to develop muscles in his chicken legs, and at age fifteen, he attended a meeting held by a local cycling club where he met and befriended Steve Johnson (who later went on to become president of USA Cycling). The cycling club's long, hard training rides of fifty to sixty miles provided Zabriskie with an escape from his difficult home life. His father had a long history of substance abuse, and after watching him deteriorate because of his drug addiction, Zabriskie vowed to himself that he would never take drugs. He saw cycling as a healthy, wholesome hobby that would keep him from following in his father's footsteps. In 1998, while still an amateur, he was invited to ride with Lance and Kevin Livingston. The ride was an initiation of sorts. Armstrong and his pals had their eyes on Zabriskie. After turning pro, Zabriskie joined the Postal team in 2000, where he remained until the end of the 2004 season. For his entire first year, Zabriskie, whose form was near perfect in time trials, refrained from doping. At hotels, he had seen his teammates and roommates getting injections from team doctors, but he had refused. He didn't know what these riders were taking, but he was worried that the injections might in fact be a doping product. But in 2002, after having a lackluster season, he began accepting what his teammates called "recovery" injections, which were provided by the team doctors. Eventually, despite his aversion to needles, he began injecting himself. He didn't really know what was in the syringes; the only ingredients listed on the package, which he read carefully, were vitamins.

In 2003, when Zabriskie was starting to show some real promise, Johan Bruyneel and Garcia del Moral summoned him, and then teammate Michael Barry, to a café in Girona, Spain, where they provided the two young cyclists with injectable liquids—"recovery," as well as EPO. Zabriskie was shocked. He hadn't expected this. He questioned them about the health risks of using EPO: Would he be able to have children? Was it safe? Would it cause any physical changes? The cheating aspect was of lesser concern, since it seemed as though the entire peloton was using.

"Everyone is doing it," Bruyneel told him, adding that if EPO were dangerous, no pro cyclists would be having kids. Zabriskie was terrified. But ultimately he ran out of questions and caved.

Then Bruyneel explained that EPO worked better in combination with testosterone, and he and Garcia del Moral left a box of testosterone patches behind for the two riders to split. Afterward, Zabriskie went home, called his mom, and cried.

Zabriskie's disillusionment with Bruyneel and the Postal team, and some bad luck with crashes, prompted him to consider giving up the sport. But in October 2004, he signed a two-year contract with CSC, becoming a key support rider for Italian Ivan Basso—one of Lance's major rivals in the 2005 Tour. While on the CSC team, Zabriskie used testosterone patches and took growth hormone and EPO, but he felt less pressure from CSC team management to use banned substances. In fact, the drugs he used at that time were provided to him by his friend and former Postal teammate, Floyd Landis, who was now riding for Phonak.

The 2005 Tour de France again opened with a prologue time trial, and Zabriskie had posted the best time of the day so far. Armstrong, as the defending champion, went last, and most people assumed that he would beat the time and put on the yellow jersey. But after Armstrong's final sprint across the finish line, the clock showed that he was 2 seconds behind Zabriskie. For the first time in more than a decade, an American other than Armstrong was wearing the yellow jersey. Armstrong was shocked. Zabriskie held on to the yellow jersey for the next three stages, all of them flat.

The Tour de France had scheduled a team time trial for the fourth day. Team time trials are entertaining spectacles. The riders wear high-tech aerodynamic skinsuits and long, pointy helmets to break the wind, and mount special, space-age bikes that look like human-powered fighter jets. And all the riders on a team stay together, taking turns being at the front of the line, heading into the oncoming winds.

Zabriskie's team was on track to potentially beat the Discovery Channel team when his bike accidentally touched the wheel of the rider in front of him, causing his front wheel to wobble. Zabriskie fell to the left, smacking into the metal barriers. The two teammates behind him swerved around him, and his team carried on. They were only 0.9 miles from the finish and they were still going for the win. They crossed the finish line 2 seconds behind Discovery. Armstrong was now the race leader. However, it wasn't the way Armstrong wanted to take the yellow jersey, and he informed Tour organizers that he would refuse to wear it. It's considered bad form in the Tour to capitalize—at least directly—on another's misfortune. The Tour de France, though, was trying to capitalize on Armstrong and they wanted him in the yellow jersey. They rejected his gambit and told him that if he didn't wear the jersey, he would be booted from the race.

Armstrong wore the yellow jersey until the ninth stage, when German Jens Voigt attacked on a mountain stage and gained enough time on him to take it.

By the fifteenth stage, although he hadn't won any of the individual stages, Armstrong was so comfortably in the overall lead that, in a rare move, he gave other riders on the team a chance to show off their skills. As they rode from Lézat-sur-Lèze to Saint-Lary-Soulan, George Hincapie saw an opportunity to get into an early breakaway. Hincapie clung to the wheel of another rider all the way up the mountain roads to conserve as much energy as possible. As the two men neared the finish line, Hincapie sprinted around the other rider with ease, winning the stage. Hincapie placed his hands atop his head in disbelief and seemed to be close to tears. It was as if he never expected to actually win a stage in the Tour de France, much less a mountain stage. He was known as more of a sprinter—good on the flats, not so good in the mountains. EPO had given him the power to climb. But Hincapie didn't feel he benefited from an unfair advantage. Any rider he beat probably was also on EPO, he figured. It was an equal playing field. The stage win was huge for his career, and he later thanked Armstrong for giving him the opportunity.

By the time the penultimate stage came around—a 34-mile time trial around the town of Saint-Étienne—Armstrong was so far ahead of everyone else that he could have walked the last mile and still won the Tour de France. But Armstrong felt he had to prove that he was still the fastest man in the race—that it wasn't just his strong team that was propelling him to his seventh win. Wearing his yellow Nike skinsuit, he darted out of the starting gate and headed on his way. As his smooth, aerodynamic silhouette blazed through the country roads, Armstrong rocked slightly back and forth on his bike, giving it every bit of energy he had. The effort was good enough to beat Ullrich by 23 seconds. It was Armstrong's only stage win of the race, and it was a sweet one. He led the general classification by 4 minutes, 40 seconds over Italian Ivan Basso.

On the final day of the race, the peloton left the town of Corbeil-Essonnes and took its leisurely time riding toward Paris. Armstrong again lifted a glass of champagne and posed for the cameras before crossing the finish line.

After the race, Armstrong gave a speech. The Tour de France had never before allowed the winner of the race to make remarks from the podium on the Champs-Élysées, and they probably regretted making that exception. Armstrong's words were bitter, aimed at those who doubted him, like David Walsh. "Finally, the last thing I'll say to the people who don't believe in cycling, the cynics and the skeptics: I'm sorry for you. I'm sorry that you can't dream big. I'm sorry you don't believe in miracles. But this is one hell of a race. This is a great sporting event and you should stand around and believe it. You should believe in these athletes, and you should believe in these people. . . . And there are no secrets—this is a hard sporting event and hard work wins it. So vive le Tour forever!"

About a week later, those words would seem oddly prescient. It was as if Armstrong had been telegraphing what was about to come—this time courtesy of the French press.

Damien Ressiot, of *L'Équipe*, had finally figured out a way to identify the anonymous rider who had tested positive for EPO on six urine samples from the 1999 Tour de France. He first contacted Armstrong's camp and asked them if Armstrong had any medical exemptions relating to his cancer that allowed him to take performance-enhancing drugs. Armstrong, through a spokesman, denied that he had ever taken any drugs using a medical exemption. Ressiot pressed the issue, by asking Armstrong to prove it. Armstrong agreed to give Ressiot permission to go to UCI headquarters in Aigle, Switzerland, to look up his medical forms from the 1999 Tour de France. Those forms contained Armstrong's rider number—which, just as Ressiot had suspected, matched the number on the six positive samples.

After Ressiot's story came out in *L'Équipe*, Armstrong denied the accusation. He called *L'Équipe* a sleazy French tabloid and he accused the French lab of spiking his samples with EPO and then leaking the results to the press.

Armstrong had many friends in the media, who either largely ignored the story or flat-out defended him.

The *New York Daily News* ran an article comparing the European and American commentary on the matter. Americans tended to blame the results of the urine tests on some French nationalistic desire to take down Armstrong.

"Because he didn't show up with a red wine hangover every morning, he was cheating," said Tucker Carlson on CNN. "I defend the Frogs at every turn, as you know. But this is a case of envy," he said.

"They don't mind us when we're buying their wine or storming German pillboxes. But aside from that, they don't really care for us," said Mike Lopresti of *USA Today*. "They have never been able to accept their sporting jewel being dominated by an American."

"It doesn't take a French poodle to sniff out the reasons why the laboratory leaked the results," wrote Gil LeBreton of the *Fort Worth Star-Telegram*. "The French, by nature, are skeptical of outsiders who come in and do what the French say can't be done."

Needless to say, the story didn't get much traction in the United States. *The New York Times* ran the to-the-point headline, A TOP U.S. CYCLING GROUP IS STANDING BY ARMSTRONG.

The six positive tests, though, didn't help Armstrong's ongoing case against SCA Promotions, which was still refusing to pay his $5 million in bonuses. Armstrong's lawyers had supplied SCA with paperwork that said he had undergone the proper drug testing. He had followed the rules. He deserved his bonus. End of story.

At an early procedural meeting in a downtown Dallas courtroom, both sides had agreed to have the case settled by an out-of-court arbitration panel. While the arbitration hearing was supposed to remain confidential, Armstrong and his advisers knew there was no way the case could be kept quiet. Perhaps it would be better for Armstrong's image to let it go. But that would mean giving up $5 million, and Armstrong was quite serious about getting that money.

Bob Hamman was aggressively pursuing every possible lead in his investigation. He first called Betsy Andreu in the fall of 2004. Hamman was serious over the phone, speaking in his deep, deliberate, almost guttural voice. Betsy was hesitant at first, but eventually grew to trust Hamman. Betsy's father owned a jewelry store in Detroit, and she sympathized with Hamman as a small business owner who, she felt, got screwed by Armstrong. The two began to talk often. Betsy would pass on any rumor or story she heard about Armstrong, and Hamman would try to chase it down. Hamman had a nickname for Betsy: Captain Ahab. "Captain Ahab, it's nice to hear your smiling voice, kid," he would say over the phone. "Have you found anything new? Anyone else who could tell the truth?"

In one conversation, Betsy brought up another potential witness: Stephanie McIlvain.

Andreu had persuaded McIlvain to speak with David Walsh and she became a significant source for Walsh's book and his reporting. McIlvain also spoke to ESPN, confirming the hospital room incident.

For McIlvain, it was one thing to tell David Walsh and ESPN about the hospital room scene. They protected her name and she felt comfortable that nobody would ever find out she was the source. It was another thing entirely to get involved in a lawsuit where she might have to testify on the record. McIlvain and her husband, Pat, still worked for Oakley, which still sponsored Armstrong. When Betsy called Stephanie and asked her to speak with

At thirteen, Lance (*center*) was a City of Plano Swimmer, along with his best friends. Here, he is at a meet at the Forest Park public pool in Fort Worth, Texas, in 1985, with his neighborhood friends Chann McRae (*left*) and John Boggan (*right*).

Lance (*right*), at fifteen, with Rick Crawford (*left*), before Lance's breakthrough performance at the 1987 President's Triathlon at Las Colinas Country Club, near Dallas. Lance placed sixth, beating many of the country's top pros. Rick became Lance's first cycling coach and, in 2012, would confess to providing EPO to some pro riders but not to Lance.

Scott Eder

Lance ran for the Plano East Senior High School Panthers for the 1988–89 season. He was the second finisher overall in this cross country meet, when he was a senior. Administrators asked him to withdraw from Plano East before graduation that spring, after Lance missed too many classes while training with the Junior National Cycling Team.

Lance and his mother, Linda, before a Dallas-area triathlon, 1989.

Hal Boggan

Hal Boggan

Lance is exhausted following a triathlon as a teenager, 1989.

Floyd Landis was raised amid cornfields of Lancaster County, Pennsylvania, in a family of Mennonite faith. Here's Landis in his hometown of Farmersville, more than a decade before he moved to California to take his shot at racing professionally.

Paul Landis

U.S. OLYMPICARDS
1992 U.S. OLYMPIC HOPEFULS

LANCE ARMSTRONG USA

31

LANCE ARMSTRONG
CYCLING

USA

Born: 9/18/71 Dallas, TX
Ht: 5'11" **Wt:** 165 lbs.
Hometown: Austin, TX
Club: Motorola Cycling Team
National Team: 1989-92

It's hard to believe the top amateur cyclist in America has been competing in the sport for only three years. A 2-time National Sprint Triathlon champion, Lance Armstrong rocketed into the cycling circuit in '91, winning the National Road Race Championship and becoming the first American ever to win the Settimana Bergamasca. His outstanding strength and aggressive riding style make him a cyclist to watch in Barcelona.

© 1992 Impel Marketing Inc. 36 USC 380.
Official Licensee of the U.S. Olympic Committee.

By the summer of 1992, Lance had been an amateur cyclist for three years. His Olympicard touted his victory in the 1991 win in Italy's eleven-day Settimana Bergamasca, which launched his career but led to bad feelings with his team, Subaru-Montgomery. He had a contract to ride for Motorola before the Olympics.

In 1993, Lance won $1 million put up by Thrift Drug, a chain owned by JC Penney, as a promotional gimmick that nobody actually thought could be won. It was reportedly the biggest prize ever offered in bike racing.

In the 1996 Olympic Games, in Atlanta, Lance finished sixth in the time trial.

In Barcelona, Lance greets his mom, Linda; J. T. Neal (with bag); and his grandfather PaPa (in sun visor), before the 1992 Olympic Games men's road race. Lance would place fourteenth.

In early 1998, Lance announced he would marry Kristin Richard, shown here in Austin that year.

Jim Ochowicz, Lance's close friend and the godfather to his son Luke. Och played a key role in Lance's career while he was Motorola team manager. Here he wears his old Motorola team kit at the 1998 Ride for the Roses, in Austin, Texas.

Lance signs posters in Austin at the first Ride for the Roses, in March 1997, raising $20,000 for the new Lance Armstrong Foundation.

Floyd Landis during the 2003
Tour de France, outside the team bus.

A testosterone patch used
by George Hincapie during
the 2003 or 2004 season.

EPO, a synthetic form of the
natural hormone erythropoietin,
typically must be refrigerated.
While in Europe in the mid-1990s,
some riders spent several hundred
dollars for one month's EPO
supply, purchased at pharmacies in
Switzerland.

The US Postal team poses during the 2004 Tour de France.

Lance (*second from left*) prepares to ring the opening bell at the New York Stock Exchange in April 2005. He is joined by NYSE President Robert G. Britz (*far left*), Bristol-Myers Squibb CEO Peter R. Dolan (*second from right*), and Lance's agent, Bill Stapleton (*far right*), of Capital Sports & Entertainment.

Lance loved his Gulfstream G-IV jet, Mellow Johnny's Aviation, shown here in 2011.

Timothy Archibald

Thomas Weisel and some of the elite, bike-loving executives who put roughly $1 million annually into USA Cycling for training young American bike racers, 2006.

Dennis Kleiman

David "Tiger" Williams of
Williams Trading LLC, 2006

Tim De Waele/TDWsport.com/Corbis

Lance (*right*), with Johan Bruyneel, the *directeur sportif*
of Team RadioShack, after his last Tour de France,
in 2010. Lance finished in 23rd place, 39 minutes
and 20 seconds behind Alberto Contador. Contador
was later disqualified after failing a doping test.

US Anti-Doping
Agency chief
executive Travis
Tygart (*left*), and
USADA general
counsel William
"Bill" Bock (*below*).

Polish defector Eddie Borysewicz, who
opened an office at the US Olympic
Training Center in Squaw Valley,
California; introduced the concept of team
tactics; and whipped American riders into
shape, often telling them they were too fat.

Edward Borysewicz

Above and below: Raftermen Photography

Betsy and Frankie Andreu at their
home in Dearborn, Michigan, 2012.

Greg LeMond with his three
Tour de France trophies in his
home in Minneapolis, 2013.

Lance Armstrong insists he never used performance-enhancing drugs during a
2005 sworn deposition in Austin, Texas. He sued SCA Promotions when it refused to pay some of his bonus money for his victory in the 2004 Tour de France.

Hamman, she balked. Eventually, SCA subpoenaed McIlvain to testify. She notified executives at Oakley, including its billionaire founder, Jim Jannard, of the subpoena.

Just days before Frankie's scheduled deposition, he received a phone call from Lance, telling him that Craig Nichols, his primary oncologist at the hospital in Indianapolis where he had been treated for cancer, was going to sign an affidavit saying that his hospital confession never happened. Lance didn't make any threats against Frankie, except to suggest that any testimony would be meaningless compared with a doctor's affidavit. But Betsy felt the call was an attempt to intimidate him—that the unspoken message was: I'm watching you. I'm in control.

In October 2005, Betsy showed up alone for her deposition, which was held in a conference room in a nondescript hotel in Romulus, near Detroit. Two surprise visitors walked in: Lance and Bart Knaggs. Betsy freaked out. "Oh my God! Oh my God! Oh my God!" she kept saying in a quiet whisper. But she went on to recount the hospital room scene—including Lance's admissions and her subsequent dramatic threat to break off her engagement to Frankie—while Lance sat on the opposite side of the conference table, alternately staring at her and looking down at his cell phone to send frequent texts.

Once Betsy finished her testimony, Lance and Knaggs left the room and headed to a small airport, boarding a private jet to New York, where Lance joined Sheryl to tape an appearance on *Saturday Night Live*. Lance was included in a skit in which he fended off a fake Frenchman who demanded a urine sample and screamed, "It's our race. Stop winning it! *J'accuse!*"

Betsy got a call from Stephanie McIlvain, who was upset. Stephanie said her husband had been called into a meeting by an Oakley executive. If Stephanie testified about the hospital room scene, the executive said, she and her husband would lose their jobs at Oakley.

Frankie and Betsy were devastated. They had been counting on at least one other person to back them up. Now they'd be exposed, isolated. It would be easy for Armstrong to discredit them as disgruntled crazies.

A few weeks later, Lance showed up at the downtown Austin office of his lawyer, Tim Herman, for his own deposition, dressed casually in a shirt with the cuffs left unbuttoned. He was ornery and difficult that day, and everything Jeff Tillotson asked him left him in a state of high agitation.

When Tillotson asked Armstrong if he thought Frankie, his old friend, was lying about the hospital room, Armstrong responded, "One hundred percent. But I feel for him."

"What do you mean by that?" Tillotson asked.

"Well, I think he's trying to back up his old lady," Armstrong said.

Armstrong said the hospital room scene never happened. "How could it have taken place when I've never taken performance-enhancing drugs?" he said.

"Okay," Tillotson said.

"How could that have happened?" Armstrong asked again.

"That was my point. You're not—it's not simply, you don't recall. Just—"

"How many times do I have to say it?!" Armstrong asked.

"I'm just trying to make sure your testimony is clear," Tillotson shot back.

"Well, if it can't be any clearer than 'I've never taken drugs,' then incidents like that could never have happened," he said. "How clear is that?"

In fact, Lance seemed so genuinely infuriated at being asked questions about his use of performance-enhancing drugs that Tillotson began to question the case. Is he pathological? Or could it be that we have it wrong?

Armstrong said he would never dope, never take a banned substance, never reinfuse his own blood—and it was preposterous to suggest otherwise. Outraged by the suggestion that he was a doper, he provided a touching rationale for why he had remained clean:

Doping would destroy the hopes of millions of his American fans. It "would all go away," Armstrong said. The "faith of all of the cancer survivors around the world. So everything I do off the bike would go away, too. And don't think for a second that I don't understand that. It's not about money for me. *Everything*. It's also about the faith that people have put in me over the years. So all of that would be erased. So I don't need it to say in a contract, you're fired if you test positive. That's not as important as losing the support of hundreds of millions of people."

Despite Armstrong's denials, the testimony in the SCA arbitration did seem damning. Frankie and Betsy Andreu had both sworn under oath that they witnessed Armstrong telling his doctors in Indiana that he had used human growth hormone, EPO, testosterone, steroids, and cortisone. Stephen Swart, his former Motorola teammate, said in a videotaped deposition that Armstrong was the instigator in the team's EPO use. Kathy LeMond, Greg's wife, said she attended a dinner party in France at which Armstrong's mechanic, Julien de Vriese told her Armstrong had paid $500,000 to get out of a positive drug test. De Vriese guessed the money must have come from Nike. And of course the recent story in L'Équipe was another powerful indicator that Armstrong had been doping at least as far back as 1999.

As the arbitration hearings entered the final phase, in January 2006, Lance's lawyers cited material from Dr. Edward F. Coyle's article in the *Journal of Applied Physiology*, extolling Armstrong's extraordinary physical gifts, to explain how he had been able to make such a spectacular comeback from cancer and go on to have such a remarkable string of successes. And they showed the arbitrators the 2005 Discovery Channel documentary *The Science of Lance Armstrong*, which also went into detail about Lance's superhuman physiology.

On a later day during those January hearings, Lance was called to give testimony. Speaking before a panel of three lawyers who were serving as arbitrators, Lance displayed a demeanor dramatically different from his behavior during the deposition in his lawyer's office in Austin. He was polite, even charming. When cross-examined about some pills he was alleged to have shown Frankie Andreu, Lance demurred, "I have to confess—if you want a confession—I'm a little bit of a coffee fiend," and asserted that what Andreu had seen were caffeine pills (which at the time were allowed at low doses)

Lance also cited the book *Lance Armstrong's War*, which Dan Coyle wrote after spending the 2004 season in Girona, Spain, with Armstrong, Hincapie, and Landis. "As you can see from that book, for a bunch of people that are trying to hide [something], there really wasn't a lot of hiding going on," Lance asserted.

To prove that Lance had been tested for drugs and found to be clean, his lawyers also submitted a 2005 affidavit from Travis Tygart, then the general counsel of the US Anti-Doping Agency, stating that Lance had taken part in USADA's testing program and was under its jurisdiction. What the panel didn't hear was that the two men had never met in person, though in 2004, Tygart had heard from Bill Stapleton, who offered the agency a donation of $250,000. Tygart had rejected the funds, saying that the agency's ethics policy prohibited it from taking gifts from people it might be testing in the future.

For its part, in addition to the depositions, SCA included testimony from an Australian scientist named Michael Ashenden, who questioned the validity of the science behind Edward Coyle's study. Ashenden who, like Coyle, was a paid consultant, said he didn't buy Coyle's conclusions. "There's inconsistencies there which, to my mind, make me question the validity of it," he said. "I still haven't seen any data that suggests there was an improvement in efficiency and, therefore, as a scientist, I couldn't take that as an explanation," he said. In part because of pressure from Ashenden, Coyle would later be forced to write a letter admitting errors in his math.

Ashenden noted several other inconsistencies in the myth of Armstrong versus the reality. Armstrong's oxygen uptake—the sheer rate at which his body is able to use oxygen—was only mediocre compared to many other top-level endurance athletes. "It struck me that, gee, that's lower than what I would have expected," he said.

Ashenden pointed out that Armstrong's body weight was about the same before and after cancer. "Something that I'd always read about Armstrong is his explanation for this improvement in performance is that during the cancer, he remodeled his body," Ashenden said. "I was given a pretty brief opportunity to review his medical records," he said. "I can't see where he lost his body weight and when, and none of the data that I've seen would make me think any different. He's virtually the same weight." Ashenden said Coyle's slide showing Armstrong to be a one-in-a-billion human being was "baseless. There was no scientific rationale for the conclusions that he reached."

Powerful as its case might have seemed, SCA's legal position was flawed. Even if the evidence against Armstrong showed overwhelmingly that he had doped, he had not been stripped of his titles. Unless the UCI, the sport's official governing body, concluded that Armstrong doped, SCA was unlikely to win its case, regardless of the evidence.

Making things more problematic for SCA was a ruling by the arbitration panel that said the company should be treated as a traditional insurance company. Under Texas law, that meant that if SCA lost the case, it would be liable for triple damages. Facing the possibility of financial catastrophe, in February 2006, Bob Hamman decided to drop the case, despite the fact that he still believed in its validity. Opting to settle, SCA was required to pay $7 million, the amount of the contested bonus plus legal expenses—the most Armstrong and Tailwind could've gotten from SCA without bankrupting it.

Lance had won, leaving Hamman furious.

The SCA case was but one of many lawsuits Tim Herman and other members of Armstrong's legal team were handling on his behalf, and it wasn't the only one in which they were successful. For example, the suit they had filed against *The Sunday Times* for an article based on David Walsh and Pierre Ballester's book, *L.A. Confidentiel,* resulted in the paper making a £300,000 settlement offer after the High Court ruled that the article had wrongly left readers with the impression that Lance was a fraud, a cheat, and a liar.

Lance's lawsuit didn't stop Walsh from working on a new book incorporating additional evidence of Lance's doping, including the material about his positive EPO tests during the 1999 Tour de France. But it seemed as though Lance was going to get away with that, too, thanks to UCI president Hein Verbruggen. Within weeks of the appearance of Damien Ressiot's story about the EPO tests, UCI announced it was hiring an independent inspector—the lawyer Emile Vrijman, who happened to be a friend of Verbruggen's—to look into the accusations in *L'Équipe.* When Vrijman's report finally came out in June 2006, it ignored the overwhelming evidence of doping by Armstrong and instead focused mainly on how the lab hadn't followed the rules when it retested old samples. It did not actually refute the claims by the French journalist. It merely said the samples couldn't be used for an "official" positive.

Most newspapers reported that Armstrong had been exonerated. "Report clears Armstrong of doping in 1999 Tour de France," the Associated Press said. Lance "got a boost yesterday toward clearing his name of doping allegations connected with his triumph in the 1999 Tour de France," reported *The New York Times.* "Vrijman stated that there was no proof that Armstrong had used EPO," the article said, citing the independent report. Armstrong's chief mythologists must have been breathing huge sighs of relief.

Despite all the serious allegations being leveled at Armstrong, nothing was having an effect on his marketability or on his reputation. Lance was on top of the world, at the height of his fame, and the money was rolling in. He still had hugely lucrative endorsement deals with Nike and Oakley and many others. He continued to serve on the White House cancer panel. He was jet-setting around the globe, meeting with world leaders to talk about cancer awareness.

In cycling circles, Armstrong's name was beginning to be sullied. On cycling message boards, anonymous posters debated the possibility that Lance had raced clean. But the debate was confined largely to those forums. The mainstream press had moved on.

Lance meanwhile had embarked on a new Casanova phase of his life. In February 2006, he and Sheryl Crow called off their engagement. She had put her career on hold for a while to support his bid for global cycling supremacy, joining him on the podium after his seventh Tour victory, and once he retired and she went back to singing, he had joined her at her concerts and TV appearances. But Lance said he didn't want more children; she did (and adopted a baby boy about fifteen months later).

In early 2006, SCA's Jeff Tillotson and his wife went to a football game in Austin, where he saw Lance seated on the sidelines with a brunette beauty. Tillotson snapped a photo of Lance and his date and sent it over to Lance's lawyer, Sean Breen. The two had developed a cordial relationship during the course of the hearings, despite their being on opposite sides of the case. Breen, who is Tim Herman's partner, replied a day later by sending Tillotson a link to a *Penthouse* magazine centerfold photo of the woman in question. He also told Tillotson via e-mail that things were now "so over" between Lance and Sheryl.

With Armstrong out of professional cycling, the Tour de France was wide open for the taking. And Floyd Landis believed he had a shot, all but his last. He had been through three hip surgeries, and doctors were telling him that, at the end of the season, he would need to have a complete hip replacement. Landis could barely walk. The only physical activity he could do, actually, was ride a bike. Of course he'd been doing that with the help of doping, and he would need to keep doping if he were to have a chance of winning the Tour. But doping had become increasingly problematic for him, as the Phonak team had no organized system for it. This meant he had had to make his own arrangements, and they hadn't always worked out so well. Midway through the stages of the 2005 Tour, for example, he'd had a near fatal catastrophe involving a transfusion. After an elaborately choreographed top secret delivery of blood, Landis connected the bag to a coat hanger in his hotel room, and inserted a needle. The next day, a rest day, Landis began to feel strange. He had trouble breathing, felt dizzy, and his entire body was in intense pain. Landis was secretly rushed to the hospital, where he was treated for serious complications stemming from the transfusion. Nobody ever found out about his brush with death, and he was back in time for the beginning of the next stage. Landis never found out what happened. Did he get someone else's blood? Was the blood tainted in some way? Landis felt he was lucky just to be alive.

Understandably concerned about avoiding such incidents in the future, Landis met with the owner of Phonak, Andy Rihs, prior to the 2006 season, to talk about his Tour de France aspirations—and what he felt he needed in order to fulfill them. Rihs is a boisterous, overweight business mogul and one of the richest men in Switzerland. In the meeting, Landis told Rihs that he believed he could win the Tour de France. But to help him do it, he wanted the team to operate more like the US Postal team—by which he meant that it should have an organized doping program. During the previous season, Landis had arranged for all of his own doping, but it was too stressful, too time consuming, and too expensive. He couldn't keep doing it alone, and he couldn't afford it. He asked Rihs if he would fund a doping program for Phonak. Rihs agreed. By asking Rihs to bring the doping in-house, Landis may have dodged a bullet. He had been thinking about hiring Eufemiano Fuentes, who operated a blood-doping clinic in Madrid. That June, Fuentes became the center of the biggest doping scandal since the Festina affair. His clinic, which he ran out of an apartment in an upscale residential building, was raided by Spanish police in what became known as Operación Puerto. Dr. Fuentes was caught with an apartment full of blood plasma belonging to half of the professional peloton in Europe. Many of the cyclists had used code names on their blood bags, but they weren't exactly mastermind criminals, and the names they had come up with were often easy for the investigators to decipher—sometimes by simply reading their blogs. Other riders used the names of their pets. The probe nabbed two of the biggest stars in professional cycling: Jan Ullrich and Ivan Basso. Also discovered was a fax sent by Fuentes to Haven Parchinski, the maiden name of Tyler Hamilton's wife, listing how much Hamilton had paid and still owed Fuentes for his treatments.

Puerto's aftermath, which brought a temporary halt to the careers of many of cycling's greatest athletes, meant Landis's chances of winning the Tour de France had improved significantly. Some cycling fans now considered him the overall favorite.

To stateside fans, Floyd Landis was still relatively unknown. It wasn't until late June 2006, just a few weeks before the Tour, that any of the American media began to pay much attention to him, when *The New York Times Magazine* ran a long piece, authored by Daniel Coyle, centered around his upcoming hip surgery. But even in a piece that was ostensibly about Landis, the underlying story was about whether another American would be able to fill Armstrong's shoes. It described Landis as "one of America's hopefuls in the race now that Lance Armstrong has retired from the sport." The article made little mention of the news of the massive doping scandal—Operation Puerto—that had just broken in Europe.

Landis's Tour de France effort began disastrously. In the opening time trial, when it was his turn to go, he wasn't there. The clock ticked down. Beep, beep, beeeeeeep! No Landis. Suddenly, he appeared, running frantically to the starting gate with his bike. He'd gotten a flat just as his turn was coming up, and he was still changing the tire when the clock chimed. Under the Tour de France rules, there are no exceptions during time trials. So Landis would be docked precious seconds from his total time.

Landis was able to redeem himself on the second time trial of the race, where he finished second, and secured a spot near the top of the standings. On stage 11, the race finally hit the mountains, and Landis found himself at the front of a small pack of riders. Top climber Michael Rasmussen put in a hard attack on the final ascent in an attempt to help his Rabobank teammate, Denis Menchov. Landis clung to Rasmussen's wheel. With him was Levi Leipheimer, the former Postal team member, now racing for the German-based Gerolsteiner team. By the time they were approaching the summit, it was only Landis, Menchov, and Leipheimer. Landis knew all he had to do was stick to Menchov's wheel. He didn't care about a stage win. Just time. But his performance was strong enough that he won the stage anyway.

When Landis donned the yellow jersey at the top of the mountain pass, Armstrong was nearby, watching as a spectator and as part owner of the Discovery Channel team. Later that day, during the Phonak team dinner, one of the Phonak riders gave Landis some disturbing information. Armstrong had offered $20,000 to any rider who could ensure that Landis would not win the Tour de France. Landis didn't know whether Armstrong had made the offer to intimidate him or mess with his head, or if he was actually taking out the cycling equivalent of a "hit" on him. He decided to keep the news within the small circle of riders at the dinner table, instead of reporting the incident to the UCI or going to the press.

During the next few days, Landis went in and out of the lead, alternating with Spaniard Óscar Pereiro. On stage 13, Landis fell behind and missed the winning breakaway. He was now 1 minute, 29 seconds behind Pereiro. But on stage 15, Landis regained the lead and the yellow jersey. He looked as if he might maintain the lead all the way to Paris.

Stage 16 was a grueling day in the mountains that included four climbs over a 113-mile course. With an average grade of 6 percent, the final climb of the day, La Toussuire, was not particularly steep, but at 11.43 miles, it was long. Landis began the climb well, keeping up with all the other top riders. But something wasn't right with him. He felt flat. As the climb began, Pereiro and the other riders pulled out ahead. Spaniard Carlos Sastre attacked, getting out of the saddle and challenging the group to a mountain duel. Landis fell behind immediately. Landis looked like he was in pain, and was "cracking," as they say in cycling. By the end of the day, his Tour de France hopes seemed to be over. Having lost a whopping 10 minutes of time, he was now 8 minutes behind race leader Pereiro.

When Landis went back to the team hotel, his hip was killing him and he considered abandoning the race. Severely depressed over the day's performance, he was sure his next surgery would dash any future hope of winning the biggest race on the planet. That night he did something few had done during the Tour de France since the 1930s, when alcohol was viewed as the best way to ease the pain of bike racing: He downed a couple of shots of whiskey and a beer. He felt he deserved it. Besides, what was the point of abstinence? Calmed by his "meds," Landis decided to stay in the race. And he decided to try something crazy.

Stage 17 went from Saint-Jean-de-Maurienne to Morzine. It included five climbs over 123 miles. As always, it was assumed that the race leaders would stay together until the final climb, where they would race all-out to the summit finish. On the first climb, less than two hours into the five and a half hour day, Landis took off and attacked. The other riders in the pack looked at each other, perplexed. Landis had no teammates with him. He was all alone. It looked as if Landis, dejected from the previous day's performance, was going out on a suicide mission—but giving up in style. As he pedaled in front of the pack, his lead grew. One minute, two minutes, five minutes.

Then, he was more than 8 minutes ahead of the pack, which included Pereiro. This wasn't necessarily good, because at some point the pack riders, who could hear in their radios how far up the road Landis was getting, were going to start organizing themselves to chase him down.

Since Pereiro was wearing the yellow jersey and had the most to lose, he was expected to organize the chase. But on this hot summer day, there was confusion in the peloton. Pereiro's team was relatively weak, and wanted riders from other teams to aid in the chase. But they all refused. Their message: You don't want to lead the chase? Fine, then don't. But you'll lose the yellow jersey.

The in-fighting delayed the pursuit of Landis long enough that as the final climb approached, he was so far ahead that he actually had a chance to come back into the race lead. However, as he began to pedal up the Col de Joux

Plane, his lead shrunk rapidly. It was 8 minutes, then 7 minutes and 30 seconds, then 7 at the top of the climb.

Landis still had to descend from the top of the Joux Plane into the town of Morzine. He tucked himself into an aero position and took every risk possible on the downhill to regain as much time as he could. As he crossed the finish line, he pumped his fist in the air. And then he waited as the clock ticked down. By the time Pereiro crossed the line, his lead over Landis had diminished from over 8 minutes to 31 seconds. Landis was in third place, and by all calculations, he would be able to regain the lead during the final time trial.

Two days later, Landis donned his skinsuit and aerodynamic bike for the final time trial. This time, he didn't get a flat tire at the start, and beat Pereiro handily, taking the yellow jersey with a lead of 59 seconds.

On the final day, on the ride into Paris, it was Landis's turn to sip champagne and pose for the cameras—his turn to take a victory lap around the Champs-Élysées.

As Landis stood on the winner's podium, he was truly happy. Not so much because he wanted to be a hero, or famous, but because the win meant money. His bills, his mortgage, his cars, his Harley-Davidson, would all be paid off now. With the endorsement money that was sure to follow his victory, he could support his family in style and comfort. The glory of it all was secondary.

The giddy feeling lasted only a few days. Floyd was in Holland to participate in a criterium race when he got the devastating call. His urine sample after the seventeenth stage of the Tour de France had registered abnormally high for testosterone. He was on the verge of being given a positive test and being stripped of his title.

Landis discussed his predicament with the team owner, Andy Rihs, and with Jim Ochowicz, who was still consulting for Phonak. Before they even had time to come up with a plan, news of the test had already been leaked to the press. It was too late.

A day after the news came out, Landis held a press conference in Spain. He showed up unprepared, not sure what he should say. When asked whether he had used banned substances, he hesitated and finally answered: "I'll say no."

The answer was a red flag—a bombshell of an answer that almost counted as an admission. Fifteen minutes after the press conference, Landis's phone rang. It was Armstrong calling with some advice. "Look . . . when people ask you . . . did you ever use performance-enhancing drugs, you need to say absolutely not." Landis agreed. He would steadfastly deny doping from that point forward.

Landis flew back to the United States and tried to figure out what to do next. He spoke with a number of confidants. For a while, he stayed in the Manhattan home of Doug Ellis, a wealthy and successful financial industry software engineer who was considering starting a cycling team. At Ellis's suggestion, Floyd met with Jonathan Vaughters, who was now team director for a semipro cycling team. Vaughters saw no easy way out of it, though. He knew that the anti-doping machinery had become too powerful. Landis would never make it through. Floyd's best option, Vaughters suggested, was to admit everything. To lay everything on the table, even if that meant blowing up the sport. If he did that, Vaughters said, the story would become about cycling, and not about Floyd. It would lift an enormous weight off of Floyd's shoulders. If he fought, as Hamilton had, he would lose, and discredit and bankrupt himself.

Vaughters of course had his own secrets, and knew all about the weight of carrying them. Having lied to his friends and family about doping for years, he was dying to disclose the truth about his own doping. But the closest he had come to doing so was to allow the *New York Times* reporter Juliet Macur to quote him anonymously in a story she had written about Frankie Andreu. In the story, she reported that both Andreu and an unnamed rider had admitted using EPO, but that neither had seen Armstrong do so. In fact, Vaughters had told Macur that he would not answer that particular question—which he thought was a clear way of saying, "Yes, I saw Armstrong dope. I'm not going to deny it, but I'm not going to confirm it, either."

Landis began to seriously consider coming clean. But when he spoke again with Armstrong as well as other people in the cycling industry, they all advised him to fight the charges. He couldn't admit to doping, they said, because a revelation could expose the entire team as well as its support staffers.

Landis still hoped to get back into the sport, and bombshell allegations would eliminate that possibility.

About a month after Landis's positive test, his father-in-law and best friend, David Witt, committed suicide, shooting himself in the head. The co-owner of a local restaurant and an avid bodybuilder, Witt had become one of Landis's drug suppliers. Witt got prescriptions in his own name for the drugs Landis needed—including testosterone and human growth hormone. Though Witt had long suffered from depression, Landis was certain his own disgrace had at least contributed to Witt's suicide.

Landis was devastated and depressed. It felt as if his life were in the middle of a massive mudslide, wiping away everything in its path.

Anguished and desperate, Landis again reached out to Jim Ochowicz. He figured Ochowicz was one of the few people who would understand the situation he was in and be able to advise him about what to do. Ochowicz had been there in St. Moritz when Landis and Armstrong were training with Michele Ferrari. And Ochowicz knew everything there was to know about the cycling world. Not only was he still the president of USA Cycling, and still an employee of Thom Weisel's, but he knew all the key players, including of course Lance Armstrong, with whom he was close.

When Landis called, Ochowicz was staying in the Hollywood home of Sheryl Crow. She was a good friend, and had remained so even after she and Armstrong split up. Ochowicz invited Landis to come and talk. Landis drove his Harley-Davidson up from Temecula. Crow brought the two men drinks and sandwiches, then left the house about ten minutes later. As they sat on her veranda overlooking downtown L.A., Landis said, "Listen, you know what's going on in cycling. You and I both know about the doping programs on every team you've ever run, certainly the US Postal team."

"Yeah, yeah," Ochowicz responded.

"I can't fight it anymore," Landis said. "I don't want to be broke and feel guilty, and that's what's about to happen. I don't mind being broke, but I'm not going to feel shitty anymore," he said. "My two choices here are either fight this or just admit to it and clear my conscience. I'll tell you what I'm not going to do. I'm not going to take the fall for this sport and walk away and just get beaten up the rest of my life. At the very least, I'm going to clear my conscience."

Ochowicz gave Landis some firm advice: He should say nothing. Nobody would believe him anyway. The allegations would drag down the entire sport and ruin not only his career but the careers of others. The only option was to fight the charges in every way he could, Ochowicz said. Floyd didn't explicitly ask Ochowicz for money, but it was clear that was what Floyd needed if he were to continue his denials. "Look, I need some support," Landis pleaded.

"Let me make some phone calls and I'll let you know," Ochowicz said.

A few days later, Landis got a call from Bill Stapleton, who demanded to know why Floyd had asked Ochowicz for money. Floyd explained that he was short on cash and could use some help. Over and over, Stapleton kept asking him, "Why should we help you out?" Landis felt that Stapleton was trying to goad him into threatening them with extortion if they didn't give him money.

Despite Stapleton's call, Armstrong did arrange to help Floyd. Not directly—Armstrong couldn't risk the association—but he connected Landis to some of his own wealthy backers, like Thom Weisel and John Bucksbaum. Tiger Williams, whom Landis already knew, also helped out.

If Landis stayed quiet about the doping, there was an enticing carrot: money to help him fight the US Anti-Doping Agency.

But if he came clean in order to clear his conscience, he knew there was a giant stick: the wrath of Armstrong. Lance, Stapleton, and their powerful friends would try to discredit and destroy him.

CHAPTER TWELVE

THE COMEBACK (AGAIN)

In winter 2006, newly single Lance was spending even more time with his celebrity pals, traveling with actor Matthew McConaughey to South Beach, where they hit the beach and the clubs, and accompanying Jake Gyllenhaal to the National Arts Awards in New York.

Lance also registered for his first marathon, the New York City Marathon—a way to fill what he characterized as the void in his life after he quit professional cycling. The marathon, held in November, was also a way for him to keep both himself and Nike, his main sponsor, in the public eye as he approached the ten-year anniversary of his initial cancer diagnosis.

Nike was already so invested in Lance that it had named a building on its corporate campus in Beaverton, Oregon, after him. The Lance Armstrong Fitness Center had an Olympic-size pool and a multistory rock-climbing wall, as well as a spinning studio, a Pilates studio, and a weight room. But now Nike was turning to Lance for a fresh boost to its flagging business. At the time Lance registered for the marathon, Nike was scrambling to meet the changing tastes and demands of consumers who could order thirty-dollar sneakers online, and its executives were under pressure to improve their profit margins. Looking for ways to capitalize on the inspirational aspects of Lance's life and incorporate them into their product line, they had come up with an ingenious new idea. With Lance now training for the world's most famous marathon, Nike arranged for him to promote a new device that had grown out of Nike's partnership with Apple. The device, the so-called Nike+iPod, made it possible for runners to collect their personal speed and distance data on Apple iPods, at a cost of about $300, which included the iPod itself as well as specially outfitted $100 sneakers that connected to a sensor. The iPod also featured a prerecorded download of Lance chanting a series of motivational mantras. When the runner accessed his results, he would hear Lance saying things like "Congratulations! You've just set a personal mileage record!"

Running was not new to Lance. In his eyes, in fact, running was his first sport; it had come before swimming, before cycling, before triathlons. When he was a rebellious teen, with a pierced ear sporting a diamond stud, he was the fastest runner on the Plano East High School cross-country team, which won Dallas district championships. He had continued to run throughout the years, even while cycling professionally, as a form of cross-training.

Just days before the marathon, however, Lance came down with a bad case of shin splints. Not to be deterred from entering the race, he took heavy doses of ibuprofen and iced his shins, ran the marathon—paced by running great Alberto Salazar, a world-renowned marathoner and consultant to Nike—and came in 868th. His time, which was just under three hours, was obviously a long way from breaking any records, but his friends were impressed, for he had run the last three or four miles of the race in intense pain, which it turns out was from a stress fracture. To this day, his close friends hold up his performance in that marathon as evidence of his extraordinary determination and persistence.

These were the qualities Lance wanted to project in his postretirement years, as he worked on expanding his image as a symbol of inspiration and motivation not only for cancer survivors but also for America's Average Joes and underdogs. His friends in Hollywood helped reinforce that image, casting him for a cameo role in the 2006 movie You, Me and Dupree, executive produced by and starring his Dallas-born buddy, Owen Wilson. In the movie, Wilson's character, Dupree, loses his job and moves in with his newlywed friends, played by Kate Hudson and Matt Dillon. Dupree's character is essentially that of a hapless loser, but throughout the film, he keeps mentioning Lance as his inspiration.

At one point in the movie, the Matt Dillon character says to his friend: "You get your first ten-speed bike, and suddenly you're Lance Armstrong." Dupree responds: "Let's leave Lance out of this. Guy's done more with one testicle than you and I could do with three."

The movie ends with Dupree having transformed himself into a successful author and a motivational speaker, and features a shot of his hero, Lance, reading Dupree's popular inspirational book, whose cover is a knockoff of *It's Not About the Bike*. Lying in the grass, wearing his trademark yellow Livestrong wristband, Lance is holding the book open and trying out different pronunciations of the word "Lance-ness."

That was not the first time Hollywood had deployed Lance as a real-life inspirational figure. Two years earlier, he had done a cameo in Rawson Marshall Thurber's movie *Dodgeball: A True Underdog Story*, starring Ben Stiller and Vince Vaughn. Armstrong, playing himself, had a pivotal scene in which he inspired the character played by Vince Vaughn to continue his David and Goliath struggle against a commercial megalith. A sample bit of dialogue:

La Fleur: "Uh, actually I decided to quit . . . Lance."

Armstrong: "Quit? You know, once I was thinking about quitting when I was diagnosed with brain, lung, and testicular cancer, all at the same time. But with the love and support of my friends and family, I got back on the bike and I won the Tour de France five times in a row."

Lance's celebrity opened all kinds of doors for him, and not just in Hollywood. He had always had a taste for beautiful women, and, single again, he was in a great position to meet whoever struck his fancy. In January 2007, he noticed a feature on socialite and fashion designer Tory Burch—who could have been Sheryl Crow's long-lost twin sister—in *Vanity Fair* magazine. He used his connections to score a date. They quickly became an item, and their relationship brought them both a lot of attention. That April, Tory was at his side when he opened his Austin home to 450 people to celebrate the tenth anniversary of the Lance Armstrong Foundation. But Lance and Tory broke up by that fall. The strain of trying to carry on a long-distance relationship—Lance had children in Austin, Tory had children in New York—was too great.

After their breakup, Lance began a brief and public romance with the petite twenty-one-year-old actress Ashley Olsen, fifteen years his junior, who was sighted perched in his lap at the bar of New York's Gramercy Park Hotel. In the spring of 2008, he began seeing the actress Kate Hudson, following her breakup with Owen Wilson. But Lance broke off the relationship just a few months later. Not long after that, he became more seriously involved with Anna Hansen, a University of Colorado at Boulder graduate and mountain-biking enthusiast, whom he had first met at a corporate speaking gig in Denver in early 2007, when she was working for a nonprofit that offered outdoor adventures to young adults with cancer.

Around this time, there was even talk that Lance might run for public office. Perhaps governor of Texas. Or even the Senate. Lance hadn't declared any party allegiance, but he was pro-choice and supported increased health care coverage and gun control—positions that might have enabled him to win favor from Democrats, who were already looking ahead to finding a strong candidate to challenge the Republican incumbent, Rick Perry, in the next gubernatorial race, in 2010.

Lance squashed the speculation that he might run for the Senate seat, however, by explaining that he didn't love the idea of spending half the year living in Washington, DC. And no wonder: He'd recently moved into an 8,000-square-foot Spanish colonial mansion in Austin, with a pool, cabana, green lawns, and a row of Italian cypress trees. He decorated his new home with huge paintings of minimalist Pop art, placing one Ed Ruscha painting—with the words *safe and effective medication* spelled out against a backdrop of storm clouds—prominently on his living room wall.

Armstrong and his agent, Bill Stapleton, also began to look for new investments and business ventures. In mid-2007, New Sun Nutrition, Inc., a Santa Barbara–based distributor of FRS energy drink, made Armstrong the FRS spokesperson and put him on the board—around the same time that it received $25 million in a funding round in which Thom Weisel participated. The sports drink company also gave Lance a financial stake. FRS, which stands for Free Radical Scavenger, hired an ad agency that had done work with Nike to play up its scientific claims. In one video on FRS's site, Lance touted the energy boost he claimed he got from the drink: "Five minutes later you feel strong, fifteen minutes later you feel strong, an hour later you still feel strong." FRS agreed to give Lance's foundation a percentage of its profits, and the foundation made it the official sports drink at its events, such as Livestrong bike races and marathons. The drink company claimed that a plant-based supplement called quercetin added to the drink provided a natural boost of energy. As is the case with many energy drinks, FRS's claims were probably a bit overblown.

Armstrong also put together an unusual deal with Demand Media, a Silicon Valley web content company, after he became friends with its co-founder, Richard Rosenblatt, the former chairman of MySpace.com. Demand Media came up with the idea of starting a website under the name Livestrong .com, which would be a for-profit company that would make money mostly from web advertising. As part of the deal, Armstrong and Stapleton's firm, Capital Sports & Entertainment, got stock options from Demand Media, which was planning its IPO. With Lance's foundation now using Livestrong.org as its website address, there were now two Livestrong addresses—one for the for-profit health website (the .com), and one for the foundation website (the .org). By the time of the IPO in 2011, the foundation ended up with 184,000 shares of Demand Media at an offering price of $17 a share, though the shares rose to as much as $25 apiece during their first day of trading. Lance received 156,000 shares, valued at about $2 million, which he donated to the foundation. Capital Sports & Entertainment received 28,000 shares, valued at about $400,000. Some donors were upset that the board of the Lance Armstrong Foundation would allow Armstrong and his agent to make personal business deals using the charity's image. The move set off alarm bells and some worried it might trigger an inquiry from government regulators.

In the spring of 2008, embarking on another commercial venture, Armstrong and his buddy Bart Knaggs opened a bike shop just west of downtown Austin, in a converted 9,000-square-foot brick warehouse about a dozen blocks from Knaggs's office at Capital Sports & Entertainment. Wedged between a trio of banks and an almost-completed high-rise condominium building, it was just north of the left bank of Lake Austin, where a bike path that was to be known as the Lance Armstrong Bikeway was then being planned.

The bike shop was called Mellow Johnny's—a riff on Armstrong's way of pronouncing *maillot jaune*, or "yellow jersey." (The actual French pronunciation sounds something like "My-Oh-Zhan.") The store was stocked with high-end merchandise from Lance's sponsors, in particular Oakley, Nike, and Trek, all of which by then had licensing agreements to develop lines bearing Armstrong's Livestrong brand. Trek had made a multiyear pledge to the Lance Armstrong Foundation worth close to $1 million; Oakley had guaranteed several hundred thousand dollars a year.

Mellow Johnny's carried Trek's Madone series of racing bikes, as well as the costly, retro "naked" single-speed bicycle with wooden rims, which is one of the only bikes Armstrong has ever bought with his own money. The store also featured a media section selling Lance-related items, such as his two books and DVDs. Mixed in among the Armstrong bestsellers were books by his friends, such as his coach, Chris Carmichael; the Postal team's former *directeur sportif* Johan Bruyneel; and photographer buddy Graham Watson. And for those who wished to linger, there was an in-store coffee shop called Juan Pelota—an alias Lance had sometimes used while traveling overseas, which itself was a tongue-in-cheek reference to his one testicle. (*Juan* sounds like *one*, and *pelota* is Spanish for "ball.") Everything about the store was in some way a reflection or a celebration of Armstrong.

Armstrong's most ambitious business endeavor was kept hush-hush. With the help of a handful of wealthy backers, Armstrong was making an attempt at a buyout of professional bike racing. Since his retirement, the Tour de France and the international governing body of the sport, the UCI, had become embattled to the point of dysfunction.

Trouble began in 2005 when the UCI, at the behest of its former president, Hein Verbruggen, who had retired in 2005, put together a series of races it called the UCI Pro Tour. The series, which included many of the oldest and most well-known races in Europe, was an effort to bring together under one umbrella all the top cycling events so that they could negotiate for television rights and marketing deals more effectively. Most of these races were owned by individuals or promotional companies. The problem was that the company that owned the Tour de France—the Amaury Sport Organisation, or ASO—would not join the Pro Tour. Without the sport's biggest race on board, the Pro Tour could never survive.

The relationship between the UCI and the ASO had long been strained. By 2006, it was absolutely hostile, and the bitter feud was tearing apart the sport. One of the main areas of disagreement had to do with drug testing. Top executives at ASO believed that the UCI had been covering up the sport's doping problem for years, which had allowed it to become rampant in the peloton.

Armstrong's camp saw an opportunity. In fall 2006, at a Manhattan bar, Armstrong, Bill Stapleton, and Tiger Williams, along with actor Jake Gyllenhaal, discussed how cycling could benefit from central ownership. Armstrong said no new organization could succeed unless it controlled the Tour de France. Soon after, Armstrong rounded up a number of wealthy cycling enthusiasts willing to help fund a potential acquisition of the Tour de France. It would have cost about $1.5 billion at the time. The group of wealthy backers, which included Thom Weisel, had occasional meetings to discuss the matter and the possibilities of making an offer to purchase the race from the Amaury family. But the financial crisis that began to manifest in mid-2007 slowed things down, and the Amaury family proved less willing to sell the Tour de France than Armstrong and his wealthy friends had hoped. Ultimately, the deal went nowhere.

Even as Armstrong transitioned from professional bike racing to a career that consisted largely of public appearances related to his cancer charity and a slew of new business ventures, his bitter feud with Greg LeMond continued and, in some ways, intensified.

In April 2008, LeMond filed suit against Trek, claiming that Trek had tried to sabotage his brand by telling dealers it was discontinuing the line and refusing to sell them LeMond bikes. Included in the lawsuit was LeMond's contention that Trek had attempted to silence him about his anti-doping stance, and specifically that John Burke told LeMond that if he did not issue an apologetic press release, LeMond's relationship with Trek would suffer.

In connection with the suit, LeMond's lawyers issued a discovery request demanding any internal documents from Trek relating to the statement that had appeared on August 15, 2001. LeMond's attorneys also demanded anything related to Ferrari, to doping allegations, or to any telephone calls Burke made on August 13. Other documents in the case included a transcript of a

2004 phone conversation between LeMond and Burke in which Burke responded to LeMond's contention that there was mounting evidence to support the allegations that Armstrong was doping by saying: "Well, I still get back to the innocent until proven guilty, and that's somebody else's job." Burke knew that Armstrong's image moved bicycle sales, and it was clear whom he favored in the dispute between the two men.

LeMond wanted the court to award declaratory judgments and financial damages. Responding to LeMond's complaint, Trek said that it had merely wanted LeMond to stop his disparagement of Armstrong, which Trek claimed was undermining not only its own bottom line but the LeMond brand as well. Citing anonymous letters from customers who claimed to be put off by LeMond's comments about Armstrong, Trek said LeMond had sabotaged his own brand, causing sales of LeMond bikes to plummet. In April, just weeks after LeMond launched his suit, Trek announced that it was dropping LeMond bicycles from its product line.

In late September 2008, after having done the Leadville 100 mountain bike race the month before in Colorado—his first bike race since retirement—Armstrong announced that he would return to professional cycling. He was joining Team Astana, based in Kazakhstan—the land of Borat Sagdiyev, the fictional Kazakhstani TV personality in the 2006 mockumentary *Borat*.

How Armstrong landed in such a far-flung, unlikely place was a tale of surpassing strangeness—and yet a familiar tale, too, because so much of it had to do with complications related to doping. Armstrong's team had last been sponsored by the Discovery Channel. But when the Discovery Channel ended its sponsorship after the 2007 season, cycling's drug scandals had become so numerous and so devastating that Tailwind Sports was unable to find a new sponsor, and it floundered. It seemed that Thom Weisel was done owning professional bike racing teams. This left Johan Bruyneel, the longtime director, without a team to run.

Bruyneel approached Team Astana, which was in disarray following star rider Alexander Vinokourov's positive drug test in the 2007 Tour de France. Bruyneel offered to move his squad and infrastructure over to Astana. Astana, which was supported financially by Kazakhstan's state holding company, Samruk-Kazyna, agreed to the deal. The result was that the 2008

Astana team roster was nearly identical to the 2007 Discovery Channel team (except for a handful of Kazakh domestiques required by the sponsor).

In 2008, Alberto Contador, who had won the 2007 Tour for the Discovery Channel team (if only because the actual race leader, Michael Rasmussen, was disqualified for dodging a drug test), went on to dominate cycling that year—this time while wearing the Astana jersey. He won the Giro d'Italia and the Vuelta a España. However, he didn't have a shot at that year's Tour de France because the Tour organizers were punishing the Astana team for embarrassing the race in the prior season with Vinokourov's positive test. But Contador's overall success made Bruyneel look like a genius. Contador was the second great Grand Tour rider Bruyneel had developed.

When Armstrong decided to return to cycling, it was almost a given that he'd return to race under Bruyneel. Armstrong, who said he was returning to cycling not out of personal ambition but to raise awareness of cancer, agreed to race on the team without a salary. The announcement that he would join the team caused a major rift on the squad. As the captain of the team and winner of the 2007 Tour de France, Contador would be the hands-down favorite to win the 2009 Tour de France (if the Astana team was allowed to participate). But Contador knew enough about Armstrong to know he would never work in support of another rider. Having Lance as a teammate would be like having a competitor on his own team. Contador considered quitting: "I think it's too premature to say just yet if I'll leave the team. I still want to see how things develop and talk to the team," he said at the time of Lance's announcement.

"I think there's room for all of us" was Lance's response.

In framing his decision as a move to bring more awareness to his foundation's fight against cancer, Armstrong showed his mastery at mixing his personal image with that of his charity: "While my intention is to train and compete as fiercely as I always have, this time I will gauge victory by how much progress we make against cancer, a disease that will claim eight million lives this year alone," he proclaimed at the Clinton Global Initiative in New York in late September 2008. "Our campaign will appeal to every person affected by cancer as well as their nations' leaders, and we intend to visit, race, and train in those countries that join our cause."

Over the years, Armstrong had indeed devoted considerable time and effort to the fight against cancer—not just on behalf of his foundation but as a political issue. As an icon in the cancer community, he had met with lawmakers, including Senator John Kerry, to lobby for more funding for cancer research, courted presidential candidates such as Democrat Barack Obama and Republican John McCain to push for more research dollars, and spoken at numerous fund-raisers around the country. His passionate testimony before Texas officials helped convince the legislature to pass a $3 billion cancer research referendum. He could rally millions of his "Livestrong Army" fans through his website to support cancer causes.

By 2008, his own foundation had raised more than $250 million for cancer-related causes, and its staff had grown to seventy-five employees. The foundation began construction on a new headquarters in a 30,000-square-foot, spruced-up former paper warehouse in East Austin. Seven of Armstrong's Tour jerseys would later hang on the wall, and a yellow Livestrong sign would be placed just inside the front door. A section of the Lance Armstrong Bikeway, also under construction, would run just behind the light-filled building.

However, as the foundation flourished, questions arose about the blurring of boundaries between what benefited the foundation and what benefited Armstrong himself. Armstrong's return to competitive cycling meant millions of dollars for him personally. For example, his sponsorship contract with Trek said that if Armstrong decided to make a comeback, Trek would pay him a bonus of $1 million a year. And he was such a star that he was able to collect huge fees just for appearing in certain races, like the Tour Down Under, for which the government of South Australia offered him $1 million.

Still determined to clear his name of the doping suspicions that continued to haunt him, Armstrong also hoped to use his comeback as a chance to silence the doubters who had questioned whether he was clean when he won, and whether he had it in him to win without doping. Toward that end, he announced the Astana team's retention of Dr. Don Catlin, a leading expert in identifying and detecting the use of performance-enhancing drugs in professional sports. Dr. Catlin, Armstrong said, would design the most comprehensive program ever implemented for a professional athlete. The goal of the program would be to make it possible for Lance to prove he was racing clean. All of Lance's blood work and testing would be posted online at www .livestrong.com—the for-profit website Demand Media had created for him.

Catlin seemed an impeccable choice for the purpose. He had overseen testing for anabolic agents at the 1996 Atlanta Olympics, and for twenty-five years had run the country's first anti-doping lab at UCLA. At the time he was hired by Armstrong, he ran a company called Anti-Doping Research, a non-profit organization he founded to research performance-enhancing drugs, uncover new drugs being used illegally, and develop tests to detect them. Although Catlin was to be paid by Astana, Armstrong characterized him as completely independent.

Not long after the announcement about his return, Armstrong held another news conference at the Interbike cycling trade show in Las Vegas, where he was joined on the podium by Dr. Catlin. Greg LeMond showed up and proceeded to attack the testing program, calling it a conflict of interest for Catlin to take payment from the team, and asking Catlin whether he would be measuring Armstrong's oxygen intake, power output, and maximum aerobic capacity—factors he described as being able to indicate doping. Catlin responded by saying that those factors were not his areas of expertise—at which point Armstrong said, "It's time for us, everybody in this room, to move on. . . . I appreciate you being here—next question."

Determined to press his point, LeMond went on: "So the whole history has just been passed over?"—a reference to the speculation that Lance had doped to win his seven Tour titles.

The exchange did little to put a dent in Armstrong's ironclad defenses against doping accusations, but it did a lot to hurt LeMond's personal brand. Most people in cycling by this point knew LeMond was absolutely right. But by crusading against Armstrong, he looked like he was unwilling to let go and move on. LeMond had gone from being ambivalent about professional cycling to wanting to fix it single-handedly.

No matter what he did, Lance could not lay such speculations to rest. In late 2008, the French anti-doping authority threw down a challenge to Armstrong. The head of the agency, Pierre Bordry, had become convinced that Armstrong had cheated and gotten away with it. He proposed that he agree to retesting of his 1999 urine samples to see whether the French newspaper *L'Équipe* had been right. Bordry, who had overseen the testing of the anonymous samples from 1999, was quoted in *L'Équipe* as saying that he wanted to act as a referee between the newspaper and Armstrong (although Bordry seemed to already have an opinion, for he referred in the newspaper to samples "which contain erythropoietin [EPO])."

A positive test from the samples could not lead to a ban from racing because too much time had passed for Lance to be disciplined. Even so, the French agency proposed that Armstrong show good faith by agreeing to the retesting. Doing so, the agency argued, would be in Armstrong's interest, for if he was really innocent, it would make it possible for him to cut short the rumors he'd been unable to shake. The tests could be carried out quickly at Bordry's lab and done in the presence of a representative sent by Armstrong, the agency said. Or, if Armstrong preferred, they could be done at another World Anti-Doping Agency–accredited European lab outside France.

Armstrong declined Bordry's offer.

And by early 2009, the strict and transparent individual anti-doping program that Lance had announced was abandoned, before it ever began. Dr. Catlin issued a statement saying that by mutual agreement, he and Lance had decided to part ways, without his ever having looked at a single blood or urine sample from Armstrong, because the program was too complex and too costly to carry out. Bill Stapleton issued a statement saying that Armstrong had been tested two or three times since December by Rasmus Damsgaard, a Danish anti-doping research scientist who ran the internal anti-doping program of the Astana team, and would continue to do Armstrong's testing throughout the season. Meanwhile, Astana had rehired Armstrong's old team doctor, Pedro Celaya.

Lance also began to back off his initial commitment to publish all of his biological data online. In late January, he headed to Australia for the Tour Down Under, his first race out of retirement. It was just a tune-up race. He wasn't seriously attempting to win it. After the race, people noted that the data about his blood work had not been posted on his website, contrary to his promise to do so as the season got under way. Armstrong explained that he was worried that publishing all his biological data would prompt unfair questions about him from the public. A layman would probably not be able to understand complex information, he said, adding that there are natural fluctuations in some blood levels when a rider races at a high altitude. His website did post seven of his basic test results, which had been obtained since he rejoined the testing pool, and stated that since he had returned to cycling, he had been tested seventeen times. But that didn't satisfy critics.

Dick Pound, the former chairman of the World Anti-Doping Agency (WADA), said: "Armstrong made all the big announcements, and the testing has dropped right off the radar. No sign that anything is actually getting done."

Notwithstanding the controversies that continued to swirl around him, many veteran cyclists, both on and off his team, were excited about Armstrong's return to the sport. They had never before seen anything like what Lance had managed to achieve in his first comeback—the crowds, the media, the electricity in the atmosphere wherever he went. Even riders from rival teams sought his autograph and wanted to have their photos taken with him. As the mayor of the French town of Manosque told one rider during a race in March: Whether the people love him or hate him, whether they like him or dislike him, they'll all come to the Tour because they want to see the best.

Several anti-doping scientists, though, had different ideas. They believed Armstrong was planning to use blood transfusions during the 2009 Tour de France, and they were in the process of developing a test they thought would be able to catch him. The new test, which was being developed in a laboratory in Barcelona, could detect plastic molecules from transfusion bags in riders' blood. The scheme would require cooperation from several organizations, including the WADA, the UCI, and the Swiss anti-doping laboratory that handled blood testing for the Tour de France. But as the test hadn't yet been perfected, the plan was to freeze Armstrong's blood and test it later. There was a small hitch, though: In order to preserve frozen specimen, a chemical needed to be mixed with the blood.

Drug testing follows strict protocols. When a rider gives a sample, the blood or urine is divided into two separate containers—an A and a B sample. Both containers are sealed. When the samples get to the lab, only the A sample is tested. The seal on the B sample remains intact. If the A sample tests positive, a rider has the right to witness the seal on the B sample being broken and the sample being tested. The procedure guards against tampering.

Armstrong would surely notice if a drug tester put something into his blood sample. Savvy veterans know to watch the sample carefully until it is sealed. The people involved in the plan decided they would take the blood test, seal both samples in front of Armstrong, and then break the seal back at the lab, add the preservative, and freeze it. Once the Barcelona test was perfected, they would test Armstrong's blood for the plasticizer. Because the seals were to be broken, the test itself could not be used to sanction Armstrong, but it could be used in conjunction with other evidence—such as witness testimony—to convict him of a doping offense. The scientists were excited. They thought they had their man.

In a separate and unrelated drug-testing incident in early March, Armstrong returned from a training ride in the south of France to discover an official from the AFLD, the French anti-doping agency, waiting for him, ready to take a urine sample. That year, the AFLD quietly stepped up its efforts to catch cheating cyclists with out-of-competition testing. Armstrong, who was with Bruyneel, got off his bike and darted inside his house while Bruyneel blocked the drug tester from entering. After twenty minutes—theoretically enough time to manipulate his bodily fluids to avoid testing positive—Armstrong came out and submitted to the test. Armstrong was in violation of anti-doping protocol, which says that athletes must stay within sight of the sample collectors at all times once they show up to do the test. The incident was all over the news. Armstrong's explanation was that, although he was used to being tested by the UCI, he hadn't expected to be tested by the French and he had wanted to make a call to be sure the tester was legitimate. But that didn't explain why Armstrong went inside and took a shower. If he had, as he said, taken four hundred drug tests, surely he knew the rules. The UCI, of course, backed Armstrong. The French anti-doping officials were not so obliging; they were considering banning Armstrong from the Tour de France over the incident, which Lance dubbed Showergate.

"I suspect this will escalate, and we'll see even more antics out of the AFLD in the near future," he said in a video he recorded and posted on the Internet. "There's a very high likelihood that they'd prohibit me from riding in the Tour. And that's too bad. The tour is something that I love dearly, something I wanted to ride in."

For his comeback year, Armstrong had decided to limit the number of races he participated in. He had done the Tour Down Under and was planning to do the Leadville 100, the mountain bike race he had done the previous year to mark his return to cycling. The only race he had committed to in Europe was the Tour de France. But now, with "Showergate," Armstrong announced that it was possible he would skip the Tour. In the meantime, he would race in the Giro d'Italia in May, a decision that was seen as a snub to the French. The huge publicity boost the Tour de France would have received as Armstrong's European comeback race would now be going to the Italians.

Later in March, Armstrong entered the Vuelta a Castilla y León, a stage race in Spain, in preparation for the Giro. On the opening day, Armstrong was caught in a crash and fractured his right collarbone, putting his Giro d'Italia berth in jeopardy. But after undergoing emergency surgery, he bounced back in astonishingly good form and was ready for the start of the race. He finished in a respectable twelfth place. Pretty good for a guy who was thirty-seven, older than practically anyone else in the field, who had just broken his collarbone, and had been out of bike racing for a couple of years.

Meanwhile, French anti-doping officials had decided to allow Armstrong to race in the Tour, and Armstrong said he'd do it. As he trained, Lance began chronicling his training rides on Twitter, posting half a dozen times a day. By May, he had about 700,000 followers. He tweeted mostly about the mundane details of his personal life: his kids, his bike, his favorite music. Occasionally, Armstrong would tweet something cancer-related, like "Spoke by phone with Prof Veronesi. 83 yr old has operated on 25k+ women with breast cancer. Amazing man and great partner on our campaign."

In June 2009, he announced the birth of his son with his girlfriend, Anna Hansen: "Wassup, world? My name is Max Armstrong and I just arrived. My mommy is healthy and so am I!"

That same month, Johan Bruyneel named Alberto Contador as Astana's leader for the Tour, meaning Armstrong would be a super domestique. Armstrong said he would do everything he could to defend Contador. However, riders on the team suspected that the hierarchy inside Astana might be fluid, and subject to adjustment as the race went on—an unusual situation in cycling. The uncertainty made Contador anxious, for he didn't buy the idea that Armstrong would act as a domestique.

Contador's suspicions were confirmed on the third stage of the race, a routine flat stage. Twenty miles from the finish line, there was an awkward bend in the road that allowed twenty-eight of the riders, including Armstrong and two of his teammates, to pull ahead of the rest of the field, while the others, including Contador, were stuck behind. Instead of telling his teammates to go back to help Contador, Armstrong instructed them to go to the front and hammer it, thus increasing the gap between them and the field. Contador finished 41 seconds behind Armstrong. Armstrong was now in third. Contador was in fourth, 19 seconds behind in the overall standings.

Armstrong now considered himself the team leader. On stage 7—the first one in the mountains—the plan was for Armstrong and Contador to stay together. But Contador ignored the plan. With 1.2 miles to the mountaintop finish, Contador attacked. Armstrong couldn't keep pace, and Contador gained back enough time to leapfrog Armstrong in the standings. He was now 2 seconds ahead of Armstrong.

The dueling teammates had to wait until stage 15 for another mountaintop finish that could separate them. The stage finished at the ski resort Verbier in Switzerland. With about 3.7 miles to go on the final climb, Contador accelerated and left everyone behind, moving into the yellow jersey. Armstrong was now in second, 1 minute, 37 seconds behind Contador. Contador held the lead all the way to the finish line in Paris, winning by 4 minutes, 11 seconds, with Armstrong in third place overall, 5 minutes and 24 seconds behind him.

Contador had won the Tour de France, but he was furious at Armstrong's behavior during the race. "My relationship with Lance Armstrong is zero," Contador said afterward. "He's a great rider and he did a great Tour. . . . [O]n a personal level . . . I have never admired him and never will."

Armstrong, who had criticized Contador as being inexperienced, responded on Twitter. "Hey pistolero, there is no 'I' in 'team.' what did I say in March? Lots to learn. Restated." (The "pistolero" stemmed from Contador's habit of celebrating victories by shooting an imaginary pistol.)

"Seeing these comments from AC [Alberto Contador]. If I were him I'd drop this drivel and start thanking his team. w/o them, he doesn't win," Armstrong said in another tweet. "A champion is also measured on how much he respects his teammates and opponents."

After the Tour, the French media alleged that both Contador and Armstrong had had an advantage in the Tour, in that the Astana team had been given advance warning of visits by drug testers.

Armstrong's blood test numbers, which he released publicly in an effort to silence critics, were immediately analyzed by hematology experts around the world. Several of them came out with public statements saying that they thought the fluctuations in Armstrong's blood looked suspicious—possibly indicating blood manipulation. Armstrong denied the claims, and once again, the UCI backed him up, calling the fluctuations within the normal range.

The attempt by anti-doping scientists to test for plasticizers in his blood had also failed. The anti-doping laboratory that was supposed to store the blood pulled out at the last minute, just before the Tour, when it came under pressure from the UCI, which said the test fell outside the bounds of normal testing procedures.

Armstrong's success—third place was considered a surprisingly good finish under the circumstances—led to massive interest in his comeback. If Armstrong could finish third in his first year back, and not long after suffering from a broken collarbone, it was within reason that he could be a favorite to win in 2010.

Even while Armstrong was riding for Astana, he and Bruyneel were actively maneuvering to start a new cycling team and to sign a title sponsor. Armstrong figured he needed $15 million—either from a US-based multinational company that might be willing to sponsor the team, or from a consortium of Americans who would own it. One of the problems facing the ownership idea, however, was that there's really no equity in a cycling team. You can say you own a team, but when the rider contracts are up and the obligations of the sponsor have ended, you're left with nothing but bikes and cars and buses and trucks. So the only realistic option was to find a title sponsor, and they found a partner in electronics retailer RadioShack, whose team, of course, would be led by Armstrong. The twenty-six-member squad would be based in the United States and include most of the riders who had been on the Astana team, with the exception of Contador. Bruyneel was named team director. Armstrong's old teammate Viatcheslav Ekimov returned as one of the managers.

Texas-based RadioShack, which was involved in several other sports sponsorships, seemed thrilled by its latest deal, and agreed to also guarantee $4 million a year to Lance's foundation. Lee Applbaum, RadioShack's chief marketing officer, said in a statement that Lance was "one of the greatest athletes of our generation, a father, a cancer survivor and a tireless advocate in the fight against cancer." He added: "Armstrong understands the power of keeping people connected, and that's why we feel he's the perfect partner for our brand."

CHAPTER THIRTEEN

BETRAYALS

At the start of 2007, six months after Floyd Landis was stripped of his 2006 Tour de France title, the clock began ticking on the two-year ban from bike racing that had been handed down to him by the US Anti-Doping Agency. USADA, based in Colorado Springs, Colorado, was a quasi-governmental entity that had been created in October 1999, when most Olympic governing bodies began separating out their drug testing to avoid conflicts of interest. USADA, a member organization of the Swiss-based WADA, the World Anti-Doping Agency, was tasked with handling drug testing and enforcement for all US Olympic athletes.

Since its inception, USADA had found only 209 possible violations in about forty thousand tests. Of those, 20 percent were dismissed after further review. Most of the violations the agency found were minor infractions involving little-known athletes, and there were complaints that the agency wasn't effective at catching the real cheaters. But with its judgment against Landis, the agency seemed to be fulfilling its mission.

Unwilling to accept either the ban or the stain on his reputation, Floyd decided he would mount a vigorous legal challenge against USADA. To raise money for his upcoming appeal, he traveled around the country, going on bike rides and attending events with cycling fans.

Floyd argued that his positive test was the result of a flawed interpretation of the data, and accused USADA of singling him out as a publicity-seeking gambit that would enable the agency to gain government funding—which was important to USADA since about two-thirds of its budget came from federal grants. But even as Landis traveled down the path of outright denial, attacking everyone responsible for the drug testing at the Tour de France, he was still considering another path—coming clean.

Floyd's appeal resulted in a surprising outpouring of support. People were willing to give him the benefit of the doubt. And even if some of them didn't believe he had been clean, they wanted to help. Fans donated an average of around $20 a pop. However, most of Floyd's defense money would come out of his own pocket. He had about $2 million saved up from his cycling salary and winnings. The bulk of the rest came from wealthy financial backers like Tiger Williams. Thom Weisel contributed about $50,000 (which Landis considered hush money and gladly accepted). Landis had also received a six-figure advance for a book, *Positively False: The Real Story of How I Won the Tour de France*, cowritten with the editor of *Bicycling* magazine, which was set to come out that summer.

At the same time that he was proclaiming his innocence, however, Landis was confiding in Williams and others close to him that he had, in fact, used performance-enhancing drugs (though he also said that he never took the testosterone he had tested positive for, and could not account for the test results—a mystery, he called it). He explained that everyone in cycling doped, including Lance Armstrong, which was why Floyd was fighting, because he felt he had to protect the reputation of the sport.

In February, Landis attended the Tour of California, an eight-day stage race that had become the major bicycle race on US soil. Landis had won the inaugural edition of the race the previous year, before going on to win the Tour de France. Now he was there schmoozing with cycling fans, signing autographs and raising money for his appeal.

During the race, Landis went out to a Santa Barbara steakhouse with

Steve Johnson, president and CEO of USA Cycling in 2006. Johnson was also the executive director of the USA Cycling Development Foundation, which Thomas Weisel had created to help fund the sport. Their foundation provided a substantial portion of USA Cycling's annual budget, pumping over $4 million into its programs over the course of about five years.

Sitting at a bar table with Johnson and Johnson's wife, Landis began to complain about his predicament. He believed that Johnson was aware of the organized doping program on the US Postal team.

Landis complained to Johnson that he was being railroaded, kicked aside by the sport. Lance, on the other hand, had gotten away with it, despite a flood of allegations that, put together, made it obvious to anyone with half a brain that he was doping. Floyd was angry, and he hinted to Johnson that he might just come clean and blow it all up.

Johnson had been part of the sport's growth, and membership in his organization was soaring, largely because Lance had put cycling on the map. Having top American cyclists on the podium of international competitions would drive more people to watch and participate. But doping was threatening to undo all of the progress Johnson and Weisel had made. First, Tyler Hamilton tested positive. That was bad enough. Landis's situation was worse because, having won the Tour de France, he was higher profile. If Landis revealed the truth, sponsors would flee, Lance would topple from his hero's pedestal, American fans would disappear, and money would vanish overnight.

Johnson told Landis there was nothing he could do. Landis had tested positive and that was that. He had to work within the adjudication process. "Do what Tyler did and you'll be allowed to be back in and racing again," he said. Landis saw Johnson's words as a veiled threat—and that if he didn't follow Hamilton's example, he would be blackballed by the sport forever. He decided he had no choice really but to continue with his plan to take on USADA.

Hearings for Landis's appeal, which was to be settled by a three-person arbitration panel, began in May 2007 at Pepperdine University in Malibu. His defense was based on some highly technical scientific evidence that he thought would convince the arbiters that there had been errors in the testing of his urine samples. His lawyer, Maurice Suh of Gibson, Dunn & Crutcher in Los Angeles, treated the case as a major courtroom showdown, mounting a costly defense that involved subpoenaing and reviewing thousands of documents and hiring expensive scientists as expert witnesses.

Landis's chief opponent was Travis Tygart, general counsel of USADA. A native of Jacksonville, Florida, Tygart was a devout Christian who had been a high school coach and teacher before attending Southern Methodist University Law School. Starting out as outside legal counsel to USADA when it was founded, Tygart had become the agency's director of legal affairs in 2002.

Landis had chosen to open the hearings to the public. His hope was that even if he lost the appeal, the public would see that the whole system was stacked against him, and the injustice would spur outrage and force Tygart to let him off the hook. The strategy backfired, however, thanks to two serious public relations blunders made by members of Landis's inner circle. First, Landis's friend Arnie Baker was accused of hacking into the computers of the French anti-doping laboratory in an attempt to uncover evidence for Landis's case. Baker was one of Landis's early cycling coaches in San Diego, and although he was now a physician, he still coached on the side. When Landis tested positive, Baker sprang into action, delving deep into the rules and protocols of the laboratory tests used against Landis. Baker's house in a sleepy neighborhood in San Diego became his HQ for getting Landis off. Piles of documents surrounded his desk and he spent hours upon hours studying them. Baker discovered, for instance, that Landis's test had originally contained the rider number of another cyclist. It was scratched off and Landis's was written in. The lab insisted that they had the correct test. Baker denied the hacking and said he had received the documents from an anonymous whistle-blower, but the French police opened an investigation into the matter anyway.

The second and much more horrific blunder had its roots in a phone conversation between Landis and Greg LeMond shortly after Landis's positive test. LeMond had told Landis to come clean because, aside from the fact that the truth would ultimately "save cycling," he said, it would also free Landis himself from the weight of his terrible secret. LeMond then confided to Landis something he had told only a very few people—that he had been molested as a child, and that carrying the secret had eaten away at him for years. According to LeMond, Landis was not convinced that coming clean would be beneficial. "What good would that do? If I did, it would destroy a lot of my friends and hurt a lot of people." LeMond later agreed to go to the arbitration hearing to recount his conversation with Landis that day, and Landis and the people in his camp were worried about what LeMond would reveal.

The night before LeMond was scheduled to testify, he received a chilling phone call from a man claiming to be the family friend who'd molested him, "Uncle Ron." The caller told him, "I'll be there tomorrow," and made reference to some of the intimate details of the molestation. First shaken and then infuriated, LeMond traced the number to Will Geoghegan, Landis's good friend and business manager. In his testimony the next day, LeMond recounted the content of the phone call—which had to be a new low in the history of attempted intimidation—in front of a stunned group of reporters, thus effectively outing a part of his past that he had kept secret for decades. Landis's attorney, Maurice Suh, spun around in his chair and told Geoghegan he was fired, effective immediately. But the damage had been done—Landis had been made to look terrible by the actions of his friend, and the hearings became a huge media spectacle.

Although Landis's legal team did later show that there had been irregularities in the testing, Landis lost his appeal in a 2-1 decision. He was immediately stripped of his Tour de France title, but the public outcry Landis had hoped for did not materialize. The scientific details that were presented in his defense at the hearing were so technical that they went right over the heads of most of the reporters and bloggers in the audience. And needless to say, they didn't get nearly as much attention as Greg LeMond's electrifying story about Will Geoghegan's call.

Landis was devastated. He had burned through nearly all of his life savings on his defense. But he had one more chance to appeal. He took his case to the Court of Arbitration for Sport, a Switzerland-based organization that offers the possibility of a second phase to the appeal process. In early spring of 2008, a three-person panel was convened in New York and heard thirty-five hours of testimony from fourteen witnesses, after which it announced that it would issue a decision in June.

Landis knew his chances of winning the appeal were slim, and he again considered coming clean. He even had an idea about how to do it: He'd make a confessional video and post it on YouTube. When he ran the idea by Tiger Williams, he told Landis that he didn't think the time was right. After all, Landis had spent other people's money on his defense, and his book, in which he denied doping, had just come out and was ranked 15th on a major nonfiction bestseller list.

Williams advised Landis to wait and let everything play out. If he still felt like making a confession in the future, they could talk about how to handle it then. Williams also offered to help Landis get back into bike racing when his two-year ban ended, which would happen soon, regardless of the results of the appeal process.

On the last day of June 2008, Floyd Landis was in his home in Temecula, California, when his lawyer, Maurice Suh, called to tell him he'd lost his final appeal. Devastated, he walked upstairs to find his Tour de France trophy—a Sèvres porcelain shallow gold-rimmed, purple bowl on a pedestal, which had been made at the former royal ceramics factory on the outskirts of Paris. Hoisting the trophy above his head, just as he had done the day he stood on the podium on the Champs-Élysées, Landis walked out onto the balcony of the bedroom he shared with his wife, paused for a moment, then threw it to the ground. The sound of the trophy colliding with asphalt and smashing into a million little pieces was oddly soothing. Landis felt better. But friends who were in the house at the time came running upstairs. They had thought the sound was a gunshot and feared that Landis might have killed himself.

His loss was followed by Armstrong's announcement that he was joining Team Astana and returning to professional cycling. This made Landis even angrier. While the entire cycling industry had bent over backward to accommodate Armstrong, despite nearly a decade's worth of doping allegations, the only person who seemed to care about Landis was Tiger Williams.

True to his word that he would help Landis get back into cycling, Williams had his new business venture, eSoles, an athletic shoe insole company, put sponsorship money into a team known as OUCH, in order to secure Landis a spot on it. OUCH was a low-level team that raced only in the United

States, and its title sponsor was a sports medicine clinic in Temecula founded by Landis's longtime friend and cycling buddy, Dr. Brent Kay.

In February 2009, Landis, his suspension over, raced in the Tour of California with seven other OUCH teammates, mostly lower-level professional riders. He finished a mediocre 23rd place out of 136. This set the tone for Landis's season. He lacked motivation. Races in the United States were more for sprinters than for European stage racers, and they simply weren't long enough or difficult enough to truly challenge him.

Under the strain of so much disappointment and disillusionment, Landis's marriage to Amber slowly fell apart. He moved out of their home in Temecula to a small cabin in Idyllwild, in the San Jacinto Mountains. And then things went from bad to worse. During the summer of 2009, while doing some home repairs, Landis fell off a ladder, breaking bones and severely injuring himself. Afterward, he spent weeks sitting around the house, drinking beer, nursing his grudges, getting ever more depressed.

That July, when Landis learned about the new RadioShack team, he swallowed his pride and called Johan Bruyneel to ask for a spot on the team. Bruyneel turned him down. He said Floyd would bring too much negative publicity, that in terms of public relations, Floyd was radioactive.

Floyd's depression deepened. He'd kept quiet, just as everyone had told him to do. Had he admitted everything and given Travis Tygart information on Armstrong and the other cyclists, his ban would have been shortened. But out of fear of being blackballed, he had continued to lie. Now he realized he'd been played. He was taking the fall for the entire sport, leaving all of cycling's other dopers unstained.

Landis had started to see a therapist in late 2009 after an article on the cycling website VeloNews painted him as a suicidal alcoholic. He thought the article was bullshit, but so many of his friends were worried about him that he had agreed to seek help. Landis was surprised at how good it felt to tell his shrink all of his secrets. Getting it off his chest made him feel light and free. It was then that he realized the true enormity of the weight he was carrying around with him.

In December, he confided his intention to come clean to Jonathan

Vaughters, who again endorsed the idea, and in early 2010 to Tiger Williams. This time, Williams advised Landis to speak out, and promised to use his influence and resources to shield him from the consequences.

Landis also found the motivation to get back on his bike and train. For the 2010 season, he joined the Bahati Foundation team, founded by Rahsaan Bahati, a star cyclist on the American circuit. Landis's good friend Brent Kay had offered to cosponsor the team on the condition that Landis be given a spot on the roster, and the team was then renamed the OUCH-Bahati Foundation team. Landis's new teammates hoped that, as a former winner of the race, he could get them an invitation to compete in the Tour of California, which had moved from its traditional February time slot to May 16 that year. But in March, Landis found out that although Armstrong and his RadioShack team would be competing in the race—in fact, the Tour was paying Armstrong to appear—his own team had been shut out. Landis assumed it was because his team had not paid a high enough fee to the race organizers.

Landis began to ruminate on the aspects of cycling that had always bothered him—the politics, his sense that cycling's rules and regulations were applied unevenly, and the financial corruption. This rejection was the last straw for Landis. He decided once again that he would do what he could to tear it all down.

Landis again talked to Tiger Williams, who again encouraged him. Williams himself had had a falling-out with Armstrong the previous year over a business deal. He and Armstrong had a handshake agreement allowing Williams to use the Livestrong brand on the product line of eSoles, in exchange for which Williams had agreed to make a large donation to the Lance Armstrong Foundation. Williams had supported Lance's charity for many years, donating substantial sums of his own money as well as holding fund-raisers, including a benefit at the Waldorf Astoria that had raised $4.7 million. But Armstrong suddenly backed out of the eSoles deal, telling Williams that it conflicted with an agreement that Livestrong had already made with Nike. When Williams protested, Armstrong dismissed him with a terse e-mail. After all their history together, Williams felt betrayed.

After talking with Williams, Landis began to draft an e-mail to Steve Johnson, the president of USA Cycling, replete with details that he knew would blow the lid off of the cycling world. Digging deep into his memory, he tried to unearth everything he could remember about specific instances of performance-enhancing drug use on the US Postal team, and then double- and triple-checked the dates against a journal he had kept to make sure he was as accurate and precise as possible. What resulted was a 1,080-word e-mail that was the equivalent of the Pentagon Papers of professional bike racing. In it he confessed to his own doping, and made accusations against Lance Armstrong, George Hincapie, Chechu Rubiera, and many other cyclists on the US Postal team, all of whom he said had engaged in years of clandestine doping, with encouragement from Johan Bruyneel. Landis didn't mention Thom Weisel in his account.

But Landis didn't send the e-mail. Not yet. First he planned to talk to Andrew Messick, an employee of the Anschutz Entertainment Group, which had founded and owned the Tour of California. Messick was in charge of promoting the race, and had a role in choosing the entrants. Landis wanted Messick to know the whole truth about Armstrong—and about cycling. He wanted Messick to face a moral dilemma, just as he himself had when he made the decision to dope. As Landis drove off down his long dirt driveway to the mountain road leading north to Los Angeles, he knew he had crossed an important threshold in his journey as a cyclist. When he arrived at the restaurant where they had agreed to meet, Messick was already there.

As Landis sat down, he pulled out a digital tape recorder and placed it on the table between them. Turning it on, he announced, "Look. I'm going to tell you some things and I'm going to record it because I'm going to be accused of extortion. That is not what this is." He told Messick how he had doped for years while he was on the US Postal team, and how Armstrong and other riders had done the same. He talked about what he saw as the injustice and hypocrisy of the cycling world. "When you're in the mafia and you get caught and go to jail, you keep your mouth shut, and the organization takes care of your family," he said. "In cycling, you're expected to keep your mouth shut when you test positive, but you become an outcast. Everyone just turns their back on you."

As he listened and ate his sandwich, Messick became so visibly rattled by what Landis was telling him that his hands shook. Messick repeatedly asked the same question: "Yeah, but who is going to believe you?"

After the lunch, Messick told Steve Johnson about the meeting—just as Landis had assumed he would. Landis knew that the two men communicated often and that Johnson had been involved in helping the Tour of California get off the ground. Landis further assumed that Johnson would in turn tell Lance, and he was curious how long it would take for that to happen, because the network of connections between USA Cycling and Armstrong made it almost inevitable. If Landis went public with detailed allegations, it could bring them all down. One of the lawyers at USA Cycling then called Bill Stapleton, who jumped into action immediately. As Landis had anticipated, Armstrong called one of the leaders of Landis's cycling team and accused Landis of extortion. Landis, Armstrong said, was threatening to level allegations against Armstrong if he did not pay up. Armstrong asked how the team was doing financially, and offered to find the team sponsorship money in exchange for booting Landis. But Landis's team was behind him. They turned down Armstrong's offer.

Landis decided to up the ante by asking Messick to set up a meeting for him with USADA. Landis wanted to see what Messick would do. Would he tell Armstrong? Would he try to stop him? To Landis's surprise, Messick actually put him in contact with Travis Tygart.

Tygart got the call from Messick on Good Friday. When he realized what the call was about, he ducked into his daughter's room for some privacy. Messick explained that Floyd Landis had some things he wanted to get off his chest. Tygart knew immediately what Messick was talking about. Floyd had been on Tygart's mind lately.

Earlier that winter, Tygart had been skiing with his kids and ended up on a chairlift with Jonathan Vaughters. At first, the two men didn't recognize each other under all the gear. After some small talk, Tygart realized who it was.

"Jonathan?!"

"Travis?" Vaughters responded.

The two had not seen each other in months. During the chairlift ride,

Vaughters brought up Floyd, who was trying to make a comeback and having a very difficult time of it.

"I told Floyd he should have talked to you," Vaughters said. "That was the right way to go."

"Wish he would have," Tygart said.

The two men went on their way, both skiing with their young kids. But the conversation made Tygart think about his mission. After Landis's arbitration, Tygart forgot about cycling. He had other high-profile doping cases to worry about. But what might Landis have said? Surely, he would know enough to have brought Armstrong down. Had he cooperated, he might have served only a six-month ban and had a chance to compete again at the highest levels. Instead, Armstrong was making a comeback and was all over TV, newspapers, and magazines with a bounty of new endorsements. Landis was struggling and was rumored to be in some kind of alcoholic depression. Was this really anti-doping justice? Tygart thought.

Looking back, Tygart realized he'd missed several warning signs that pointed to a vast doping conspiracy centered around Armstrong. There was the time in 2002 when Armstrong missed a drug test. Instead of accepting a warning, Armstrong fought USADA tooth and nail. Stapleton had called up Tygart and tried to intimidate him. *This is not the way an innocent person reacts*, Tygart thought at the time. Eventually, Armstrong himself had called Tygart, complaining about the circumstances of the missed test.

"This is bullshit," Armstrong said.

"You know what," Tygart shot back, looking at a poster of Lance on his wall, "if you're clean, you should love us. Because we're the ones who can show that with an aggressive and thorough testing protocol."

After the conversation, Lance began using Tygart's logic in interviews, claiming to be the "world's most tested athlete." Tygart thought it was savvy but disingenuous.

There were also Tygart's odd interactions with Chris Carmichael, who lived nearby in Colorado Springs. Around the time of Tyler Hamilton's positive test, in 2004, the Carmichaels invited Tygart and his wife over for dinner. During the evening, Chris began pressing Travis for information on Tyler.

"What do you think he's gonna do?" Carmichael kept asking. Thinking back on it now, Tygart could see that Carmichael had been pressing for information to relay to Lance's camp. They were worried Hamilton was going to roll on Armstrong.

On another occasion, in 2005, Travis saw Carmichael at a barbecue. Carmichael had been drinking and went off on Betsy Andreu, tearing her to shreds and using language that Tygart found offensive.

Then there was, of course, Stapleton's offer of a donation in 2004.

In a nutshell, Tygart had been used and duped by Armstrong for years, and he was only now beginning to realize the extent of it.

When he got the call from Landis, Tygart sensed that he was about to tell him something important. He agreed to meet with him immediately. He flew from Colorado to L.A. for the meeting, which was held at the Marriott near LAX on April 20.

Landis wasn't sure he trusted Tygart. He didn't know if USADA was in cahoots with USA Cycling and, therefore, with Armstrong. But he took a leap of faith. He told Tygart everything. He asked Tygart to keep the details of their meeting secret from anyone at USA Cycling, and Tygart agreed. Landis was testing him. If Tygart told Armstrong about the meeting, Landis would know, because if history was any guide, he'd hear from someone in Armstrong's camp almost immediately.

There was now a flurry of e-mails going back and forth between Landis, Andrew Messick, and officials from USA Cycling. In an April 24 e-mail that was addressed to Messick but copied to Steve Johnson (and others), Landis taunted Johnson:

> I've taken the liberty . . . to copy Steve Johnson on this note and
> I'm hopeful that unlike in the past he'll also be willing to join and
> be forthcoming about what he knows about the history of doping
> in cycling.

Johnson was evasive in responding to Landis. He told him that, if he was going to come forward with allegations, he had better have the details to back them up. After all, Johnson said, Landis was reversing his long-standing position that he'd never doped.

Landis decided it was time, finally, to send his e-mail to Johnson, copying a small number of officials from USA Cycling and the UCI. On Friday, April 30, 2010, at about 6:20 in the evening, he hit the send button on the 1,080-word e-mail, which portrayed the US Postal team for what it was: a sports team with a sophisticated doping program, with Armstrong at its center, the ringleader.

His own history of doping had begun after the Dauphiné Libéré in June 2002, he wrote, when Bruyneel instructed him on how to use testosterone patches. And from that beginning Landis proceeded to lay it all out: Lance handing him the box of 2.5-milligram testosterone patches in front of Lance's wife, Kristin; Dr. Michele Ferrari extracting half a liter of blood from him, which was to be reinfused during the Tour; the discussions he and Armstrong had had in which Armstrong described using EPO, then testing positive for it after ignoring Ferrari's warnings about the existence of a new test; the bribe that had been paid to Hein Verbruggen, then head of the UCI, to keep Armstrong's EPO test results secret; all the details about the Postal team blood bags that had been stored in Armstrong's apartment in Girona, Italy; the injections of Andriol, a form of ingestible testosterone, which the team doctor had given Landis and his roommate, George Hincapie, two out of every three nights for the duration of the Tour; the blood transfusions administered during the race to him and other members of the Postal team—including Armstrong, Hincapie, and Rubiera, whose transfusions he said he had personally witnessed.

Landis continued with details about being told to take EPO to raise his hematocrit level and going to Lance's home to get it. He described the blood draws and reinfusions during the Tour de France, including the one on a bus on a remote mountain road in France where he "saw the entire team [including Armstrong and Hincapie] being transfused in plain view of all the other riders."

Landis ended the e-mail by telling Johnson: "There are many many more details that I have in diaries and am in the process of writing into an intelligible story but since the position of USA Cycling is that there have not been enough details shared to justify calling USADA, I am writing as many as I can reasonably put into an e-mail and share with you." He said his goal was to figure out "what is the process which USA Cycling uses to proceed with such allegations." He added that he would provide "much more detail as soon as you can demonstrate that you can be trusted to do the right thing."

His next step was to hold a press conference. So within roughly a week, Brent Kay rented a hospitality tent during one of the stages of the Tour of California, which was to take place in downtown Los Angeles. The plan was that Landis would make his announcement there and confess to the world about his doping.

When Lance got wind of Landis's plan, he called Kay and told him that if he helped Landis, he would find ways to have malpractice claims leveled against him that would destroy his medical practice. Lance also wanted Kay to relay a message to Landis: that it was no use going to USADA. Armstrong said he had "sources" at USADA and he would know as soon as Landis contacted them.

On May 6, Landis wrote Armstrong an e-mail, informing him that he had already gone to USADA; Lance's sources weren't as good as he thought.

After speaking to Landis, Travis Tygart called up a friend in the criminal investigation unit of the Food and Drug Administration, Jeff Novitzky. Although Tygart's job was with the US Anti-Doping Agency, he had worked closely with Novitzky on investigations involving the use of performance-enhancing drugs by professional athletes. Over the years, the two men had cooperated on cases involving Major League Baseball, pro football, swimming, and Olympic track events, but in 2008 they had begun to look into cycling.

Novitzky had a reputation as the Eliot Ness of steroid outing, which he had earned on a signature prosecution dating back to his time with the Internal Revenue Service. The son of a high school basketball coach, he graduated with an accounting degree from San José State and joined the IRS the following year, 1993, eventually becoming a special agent with its Criminal Investigation unit. Novitzky spent years working routine investigations in the San Francisco area, often helping drug agents by handling the financial angles of cocaine and heroin cases. That changed in 2002, when he began looking into a pharmaceutical laboratory called the Bay Area Laboratory Co-Operative, or BALCO, in Burlingame, California.

Novitzky had first heard of BALCO founder Victor Conte Jr. in the late 1980s when, as a teenage jock growing up in nearby Silicon Valley, he heard about Conte's lab, which catered to elite athletes. A few years later, Novitzky, by then a college basketball player and an avid reader of fitness magazines, began to notice ads for Conte's nutritional supplements and articles about them showing up in those publications. In the late 1990s, several years after he had joined the IRS, Novitzky heard vague rumors from local athletes and coaches that BALCO might be providing athletes with banned performance-enhancing drugs. But he didn't do anything to follow up on them until after hearing Conte's defense, at a televised news conference during the Sydney Olympics, of Cottrell James "C.J." Hunter III, an American shot put world champion. Hunter had withdrawn from the competition due to a knee injury, but he kept his coaching credentials and attended the games to support his wife, the Olympic sprinter Marion Jones. Shortly after Jones won her first of what would be five medals, however, the International Olympic Committee announced that Hunter had failed four out-of-competition drug tests, testing positive for the steroid nandrolone. Hunter was ordered to surrender his on-field coaching credentials. During the news conference, Conte claimed Hunter's positive tests were the result of an iron supplement. After the Olympics, Novitzky began researching Conte, checking out his posts on Internet message boards devoted to bodybuilding, and taking note of how much Conte seemed to know about anabolic steroids, what they cost, and what they could do for athletes.

In August 2002, Novitzky and the IRS Criminal Investigation unit opened an investigation into a personal trainer believed to be distributing steroids, and the trainer's suspected supplier, the BALCO lab. The probe began as a drug-and-money-laundering investigation, focused on BALCO's profits from the distribution of steroids. So Novitzky ran BALCO through an IRS financial database designed to pinpoint possible money-laundering operations by tracking cash transactions larger than $10,000. When he found a $14,000 cash withdrawal, he was sure they were on to something.

Novitzky began a weekly Monday night "trash recon," picking through BALCO's garbage. Legal since a Supreme Court ruling in 1988, such investigations can be done without bothering to obtain a search warrant. He found wrappers for syringes and boxes that had contained human growth hormone, testosterone, and Epogen (a prescription version of EPO). The trash in BALCO's Dumpster also contained notes to Conte from elite track and field athletes who had obtained the drugs, documents showing that a sample of San Francisco Giants home run champion Barry Bond's blood had been sent to a lab for steroid pretesting (to make sure the drugs would go undetected by drug testers), and FedEx receipts for drugs shipped to a professional baseball player. One of his trash runs turned up evidence that Conte was buying epitestosterone, or "Epi," a masking agent used by doping athletes, by mail from a company in the Midwest.

Eventually, Novitzky obtained subpoenas for Conte's bank records and discovered that he had withdrawn more than $480,000 in cash during the course of two years. BALCO's subpoenaed bank records also led Novitzky to Stericycle, the medical waste management company BALCO employed to pick up its used vials and needles and other detritus. He then obtained a subpoena to search the drums at Stericycle for the medical waste from seven separate pickups at BALCO labs. From December 2002 through July 2003, he combed the medical waste that came from BALCO on a monthly basis. The BALCO trash at Stericycle was, if anything, even more revealing than what he picked up at the BALCO site itself. There were empty vials of EPO, testosterone, and growth hormone, and more than sixty used syringes.

The evidence Novitzky collected was enough to allow him to conclude that Conte's lab was a front for a massive steroid ring that supplied athletes in Major League Baseball, the National Football League, and Olympic track and field. He obtained search warrants, and in September 2003, a group of more than two dozen agents and officials from a variety of agencies raided the lab as well as Conte's home and three private mailboxes. Novitzky arranged for USADA's medical director to be on hand during the raid to provide technical assistance.

Conte spent three months in prison after pleading guilty to distributing illegal steroids and laundering money, based on the evidence that Novitzky gathered and turned over to prosecutors. The investigation also led to criminal convictions of Barry Bonds and sprinter Marion Jones, who was forced to forfeit the three gold medals and two bronzes that she won at the 2000 Sydney Olympics. In October 2007, Jones pleaded guilty to lying to Novitzky and an assistant US attorney about doping and her part in a check-cashing scheme, and was sentenced to six months in prison. In 2011, Bonds was found guilty of obstruction of justice dating back to his 2003 testimony to the grand jury investigating BALCO; he was sentenced to thirty days of home confinement, two years of probation, 250 hours of community service in youth-related activities, and a $4,000 fine.

But Novitzky was controversial. Critics questioned the appropriateness of using the IRS to target athletes for drug use. Lawyers for some of the athletes targeted by his investigations described him as out of control, and said he sometimes put words into suspects' mouths.

In spring 2008, Novitzky left the IRS and joined the Food and Drug Administration's Office of Criminal Investigations, where he felt his anti-doping zeal would be better appreciated. The FDA had responsibility for overseeing the misuse of prescription drugs, and it was because Travis Tygart knew of Novitzky's interest in the off-label use of Epogen, the prescription form of EPO, that Tygart told him about Floyd Landis and asked if he would like to talk to him. During the first week of May, Novitzky called Floyd and set up a meeting.

Six days later, Landis met with Novitzky and Tygart in a hotel in Marina del Rey for six hours, and for an additional two the next morning. Landis also brought along Brent Kay, because he wanted Kay to tell Novitzky of Lance's threatening phone call. While Lance hadn't threatened him with violence, Kay was so freaked out that he had hired an armed guard to watch his Temecula house anyway.

During those long hours of testimony, Landis told the men everything he knew—everything he could think of—about doping on the US Postal team, and he gave them his diary, which included doping schedules that he'd written in code, in order to corroborate his account. He was worried that if anything he said was inaccurate, he could face criminal charges.

At the meeting, Novitzky asked Landis if he would be willing to help him with an investigation, in exchange for which he would protect Landis from criminal prosecution. Landis agreed, but he also had to agree to keep quiet about his allegations. His plans to go public with his story would have to be put on hold.

Flirting with the idea of having Landis go undercover, Novitzky told Landis that he was currently investigating a California cycling team called Rock Racing. The brainchild behind the team was Los Angeles fashion designer Michael Ball, owner of Rock & Republic jeans, who had set out to build a domestic racing team that would embody a bad-boy image. Its riders wore all black with white skulls on their chests, and many had extensive tattoos—as well as histories of suspensions for failed doping tests. The team had hired Tyler Hamilton, who had come back from his own two-year doping suspension only to fail again in an out-of-competition check in 2009, when he tested positive for dehydroepiandrosterone, or DHEA, a multifunctional steroid. Hamilton claimed it was in an herbal remedy he took after he had stopped using prescription antidepressants. Another Rock Racing rider had recently admitted to being in possession of EPO.

Michael Ball had dark, handsome features and kept in shape. He looked about thirty-five but was actually over fifty. He acted like he was twenty-five, chasing models and partying as if it were the 1970s. Ball referred to anti-doping officials as the Gestapo and felt drug-testing was something that should be handled internally, as it is in the National Football League and Major League Baseball. "This sport is eating its young," he told *Outside* magazine in May 2008. "You have to close ranks and take care of your own."

Novitzky believed Ball was profiting by supplying riders with EPO and other drugs, much as BALCO's Victor Conte had. An investigation of Ball was already under way, and Novitzky hoped to gather enough evidence to obtain a search warrant for his house. He already had teamed up with officers from other agencies, including the Federal Bureau of Investigation, to gather information.

Floyd Landis knew Ball. In fact, he had been to parties at his house where he'd seen guests snorting cocaine, and he was actually in negotiations with Ball about a spot on the Rock Racing team, which was considerably higher profile than his current squad. Novitzky asked Landis if he would wear a recording device and gather evidence.

Floyd felt a bit of queasiness about being an informer. It was one thing for him to have outed himself and his former teammates, especially when he felt he had been so badly treated by Lance, Johan Bruyneel, and Jim Ochowicz. But it was another thing to do something that could potentially incriminate someone with whom he was in negotiations for a job and who had done him no harm. Plus, he didn't think Ball was selling EPO, let alone profiting from it. Still he wanted Novitzky to take him seriously and had given his word that he would help. So he quieted his doubts and agreed to wear a wire.

I am committed, he told himself.

CHAPTER FOURTEEN

THE CHASE

Just after the Tour of California began on May 16, 2010, Floyd Landis called Michael Ball to say that he was passing through Los Angeles and would like to get together. On the designated night, several agents from the Federal Bureau of Investigation, who had been assigned to work with Novitzky on the case, met Landis in his hotel room in Marina del Rey and began strapping an audio recording device to his body, using thick elastic.

By the time they completed the process, which took over an hour, Floyd's torso was wrapped up like a mummy. Shortly before he was to leave, however, Ball began texting him, each time asking to push the meeting back. By midnight, six hours had passed, and Novitzky, who was monitoring the sting from San Francisco, was worried.

"I think he's onto us," Novitzky told Floyd on the phone. "He's definitely figured it out. Let's call it off."

Floyd dismissed Novitzky's concerns, telling him that Ball was probably just out on the town partying with his girlfriend. He said he'd set up another meeting with Ball for the following morning. After making a plan with the FBI agents to have the mummy-wrapping process repeated the next day, Landis went to the hotel bar and had a drink. He was nervous about what he was about to do. Not only was he wearing a wire, but the FBI had stationed agents wearing concealed guns around Ball's condo. What had he gotten himself into? One drink led to another, then another. Pretty soon he was completely hammered.

The next morning, after the FBI agents attached the wire to him again, Floyd crossed the street from his hotel to Ball's high-rise. Floyd had a severe hangover—and apparently Ball did, too, because after the doorman let Landis in, he discovered that Ball was still in his bedroom, half asleep. When he emerged, still only half dressed, the two men began chatting while Ball logged on to his computer, only to see the headline: CYCLIST FLOYD LANDIS ADMITS DOPING, ALLEGES USE BY ARMSTRONG. The story went on to recount the highlights of a scoop in *The Wall Street Journal* about the e-mails Landis had sent to USA Cycling and others in the cycling world.

Landis was caught completely off guard. He knew the *Journal* had been working on a story because Reed had recently been calling him for comments, but on the instruction of federal investigators, Landis had not returned the calls and he had figured it would take the *Journal* a lot longer to get ahold of the e-mails and authenticate them. The story had gone online at 1:27 A.M., the morning of May 20, just about the time Landis was passing out drunk in his hotel room.

"What's going on with this?" Ball asked. But he didn't seem angry. Instead, he expressed support for Floyd. His outing of himself, Lance, and other riders on the Postal team was the best thing that could happen to cycling, Ball said. "Somewhere in this country, there's a federal investigator that will see this and open an investigation," Ball added.

"You think?" Floyd said.

Floyd felt bad at that moment, but he also felt that it was too late to turn back. He had made a commitment to Novitzky and he intended to keep it. He asked Ball if he could help himself to a drink and opened Ball's fridge.

When Floyd opened the fridge, he saw packages of human growth hormone. Armed with a key chain video/audio recorder that the FBI agents had given him that morning, he began filming close-ups of the labels of each—video that Novitzky later used to obtain a search warrant of Ball's apartment and to seize the drugs Floyd had seen.

But the prosecutors never charged Ball. He was just the sponsor of a minor cycling team, and clearly not the mastermind of a doping ring. He turned out to have a prescription for HGH. The information that Landis had supplied about the US Postal team, on the other hand, pointed the way to a far bigger target. Once Novitzky and Tygart had thoroughly debriefed Landis and concluded on the basis of what he told them that there was good reason to believe that doping was going on in the highest echelons of the sport, involving cycling's biggest star, Novitzky began planning a much more ambitious investigation—which meant getting federal prosecutors who would work with him and ultimately bring criminal charges. He was assigned to work with two prosecutors in the US Attorney's Office at Los Angeles—Doug Miller, a methodical, thirtysomething assistant US attorney, who had a decade of experience prosecuting criminal cases, including bank frauds, and Mark Williams, a young, energetic lawyer who arrived at the office in 2008.

Meanwhile, Armstrong, knowing nothing of the criminal investigation that was already in motion and completely blindsided by the *Wall Street Journal* story, which broke while he was in the middle of the Tour of California, did what he had done so many times before—denied the allegations and attacked the character of the accuser. Armstrong and his army of publicists wrote off Landis's remarks as the nonsensical ramblings of a disgruntled teammate who was a proven liar. "Floyd lost his credibility a long time ago," Lance told reporters outside the RadioShack team bus at the Tour of California. "This is a man who has been under oath several times and had a completely different version, wrote a book for profit with a completely different version . . . someone that took, some would say, close to $1 million from innocent people for his defense under a different premise. Now, when it's all run out, the story changes."

Armstrong also accused Landis of harassing and threatening him for years. But Armstrong and his associates knew the truth: Landis's allegations were the most detailed and damning of Armstrong's career. If they led to a federal investigation—and if there were any doubts about that, they would have been dispelled by a second story that appeared in the *Journal* the next day, on the twenty-first, stating that such an investigation was indeed under way—it might prove impossible for them to control the story and the flow of information.

On May 25, just two days after the conclusion of the Tour of California, David Zabriskie met with Doug Miller and Mark Williams to tell *his* story about using EPO and other drugs, which he testified that team director Johan Bruyneel had pressured him to do. Zabriskie was one of the first of many who would step forward in response to a request from Novitzky, who had begun contacting many of the key riders and people close to them, seeking interviews and proffering limited immunity—a standard legal arrangement that allows a cooperating witness to provide testimony while being guaranteed protection from prosecution based on any admissions he might make, provided he tells the truth.

Kristin Armstrong, Sheryl Crow, Frankie and Betsy Andreu, Jonathan Vaughters and Christian Vande Velde of the Garmin-Sharp cycling team, and Levi Leipheimer of the RadioShack team, all heard from Novitzky that summer, and all accepted the proffers and agreed to talk. Potential witnesses who initially refused to talk with investigators were issued grand jury subpoenas. Those people included Armstrong's USPS teammates George Hincapie, Tyler Hamilton, Kevin Livingston, and Yaroslav Popovych; Armstrong's longtime friend, Oakley sunglass representative Stephanie McIlvain and her husband; and Allen Lim, a physiologist who had worked for Armstrong. That meant they would be forced to testify—without a lawyer—in front of a sitting grand jury in Los Angeles.

Armstrong lined up his own high-powered lawyers to try to stymie the investigation. His Austin attorney, Tim Herman, flew out to California and hired Bryan Daly, a Los Angeles attorney who was a former prosecutor in the US Attorney's Office there and understood how it worked. While in L.A., Herman called the prosecutors who were handling the case to see if he and Daly could come in to speak with them. The prosecutors turned them down, saying it was too early in the investigation for such a meeting to be productive.

Armstrong also got a tip from Karl Rove, who lived in Austin, knew Armstrong, and wanted to help. He suggested Armstrong contact Robert D. Luskin of Patton Boggs in Washington, DC, a Democratic lawyer with connections at the US Justice Department. With his gold hoop earring, buff body, shaved head, and Ducati Monster motorcycle, the sixty-five-year-old Luskin was hardly the typical white-collar Washington, DC, lawyer. He was known around Washington as the first male attorney to wear an earring in the Supreme Court. But that hadn't kept him from the avenues of power in that town. It was he who had represented Rove—and gotten him off—when he was accused of outing covert CIA operative Valerie Plame.

Armstrong also hired a crisis management consultant, Mark Fabiani, a silver-haired lawyer in San Diego who had earned the nickname the Master of Disaster when he served as special counsel to President Bill Clinton during the Whitewater investigations in the early 1990s. After that, Fabiani had acted as deputy campaign manager and spokesman for Vice President Al Gore's presidential election bid, including Gore's postelection challenge of Florida's vote count. As it happened, his firm had also represented Marion Jones throughout the BALCO affair.

And there were more: Lance retained the services of John Keker of San Francisco–based Keker & Van Nest, and his partner, Elliot Peters. Known as a confrontational bulldog in the courtroom, Keker had represented Enron Corporation's former chief financial officer Andrew Fastow, and specialized in getting Wall Street executives off the hook for their alleged transgressions. In an effort to influence the outcome of the government's probe, Armstrong began offering to pay for legal representation for some of his former teammates. Tyler Hamilton turned down Armstrong's offer. Hamilton already had an attorney, Chris Manderson, and Hamilton wasn't planning on protecting Lance. In fact, Manderson made it clear that if Hamilton lied in front of the grand jury, he would refuse to represent him. Hamilton had two choices, Manderson said: Tell the truth or risk going to prison. Hamilton was the epitome of a flawed witness. After his comeback from his positive test for a blood transfusion in 2004, he had tested positive again in 2009. Meanwhile, he had also been implicated in Operación Puerto, the raid on the Spanish doping lab that occurred in 2006. In a sport where doping was prevalent, Hamilton had been one of the most aggressive users of blood transfusions and other performance-enhancing tactics. Even Lance thought of him as a doping extremist.

So Hamilton was a known liar. Any testimony he gave would also be compromised by the fact that he had an obvious personal grievance with

Lance, having heard that his ex-wife, Haven, had dated Lance shortly after they divorced.

But prosecutors figured his one saving grace as a witness was that, while he had lied to the public and even to his closest friends, he had never lied in a court of law. And just as they hoped, now that Hamilton had a federal subpoena to answer to, he decided the lying would have to stop. He wasn't willing to risk going to prison to keep his secrets.

In July, in the federal courtroom in downtown Los Angeles, Hamilton spilled his guts to the grand jury, testifying among other things that he had seen Armstrong inject EPO. Hamilton's testimony went on for nearly four hours—so long that the prosecutors weren't done with him by the end of the day when it was time to send the jurors home. Proseuctors offered Hamilton limited immunity if he would talk to prosecutors outside of the grand jury. Hamilton agreed. In a room with his own attorneys present, Hamilton proceeded to give Novitzky more details that would be helpful in the investigation.

For Hamilton, it felt good to give his testimony. To finally tell the truth. And then, having told the truth to the US government, he decided it was time to tell the truth to the world. He began shopping around a book proposal.

One early morning that summer, Novitzky approached Stephanie McIlvain at her home in Southern California. Novitzky was aware that McIlvain had visited Armstrong during his cancer treatments in Indiana, and he believed she overheard his 1996 hospital room discussion with doctors about his previous drug use, and that she lied under oath in her SCA testimony. McIlvain was home with her son; her husband, Pat, had already left for work. Standing on her doorstep, Novitzky, who was accompanied by one other federal investigator, went for the jugular. "You lied and you could go to jail if you don't allow us to come into that house and speak with you," he said. "You're in a lot of trouble."

"I'm sorry," McIlvain said, terrified. "I need to get with a lawyer."

A few weeks later she spent more than four hours before a Los Angeles grand jury, recounting what took place in the hospital on the day Armstrong allegedly confessed to doping. She wasn't the killer witness Novitzky had hoped for, however. She told jurors that she had lied to Betsy, to David Walsh, to ESPN, when she said she remembered the hospital room scene. She had heard rumors, she said, of Lance Armstrong's doping, but didn't have any firsthand evidence. She was going through a difficult time, she said, and made up stories about Armstrong because, in some strange way, it made her feel good. She was ashamed. She said nobody at Oakley pressured her in any way with regard to her SCA testimony. She made that story up, she said, to get Betsy Andreu off her back.

Her husband, Pat, also spent considerable time in front of the grand jury. Prosecutors grilled him about whether he was coerced by executives at Oakley to pressure his wife into lying during the SCA testimony. Pat swore under oath that nobody at Oakley ever weighed in.

Greg LeMond was also issued a subpoena in mid-July. He wasn't a subject of the investigation, but prosecutors said they were seeking the documents he obtained in the discovery phase of his lawsuit against Trek, which had been removed to the US District Court in Minnesota in April 2008 and by then settled. LeMond had wanted to go to trial against Trek, but the case unraveled. Although LeMond had recouped minor damages in the settlement, he considered the litigation an outright failure. He was happy to comply with the subpoena, in the hope that those documents might prove helpful in going after Armstrong, even though they hadn't done LeMond much good.

Part of the documentation that LeMond sent to federal prosecutors was his 2004 recording of a conversation between himself and McIlvain in which she admitted that she had, indeed, overheard Armstrong confess to using performance-enhancing drugs in the Indiana hospital room in 1996. LeMond had recorded the phone call with her because he thought McIlvain might be called to testify in a lawsuit with Trek, and he was worried she might try to cover for Lance. He had heard from Betsy that McIlvain was balking and was planning to lie in the hearing.

LeMond also offered to be helpful in another way. He was going to lend his support to Floyd Landis. Now that Landis had come clean about doping, he wanted to do what he could to help him with any legal issues he might still be facing. As a favor to LeMond, two of his own laywers—Leo Cunningham and Mark Handfelt—agreed to represent Landis and assist him with navigating the federal investigation. LeMond and Landis were now allies in the fight against doping, and against Armstrong.

Meanwhile, Landis was secretly working on a legal case of his own. He possessed an acute understanding of the interwoven relationships and commercial forces that had made it possible for Armstrong and his associates to keep Armstrong's doping secret. Turning to a law that private citizens have used to bring civil lawsuits against major companies, including tech giant Oracle Corporation and drugmaker Pfizer Inc. for allegedly defrauding the government, Landis sued Armstrong and other key players—including Thom Weisel, Bill Stapleton, Johan Bruyneel, and Bart Knaggs. On June 10, he had filed his federal whistle-blower lawsuit, under seal, claiming Armstrong and his closest backers defrauded the federal government when they took money from the United States Postal Service. The team's contracts with the Postal Service specifically prohibited doping, and it is a violation of the federal False Claims Act to knowingly violate a government contract. If found liable, the men could be responsible for up to triple the amount of money paid out on the US Postal contract, which was somewhere north of $30 million all told. The suit had come about in an interesting way. After the *Wall Street Journal* story broke, the cycling website VeloNews had run an article entitled EXPERT: FLOYD LANDIS COULD BE PROTECTED, AND REWARDED, BY WHISTLE-BLOWER LAW. Landis saw the article and called the whistle-blower lawyer quoted in the story. The lawyer, Paul Scott, agreed to take the case on a contingency basis, since the potential rewards were great. As a US citizen, Landis could sue the men under the False Claims Act on behalf of the US government and be rewarded with up to 30 percent of any money recovered by the government. Justice Department lawyers in Washington, DC, began weighing whether to join Landis's lawsuit and launched an investigation of his claims. If they joined in, Landis would have a much better chance of receiving a payout.

Novitzky and the federal prosecutors thought that if they could get George Hincapie to talk, they would have the story of doping nailed down. Hincapie was the only American rider who was close to Armstrong during all of his seven Tour de France wins. He knew everything. And unlike almost every other close teammate of Armstrong's, Hincapie was a credible witness.

He had never tested positive, never publicly proclaimed his innocence. He had never even had a falling-out with Armstrong. He had no motivation to lie. In fact, his lawyer, Zia Modabber, was a close friend of Lance's.

But once it became clear that the prosecutors were serious, Hincapie began to think that he should find a lawyer without any connections to Lance. Hincapie's friend, William Crowley, the second in command for billionaire hedge fund owner Eddie Lampert and an avid cyclist, hooked Hincapie up with Crowley's own lawyers at the white-shoe boutique law firm Wachtell, Lipton, Rosen & Katz, in New York. One of the partners assigned to help Hincapie figure out his next move was David Anders. Anders, a former federal prosecutor known for highly publicized takedowns of Wall Street titans and for his WorldCom prosecution, understood how to navigate the situation. It was unlikely Hincapie was in any legal jeopardy himself, he explained, so long as he cooperated and didn't lie to prosecutors. They agreed that Anders and Hincapie would fly to Los Angeles together and meet with the prosecutors—*after* the 21-day Tour de France, which Hincapie was scheduled to race in later that summer.

The race that July was a disaster for Armstrong. Even sports channels like ESPN and Versus had begun mentioning in their coverage the investigation under way in Los Angeles. Armstrong fell out of contention after crashing just before a pivotal mountain stage. He tried to win just a single stage, but, in the end, he couldn't even manage that. When Lance stepped foot outside the bus, he was mobbed by reporters asking him about Floyd's more detailed allegations. Instead of holding post-race press conferences each day, Lance gave interviews to a Team RadioShack public relations manager, who played a tape of the interview in the press room. Reporters covering the event were forced to huddle around a tiny speaker and jot down notes from the recording.

By the end of 2010, federal prosecutors had interviewed dozens of witnesses. In grand jury testimony and informal proffers, they learned of the widespread doping and trafficking of controlled substances. They had even procured the testimony of Sheryl Crow, after she had agreed to their proffer. Crow had witnessed doping firsthand, she said. She told investigators that in 2005, she had flown with Lance on a private jet to Belgium, where she watched him receive a blood transfusion.

Michael Ball was cooperating against Armstrong, too. But Ball had something Novitzky wanted. Some members of Ball's Rock Racing team told him that they had stayed in a house that Lance had once lived in and had found an old blood testing device made by Quest Diagnostics called a HemoCue—a small, red gadget the size of a paperback book that can instantly analyze blood. By pricking one's finger and placing a drop of the blood onto a tiny piece of clear plastic and inserting it in the HemoCue, a rider could derive an instant hematocrit reading. The riders told Ball that Armstrong's red blood cell percentages were still stored in the device and they were abnormally high. The riders gave the HemoCue to Ball, who ended up keeping it at his office. Ball handed it over to Novitzky, who analyzed it for possible evidence against Lance. Ball was never charged. Novitzky, Miller, and Williams began to put together the pieces of a charging document against Armstrong. For months, ever since hearing the allegations Landis had made, they'd been discussing how they might build a criminal case against Armstrong and the managers of the Postal team. Assuming Landis's allegations were true, which all the evidence seemed to substantiate, the challenge would be to find out how they violated federal criminal law. Doping itself is not a crime in the United States, so they had to look for ways the team's sophisticated conspiracy could have violated federal laws. They figured wire fraud might be one potential criminal charge because it covers any communications by mail, fax, or e-mail. Another option was a conspiracy charge for allegedly covering it all up. Then there was good old-fashioned drug trafficking.

There was also a more creative option: that Armstrong and the US Postal team had criminally defrauded their sponsors by violating their contracts with criminal acts, such as transporting controlled substances across state and international borders. (Every one of the team's major sponsor contracts included clauses that prohibited the team from doping. Some of the contracts were more explicit than others.) And that, ultimately, was the legal strategy the prosecution settled on: to charge Armstrong, and perhaps the US Postal team managers, with having defrauded their sponsors—not just the US Postal Service but the Discovery Channel, Trek, Nike, and so on—when they signed off on contracts. This was unique in the annals of professional sports. Though other athletes like Barry Bonds and Roger Clemens had been charged with lying under oath and obstruction of justice, none had ever before been charged in federal court with defrauding sponsors by doping.

The investigation took a heavy emotional toll on Lance, who was worried what the public thought of him. He was desperate for information not just about Novitzky and his latest moves but about the reporters covering the story, too—and he would stew over their coverage, dismissing them, including us, as hacks who were completely wrong on the facts. Despite the headlines, Armstrong found some measure of consolation in telling himself that he was still able to pass the Starbucks test: When he walked into Starbucks to get his morning coffee, nobody shouted, "Doper!"

Lance was trying, so far as possible, to lead a normal family life. His ex-wife, Kristin, had been subpoenaed and later testified, but one afternoon in August, at the Four Seasons in Austin, he bumped into her lunching with friends, and they greeted each other cordially. With his girlfriend, Anna Hansen, who is ten years his junior, he was planning for the arrival of a baby girl, his fifth child, due in October.

Lance did believe, however, that there was a real possibility the grand jury in Los Angeles would hand down an indictment. The thought that he might face a criminal trial unnerved him. But everyone else in his world seemed confident that he would emerge unscathed, just as he always had. Lance's agent, Bill Stapleton, continued to keep in close touch with all of his major sponsors and paid a visit to Nike headquarters that summer. By late August, two of his sponsors—Michelob and RadioShack—had filmed new ads starring Lance. And Nike was in the midst of planning an aggressive expansion of the Livestrong brand overseas, particularly in Europe.

As the federal investigation dragged on for months, it hit a number of snags.

One problem was that George Hincapie wasn't the star witness prosecutors had hoped he would be. In a five-hour meeting in a private room at the courthouse in Los Angeles, Hincapie told Novitzky and the prosecutors that he had doped and that he was generally aware that his friend Lance had doped—engaging in blood transfusions, using EPO and other banned drugs.

Hincapie said Armstrong had even provided him with vials of EPO. But Hincapie said he hadn't seen Lance doping firsthand. And some of Hincapie's testimony contradicted Floyd Landis's account.

Kevin Livingston, who now ran a training business in the basement of Armstrong's bike store, denied almost all knowledge of Armstrong's use and the team's sophisticated doping regimen. Kevin was represented by Lance's friend Modabber.

Beyond that, nearly all of the cyclists who provided testimony had serious credibility issues. Even Jonathan Vaughters, now managing a team committed to clean cycling, was compromised because he had become bitter enemies with Armstrong, which meant he might have an axe to grind.

In 2011, Lance announced his second retirement from professional cycling. Then thirty-nine years old, he said he intended to spend more time with his children and dedicate more energy to the Lance Armstrong Foundation.

Armstrong's image, though, was about to suffer from another assault. In May 2011, almost exactly one year after the *Journal*'s story about the Floyd Landis e-mail, Tyler Hamilton appeared on *60 Minutes* and confessed to doping. In a message he sent by e-mail to his friends and family just before the broadcast, Hamilton said the federal investigation had triggered him to tell "the whole truth" for the first time, because he had concluded that "this was the way forward" for him. During the TV interview, he described his own doping as well as that of many of his teammates, including Armstrong, who he said had injected EPO more than once in his presence. Hamilton also repeated an allegation Landis had made—that Armstrong had paid a bribe to quash the positive test after the 2001 Tour de Suisse.

The day after the show aired, Mark Fabiani made a statement: "Tyler Hamilton is a confessed liar in search of a book deal—and he managed to dupe *60 Minutes*. . . . Most people, though, will see this for exactly what it is: More washed-up cyclists talking trash for cash." At Fabiani's suggestion, Lance created a website, www.Facts4Lance.com, to counter Hamilton's allegations.

Hein Verbruggen chimed in, too. In an interview following the show, Verbruggen said Armstrong "never, never, never" doped. He denied that there had ever been a cover-up of any positive test. "I repeat again: Lance

Armstrong has never used doping. Never, never never. And I say this not because I am a friend of his, because that is not true. I say it because I'm sure. Even if we would like, it would not be possible to bury a positive test."

A few weeks later, Hamilton went to visit friends in Aspen, where he ran into Lance at Cache Cache, a fashionable restaurant in town. According to Hamilton, Lance bumped his shoulder aggressively, and remarked that nobody would ever believe him. He then told him that his lawyers would chew him up and spit him out; his life would become a living hell. Hamilton described the encounter to his lawyer, who complained to the prosecutors that Lance was trying to intimidate a witness. Though both Lance and the owner of the restaurant described the incident as a non-event, it was taken seriously enough that the FBI showed up at Cache Cache a few days later to take possession of its surveillance tapes. Since the tapes captured only the kitchen area, they had no firm evidence.

This was at least the second incident of what investigators believed was witness intimidation. Armstrong had sent an e-mail to former US Postal teammate Michael Barry, asking him to lie to the grand jury. Barry refused, and informed investigators of the exchange.

Despite the scrutiny, Lance had no intention of leaving the public stage. His plans involved competing in marathons in 2011 and 2012, and eventually in the Ironman Triathlon. During 2011, he made his first forays into off-road tri events and met with only mixed results. He took it hard. But he intended to keep training with Michele Ferrari still by his side.

As of the end of 2011, Armstrong was still actively working for a large stable of sponsors that included Nike, Nissan, Demand Media, FRS, and Anheuser-Busch. "Our relationship with Lance remains as strong as ever," a Nike spokesman told *The Wall Street Journal* that summer. Anheuser-Busch continued airing the Michelob Ultra ad that Lance had taped the previous summer, showing it during both the US Open golf broadcast and the 2011 Tour de France. "Lance has performed as an extraordinary athlete in a demanding sport, making him admired by millions who lead active lifestyles," a spokesman for the company said. "That was our opinion when we signed him and that is our opinion today." There was a slight drop in requests for Lance to make speeches and public appearances, compared with a year earlier.

His agent, Bill Stapleton, even got on the phone with Vanessa to say, "That's typical of a retired athlete."

Sitting in his living room in front of his fireplace in Durango, Colorado, in January 2012, Rick Crawford checked the Twittersphere for the latest posts about Lance Armstrong. The two men hadn't spoken since the late 1980s, back when Rick had invested a couple of years of his time in helping Lance to make the transition from swimmer to triathlete.

After working with Lance in Plano, Rick had become a cycling coach to elite riders, including Levi Leipheimer, who later joined Armstrong's teams. Between 1999 and 2002, Rick also helped Leipheimer procure EPO. The blood booster provided Levi the edge he needed to get a job offer in 2000 from Lance's US Postal team. But Rick's beef with Lance had nothing to do with doping. Rather, it had to do with his bitterness over the sense that he had been used by Lance to get to a certain level—then, once Lance reached his goals, Lance had tossed his old coach aside. *You steamrolled me, Lance,* Rick thought to himself. *You have no regard for feelings or relationships.*

After a few glasses of wine, Rick jumped into the Twitter conversation himself, adding: "Lance isn't what he says he is. He's kind of a dick. And the foundation is a shell, just another thing Lance has learned to control."

Within a day, Rick received a direct message on Twitter from Lance, seeking his phone number. When Lance called Rick the next day, Rick recalls him saying, "Hey, dude, I just saw your boss-to-be, here in Austin. He was here for a fund-raiser." At the time, Rick was up for a job as collegiate cycling director at Colorado Mesa University. It just so happened that the head of CMU's athletic program had brain cancer and recently had become a Lance Armstrong Foundation donor.

"I don't think this is looking good for your job prospects at CMU. I'm just going to tell him you've been talking shit. This doesn't look good for you," Lance added, according to Rick.

Rick was repentant. "I had one wine too many. The tweets were immature," he said, and he apologized. But as he spoke, he had the sense that he might never get to talk to Lance on the phone again in his life. So just before hanging up, Rick decided he would use the moment to cleanse his soul, to tell Lance what he really thought: "You smashed me. You have no right to ask me to be nice to you. You're not nice to me. And I am not happy about it." Lance demanded that he erase the tweets, and Rick obliged.

A few days later, Rick met with the head of CMU's athletic department, who asked him to explain himself. He apologized for sending the tweets. "Look," Rick said, "this is personal. It's between me and Lance. To me, he isn't a hero." Rick got the job.

At the time, Lance, Anna, and their two young children were living part-time in Austin and part-time in their $9 million five-bedroom home in Aspen, Colorado, with views of the Rocky Mountains.

He traveled a lot for foundation-related events. When he popped in at a Canadian Tire store in Toronto, after the chain agreed to carry Livestrong ellipticals, treadmills, and exercise bikes and to make a minimum $4 million donation, an adoring throng was there to greet him. He flew to New York, where he met with Nike CEO Mark Parker to don a flashy new $150 Nike wristband. He and Stapleton reached a deal with two-year-old Israeli start-up Mobli, a visual social media platform based in New York, that would allow Armstrong followers to watch moments from his training sessions as well as his work with the foundation. Both Armstrong and Stapleton joined Mobli's board.

And suddenly things seemed to be again looking up. In early February 2012, André Birotte Jr., the US attorney for the Central District of California, announced, without any explanation, that his office was ending its two-year investigation into alleged fraud by the US Postal team. Doug Miller and Mark Williams, the line prosecutors, who had put so much energy into this investigation and felt they had built a strong case, were very upset. So was Jeff Novitzky, who had been informed of Birotte's decision only minutes before he sent out a press release.

Armstrong had a quiet celebration in Austin, with his kids, his girlfriend, and a cold beer. The end of the investigation didn't just seem to exonerate Armstrong; it also provided his lawyers with ammunition against the media, who, they argued, had gone too far in asserting that there had been illegal behavior and had failed to ask tough questions about the government's legal theory. With the probe now having been dropped, Armstrong's lawyers seemed to have a point.

Travis Tygart, undeterred by the inaction of the US Attorney's Office, decided to proceed with his doping case. Though USADA couldn't press criminal charges, it exercised a great deal of power in the world of elite sports. Tygart had already spoken to a number of the witnesses—not just Floyd Landis but also Tyler Hamilton, and Frankie and Betsy Andreu, with whom he had had extensive conversations. Now he needed more evidence.

Tygart knew the daunting odds. One problem was the eight-year statute of limitations in the anti-doping code. He wanted to bring the case quickly so that Armstrong's final two Tour de France wins in 2004 and 2005 would fall within the statute window. In any case, Tygart planned to argue that the eight-year statute did not apply.

To prepare their case, Tygart and USADA's general counsel, Bill Bock, initiated a series of meetings with about a dozen former Postal riders, promising them leniency if they testified truthfully.

In March, they sat down with David Zabriskie at his lawyer's office on Park Avenue in New York City. As Zabriskie described the moment that Bruyneel told him to start to use EPO, he began to weep. They took a break to allow him to recover.

Tygart and Bock looked at each other before resuming their questioning.

"This is why we're doing this," Bock said quietly to Tygart.

CHAPTER FIFTEEN

SCORCHED EARTH

In February 2012, Lance joined some of the world's fastest and most masochistic athletes, including several Olympians, for a triathlon in Central America. Donning goggles and a bright yellow swim cap, he freestyled 1.2 miles in a strong current on the banks of the Panama Canal. After getting caught in a pack behind American Matty Reed, a 2008 Olympian, he managed tenth place in the swim, in 19 minutes and 22 seconds. Peeling off his black swimskin, he then biked fifty-six miles through the jungle and rain forest on his new Trek Speed Concept, wearing a tight, black custom-made Nike triathlon suit. Unsure of how to pace himself, he came in second on the bike course. Next he ran 13.1 miles on a sunbaked oceanside causeway. After just a few miles, he picked up his pace, flying past pro Chris Lieto to take the lead. For most of the run, it seemed Lance might win. But around the ninth mile, his pace slowed, and in the final mile, an Olympic triathlon bronze and silver medalist overtook him. New Zealander Bevan Docherty crossed the finish line in 3 hours, 50 minutes, and 13 seconds—42 seconds ahead of Lance, who was runner-up. Not too shabby for his first professional triathlon since his retirement from cycling.

Triathlons, Lance figured, would now be his calling—his future livelihood and the source of renewed athletic glory. He felt he was on his way to proving to the world that he was not just the best cyclist of all time but a badass swimmer and runner, too. Lance vowed to himself that he would lose a little weight and work on his stride. He also changed his diet, going vegan for breakfast and lunch. That spring, he entered five middle-distance events, showing up for them with his posse of coaches and handlers, his own personal photographer, and sometimes his girlfriend, Anna, and his kids in tow. Fans mobbed him at the finish lines. His popularity, he gloated to himself, must be driving Novitzky nuts.

In May, he traveled to the small town of Haines City, in the heart of central Florida. Competing against two thousand other participants, he came out of the swim in Lake Eva in fifth place. Then he biked through rural Polk County, easily passing the top four competitors, before running laps at Lake Eva Park. He won, beating his nearest competitor, a Ukrainian pro, by 11 minutes.

Two weeks later, he competed against a field of triathlon veterans in Kailua-Kona, Hawaii—considered the spiritual home of the sport and Lance's new favorite retreat. He completed the entire event in just 3 hours, 50 minutes, and 55 seconds overall, breaking the course record by nearly 7 minutes.

The next goal: to win the Ironman World Championship, the culminating event in the season's series of Ironman competitions, to be held in Kailua-Kona that October, when he would be forty-one years old. It begins with a 2.4-mile swim, followed by a 112-mile bike leg and then a 26.2-mile run—double the distances of any of the run-bike-swim events in which Lance had competed to date. His cancer foundation had formed a partnership with the World Triathlon Corporation, a privately held company that owns all the Ironman events. Their deal would raise more than $1 million for the foundation, which would bring hefty financial benefits for Lance, too. He would score payments ranging from $3,000 to $120,000 for every event he won. Even more important, the world championship would bring him an entirely new fan base, making him attractive to sponsors, especially because the Ironman has the most desirable demographic in sports, drawing a disproportionate share of wealthy entrepreneurs, CEOs, doctors, and lawyers—just the kind of sports enthusiasts who happily spend thousands of dollars on high-end athletic gear, equipment, and training. Still solidly behind Lance as he planned for the Ironman, Nike provided him with a series of custom-made triathlon suits in gray and black, with LIVESTRONG down the front and yellow Nike swooshes. Because of Lance's participation, NBC made plans to broadcast two hours of the championships, up from the usual ninety minutes. It would show the event on the airwaves in October instead of December, as it had in the past.

Lance had been a part-time resident in Kukio, Hawaii, with its golf and beach club surrounded by white sands and lava rock, since 2008. Once he went into training for the Ironman, he and Anna and their young kids relocated to a friend's luxury private home in Kona. He planned to spend at least six weeks of 2012 there, arranging to have his older kids—Luke, Isabelle, and Grace—flown in from Austin on his Gulfstream, during their spring breaks.

To train, Lance rode over the Kohala volcano into the Pololu Valley, with its black sand beach, and alongside the Queen Ka'ahumanu Highway, the stretch of road that comprises a key part of the Hawaiian Ironman, sometimes passing his triathlon rival, the pro Chris Lieto, or his friend Michael Dell, the founder and CEO of Dell Inc., on their bikes. Lance swam in Kailua Bay, an inlet on the west coast of the Big Island of Hawaii, with his coach, Jimmy Riccitello, nearby on a stand-up paddleboard. He also became a member of the Kona Masters elite swimming team, adding pool workouts at the Kona Community Aquatic Center of between 2,000 and 3,000 yards three days a week.

For Lance to earn one of the 1,700 slots in the Kona championships, he would have to participate in one of the 140.6-mile qualifying events. He selected the France Ironman to be held in Nice in June. Wanting to familiarize himself with the course beforehand, he flew to Kortrijk, Belgium, on his Gulfstream jet in April, met up with Johan Bruyneel, who was then the manager of the RadioShack-Nissan team, and they both headed south to Nice. The France Ironman course took Lance through seventeen towns and into the mountains near the French Riviera, while Johan rode in a follow car beside him.

Now that the US attorney in Los Angeles had dropped the criminal fraud investigation against Armstrong, life returned to the Lance version of normal. He rented a villa in Cap-d'Ail for the month of April and returned to the States briefly in May, to deliver a keynote speech at a corporate event and to train and compete in Half Ironmans in the States.

However, the legal battles were far from over. Lawyers with the Justice Department's Civil Division in Washington, DC, were still considering whether to join Floyd Landis's whistle-blower lawsuit. One of those lawyers was Robert Chandler, from the department's Commercial Litigation Branch, who had worked closely with the US Postal Service Office of Inspector General in connection with the civil case for at least a year. In June 2011, the USPS OIG had issued Lance a subpoena, asking him to provide, among other things, a long list of records related to his business relationship with Tailwind Sports and Capital Sports & Entertainment from the mid-1990s to 2004, when the USPS sponsored Lance's cycling teams. The subpoena also requested Lance's correspondence with Michele Ferrari, and with any employees of the US Anti-Doping Agency, the World Anti-Doping Agency, testing laboratories, the USPS, and "any person (including any companies or other organizations) that at any time manufactured or distributed any substance believed to have the potential to enhance an athlete's ability to compete in endurance sports." On top of all that, it also sought Lance's training journals and medical records, including hematocrit and hormone levels, and any financial records reflecting payments to Ferrari, the UCI, USA Cycling, WADA or USADA, and any USPS employees, including fellow riders.

But Lance still hadn't answered the government's request for documents. His lawyers sought—unsuccessfully—to quash the subpoena, and then later tried to sidestep it, arguing that complying with the subpoena during the criminal investigation would have violated Lance's Fifth Amendment rights against self-incrimination. In mid-2012, nearly a year later—and several months after the threat of criminal investigation ended—Lance's lawyers now fought vigorously to keep the court record from public view. If the public found out that Lance had intended to assert his Fifth Amendment rights, well, that in itself would damage Lance's reputation, his lawyers asserted.

Thom Weisel had received a similar subpoena, and on the advice of his lawyer at Sullivan & Cromwell, he had complied, providing documents, including evidence that Weisel had lost a significant amount of money on his backing of the team. Weisel's lawyers said he hadn't known about any doping by Lance or others on the team.

Johan Bruyneel was subpoenaed when he flew back to San Francisco in mid-May for the start of the Amgen Tour of California, in which RadioShack-Nissan was competing. He was served at the airport, and later met with federal investigators, providing a videotaped deposition. What he said during the taped deposition hasn't been made public so far.

While he was a pro cyclist, Lance had developed a lucrative side business of hosting so-called once-in-a-lifetime Ride with Lance experiences. Small groups of fifteen to fifty people paid $5,000 to $20,000 apiece for the privilege of working out with Lance for an hour or a morning, with all proceeds going to various charities, or so many participants thought. Some donors who neglected to read the fine print were angry when they learned that Lance himself was pocketing some of the money in the form of appearance fees, and collecting anywhere from $75,000 to $400,000. And now, Lance agreed to spend Memorial Day weekend hosting Swim Bike Run with Lance & Friends, a training camp to be held at a Kona resort hotel whose golf course was situated on the running leg of the Ironman course. Up to fifty participants would pay $25,000, not including the cost of getting to Hawaii, with the proceeds going to a juvenile diabetes charity in Hawaii. Uniforms emblazoned with the name Mellow Johnny's were to be courtesy of his shop in Austin. Lance was to be paid handsomely to participate in the weekend event, which also advertised Ironman stars Dave Scott and Chrissie Wellington, both new friends of Lance's, as guest coaches.

Other events were in the works, too. The Lance Armstrong Foundation began crafting a plan to take bids on eBay for the Ultimate Kona Ironman Experience with Lance Armstrong, to be held during the world championships in October. The package included a coveted spot in the race, five nights in a hotel, and a chance to go on a training ride, swim, or run, and dinner, with Lance. Bidding would start at $40,000.

Anheuser-Busch, which used Lance to promote its Michelob Ultra line, meanwhile began planning a sweepstakes that it would advertise in two-page spreads in *Sports Illustrated* and *Runner's World* magazines. Entrants had the chance to win a $19,000 package highlighted by a trip to Kona to "hike, kayak or even take a ride" with Lance at some point between October 13 and 18. The tagline for the campaign seemed intended to taunt Jeff Novitzky: "Ultra invites you to catch Lance . . . if you can."

The organizers of the Kona training camp ended up canceling it, however, blaming low enrollment of fewer than twenty people due to too many overlapping events occurring during and around the Memorial Day weekend. That may have been disappointing, but Lance's long-range plans were about to encounter a much more serious obstacle, in the form of a roadblock thrown up by Travis Tygart's US Anti-Doping Agency.

Earlier that May, USADA's general counsel, Indiana-based Bill Bock, had placed a phone call to Lance's longtime attorney Mark Levinstein of Williams & Connolly in Washington, DC. Levinstein had represented Lance for many years. When it surfaced that Lance's urine samples from the 1999 Tour had tested positive for EPO in 2005, Levinstein, together with Lance and Bill Stapleton, had launched a fusillade of unverifiable accusations, including sabotage, against multiple targets. This was a man who was unafraid to go on the attack.

When Bock reached Levinstein on the phone, he said that it was clear to USADA that there had been a massive doping scheme and conspiracy on the US Postal team, and that they wanted Lance to come clean about his role. "We're prepared to bring a case but we'd like to give him an opportunity to be on the right side of this thing, and to tell the truth, and to be a part of cleaning up the sport, like some former teammates of his have done." Bock didn't name the teammates.

Bill Bock and Travis Tygart were both regular church goers, but they had vastly different personalities. Tygart tended to display the characteristics of the stern god of the Hebrew Bible, whereas Bock seemed more like the compassionate, New Testament version. Both men viewed doping in sports as a black-and-white issue. Dopers are cheaters and they need to be punished. Bock, however, was fond of saying that he sins every day, and though he'd like to think he would never try performance-enhancing drugs, he couldn't possibly know what it's like for professional athletes faced with the decision of whether to dope or risk career-altering consequences.

USADA was offering Lance a chance for a deal: Come forward and admit to everything and face a relatively modest punishment. USADA intended to strip Armstrong of his final two Tour de France wins—they were within the official eight-year statute of limitations—and suspend him from competition for six months.

To Bock, it seemed this would be a good, face-saving trade-off for Lance. By coming clean, he could hold on to most of his Tour wins, and he would probably be able to keep at least some of his sponsors. He could then use his role as a crusader against cancer to rehabilitate his public image. Bock told Levinstein that Lance had a limited window of time in which to respond, that he'd have to sit down with him and Travis Tygart in the coming weeks. If he didn't, they would proceed with a case against him, leaving Lance with only two choices: He could accept whatever further punishment they decided to mete out, or challenge their findings in an arbitration before a three-person panel. Levinstein punted. He told Bock that he didn't represent Armstrong "for this purpose" and referred Bock to Tim Herman. A few days passed. When Herman didn't call Bock, Bock began to wonder whether Levinstein had even passed along his message, or whether the delay was an attempt to stall the agency's case. Finally, Bock called Herman, who made a proposal: He wanted to set up a conference call and put Lance's entire legal team on the line with Bock.

Herman reconvened several of the lawyers who had defended Lance in the criminal case. The various attorneys had a wide range of skills and had played different roles during the criminal investigation. Robert D. Luskin, the lawyer referred to him by Karl Rove, took the lead. Lance also again retained the services of John Keker and Elliot Peters of San Francisco. During the criminal investigation, Keker and Peters had accused Novitzky of "repeated and flagrant" disclosures of secret grand jury information to the press and had asked a federal court in Los Angeles to hold law enforcement officials accountable for the leaks. The move was intended to discredit Novitzky in anticipation of a possible indictment by the grand jury.

Lance's lawyers were among the who's who of $1,000-an-hour litigators. When they found themselves on the phone with Bill Bock and USADA's legal affairs director, Chinwuba "Onye" Ikwuakor, they must have assumed they'd be in the power seat. After all, as general counsel of USADA, Bock was being paid by a nonprofit whose total annual budget was only $14 million,

$19 million of which was funded by an annual government grant. USADA's entire legal budget was less than what a month's work on a big case by one of Lance's two primary outside law firms would cost. USADA's 2011 Form 990 income tax statement showed that it had paid Bock's Indianapolis law firm $343,054 that year.

Robert Luskin and John Keker went on the attack immediately, bombarding Bock with accusations of impropriety. They accused USADA of basing its case on witness testimony that was given to the grand jury in secret, which they said USADA should never have gotten their hands on in the first place. Although Novitzky and Tygart had worked together closely during the criminal investigation, Tygart always denied receiving any grand jury information from his friend. For their part, Armstrong's lawyers denied that their client had ever used performance-enhancing drugs, and threatened a federal lawsuit that would sink USADA in a legal morass and devour its budget, should it take action. By the end of the forty-five-minute conversation, it was clear that Lance wouldn't be meeting with Bock or Tygart.

Armstrong was in a no-win situation. USADA wouldn't tell him the specific punishment it woud dole out if he did come forward and admit everything. Would they ban him for two years? Four years? He had no idea. He knew that if he did come forward, it would surely end his lucrative endorsement deals and sully his public image. Armstrong believed fighting USADA was the better option. Even if he lost, there was a good possibility, he thought, that he could convince the public that he had been wrongly accused and that he had been unfairly targeted by USADA.

However, with or without Lance, the USADA investigation was going forward. Ten of Lance's former teammates and team employees, including his close friend George Hincapie, had already testified about doping on the US Postal team and the Discovery Channel team. All of those men had agreed to accept a deal: In exchange for a relatively minor suspension, they had come clean—not only about themselves and about Lance, but also about Johan Bruyneel and the three doctors, Michele Ferrari, Pedro Celaya, and Luis Garcia del Moral, as well as the assistant and drug courier, Pepe Martí.

And now Lance was about to learn the consequences of refusing to negotiate with USADA on its terms. So was the public.

On June 13—a day after the Lance Armstrong Foundation began promoting the "Ultimate Kona Ironman Experience with Lance"—Vanessa obtained a copy of USADA's fifteen-page notice letter from a source with knowledge of the investigation, and the *Journal* published it, in its entirety, on its website that day. The letter, which was dated June 12 and written by Bill Bock, was addressed to Lance and the five other men, and accused the six of engaging in a conspiracy to cheat, and of pushing dangerous, performance-enhancing drugs on other riders on the team.

The letter read, in part: "*This action is being brought as a single consolidated action because for a significant part of the period from January 1, 1998, through the present, each of the Respondents has been part of a doping conspiracy involving team officials, employees, doctors, and elite cyclists of the United States Postal Service and Discovery Channel Cycling Teams who committed numerous violations of the Applicable Rules. The purpose of the USPS Conspiracy was to engage in the use of doping substances and techniques, which were either undetectable or difficult to detect in routine drug testing in order to advance the athletic and sporting achievements, financial wellbeing and status of the teams and their riders, employees, members and investors . . . as well as to prevent the truth regarding doping . . . from being revealed.*" Under the subheading COVER-UP, the letter said that "*beginning in 1999 and continuing through the present it has been an object of the Conspiracy to conceal and cover-up the doping conduct. . . . Numerous witnesses will testify that . . . Johan Bruyneel, Pedro Celaya, Michele Ferrari, Lance Armstrong and other co-conspirators engaged in activities to conceal their conduct and mislead anti-doping authorities including false statements to the media, false statements and false testimony given under oath and in legal proceedings, and attempts to intimidate, discredit, silence and retaliate against witnesses.*"

Lance was the lone cyclist who was still clinging to the lie, the letter said. "*With the exception of Mr. Armstrong, every other US rider contacted by USADA* [the document did not say how many of them there were or name any of the ten] *regarding doping in cycling agreed to meet with USADA and to truthfully and fully describe their involvement in doping and all doping by others of which they were aware. Mr. Armstrong was likewise contacted through his legal counsel and given the opportunity to meet with USADA to fully and truthfully disclose all knowledge of anti-doping rule violations committed in the sport of cycling. However, Mr. Armstrong declined USADA's offer."*

The letter also cited "data from blood collections obtained by the UCI" in 2009 and 2010 that showed signs that Lance had used EPO or taken blood transfusions during his cycling comeback, too. As punishment for his transgressions, USADA suggested that Armstrong lose all his titles and receive a lifetime ban from competition—and it provided copies of the letter to both the World Triathlon Corporation and the USA Triathlon, the sport's governing body in this country. It also suggested lifetime bans for Bruyneel, Ferrari, Celaya, del Moral, and Martí.

With the important Nice event just weeks away, Lance had returned to France to train on the Ironman course. He continued to maintain his innocence after USADA's notice letter became public, saying in his statement to the press: "I have never doped, and, unlike many of my accusers, I have competed as an endurance athlete for twenty-five years with no spike in performance, passed more than five hundred drug tests and never failed one. . . . Any fair consideration of these allegations has and will continue to vindicate me."

On June 23, Lance spoke to Vanessa on the phone, complaining about USADA but acknowledging for the first time—in an indirect way—that he had in fact doped. "Say what you will about what I did or didn't do ten years ago, they're not playing by the rules," he told her. "Here's the deal: Athletes cheating in sports, that's bad. But what these guys are doing is far worse!" USADA had a vendetta against him, he insisted. "The levels they have gone to try to fuck me and rig this thing are far worse than any athlete taking a transfusion or some EPO. This is far dirtier."

Our conversations with him, as well as with several people close to him, left us with the sense that he was of two minds about the punishment that USADA threatened to hand down. He knew that all seven of his titles were at risk; but he seemed to have convinced himself that that wouldn't matter because, in the end, people would *know* who won the Tour de France. After all, his trademark yellow jerseys were everywhere: Seven of them decorated the walls of his foundation; another seven were tucked away in the upstairs media room of his 8,000-square-foot home in Austin, Texas; yet more hung on the walls of Thom Weisel's San Francisco offices; still others were framed and on display at Mellow Johnny's.

However, it was clear to us that there was something else Armstrong wasn't taking into account. It wasn't just his titles that were at risk. When USADA sent its letter to Armstrong, along with copies to the World Triathlon Corporation and USA Triathlon, it was setting in motion a series of events that would block Lance from competing in pro-level triathlons. Armstrong had just rediscovered his love for the sport he had competed in as a teenager and was, he told friends, in the best shape of his life. But his plan was about to be scuttled because just after the release of the letter, the two major governing bodies of the sport announced that they were suspending him. According to the rules of both the World and the USA triathlon organizations, any athlete who is facing a sanction from USADA is immediately suspended from competing in events that they sponsor until the doping case is resolved.

The ban meant that Lance wouldn't be able to compete in the races that really mattered to him—those that can confer or deliver points toward world champion status. All year, he had been pursuing the dream of a slot in the 2012 Ironman World Championship. Now that was out of the question. No Ironman race would give up its certification by USA Triathlon to embrace Armstrong, and neither would any other competition that hoped to attract world champion contenders. The Chicago Marathon also rejected Armstrong's bid to run in its October 7 race.

Lance was furious. He told his friends that he felt like an artist who had been told he couldn't paint another masterpiece.

Lance had been stressed, perhaps even scared, during the twenty-one months when Jeff Novitzky was on his trail. The possibility that the grand jury seated in a Los Angeles courtroom might indict him and that the government might choose to go to trial must have been deeply alarming to him. But he had won that battle. That left USADA's Travis Tygart as his only real opponent. Having retired from cycling, Lance felt initially that there was nothing much USADA could do to hurt him, so he had been relatively indifferent to any threat that Tygart represented. Now he was beginning to understand that Tygart might have it within his power to destroy his plans for the future.

Lance still held out hope that public sentiment would turn against the

USADA—particularly with the 2012 London Olympic Games only weeks away. Perhaps people would read the headlines about the agency's move to charge him and ask themselves: *What? I thought this shit was over and done with in February! With the Olympics about to begin, doesn't USADA have better things to do?*

Lance also figured that the public would eventually tire of what he himself thought of as USADA's publicity stunts. Tygart, in his mind, had tried to weasel his way into everything—baseball, football, and even boxing disputes. His charges against Lance, Lance believed, were motivated by his desire for public recognition and were advanced through testimony that Lance argued was bought and paid for by promises of anonymity and immunity for Lance's former teammates.

Nonetheless, Lance was seriously worried. He likened the prospect of going through USADA's arbitration process to looking down the barrel of a shotgun. He knew that, in the ten years that the World Anti-Doping Agency code had been in place, athletes had rarely won in arbitration. The prospect of losing any case where Floyd Landis and Tyler Hamilton would be witnesses against him outraged him. He viewed himself as normal, and saw them as hypocrites, crazies—cycling "wing nuts." If USADA could make a case, using a mountain of circumstantial evidence, and two of the three arbitrators agreed, he was done for. He'd already spent hundreds of thousands of dollars a month for more than a year on legal bills during the federal criminal investigation, and a lengthy arbitration with USADA would cost him millions more.

The dilemma for Lance and his lawyers at this point was how to force USADA to operate in a way they believed was "fair." From the perspective of Armstrong's lawyers, the agency had way too much power. A three-person arbitration panel doesn't need the kind of evidence required for a conviction in a criminal case; it just needs two out of three to agree on "a preponderance of evidence" against him, and USADA could strip Armstrong of his titles and deprive him of his livelihood. This was a much lower bar than required to convict someone in a criminal case, where the legal burden of proof consisted of convincing jurors of guilt "beyond a reasonable doubt." Luskin and Keker were used to operating within the realm of the criminal justice system and federal courts, where they could exploit obscure laws to get cases dismissed and keep evidence away from jurors. Now they were fighting in the realm of arbitrations, where basic common sense ruled and the legal hurdles to such commonsense judgment were nonexistent. And they probably realized that to any person with half a brain, it might seem patently obvious that their client had cheated in cycling. Lance didn't stand a chance.

The strategy became simple: In an attempt to sway public opinion to Lance's side, his lawyers would set out to trash USADA, accusing the agency of not playing fair, and suing it in federal court. The attack team kicked into immediate action. They called USADA's investigation a witch hunt aimed at bringing down a hero, and accused Tygart and Bock of buying the testimony of riders by offering them reduced suspensions for cooperation. Luskin began publicly blasting USADA, calling its leaders "arrogant and craven." In his statements to the press, he repeated Lance's denials that he had ever doped.

On July 9, Lance's legal team filed a lawsuit in federal court in Austin, challenging the agency's effort to bring its charges. The 109-page lawsuit read more like a college thesis on why the agency should not exist. It was filled with personal attacks on Travis Tygart. "Defendant Tygart shares with Agent Novitsky [sic] a well-publicized obsession with 'getting' Mr. Armstrong," the complaint said. "Tygart evidently believes that USADA needs to bring a big case against a 'big fish' to justify its existence. One of, if not the primary, goals of this effort is to convince the United States government to continue and increase the tens of millions of dollars of unsupervised grants that the government already provides to USADA." Tygart and Novitzky, it added, "offered other cyclists corrupt inducements—offers some cyclists could not refuse—to implicate Mr. Armstrong in exchange for saving the cyclists' careers. If they refused to do so, USADA would work to ruin their careers, just as it is now attempting to end Mr. Armstrong's career." The lawsuit said that it is "a testament to USADA's brazenness and callous disregard for its own mission that it seeks to strip Lance of his life's work and his future livelihood"—elite competitive sport—"absent a single positive test." The complaint also included massive amounts of information on the Lance Armstrong Foundation, which, it noted, provides free services to cancer survivors with "financial, emotional and practical challenges," and said that Lance had been the foundation's biggest individual donor, with contributions of more than $6.5 million. Lance's legal team referred to the lawsuit strategy as a long shot, but one that was worth it because, in the very least, it sent a message to Lance's sponsors that they were serious about taking on USADA and it might at least delay the process. The legal strategy turned out to be even less effective than they had hoped.

Later that very same day, US District Judge Sam Sparks, to whom the case had been assigned, dismissed the suit. The crusty judge called it a "lengthy and bitter polemic" filled with "boilerplate" allegations. Basically, Judge Sparks was telling Armstrong's lawyers he did not appreciate their use of the federal court's time to try to advance their public relations agenda. "Armstrong is advised, in the strongest possible terms . . . to omit any improper argument, rhetoric, or irrelevant material from his future pleadings," Judge Sparks wrote.

A few days later, Armstrong's lawyers refiled a significantly shorter suit that focused on challenging the constitutionality of the global Olympic anti-doping infrastructure. They argued that because USADA had worked alongside law enforcement, it should be considered a "state actor" and subject to constitutional restrictions that would prevent it from bringing its case against Armstrong.

Shortly after filing the lawsuit, Lance enlisted his cancer charity to lobby Congress on his behalf. Armstrong wanted USADA's $10 million federal grant from the Office of National Drug Control Policy to be yanked. The foundation hired lobbyists from Patton Boggs, Luskin's law firm, to represent it. On July 12, Wisconsin Republican Jim Sensenbrenner sent a letter—using arguments similar to those in Armstrong's lawsuit—to the Office of National Drug Control Policy, describing USADA's right to exert authority over Armstrong as "strained at best."

Congressman Sensenbrenner, whose district encompasses the Waterloo, Wisconsin, headquarters of Armstrong sponsor Trek, said that it was the International Cycling Union (UCI), not USADA, that had jurisdiction over his titles. He also pointed to USADA's eight-year statute of limitations, which he said precluded it from stripping Armstrong's titles from 2003 and before. "While USADA's charging letter accuses Armstrong of a vast conspiracy involving numerous riders, the agency has not charged any associated athletes other than Armstrong," Sensenbrenner wrote.

Armstrong's lawyers, meanwhile, turned to yet another attempt to undermine USADA—by going after its review board. All anti-doping cases USADA brings are first approved by an independent review board made up of three panelists chosen from a pool of approved people. Looking for dirt on the review board assigned to Armstrong's case, the lawyers struck gold. It turned out that one of the members of the board, Minneapolis attorney Clark Calvin Griffith, a seventy-year-old sports lawyer and adjunct professor at the William Mitchell College of Law in Minneapolis—and the son of former Minneapolis Twins owner Calvin Griffith—had been charged with indecent exposure. The previous March, a twenty-four-year-old female student had complained to the college that Griffith had unzipped his pants and told her to touch his penis. She also complained to the police, who subsequently recorded a phone call he made to her, during which he apologized and said he was in "an absolute daze" when "I unzipped." Shortly afterward, he was charged with indecent exposure, and in July, he entered into a plea agreement in which he admitted no wrongdoing but agreed to undergo sex offender counseling.

"Wow. @usantidoping can pick em," Armstrong tweeted to his nearly four million Twitter followers. "Here's [link to story] 1 of 3 Review Board members studying my case. #protectingcleanathletesandpervs."

Tygart knew that American public opinion was mixed—and that some saw him as the bad guy persecuting their hero. He had received three death threats, he said, including a chilling warning that he would get a bullet to his head. But he was not willing to let a celebrity athlete off the hook.

On August 20, Judge Sparks dismissed Armstrong's lawsuit—this time, for good. He said Armstrong's central argument—that USADA was a "state actor" and that its appeal process was unconstitutional—had no merit. USADA was part of the widely accepted arbitration process recognized by the United States courts. Judge Sparks said that if Armstrong were truly innocent of USADA's charges, he should go to arbitration and argue his point. "This court simply has no business telling national and international amateur athletic organizations how to regulate their respective sports," he wrote. After all his legal and public relations maneuvers, Lance was back to the two choices Bock had originally offered: Fight USADA in arbitration or back down and accept his punishment. Armstrong had three days to make his decision.

Just a few hours before his midnight deadline, Armstrong bowed out of the fight. His decision not to challenge USADA's charges—which he said was not an admission of guilt but a protest of its unfair process—seemed, at the time, shrewd. He avoided the embarrassment of an arbitration hearing in which his former teammates were poised to accuse him in person. The agency that night said it would strip him of all results dating back to August 1, 1998. That was roughly a year before his first Tour de France victory, and also included his wins in other races such as the Tour de Suisse and France's Critérium du Dauphiné Libéré.

The day after the announcement, donations to the foundation rose to twenty-five times their typical daily levels, and Nike made it clear that it would continue to stand by him: "We are saddened that Lance Armstrong may no longer be able to participate in certain competitions and his titles appear to be impacted," it said. "Lance has stated his innocence and has been unwavering on this position." Other sponsors, including Anheuser-Busch and Oakley fell into place, too—in fact, nobody was ready to drop Lance.

Many journalists and fans continued to back him, too. "Sad day," tweeted ESPN's Rick Reilly—an eleven-time Sportswriter of the Year who had defended Lance against doping allegations for fourteen years—adding that he couldn't believe Lance was "giving into doping charges. Never thought he'd quit." Graham Watson, an established cycling photographer who published a 2004 pictorial book with Lance, *Lance Armstrong: Images of a Champion*, also weighed in, writing on his blog, "Lance did what he had to do to win, and he clearly did it very well. . . . All I do know is he's not the manipulative 'bully' certain members of the media have tried to portray him as in their tabloid stories. He was ambitious, ruthless, highly talented, tough, he knew how to lead his teammates and intimidate his rivals to make sure he won. But is he any different from a President, an army General, a corporate leader of industry, a career politician, or any other sporting great?" Sally Jenkins, the *Washington Post* columnist who coauthored Lance's autobiography, wrote an editorial sticking up for Lance: "I don't know if he's telling the truth when he insists he didn't use performance-enhancing drugs in the Tour de France—never have known," she wrote. "I do know that he beat cancer fair and square, that he's not the mastermind criminal the US Anti-Doping Agency makes him out to be, and that the process of stripping him of his titles reeks." Author Buzz Bissinger wrote a cover story for *Newsweek*, saying: "I still believe in Lance Armstrong. I believe his decision had nothing to do with fear of being found guilty in a public setting before an arbitration panel, but the emotional and mental toll of years and years of fighting charges that have never been officially substantiated—despite stemming all the way back to 1999." Bissinger quoted Lance saying he wouldn't fight USADA for the sake of his own mental health, for his family, and his foundation, and for cycling. Cycling, Lance told Bissinger, "doesn't need this." NASCAR driver Max Papis tweeted to Lance, "Too many people too jealous of what u did. Revenge is always sad to see."

Lance even had legislative support. Or perhaps it would be technically more accurate to say that USADA had some serious detractors within government circles. Just after Labor Day, a group of California legislators took aim at USADA, sending a letter to the state's two US senators, Dianne Feinstein and Barbara Boxer, asking them to launch "a comprehensive review of USADA's operations and finances, with special attention to USADA's unilateral changes in rules for dealing with athletes who have never failed a drug test." The letter, dated September 4 and written by California state senator Michael J. Rubio, didn't mention Lance, and Rubio said at the time that his interest in the issue grew out of concern for US Olympic athletes. The letter, which noted that USADA receives "a majority of its funding from taxpayer dollars," was signed by twenty-two other California state senators from both major parties, who were in agreement that the process of suspending athletes was inherently flawed.

However, the reactions were not all pro-Lance and/or anti-USADA. One person in particular was very troubled by Lance's apparently Teflon-like ability to deflect charges: Lance's old Subaru-Montgomery teammate Paul Willerton. He'd assumed that after Lance chose not to fight USADA, his popularity with the public and his corporate sponsors would end. To him, the decision not to fight seemed like a clear admission of guilt and he didn't understand why others didn't see it that way. Willerton, who had retired from the sport in 1993 but kept his ties to many of his former teammates, viewed himself as a cycling insider, someone who knew most of the key players, the good guys and the bad guys. As Willerton monitored the reactions to Lance, he paid particular attention to brand experts who were saying that Lance still had value in the marketplace because Nike still backed him. It bothered him that Nike, which had played such an active role in creating Lance's image over the years as a squeaky-clean athlete, hadn't taken a public stance against either Lance or doping—and he decided to try to do something about it.

Using his girlfriend's e-mail account, and not disclosing his name, Willerton began e-mailing Nike's head of corporate communications each week, asking for specifics about Nike's stance on Lance. Each time, the reply was that Nike would stand by Lance. Willerton, who was friendly with a couple of lower-level executives within Nike, also began calling his two friends, asking them why Nike hadn't stepped away from Lance. These executives told Willerton that they themselves didn't get it. Throughout September, Willerton kept on sending e-mails, hoping to erode some of that support.

Popular and corporate support notwithstanding, Lance was still in a very tough spot—banished from competing in the highest-level triathlons. Lance now turned to small-time races that hadn't signed on to the World Anti-Doping Agency code and didn't have to recognize his suspension.

These triathlons were happy to accept Armstrong because it meant media attention they would otherwise never get. In fact, some events actually gave up their certification with the sport's governing body, USA Triathlon, so they could allow Armstrong into the race. This was no small thing for these races. Having certification from the USAT lowers insurance rates for race organizers and helps attract higher level triathletes. But for some, the trade-off seemed worthwhile. Half Full Triathlon in Maryland, for example, decided to allow Armstrong in the race, and enrollment jumped 20 percent.

The Superfrog Triathlon was still working on getting its USAT certification when Armstrong applied for entry. The race, which raises money for the Navy Seal Foundation, quickly dropped its USAT bid, announced that Armstrong would compete, and saw a spike in registration to a record 825 entrants, at a registration fee as high as $275. When the day came, Lance's sponsors made their presence known; Nike donated Livestrong T-shirts to race volunteers and spectators; Trek sent a representative to observe.

The Superfrog, held at Silver Strand State Beach near San Diego, is the longest-running Half Iron distance triathlon in the world, and its events—a 1.2-mile cold Pacific Ocean swim, 56-mile windy bike ride on Highway 75, and 13.1-mile run on soft sand, hard sand, and pavement—are among the world's most challenging. The course was in territory familiar to Lance, near Ramona, where he had cut his teeth riding with Eddie B when he joined the Subaru-Montgomery team.

Lance hadn't swum much since leaving Nice in June. When the event started, he was rolled by a couple of big waves, and by the time he got out of the ocean, he was a couple of minutes behind the event leaders. But he made up for lost time during the bike ride, and by the end of the first mile of the run, he was in the lead. Lance's 2-hour, 2-minute, and 48-second bike split broke the course record, as did his overall finish time of 3 hours and 49 minutes. After the race, Lance signed the Livestrong T-shirts of spectators. One wore a homemade badge that said F U USADA. Lance added an exclamation point to the end of her badge.

By continuing to find a welcome into certain nonsanctioned competitions, Lance hoped to be the first athlete to face a serious doping case without losing his popularity. And he was doing reasonably well in them, too. He took first place in a trail marathon in Steamboat Springs, Colorado, finishing in 3 hours, 18 minutes, and 10 seconds in what was only the fourth marathon he had ever run in his life. He entered and, finishing behind a local sixteen-year-old, took second place in a 4-hour mountain bike race near his part-time home in Aspen. In September, he completed the GoldenLeaf Half Marathon, with its 13.1-mile course, from Snowmass ski area down to the town of Aspen in 1 hour, 30 minutes, and 51 seconds, to place fourth.

Lance continued to hold out hope that his Tour de France titles could be restored to him and the ban on competition lifted. The UCI, which had always backed him in every other drug scandal in the past, still had to ratify USADA's sanctions for them to become permanent. If the UCI decided to appeal USADA's decision, USADA and the UCI would then have to argue their respective cases in front of the Court of Arbitration for Sport. Over the years, the UCI had been paid handsome sums of money by Armstrong and his camp—including $150,000 in donations the UCI acknowledges, plus, according to Kathy LeMond's sworn account of her conversation with Julien de Vriese, another $500,000 that it doesn't acknowledge. The UCI also helped smooth over at least three suspicious drug tests for Armstrong, which it also denies. Within days of USADA's charges, the UCI, which referred to the charges as "worrisome," requested USADA's "reasoned decision" on banning Armstrong. It said it wanted to see USADA's evidence before it made its own final decision.

Meanwhile, Armstrong continued to flout USADA's power. He kept making statements on Twitter challenging their legitimacy. In late August, for example, he had tweeted a response to what he described as USADA's "pitiful charade": "There comes a point in every man's life when he has to say, 'Enough is enough.' For me, that time is now. I have been dealing with claims that I cheated and had an unfair advantage in winning my seven Tours since 1999. Over the past three years, I have been subjected to a two-year federal criminal investigation followed by Travis Tygart's unconstitutional witch hunt. The toll this has taken on my family, and my work for our foundation and on me leads me to where I am today—finished with this nonsense."

By going on the attack in such a public way, Armstrong and his lawyers were unwittingly opening themselves up to a new problem. USADA had been bashed in the press by dopers before. But in the past, its bylaws did not allow its officials to speak publicly about the details of its cases. To combat the public relations dilemma, USADA changed its bylaws during its 2005 battle with Tyler Hamilton over his two-year doping suspension. The change meant that now Tygart and others in the agency could feel free to address any inaccuracies spread by athletes and their representatives.

Tygart began to have conversations with lawyers for the cooperating cyclists about making USADA's entire investigation of Armstrong public. And he told them that when he sent the agency's "reasoned decision" to the UCI, he would release that to the public, too, perhaps along with supporting documents from his witnesses. Tygart quickly asked the witnesses—including Hincapie, Leipheimer, Vande Velde, and Zabriskie—to sign affidavits of doping by Armstrong and the team leaders and doctors. Their affidavits provided numerous graphic accounts of Armstrong's alleged cheating over a period of fourteen years.

Christian Vande Velde said Lance had called him in 2002 and asked him to come to his apartment in Girona to discuss his role with the team. When Vande Velde showed up, he found Michele Ferrari there with Lance, and Lance informed him that if he were to continue to ride for the Postal team, he would have to follow Dr. Ferrari's program to the letter. The conversation left Vande Velde in no doubt that he was in the doghouse and that the only way out was to follow the prescribed doping program. He subsequently began using EPO and testosterone on a schedule prepared by Ferrari.

Jonathan Vaughters described going to Lance's hotel room in 1998 to borrow his laptop, when Lance stepped out of the bathroom and injected himself with a syringe in his presence, saying: "Now that you are doing EPO, too, you can't go write a book about it."

Tyler Hamilton described how a personal assistant to the Armstrongs at their villa in Nice—"Motoman," Philippe Maire—supplied him, Lance, and Kevin Livingston with the EPO they needed during mountain stages. They would put the empty EPO vials in soda cans to be taken away and crushed.

The affidavit of George Hincapie was particularly damaging, because he was once one of Lance's closest friends and he hadn't previously confessed or acknowledged using banned substances. At the time Hincapie provided that affidavit, he was still very much involved in pro cycling, racing in Europe for the BMC racing team, and preparing for a record seventeenth Tour de France—thanks to an arrangement his lawyer had worked out with USADA's lawyers back in June when they had first approached him about testifying. In his affidavit, he testified that in the early 1990s, after Lance's team was badly defeated in a race in Italy, Lance had been upset and announced that something needed to be done—which Hincapie understood to mean that Lance felt the team needed to use EPO. Hincapie also stated that he was "generally aware" that Lance was using testosterone throughout the time the two were teammates. On one occasion, during a race in Spain in 2000, he recounted that after Lance had told him he had taken some "oil"—referring to a testosterone-olive-oil mixture Lance had swallowed—he had texted Lance to alert him to the presence of drug testers and Lance then dropped out of the race.

USADA's evidence also suggested that while some of the riders' wives, such as Betsy Andreu, had worked to undermine or expose the doping scheme on the Postal team, Lance's ex-wife, Kristin, had participated, wrapping cortisone tablets in foil and handing them out to cyclists, and had seen Lance handing testosterone patches to Landis.

Bill Bock's summary of all the evidence compiled by USADA was sent to the UCI on October 10, and released to the public the same day. The agency also set up a website that offered links to thousands of pages of documents, photos, videos, and affidavits from Armstrong's former teammates. Suddenly, USADA's investigation came to vivid life. There were riders' e-mail exchanges, video footage showing doping doctors at team celebrations, and receipts of Armstrong's payments to Ferrari totaling more than $1 million. The UCI made no immediate response.

The public did, however. Hundreds of thousands of people around the world logged on to read USADA's reasoned decision, and the hundreds of pages of additional testimony, in the hours after it was released. Cycling bloggers and journalists, including us, dug through it, and used Twitter accounts to share bits of the new information with one another. "Dave Z affidavit is disturbing. Avoided drugs as they had killed his adict [*sic*] father. . . . Pushed by Johan until he broke," tweeted Race Radio, a cycling blogger. "Hey triathlon, @lancearmstrong continued to use Ferrari to prepare for tri's. page 86. Sure you still want him?" wrote nyvelocity. "OH but wait!!! @johanbruneel gets in on the act. He has Lance's money! How does Michele want it? Oh my," tweeted another blogger, who included a link to a November 4, 2009, e-mail from Bruyneel to Ferrari, in which Bruyneel wrote that "our boy has some cash for you," asking Ferrari whether he preferred cash or a wire transfer.

Not all of the Twitter and blogosphere reaction was negative, however. There were those who stood up for Armstrong. Some persisted in seeing Lance as one of the greatest athletes of all time; others noted that Lance's description in his first book of his fight to recover from cancer and his wife's ordeal of going through IVF treatments had helped them during difficult times in their own lives.

Amazingly, most of Lance's sponsors stuck by him at first. RadioShack and Anheuser-Busch, among others, said they would keep on backing him, prompting Bill Stapleton to proclaim that the authenticity of Lance's achievements shouldn't even be questioned. "Lance's primary sponsors have been incredibly supportive and have remained supportive throughout," Stapleton told the *Financial Times*. "Brands are looking for an authentic endorser and at the end of the day they depend on the authenticity of the athlete," he added.

Lance himself, who was back in Austin, holed up in his Spanish-style mansion, pronounced himself to be "unaffected," saying in a Tweet after the documents were released that he was currently spending time with his family and getting ready for the upcoming celebrations of the fifteenth anniversary of his foundation—an evening gala, a bike ride, and a University of Texas football game against Baylor University, to be cosponsored by Nike.

His relationship with Nike in the days leading up to the USADA report's release was as close as ever. He spent October 2, the sixteenth anniversary of his cancer diagnosis, at Nike's Beaverton, Oregon, headquarters, delivering a speech to hundreds of Nike employees, who hung on his words and seemed to adore him. While he was there, Nike executives sought Lance's views on new Livestrong merchandise, as well as on the 17,000 black, yellow, and orange Livestrong T-shirts it had agreed to provide free to those attending the University of Texas "cancer awareness" football game. Before he left, he also had the opportunity to pop in at the Lance Armstrong Fitness Center, on Nike's campus, to admire the plaque Nike had put up for him, praising his "fearlessness and confidence."

It seemed that none of this enthusiasm was diminished by the USADA decision. In fact, on the day the decision was made public, Nike rushed to rerelease the same exact statement it had first issued in August. "Nike plans to continue to support Lance and the Lance Armstrong Foundation," it said.

CHAPTER SIXTEEN

NOT A SNITCH

For one brief moment in time, Armstrong may actually have believed he was "unaffected," but his protective cocoon would disintegrate within days.

After the USADA decision, as Nike and other sponsors continued to stand behind Lance, Paul Willerton began waking up in the middle of the night, thinking he just couldn't take it anymore. Inspired by the Occupy Wall Street movement of 2011, Willerton called his two friends at Nike in mid-October and told them that he was planning to show up at headquarters, alone, to stand in front of its entrance gate and demand the company drop Lance. He got out his black Sharpie pen and made several posters. FOR CLEAN SPORT, NO DRUGS, NO BULLIES and DO THE RIGHT THING: SACK LANCE. Then, he called local radio stations and TV news outlets, inviting them to come interview him.

The next morning, October 16, Willerton drove 172 miles from his home in Bend, Oregon, and arrived at Nike's Beaverton campus at 6:00 A.M. The weather was miserable, cold and rainy. A handful of other cyclists showed up to join him, and the city of Beaverton sent a squad of police cars to monitor them. Willerton stood in the wet weather with his cell phone in his ear, granting interviews to radio stations around Oregon.

Nike wasn't going to be swayed by a handful of disillusioned cyclists, but soon executives on Nike's campus up the hill were confronted with a serious problem. It had taken a few days, but reporters had finally dug deep enough into the thousands of pages of documents and discovered the testimony Kathy LeMond had provided, accusing Nike of a payoff to former UCI president Hein Verbruggen to cover up Lance's positive test for corticosteroids in the 1999 Tour.

Although these allegations had been known by some journalists, including us, for years before the release of USADA's report, most people were unaware. But suddenly, journalists at several news outlets, including the *New York Daily News* and *Cycling News*, decided to run stories pegged to Kathy's allegations. LIVEWRONG? the *Daily News* headline asked. NIKE MAY HAVE LEFT FOOTPRINT ON LANCE SCANDAL. Some stories quoted Paul Willerton saying that Nike should cease condoning Lance's behavior. Sure, Nike had a history of publicly supporting embattled athletes. That wasn't news. What was news, the journalists noted, was that in this case, there were allegations that Nike itself was an active participant in the doping program. And perhaps that was the *real* reason Nike was so reluctant to sever its ties with Lance. That night, when the stories appeared online, Nike executives felt they had no choice but to respond. They issued a statement saying: "Nike vehemently denies that it paid former UCI president Hein Verbruggen $500,000 to cover up a positive drug test. Nike does not condone the use of illegal performance-enhancing drugs."

John Slusher, Nike's executive vice president of global sports marketing, placed a call to Stapleton, who was in Austin. Slusher needed to ask Stapleton an important question, he said. Slusher then asked Stapleton to personally assure him that nothing in the USADA report was true. Stapleton said he could not do that, so Slusher then requested that Stapleton put Lance on the phone. Stapleton said no, explaining that he wouldn't put Lance in that position. Slusher hung up the phone. An hour later, he called Stapleton back to tell him that Nike would be dropping Lance.

Meanwhile, members of the board of the Lance Armstrong Foundation (which had a partnership arrangement with Nike under which it benefited from the sale of Livestrong paraphernalia) were also becoming alarmed. The foundation had been inundated with phone calls, e-mails, and letters, including some from people who had been active fund-raisers on the foundation's be-half, who now felt cheated and resentful.

The volume of criticism was so overwhelming that members of the foundation's board asked Lance to step down, and they prepared a statement for release on the foundation's website the following morning. On October 17, at 8:00 A.M., central time, Lance's statement went online: "I have had the great honor of serving as this foundation's chairman for the last five years, and its mission and success are my top priorities," it read. "Today, therefore, to spare the foundation any negative effects as a result of controversy surrounding my cycling career, I will conclude my chairmanship." Nike issued its own statement only minutes later, without so much as a personal heads-up text or phone call to Lance from Phil Knight or any other executive. Nike condemned Armstrong, saying that he had misled them for decades and that it was now ending its long association with him but would keep the Livestrong merchandise partnership that generated millions for Lance's foundation.

The fallout from Nike's move to ditch Lance was stunning, concussive. Over the course of a few hours, Anheuser-Busch dropped him, followed by Nissan, RadioShack, as well as the firms that made Armstrong's helmets, his energy bars, and his recovery drinks. Lance lost $75 million in endorsements by the end of that single day.

Lance's ex-wife, Kristin, had her own issues to deal with that day. She quickly called off her plans to travel to Bethlehem, Pennsylvania, for a running festival sponsored by Rodale Press, publisher of *Runner's World* magazine, for which she was a contributing editor. She didn't want to risk the chance of running into reporters who might ask her about Lance's downfall or, worse yet, about the foil-wrapped cortisone tablets. As part of her $15 million divorce settlement with Lance, Kristin had signed a nondisclosure agreement, and she wasn't about to violate it. On October 18, in part to explain her absence from the *Runner's World* event, she wrote a blog post about morality. "I know what truth is. I know my past. Not telling or selling my tales to the press is my choice—one that I made primarily for my children," she said. "There are many things that I am not free to discuss because I am constrained by legal principles like marital privilege, confidentiality and non-disclosure agreements." She added: "To the world, Lance may be a source of admiration or suspicion, but to me he is simply my wasband and the father of my children. His choices were, and are, his. And mine are mine. And they haven't always been pretty." And in a line that seemed slightly condescending, given the circumstances, Kristin told her fans: "I am sorry if this is disappointing to you."

Once Nike dumped Lance, and the other sponsors fled, Lance's agent, Bill Stapleton, had to downsize his Austin agency, laying off half of the staff.

Still more piled on: On Monday, October 23, the UCI ratified USADA's sanctions against Armstrong, officially revoking his titles, in what must have been a great surprise to him and what was left of his camp. "Lance Armstrong has no place in cycling," UCI president Pat McQuaid said at a press conference in Geneva. McQuaid went on to say that the UCI had nothing to hide over the Armstrong donations, and he denied that they were connected to any cover-up of a positive test.

The Amaury Sport Organisation, owner of the Tour de France, erased Armstrong's name from its record books. Tufts University rescinded his honorary degree. Six gyms that had been named after him, including four in Austin, one in Denver, and one in Tigard, Oregon, removed his name. *Sports Illustrated*, which had placed him on its cover no fewer than eleven times, pronounced him the "Anti-Sportsman" of the Year.

As the sponsors deserted in droves, Lance's lawyers began calculating his possible financial exposure. Aside from the loss of any future sponsorship income, there was a question of whether any of the sponsors could sue him to reclaim money paid to him in the past. The lawyers figured that none had a legal claim against Armstrong, however, because they had all gotten their money's worth from the huge exposure their brands received during the Tours. In fact, during happier times, some of Lance's sponsors had made a point of telling him, his agent, and executives of Tailwind Sports that they felt they had gotten a great deal because their companies had benefited so much from the worldwide media coverage. In September 2004, just before the Postal Service finally ended its $31.4 million sponsorship of the team, for instance, the advertising agency Campbell Ewald studied the value of the media exposure it had received through the sponsorship. The ad people tallied up all the coverage from July 1 through August 31 and used a "valuation process" that showed that the 17,400 articles about Lance containing mentions of the US Postal Service cycling team were worth $18.2 million in print advertising; TV news coverage of Lance and the team was worth $13 million; and the coverage of the Tour de France, on OLN, the Outdoor Life Network, as well as CBS, was worth $3.3 million. The Postal Service marketing executives had provided Bill Stapleton with a copy of the thirteen-page report, which concluded, in summary, that the $34.6 million in media exposure for those two months in 2004 was 11 percent higher than during the same period in 2003, because of excitement over Lance's victories, as well as his relationship with his then girlfriend, celebrity rock star Sheryl Crow.

Trek's president, John Burke, Lance's longtime supporter, had credited Lance with bringing men into the sport who might otherwise have taken up, say, golf. Trek roughly tripled its revenues during the time it sponsored Lance, rising from roughly $300 million in the mid-1990s to an estimated $900 million by 2012. At Discovery Channel, which spent $31 million on a four-year sponsorship of Lance and the team, one top executive tallied up the value of the media exposure for the Discovery brand as being more than $100 million in the deal's first year, 2005. Every single day for the month of July during that year, Lance Armstrong had been on the covers of newspapers all over Europe and in sports pages in the United States.

All in all, the lawyers concluded that they didn't have much to fear from Lance's past sponsors. Much more worrisome was a claim made by the Dallas firm SCA Promotions, which had insured Lance's Tour de France victories and settled a lawsuit with him several years earlier. Shortly after USADA released its evidence, SCA lawyer Jeff Tillotson jumped into action and sent a letter to Armstrong, saying that it was clear he had lied under oath about doping during the arbitration case, and informing Armstrong that SCA now wanted him to repay not just the millions he had collected—but legal fees and interest, too. A sum of $12 million was mentioned, and it was a sum they seem to have arrived at with some care. After struggling to identify all of Lance's assets, Tillotson calculated that by the fall of 2012, Lance's net worth was at the very least somewhere between $15 million and $20 million. But after deducting those assets that are protected by law from collection (like one's home, which in Lance's case was valued at more than $3 million), Lance's collectible assets totaled only $10 million to $12 million. Tillotson appeared determined to get all of it.

Lance, still convinced that he was the victim of a massive injustice, could only see this as evidence that SCA was colluding with USADA. He assumed that SCA's founder, Bob Hamman, had called Travis Tygart to propose that USADA strip Lance of his titles. That way, SCA would get its money back, and then pay USADA a kickback.

SCA wasn't the only organization that went into action against Lance. *The Sunday Times* of London, which had paid Lance the equivalent of about £300,000 in 2006 to settle its libel case over the Walsh book, sent a letter to Tim Herman, stating that Lance now owed the paper more than £1 million, including reimbursement of legal fees. "It's clear that the proceedings were baseless and fraudulent" and that his representations that he never doped were "deliberately false," the letter said.

Three days after Lance's resignation as chairman of his foundation, its fifteenth anniversary gala took place at the Austin Convention Center. As Lance took the stage to give a speech, the audience, made up of fund-raisers, patrons of the foundation who had spent $1,000 a head on tickets, most of them cancer survivors, looked on grimly. Surrounded on stage by ninety members of the foundation's staff, Lance began: "It's been a difficult couple of weeks, for me, for my family, for my friends, for this foundation. . . . I get asked a lot, 'Man, how are you doing?' And I say this every time, and I mean it: I've been better but I've also been worse." Over the course of the five minutes, Lance spoke about the genesis of the foundation, mentioning that he got the idea to start it in October 1996 while out for TexMex food at Z'Tejas with a group of five friends, who discussed planning a bike ride they hoped would raise $1,000 to give to an existing cancer nonprofit. "This movement" that started in Z'Tejas "touched the lives of two and a half million cancer survivors around the world," he said, adding that the foundation had raised half a billion to "fight this disease around the world." He continued, saying that fifteen years ago, he never thought he'd still be "standing here talking about this global epidemic that takes one American every minute." He concluded by telling the crowd that the foundation's work for cancer survivors must continue. And then he left the stage to the star performers of the night, who included Norah Jones, Stephen Marley, the son of reggae legend Bob Marley, as well as Sean Penn and Ben Stiller—all of whom were performing without pay, and at Lance's personal request. Robin Williams, Lance Armstrong's longtime close friend, provided comedic relief by jumping in to help out during the silent auction. But Robin had asked the organizers to agree not to film him during that event.

Within weeks, the foundation would cut all ties with Lance. It had already filed paperwork with the Texas secretary of state for a name change, effective October 30, renaming itself the Livestrong Foundation. And on November 12, the divorce was made official. Foundation staffers took down the seven yellow jerseys that had adorned the walls of its headquarters, and put them in storage. But the fallout from Lance's disgrace was hard to staunch. Perhaps the most serious hit occurred when a pro soccer club pulled out from a lucrative multiyear deal it had made with the foundation in 2011. Sporting Kansas City, an American soccer club based in Kansas, had promised to donate $7.5 million from ticket, concessions, and souvenir revenue over six years, in exchange for the right to name its new $200 million soccer-only sports facility the Livestrong Stadium. It still owed $750,000 of the $1 million the foundation believed it had promised for that year. But Sporting Kansas City wanted out. The soccer team removed the Livestrong name from the stadium sign and renamed itself Sporting Park.

The day after the gala, Lance huddled with friends and advisers at his home in Austin and told them he was considering coming clean about doping. One person who was there said he laid out several options, which ranged from granting a newspaper interview to incorporating a confession into a Lance Armstrong documentary. He was also thinking about writing a new book, in preparation for which he had begun reading his friend Walter Isaacson's biography of Steve Jobs—a man who had had to make a comeback of his own, after having been ousted from the company he founded. Lance seemed confident that over time he could reemerge and rebuild his popularity. He saw his situation as comparable to that not just of Steve Jobs but even of President Bill Clinton, who, in 1998, denied allegations of a sexual relationship with White House intern Monica Lewinsky with the infamous lie: "I did not have sexual relations with that woman." If Clinton could weather that scandal and go on to become one of the most popular people on the planet, then surely Lance could redeem himself, too. The question was: How?

While Armstrong was thinking about his public reputation, his lawyers were worried about his growing legal problems—and with good reason. Jeff Novitzky and the prosecutors from the US Attorney's Office in Los Angeles were trying to see if they could find grounds for reopening the criminal case. After digging, however, what the prosecutors found didn't rise to the level of obstruction of justice, and there seemed to be nothing they could do.

But another branch of the Department of Justice—the Civil Division in Washington, DC—was continuing its deliberations on whether to join Floyd Landis's whistle-blower lawsuit. With the release of the USADA documents, the Civil Division lawyers began looking into the possibility of making a claim that the owners of the US Postal Service team, including Armstrong, had defrauded the federal government by accepting sponsorship money from the US Postal Service while running an organized doping operation. Over at the FDA, Jeff Novitzky began to assist the Civil Division lawyers in gathering evidence in support of the case. Robert Chandler, the DOJ lawyer leading the government's review of the Landis lawsuit, had been calling up potential witnesses for months, and shortly after the release of USADA's report, he petitioned a federal court to force Lance to comply with the 2011 subpoena for documents relating to, among other things, any payments he had made to the UCI and Michele Ferrari. Lance did finally satisfy his obligation to the subpoena that fall.

SCA Promotions' legal action was particularly worrisome to Lance's attorneys. It wasn't just a large sum of money that was at stake. Tillotson hinted that he would ask a court to allow him to question Armstrong under oath about whether he had doped to win. That legal approach would leave Lance with two unpleasant options. He could defend himself and claim he hadn't committed perjury in the earlier deposition, which would mean claiming, under oath, that he had never used performance-enhancing drugs—which would in turn expose him to new perjury charges by the federal government. Or he could take the Fifth on the stand. However humiliated and disgraced Lance had been over the previous two months, nothing could compare with the damage that would be done by his publicly taking the Fifth. That would restart the news cycle and damage Lance's brand, perhaps beyond repair.

Frustrated, Lance took to Twitter again, sending general fuck-you messages to all the people and organizations that were hounding him. He spent the next two weeks in Hawaii, tweeting photos of the breathtaking orange and yellow sunset, over the palm trees of the Kukio golf course, and of himself hanging upside-down during a workout at the Kukio gym, with the notice that he was "hangin' in there." His tweets linked to the images on Mobli. Once he returned to Texas, he arranged to be photographed lying on the red couch in the media room on the third floor of his home, with seven yellow jerseys on the wall, glowing under the ceiling lights. "Back in Austin and just layin' around," he tweeted Saturday, November 10. Viewers' reactions were mixed. By Monday afternoon, his "layin' around" tweet had more than 6,000 retweets and 1,700 favorites. Some expressed their support, telling Lance he had earned all of the jerseys; others dismissed him as smug and deluded.

Despite his potential legal and financial troubles, and the fact that his net worth was in jeopardy and could potentially disappear in a legal bonfire, Armstrong was still myopically focused on one goal: getting back to competing in triathlons. His good friend Bill Ritter had begun making overtures on his behalf to USADA about striking some kind of deal—admitting to past doping in exchange for a reduction in his lifetime ban. Ritter, the former governor of Colorado, now the head of the privately funded Center for the New Energy Economy at Colorado State University, had gotten to know Lance three years earlier, in 2009, when Lance, having just bought property in Aspen, placed a cold call to the governor's office. "Why don't we have a pro stage race in Colorado?" Lance had suggested to Ritter. Ritter, an influential Democrat, then selected a group of people who helped create a new multiday stage race that would eventually be known as the USA Pro Challenge. The two men became friends as they worked on the project, and would often get together in Aspen over beer. In their conversations following USADA's ban, Lance told Ritter about his hopes of being able to compete again. That fall, Ritter called Travis Tygart, whom he hadn't previously met, explaining that he knew Lance wanted to get back into sport. "Is there any reason to talk to Lance? Is there a possibility of some kind of reconciliation involving anything other than a lifetime ban?" Ritter asked Tygart. Tygart told Ritter there was hope. Under the World Anti-Doping Code, athletes can get as much as a 75 percent reduction of a ban if they provide the kind of substantial help to anti-doping authorities that enables them to build cases against others. From there, Lance asked his lawyer, Tim Herman, to pick up where Ritter left off.

Herman called Tygart and offered to dispatch Lance's legal team to USADA's headquarters in Colorado Springs to meet with him. Tygart said he wanted Lance himself to come. When Herman pushed back, Tygart said he'd be willing to discuss the plan with Armstrong in person, but he was tired of dealing with Armstrong's legal attack dogs. He would only schedule a meeting if Armstrong showed up and talked with him, face-to-face.

At least one of Lance's lawyers, John Keker, was opposed to the meeting. Keker, who was proud of his work in getting Armstrong's criminal investigation dropped, thought the meeting could only hurt, possibly undoing his good work. But Armstrong's legal team had been divided over how to handle USADA's allegations from the beginning. Mark Fabiani supported the idea of a meeting, as did Tim Herman, who hoped that if Lance agreed to it, USADA's Tygart might be willing to send a letter to the Justice Department suggesting they abandon the possibility of picking up Floyd Landis's whistleblower lawsuit. Armstrong decided to go with his gut and take the meeting.

Neither Armstrong nor Herman wanted to meet with Tygart at USADA headquarters in Colorado Springs, where they'd surely be noticed, so they asked Ritter if he would allow the December 14 meeting to take place at his CSU offices in downtown Denver. Ritter agreed, as did Tygart. Having sold his private jet, Lance chartered a plane to Colorado, bringing Anna and his two youngest children along, so they could spend time with Anna's parents in Boulder.

The meeting began without Lance present. Tim Herman was going to scope out the situation to determine whether it was worth the disgraced cyclist's while to take part. In addition to Herman, there was Tygart, who had come in from Colorado Springs; Bill Bock, who had come in from Indiana;

Bill Ritter; and Steven Ungerleider, a psychologist and visiting scholar at the University of Texas who had suggested that he could serve as an honest broker between the two sides. Having written a book on the state-sponsored East German doping program in the 1970s, and served on the education and ethics committee with the World Anti-Doping Agency, Ungerleider was familiar with the world of doping control. He even brought a copy of his book to the meeting and placed it on the table.

The meeting had a down-to-business feel. There was no spread of food or even coffee for the participants, just bottles of water. But Bock and Tygart wanted Herman to know they were concerned about Lance's well-being. They had actually been shocked at the magnitude and velocity of Lance's downfall, and they had talked with each other several times about how Lance was dealing with it emotionally. Lodged permanently in the back of their minds was the memory of Antonio Pettigrew, a track athlete who committed suicide on an overdose of Unisom sleeping pills in 2010, at age forty-two, two years after losing his gold medal following a USADA doping ban.

Herman, who seemed to consider himself something of a father figure to Lance, said Lance was doing fine but that he'd be a lot better if he could get back to competing in triathlons. He said that Lance would be willing to come in and talk, to lay it all out on the table, but that in exchange he wanted to be back competing within a year.

Tygart and Bock explained that such a quick return was impossible within the rules of the sport. But they tried to make a case for other reasons for Lance to come clean. "There are many more benefits to getting on the side of the truth than simply competing in sport," Bock said. "Doesn't he want to leave a legacy of helping to repair the sport?" Coming clean to USADA would be part of the repair, and they also suggested that Lance arrange to meet with people like Floyd Landis and Greg LeMond to make amends.

Herman said he understood. He, too, was concerned about Lance's legacy and reputation. But Herman wanted something more tangible from USADA: help with the whistle-blower lawsuit against Lance. Tygart and Bock agreed that if Lance provided details about his past doping, they'd be willing to write a letter to the Department of Justice explaining that Armstrong was playing a role in cleaning up the sport. They couldn't guarantee one way or another that it would affect the whistle-blower case, but it might help. At that point, Herman agreed to call Lance, who said he'd join them in an hour. Bock and Tygart went across the street to a deli for coffee and muffins and then came back to the meeting room, where they all waited.

About ninety minutes later, Lance walked in, wearing a baseball cap and a North Face parka. His facial hair was grown out, almost to the point of being a beard. He looked nothing like the famous clean-shaven athlete with the beaming smile and the buzz cut.

Lance spoke as if it were a foregone conclusion that he had doped. He didn't bother denying anything, but he didn't offer any explicit details, either. He referred to what Ungerleider had written about the systematic doping of athletes in the former East Germany and said that whatever he had done was nothing compared to that. Tygart, who was meeting Lance for the first time, noticed that all the people surrounding him seemed to be coddling him, which had probably allowed him to infer that he could avoid the ban completely. It became clear to Tygart that none of Armstrong's lawyers had given him the "come to Jesus" talk—the kind of frank discussion with no sugarcoating that apprises the client of the true dimensions of his predicament. Lance seemed to be laboring under the false impression that he could still get out of this mess with minimal damage. He said he would be willing to talk about others who might have helped him dope. But in exchange, "You have to give me a fair punishment." That "doesn't have to be six months, but a year." Tygart actually began to feel sorry for him. Lance still thought he could take charge of the situation, but this was one of the few times in Lance's life when he was no longer in control of his fate.

Tygart told Armstrong that he had already had his chance to come clean and he'd blown it, that, at best, if he gave full cooperation, the ban would be eight years. The offer was so far from a sweetheart deal that it didn't seem to create much of an incentive for Armstrong to talk. He'd be forty-nine before he could compete again in elite competition. Lance tried to convince Tygart that he was just another rider on the US Postal team, that he had done what was required of him by a sport in which doping was rampant. In fact, he said, every sport has similar problems, including the National Football League and Major League Baseball, but those athletes hadn't been singled out by USADA.

As the discussion wound down, Tygart didn't budge. He told Armstrong he stood accused of offenses that stretched beyond doping to a cover-up marked by nearly fifteen years of denials, as well as threats and actions against anyone who told the truth.

Equally un-budging, Armstrong told Tygart that he held the keys to his own redemption. Armstrong said he could create his own "truth and reconciliation commission," laying out the facts as he saw them. Armstrong believed such a plan would put so much public pressure on USADA that it would have no choice but to allow him to compete again—to which Tygart responded: "That's bullshit! People will see it for what it is—a ploy for you to get back to competition." Lance shot back that he would compete in unsanctioned races. And with that, the negotiation was over. Lance thought Tygart's refusal to budge on the eight-year ban was bullshit. If Tygart was really interested in hearing what Lance had to say, Lance thought, he could just give him a shorter ban.

Tygart was livid. A few weeks later, he quietly sent an impassioned e-mail to US Attorney General Eric Holder in Washington, DC, requesting that the Justice Department join in Landis's civil action: "In light of the outcome of recent sport-related federal criminal cases, it is understandable that the government would have some reluctance to spend public dollars going after another sports case. This situation is different," Tygart wrote. "USADA has already done the work in the sports case and won. Indeed, Mr. Armstrong and his representatives have admitted that doping took place. . . . The central fact of doping is no longer an issue" in the Lance affair, Tygart said. "What remains unresolved is the massive economic fraud perpetrated by individuals who are outside USADA's jurisdiction."

With the holidays approaching, Lance retreated again to Hawaii's Big Island with Anna and their children. He played golf on the ten-hole Tom Fazio–designed course, swam in the local pool, and visited Hawaii Volcanoes National Park. He seemed to be trying to get back to a sense of normalcy. But clearly things had changed, including, most notably, his relationships with his sponsors. Now when he went for a ride, he opted for a Crumpton or Moots, small bike makers from Austin, over his iconic Trek. And when he went for a jog, he wore Asics running shoes, not Nikes. Lance was particularly bitter about Nike. During a long wine-soaked evening he and Anna had shared with Adam Wilk, an old friend from Plano, he had told Adam to go into the closet and take all of his Nike swag, including his new Nike tri suits. As Adam packed the clothing into a duffel bag, Lance handed him two pairs of Nike Air Force 1 sneakers, designed by the Los Angeles tattoo artist Mister Cartoon and released in July 2009. These limited edition sneakers—emblazoned with a skeleton, spiderwebs, and L.A.—were among the most coveted releases in Nike's history, and Adam found Lance's relinquishment of them particularly poignant because he knew that Lance had a friendship with Mister Cartoon.

During this period, we, like many people in the press, tried to get to Lance. Vanessa had been pursuing him aggressively for a confessional interview for several months, and continued her efforts while he was in Hawaii. To make her case, she argued—in notes to Lance, as well as Tim Herman—that, by talking to us, Lance would send a strong message to the world that he was interested in coming clean with the public about his actions, rather than simply looking for a willing outlet to take dictation. After all, we had shown ourselves to be hard-hitting reporters of the events in Lance's downfall, beginning with the story we broke on Floyd Landis's explosive allegations.

One evening in early December, over drinks with Tim Herman in Austin, Vanessa suggested Lance call our editor, Sam Walker, and Lance then began talking to Sam about coming forward. But Lance was wary. The *Journal*, his lawyers noted, was owned by Rupert Murdoch's News Corporation, the same entity that owned London's *Sunday Times*, which had threatened a lawsuit against him, seeking almost $1.6 million for the return of the 2006 settlement payment the *Times* made to him in a libel case, plus interest and lawyers' fees. The *Times* had no connection to us, but Lance viewed us as allied.

We also got the message that Lance didn't like us much personally. He described Reed as a C-level journalist and even made insulting comments about his appearance. He had a general but less intense loathing toward Vanessa, whom he seemed to find relentless and annoying.

Also, he had other ideas about how he could use the press to get his own version of the story out. One late December afternoon, after the *Times* filed its lawsuit, Lance flew over to the Hawaiian island of Maui to have lunch with Oprah Winfrey, an old acquaintance, at her large ranch in Kula. Oprah had e-mailed him a few months earlier seeking an interview for her cable channel OWN (Oprah Winfrey Network), which was struggling for ratings at the time; he had responded that he wasn't ready to talk. But then he e-mailed and suggested they get together over the holidays. Hoping to negotiate his cooperation to do an on-camera interview with her, Oprah had stayed in Hawaii a couple of extra days to accommodate his schedule.

Sitting at Oprah's mansion in Maui that day, Lance found that he felt comfortable talking to her about his problems. He began to think he was finally ready to acknowledge his past lies. An appearance on Oprah in January might be the first step in his public rehabilitation.

If he confessed on camera, he believed he would be able to charm America into loving him again, and to turn public opinion against USADA. That, he thought, would be the only way he would be allowed back into racing. Confessing publicly might also make things easier for his children. During the long night that Lance and Anna had spent with Adam Wilk and his girlfriend, he had talked about the toll the doping scandal was taking on his kids. Lance told Adam that his son Luke had gotten in a fight at the bus stop when a schoolmate teased him, saying, "Your dad does dope! Your dad does dope!" If Lance appeared on Oprah, he would be able to level with his children for the first time, without burdening them with having to keep his secret.

So he flew back to his home and called his lawyers to discuss the plan.

They were vehemently against a TV interview. Considering the serious legal jeopardy he was in, they thought it was reckless. If Armstrong had any leverage in the whistle-blower case or other civil suits that he was facing, it was that anyone taking him on in court would have to prove he had doped. By admitting it on television, he would be removing one of the obstacles keeping his enemies at bay and away from his net worth, which now seemed very much in jeopardy.

But Armstrong continued to believe the interview might be the best course of action for him—the only way he could begin to regain his reputation, and his only route back to the possibility of competing again. For him, those considerations seemed to outweigh any others. He told Oprah he would sit down with her the following week in Austin.

In January, Armstrong flew back to Austin to speak to his older children, ex-wife, family, and friends in advance of the interview. When he met with Luke, he told him that there had been a lot of questions about him over the years, about whether he doped or not. And he explained that he had always denied that. But the rumors were true, he now told Luke. He told him, "Don't defend me anymore. Don't."

Luke told Lance that he loved him. "You're my dad. This won't change that."

On the day of the interview, January 14, as he was on his way to the taping at a local hotel, Lance paid a visit to what was now called the Livestrong Foundation, where the staff of seventy-five crowded into the boardroom for a hastily convened meeting with their founder. Without acknowledging he had lied, he apologized to the staff for the damage the scandals had done to their morale. Several people wept. Lance himself choked up a bit. Some of the staff told him they were grateful to him for starting the foundation, even if he had been lying to them all along.

The interview with Oprah went on for nearly two and a half hours. Armstrong's legal team, including Tim Herman and Mark Fabiani, waited in the green room and watched the filming live. There was so much material that Oprah's producers decided to spread it over two nights. The first segment would run on Thursday night, for an hour and a half. The second segment would be broadcast the next night for an hour. Because Oprah was so determined to keep the content top secret, she carried the videotapes of the footage in her handbag on the plane instead of transmitting them by satellite as she would ordinarily have done.

With Oprah and Lance seated side by side, their chairs angled toward each other, the interview began on a dramatic note. She instructed Armstrong to answer yes or no to the following questions: Had he ever used performance-enhancing drugs? "Yes," he replied. And then, as Oprah ticked them off, one by one, had he ever used EPO, human growth hormone, testosterone, corticosteroids, blood transfusions? Yes to every one. Oprah wanted to get that out of the way. The rest of the show, she said, would be about the details.

It was in the details part of the interview that Armstrong failed miserably. He showed very little contrition, blaming his use of performance-enhancing drugs not on himself but on the sport of cycling. He downplayed his own doping, saying that drug use among cyclists was so prevalent, it was "like saying we have to have air in our tires or water in our bottles. It was part of the job." He also claimed that his elaborate doping scheme hadn't given him an unfair advantage: "I looked up the definition of *cheating* and the definition is 'to gain an advantage on a rival or foe.' I did not view it that way." He said he viewed it as leveling the playing field.

Lance specifically denied doping after his comeback in 2009 and 2010, saying that his ex-wife, Kristin, a "spiritual person," had supported him in his quest to return to cycling only on the condition that he do it clean.

He refused to give details or implicate others, and he refused to validate Betsy Andreu's account of the 1996 hospital scene. When Oprah asked him about the attacks he had made on Betsy over the years, he ventured an extremely ill-advised attempt at humor. Smirking at the camera, he told Oprah that when he'd called Betsy to apologize, he said he was sorry for calling her a crazy bitch, but he'd never called her fat. Oprah was visibly not amused.

As for Kristin, Lance didn't provide many specifics other than to say that she knew about the doping. He said simply that she "wasn't curious," adding "perhaps she didn't want to know."

Most people came away from the first interview appalled by Armstrong's lack of contrition. The word *sociopath* was used by more than one media observer to describe what many viewed as a personality disorder.

Oprah's Thursday night interview drew 3.2 million viewers, the second-biggest audience for her then two-year-old OWN cable channel. But many people didn't bother tuning in for the next evening's installment, which drew just 1.8 million viewers. The only people who seemed to benefit from the show, aside from Oprah herself, whose floundering cable network's ratings had skyrocketed, were late-night comedians.

By the time the show aired, Lance was back in Hawaii, somewhat disconnected from the fallout. On the night the second interview aired, Armstrong sent an e-mail to a friend. He wasn't feeling relieved and he wasn't contrite. What he was was angry, he said, and his wrath was directed at USADA. "At some point they will have to admit (like I just did) that they lied, bullied, and embellished," Lance wrote. Although Lance had hoped his appearance would help restore his public image, it did quite the opposite.

People who knew Lance personally were mixed in their responses to the interview. Triathlon star Chrissie Wellington, with whom he had become friendly, said she was angry that Lance had made his doping sound so banal during his Oprah interview. She also expressed regret that she'd asked him to write the foreword for the North American edition of her autobiography. "Please, if you have the North American edition, rip out the foreword," she was quoted as saying in one interview about her book.

The Oprah interview infuriated Travis Tygart and Bill Bock, mostly because of Lance's denials about doping during his comeback in 2009 and 2010, despite what USADA considered to be strong evidence to the contrary: blood samples showing markers consistent with doping, as well as a series of e-mails between Lance and Michele Ferrari's son, Stefano. The e-mails to Stefano—obtained by USADA from Italian prosecutors investigating Ferrari—showed that Lance had sought Ferrari's guidance not only for his comeback to cycling but also during his transition to the triathlon. Tygart was also incensed that Lance had explicitly denied trying to bribe USADA in 2004.

In many ways, the interview raised more questions than it answered. Lance didn't say anything about the others who had backed him—such as Bruyneel, Weisel, Stapleton, or Ochowicz. Nor did he address his power to pull strings at the UCI, even though his influence over the sport's governing body had been a key factor in his ability to avoid the consequences of positive drug tests for fifteen years.

Picking up right where they'd left off before Oprah, Bill Bock sent a letter to Lance giving him until early February to cooperate fully in an effort to "clean up cycling." He asked Lance to sit down with USADA, with the inducement of perhaps reducing his lifetime ban from competition to an eight-year suspension, as they had offered him before. But Lance's lawyer, Tim Herman, told them Lance wouldn't be able to meet their time frame and would prefer to speak to the World Anti-Doping Agency instead.

In the weeks following Oprah, Lance spent time at home, texting and calling a range of friends and associates for their reactions. When he reached

Jonathan Vaughters, with whom he hadn't spoken in eight years, Vaughters told him that he should talk to Tygart. Again, Lance refused.

Armstrong did agree to answer a series of questions from the Cycling News online. Asked if he felt like the fall guy for the entire sport, Lance responded: "Actually, yes I do. But I understand why. We all make the beds we sleep in." He also said that full amnesty for himself and other cyclists was the best way of getting the full truth.

Back in Austin, Lance went into hermit mode. Although he continued running, he often did so in areas where he could avoid crowds, such as on the Barton Creek greenbelt trail rather than in Austin's popular public parks. He seemed to have lost his taste for gestures of public defiance. During the Livestrong Austin Marathon in mid-February, a race that drew thousands of participants, his friend Adam Wilk suggested Lance make a surprise appearance by showing up at a water station, handing out cups to runners. But instead, Lance skipped the run and stayed in his house during the race.

Just days later, the government finally joined Floyd Landis's whistleblower lawsuit—a move that significantly increased Floyd's chances of winning. Floyd had been keeping a low profile for more than two years. Now he was figuring out how to get his life back on track. Floyd had left California and was living in Tiger Williams's guesthouse in Norwalk, Connecticut. At a party over the holidays, he had met Alexandra Merle-Huet, an officer in the special investments management group at the Federal Reserve Bank of New York, who earned a master's degree from Columbia University's School of International and Public Affairs. Although she wasn't a cycling fan, Floyd spent their first few dates talking almost nonstop about his past. Alex, the mother of a young son, listened and was supportive, though she worried that Floyd wasn't yet ready to let go of the past.

A few weeks after they met, the two watched Lance's Oprah interview at Alex's Upper East Side apartment in Manhattan. In the interview, Oprah mentioned Floyd, describing him as Lance's protégé and remarking that many people thought the real "tipping point" for Lance had been Landis's decision to come forward and confess. Lance actually agreed, but said that his 2009 comeback was tough on Floyd. He went on to say Floyd had been sending him text messages claiming "I've recorded everything" and threatening to out him on YouTube. But instead of YouTube, Lance said, Floyd had gone to *The Wall Street Journal* with the story.

As Lance spoke his name, Floyd felt himself growing nervous. What if Lance apologized to him on the air? If that happened, he thought, then under the principles of his Mennonite upbringing, he would have to forgive him. He didn't feel ready for that. He needn't have worried.

Floyd was moving on with his own life. At the suggestion of one of his friends, Floyd had begun making plans to seek admission to a special program at Yale University for nontraditional students whose education had been interrupted for five or more years. Floyd agreed to appear on a panel at Yale Law School with Travis Tygart and Jonathan Vaughters, on the culture of doping in sport. However, during the hour-long panel, held February 28, Floyd was tight-lipped. Because of the pending whistle-blower lawsuit, Floyd's lawyers, one of whom was seated in the audience, told him to avoid going into too many specifics. Tygart was the rock star at the event. When he said he had used the truth from Landis to "dismantle" the doping system, the audience of two hundred broke into applause. He defended the light penalties on the riders who came forward, explaining that he saw them as victims of the doping culture. When the first audience member stepped up to the mic, she said: "Travis, you're my hero."

EPILOGUE

Lance Armstrong's fourteen-year-long deception was an elaborate, many-tentacled enterprise requiring complicated logistics, scores of people to execute them, and an iron-willed determination to keep it going. Lance relied on his teammates, doctors, lawyers, financial backers, sponsors, assistants, and associates to help him cheat—or at the very least to ignore the evidence that he was doing so—and on the complacent, hero-worshipping media to celebrate his victories without looking into how he achieved them. The few who did raise questions were publicly attacked, sued for large sums of money, and generally vilified by Lance and his well-trained army of supporters.

Some of the people in his network of allies directly aided and abetted him in his doping. And everyone from his ex-wife to his friends, sponsors, and former girlfriends turned a blind eye to it—until almost the end. Of course, once the USADA decision was released, the defections were virtually unanimous—the proverbial rats fleeing the sinking ship.

During the glory years, agencies like UCI, which is specifically charged with keeping the sport clean, and USA Cycling, which promotes the sport, were co-opted to Lance's ends. And ironically, the drug testers themselves turned out to be one of Lance's most persuasive defenses against his accusers.

Lance figured out, shrewdly, that most Americans put a lot of stock in the effectiveness of drug testing, so all he had to do was cite the hundreds of times he had been tested, and people would believe he was clean. Indeed Lance *was* tested hundreds of times—if not as many times as he claimed. Though he told us on many occasions that he had passed more than 500 doping tests in his career, USADA's records indicate he was tested no more than 250 times. John Burke, the president of Trek bikes, once said publicly that Lance had passed more than 800 tests. These figures became a key pillar supporting Lance's big lie. Of course the number of times he was tested is irrelevant if, as has proved to be the case, he and his doctors knew how to manipulate some of the test results, and he and his handlers were able to suppress other results that revealed truths he couldn't manipulate.

The question is why so many people would have participated in this elaborate scheme for so long. And the answers are not hard to find. For many of his teammates and coaches, it was all about glory—and money, too, of course. They did what it took to win and, in some cases, just to stay on the team, because if they refused to dope, they risked Lance's disapproval and the possibility of being fired from the team.

For Lance's financial backers and sponsors, it was all about money—and the glory of it, too, of course. Lance Inc. was big business. Sponsors such as Nike, Oakley, Trek, and others actively advanced Lance's career, fame, and wealth, capitalizing on what they stood to gain from his successes. When Lance's critics accused him of cheating to win—and over the years, there were many such allegations—the sponsors asked no questions. Instead, acting as enablers, they offered Lance their unwavering support and continued to feature him in their marketing efforts, making him ever more visible in the public eye. In the weeks after Lance's Oprah confession, some of Lance's sponsors and supporters, including John Burke of Trek and Doug Ulman, CEO of the Livestrong Foundation, conceded that they had never once asked Lance directly if he had doped. Only when the anti-doping officials of USADA released their mountain of evidence against Lance, tainting his public image irrevocably, did his sponsors finally dump him.

What will happen to Lance in the years to come is impossible to say. It's true that, F. Scott Fitzgerald to the contrary, there *are* second acts to American lives, but it's hard to imagine Lance making a comeback to the world of sports, given the legal obstacles he still faces—not least of them the lifetime ban against elite competition. In responding to some of those suits, he may end up doing even greater damage to his reputation—whether by admitting to what he has so long denied, by outing others, or by stonewalling. None of these options look good for him. By early 2013, Lance's lawyers were negotiating with the US Department of Justice lawyers about the possibility of his providing evidence against some of the people in his inner circle, including Johan Bruyneel and his former partners at Tailwind Sports. But those talks fell apart, and by late April, the government joined the whistle-blower suit, filing claims seeking $30 million. Its complaint accused Lance and Bruyneel of "unjust enrichment," and their former Tailwind partners of breach of contract for failing to take action against riders who used prohibited substances. Much of the government's case, which alleges that the Postal Service was defrauded of $40 million, is based on Floyd's testimony.

Floyd's claims against Tailwind had put scrutiny on Thom Weisel. But Weisel's lawyers maintained that he didn't know about the doping, and pointed out that he had, in fact, lost millions of dollars over the years while he bankrolled Tailwind and the Postal team. If the Justice Department case goes to trial, then it's possible the government may call Lance to give testimony under oath. Lance may also be subpoenaed as a witness in a case that Tygart is currently planning to bring against Bruyneel.

But it could be many years—if ever—before Lance provides full and specific details to the general public about what he did, and who helped him do it. Lance has long had a psychological aversion to examining his past mistakes, a trait he has said he inherited from his mother, who didn't like to talk about her teenage pregnancy and other difficulties. Justifying his reluctance to come clean, Lance has told many people that he prides himself on being loyal to his friends—including Michele Ferrari, whom he continues to regard as a genius. In the weeks following his confessional interview with Oprah, Lance proudly proclaimed to Adam Wilk that, despite all he had been through in recent months, he had never "ratted anybody out." Some of Lance's supporters cite his stated revulsion against betrayal as evidence that Lance has a moral core. Yet that runs counter to Lance's private actions over the years, when Lance dropped many people who loved him and who dedicated themselves, sometimes without compensation, to helping him succeed.

The whistle-blower suit isn't the only legal battle he's facing. Within just a couple of months of the sit-down with Oprah, just as his lawyers feared would happen, he was hit with two more lawsuits. One alleges that Lance and FRS, a nutritional drink maker for which Lance served as a spokesman, had engaged in false advertising by linking his Tour victories to FRS drinks. The second was filed by another prize insurance company, Acceptance Insurance, which is suing him for $3 million for bonuses paid to him after he won the Tour de France races from 1999, 2000, and 2001.

Lance's financial future is also a big question, given the millions he has already spent on legal bills, the claims on what remains of his fortune, and the loss of sources of income from both sponsors and competitions. His friends say that he has told them he has enough money to live comfortably for the rest of his life, though his mother, Linda, has worried about his financial future. In mid-April, he sold his Spanish-style villa, valued at $3 million, and within weeks purchased a 1924 Mediterranean-style home in Austin's Old West neighborhood. The home is on county tax rolls for $2.7 million.

What role, if any, Lance can play in public life is another issue still to be resolved—though Lance himself seems optimistic. In early 2013, he told friends that he would like to become involved in his cancer foundation again. Because of the foundation's work on behalf of cancer survivors, many people viewed him as a humanitarian, and many still do. And Lance clearly sees himself that way, too.

Certainly, to many of those suffering a cancer diagnosis, Lance's foundation has been a valuable resource, and Lance himself something like the second coming of Christ. Through numerous private gestures he has made over the years, which he did not try to publicize, he boosted the spirits of strangers living through their darkest moments, and sometimes offered concrete assistance, too. Responding to messages from cancer patients, he has sent personal e-mails and practical advice, often with specific recommendations about which doctors to consult. Occasionally, he'd go beyond that. If a testicular cancer patient couldn't get in to see the best doctors, well, he might send an e-mail or a text to the doctor himself, paving the way for a patient to get an appointment.

Yet a return to his foundation seems unlikely in the near term. In fact, the foundation has taken yet more steps to distance itself from Lance. In early 2013, it moved its yearly Livestrong Day from the October 2 anniversary of Lance's cancer diagnosis, to the May 11 date when Nike introduced its yellow Livestrong wristband.

The foundation's effort to create an identity completely separate from Lance may be a necessary part of its survival strategy. Due to flat contributions, the foundation board slashed its 2013 budget by about 10 percent, forcing it to end its title sponsorship of the Austin Marathon just three years into what was a planned ten-year partnership. CEO Doug Ulman told Vanessa that he felt certain the foundation would survive, but that for a while it was likely that things would be "bumpy, challenging, turbulent."

And that was before the most recent round of bad news, which was delivered in late spring. With consumers starting to turn against the Livestrong brand, Nike executives made the decision to pull the Livestrong clothing and sneakers line. Since the foundation had licensed the Livestrong brand to Nike, in an arrangement that had accounted for about a quarter of its average yearly revenue from 2004 to 2012, this will constitute a formidable blow to its budget.

For a long time, Americans just couldn't get enough of Lance. His yellow bracelet was ubiquitous; his sayings like "Pain is temporary, quitting lasts forever" were quoted like gospel. His relationships were constant tabloid fodder. Millions persisted in believing in him until it became impossible to do so. Why?

That may be a question harder to answer than why his teammates and coaches, his sponsors and financial backers, collaborated in the lie. But society's gullibility in the face of ever-mounting evidence probably has something to do with its need for a certain kind of hero. Looked at this way, Lance is the inevitable product of our celebrity-worshipping culture and the whole money-mad world of sports gone amok. This is the Golden Age of fraud, an era of general willingness to ignore and justify the wrongdoings of the rich and powerful, which makes every lie bigger and widens its destructive path. Having put Lance up on a pedestal, the public was reluctant to depose him, until, of course, it had to—at which point it fell upon him with such fury that even Travis Tygart and Bill Bock were shocked by the rapidity with which he was toppled, the speed of the desertions.

Within our culture, there is a tendency to instantly vilify those whom we have idolized, and that is certainly what has happened to Lance. But as we hope our book has made clear, Lance does not bear sole responsibility for the enterprise that became Lance Inc. And the fact that he is the villain of the moment doesn't mean that he is necessarily finished, either. Just as Lance said to Travis Tygart in a moment of fury back in December 2012, he really *does* hold the keys to his own redemption. Whether he will use them, for the sake both of his own soul and the soul of the sport he once loved so much, remains to be seen. He is a man of great strength, determination, and resilience, and we truly hope that he will use those qualities to make a moral comeback as complete as the physical comeback he effected from the cancer that nearly killed him. Time will tell.

ACKNOWLEDGMENTS

Wheelmen, at times, felt like our own version of the Alpe d'Huez climb, with our hearts pumping our vast quantities of blood and our VO_2 max sustaining us. We never would've made it to the ARRIVEE banner without the contributions of many people who played significant roles in helping us get there.

Thanks to Sam Walker foremost for giving us a flying start. As *The Wall Street Journal*'s sports editor, Sam first brought us together as partners in the newsroom years ago, and he edited all of our coverage in the *Journal*. When we began working on *Wheelmen*, Sam kindly spent many hours reading drafts of what we wrote. His pep talks and nurturing support motivated us. He was wise, warm, funny, and incredibly generous. We owe Sam our heartfelt gratitude.

Thanks are also due to our literary agent, Elyse Cheney, and to Alex Jacobs at Elyse's firm, for their help. Elyse and Alex strategically spread the word about our project, and they patiently offered us guidance about the journey ahead.

We owe thanks to Bill Shinker, president and publisher of Gotham Books, for pulling the trigger on the start gun. Our talented book editor, Megan Newman, was our valuable literary *directeur sportif*. She helped to shape the finished work, and Gabrielle Campo, editorial assistant at Gotham Books, assisted us with a multitude of details in our final spurt.

Our newsroom bosses Joanna Chung and Gabriella Stern allowed us to take occasional vacation days from our day jobs, making it possible for us to travel to meet with sources and to write. We thank them for their patience and understanding. We are grateful to News Corp chief executive Robert Thomson, who allowed us to go forth with our idea for a book, and to several members of our family and friends, including Ellen Schultz, Geoffrey Blatt, Shelly Branch, and Jason Gay, who read drafts of our manuscript, offering suggestions for improvement.

Most of all, however, we are indebted to the many people who shared their insights, knowledge, memories, and personal photos.

We thank you for your time, your trust, and for your understanding that we couldn't write exactly the book that any of you might have liked. We are humbled by your generosity and we hope you recognize your contributions in making *Wheelmen* as fair and balanced as possible.

NOTES AND SOURCES

OUR APPROACH

Our account is based mainly on interviews with people who were directly involved in the events described. When possible, we searched for documents, such as e-mails, financial records, and photos, to back up their accounts. In many cases we are drawing from sworn statements given by people intimately familiar with the situation and from publicly available court documents.

When Jeff Novitzky of the Food and Drug Administration began investigating Armstrong and his former cycling team in the spring of 2010, he interviewed dozens of witnesses, imploring them to keep their discussions with him, as well as any testimony before the grand jury, secret. In February 2012, the US attorney in Los Angeles closed its criminal investigation. There was never a courtroom hearing or a single public document filed in relation to the case. In fact, the only official, public evidence that there ever was an investigation came in the form of a US Attorney's Office press release—announcing that it was over.

We pieced together many of the details of the investigation by, in large part, interviewing witnesses. We agreed to grant anonymity to those who could make a good case that it was warranted. Under federal law, witnesses in a grand jury investigation are free to talk about it, but their lawyers generally advise against it because they believe prosecutors and judges will punish their clients for going public.

In October 2012, the US Anti-Doping Agency released its "reasoned decision" in the Lance Armstrong case, together with supporting information. Its file is in excess of one thousand pages and includes sworn testimony from twenty-six people, including fifteen riders with knowledge of the US Postal Service team and its participants' doping activities. The documents can be found online at www .cyclinginvestigation.usada.org, and include documentary evidence of financial payments, e-mails, scientific data, and lab test results. The file also includes links to the hearing transcripts and exhibits in the 2005 arbitration case brought by Armstrong and Tailwind Sports against SCA Promotions. For some of our narrative, we consulted newspapers, magazines, and books to glean information about the personalities and points of view of characters. Many of the races and triathlons in this book were widely reported by dozens of publications, and video of the events exists in abundance on sites like YouTube. In addition to interviews with people who were there, we relied on these sources in order to recount what happened.

Abbreviations of Sources

AP—Associated Press
AAS—*Austin-American Statesman*
CN—Cycling News
DMN—*The Dallas Morning News*
HC—*Houston Chronicle*
IHT—*International Herald Tribune*
LAT—*Los Angeles Times*
NYT—*The New York Times*
VN—VeloNews
WSJ—*The Wall Street Journal*

Tailwind Sports, "due diligence contract binder," April 2002, showing team financial information, sponsor contracts, and riders' salaries for the US Postal Service team.

Tailwind Sports, board meeting presentation, 2/1/02, Scottsdale, Ariz., which includes Tailwind capitalization table, and fiscal 2002 financial results.

Books

Armstrong, Kristin. *Lance Armstrong*. Grosset & Dunlap, 2000.

Armstrong, Lance. *Comeback 2.0*. Touchstone, 2009.

Armstrong Lance, with Chris Carmichael. *The Lance Armstrong Performance Program*. Rodale, 2000.

Armstrong, Lance, with Sally Jenkins. *Every Second Counts*. Broadway Books, 2003.

Armstrong, Lance, with Sally Jenkins. *It's Not About the Bike*. G. P. Putnam's Sons, 2000.

Armstrong, Lance, with Graham Watson. *Images of a Champion*. Rodale, 2004.

Brandt, Richard L., with Thomas W. Weisel. *Capital Instincts*. John Wiley & Sons, 2003.

Bruyneel, Johan. *We Might As Well Win*. Mariner Books, 2009.

Burke, John. *One Last Great Thing*. Free Press, 2012.

Coyle, Daniel. *Lance Armstrong's War*. HarperCollins, 2005.

Drake, Geoff, with Jim Ochowicz. *Team 7-Eleven*. VeloPress, 2012.

Dzierzak, Lou. *The Evolution of American Bicycle Racing*. Falcon Guides, 2007.

Fainaru-Wada, Mark, and Lance Williams. *Game of Shadows*. Gotham Books, 2006.

Hamilton, Tyler, and Daniel Coyle. *The Secret Race*. Bantam Books, 2012.

Kelly, Linda Armstrong, with Joni Rodgers. *No Mountain High Enough*. Thorndike Press, 2005.

Landis, Floyd. *Positively False*. Gallery Books, 2007.

Millar, David. *Racing Through the Dark*. Touchstone, 2012.

Ungerleider, Steven. *Faust's Gold*. Thomas Dunne Books, 2001.

Walsh, David. *From Lance to Landis*. Ballantine Books, 2007.

Walsh, David. *Seven Deadly Sins*. Atria Books, 2013.

Wilcockson, John. *23 Days in July.* Da Capo Press, 2004.

Wilcockson, John. *Lance.* Da Capo Press, 2009.

ENDPAPER

The artwork, by Otto Steininger, presents a sampling of Armstrong's business and personal links from 1997 to fall 2012. Because it is intended to reflect past relationships, before Armstrong's downfall, some of the links shown may no longer be current, including the links between Lance Armstrong and the foundation, as well as the links between Armstrong and his sponsors. Although this illustration is based on our own reporting and research, it was inspired by the work of Dave Marsdin, who created a comprehensive network of Armstrong's business ties, and posted his rendering on the website Cyclismas in 2012.

Attempted donations to USADA: Interview with Tygart and former USADA CEO Terry Madden; in an interview with *60 Minutes Sports* that aired 1/9/13, Tygart said an individual "representing Armstrong tried to give USADA a large sum of money sometime in 2004." Tygart called the gesture "totally inappropriate." Armstrong, in his Oprah interview, denied that his representative made the offer to USADA, saying he "asked around" among his camp and "would know" if such an offer had been made. Bill Stapleton said he didn't recall making an offer. A spokeswoman for Amgen, which manufactures Epogen brand EPO, said, "To date, Amgen hasn't provided a direct donation to USADA."

Armstrong, Capital Sports & Entertainment, and Bruyneel ownership stakes in Tailwind Sports: A variety of news stories, including "Armstrong's Discovery Channel Team Closing Down," *USA Today*, 8/11/07, described Armstrong, Stapleton, and Bruyneel as part owners of Tailwind. According to Floyd Landis's second amended complaint for violations of the federal False Claims Act, Tailwind raised $2 million in May 2004, by issuing 1.25 million shares of its convertible Series C preferred stock at a purchase price of $1.60 and a par value of $0.001 per share. This transaction resulted in Armstrong, CSE, and Bruyneel becoming shareholders, with approximately 12 percent shares each in the company, while Weisel still remained chairman of the board. In sworn testimony, 9/1/05, Stapleton said CSE, of which Stapleton was an owner, had an 11.5 percent ownership stake in Tailwind and that Armstrong had been an owner of Tailwind since 2004, with an 11.5 percent stake. In 2004, CSE entered into a management contract with Tailwind, Stapleton said under oath. In sworn testimony, 11/30/05, Armstrong said under oath that he owned a small stake in Tailwind of "perhaps 10 percent." In an e-mail to the authors, Johan Bruyneel said that the characterization in Landis's lawsuit of his alleged ownership stake in Tailwind is "not accurate at all."

Ochowicz, a broker at Thomas Weisel Partners, managed personal assets for Verbruggen: Interview with Jim Ochowicz, 2013.

Lance Armstrong Foundation lobbied against USADA: Interview with spokesman for US Representative José Serrano (D., NY), who said the foundation lobbyist laid out his concerns about the fairness of USADA's process; a foundation spokeswoman called this description of the lobbyist's July 2012 visit "inaccurate," and said the purpose of the visit may have been misconstrued because the topic of USADA may have come up in passing.

Weisel, Garvey donors to USA Cycling: They donated money to the non-profit USA Cycling Development Foundation.

Consulting fees from USA Cycling to Tailwind: USA Cycling 990s 2001–2004; Tailwind Sports board meeting presentation.

Armstrong donated at least $125,000 to UCI: "McQuaid Reveals Armstrong Made Two Donations to the UCI," CN, 7/10/10.

Foundation, CSE shareholdings in Demand Media: Shareholder status as of the 1/11 Demand Media IPO. "Armstrong Foundation Makes Millions from IPO," AAS, 1/27/11.

Jeff Garvey shareholding in Mellow Johnny's bike shop: less than 10 percent as of 2013.

"Tiger" Williams, investor in Tailwind, former friend of Armstrong: Tailwind Sports, minutes of board meeting, 2/1/02; "For Cycling's Big Backers, Joy Ride Ends in Grief," WSJ, 12/18/10.

FRS links: "Armstrong's Business Brand, Bound Tight With His Charity," NYT, 1/13/13. A spokeswoman for the foundation said in response to the *New York Times* story that it "has never been the foundation's aim in any activity, including lobbying or marketing agreements, to shield, protect, or benefit" Armstrong in any way.

USA Cycling relationship with UCI and USOC (United States Olympic Committee): Per the Amateur Sports Act, the international sport hierarchy has the IOC on top; the UCI and the USOC on the next level; and USA Cycling one more level down with lines up to both the UCI and the USOC; interview with Steve Johnson, who said USA Cycling is "accountable" to both the UCI and the USOC.

Weisel donor to Landis's defense fund: Weisel chipped in $50,000 to the Floyd Fairness Fund, according to Landis, and as reported in "For Cycling's Big Backers," WSJ, 12/18/10.

Armstrong's stake in Trek: After his first Tour victory, Armstrong was given shares of Trek, in part to recognize his achievement coming off his battle with cancer and winning the race. His stock in Trek is less than one-third of 1 percent of Trek's outstanding stock. Armstrong didn't serve on Trek's board.

INTRODUCTION

Greg LeMond's salary: "LeMond Gets $5.7-Million Salary from French Team," AP, 8/31/89.

Armstrong's salary and bonuses: A $4.5 million base salary for 2004 was specified in a 10/10/00 letter agreement from Bill Stapleton to Mark Gorski, general manager of US Postal team; an addendum to that agreement specified that Armstrong would get a $10 million bonus if he won the Tour de France each year from 2001 to 2004.

Armstrong's endorsements*: Sports Illustrated* published a survey in May 2004 ranking Armstrong's $16.5 million in endorsements fourth among then-active US athletes, behind Tiger Woods at $70 million, LeBron James at $35 million, and Andre Agassi at $24.5 million.

Landis comes clean: "Cyclist Floyd Landis Admits Doping, Alleges Use by Armstrong and Others," posted 1:27 A.M, 5/20/10, WSJ.com.

CHAPTER ONE

Details of the Tour de France stage 13: Cycling News details on Tour de France race format: Tour de France website.

USPS's myopic focus on Armstrong: Interviews with teammates; *We Might As Well Win*, J. Bruyneel.

Landis's physiological ability: Interviews with Landis, corroborated by an account in *Lance Armstrong's War*, D. Coyle.

Landis's meeting with Novitzky and Tygart: Interview with Landis and one person familiar with the meeting.

The blood transfusions on the US Postal team: Interview with Landis; affidavit of George Hincapie to USADA.

Delivered the blood: Bruyneel's assistant Geert Duffeleer brought the blood to a hotel room where the team was staying, before a July 2004 transfusion, according to Landis's second amended complaint for violations of the federal False Claims Act, February 2013. We made a big effort to get in touch with Geert "Duffy" Duffeleer while we were reporting for *The Wall Street Journal*. We sent the *Journal* reporter John Miller to Duffy's house in Belgium. We also tried to contact him through the RadioShack squad, which declined to make him available for an interview. At the time, Duffy had a Twitter page, @chefduffy, but he has subsequently taken it down. We're not aware of any public statements he has made on the subject of doping.

All the riders got transfusions, including Armstrong: Landis's second amended complaint.

Bruyneel orchestrated transfusions: Landis's second amended complaint reads, "Mr. Landis and defendant Armstrong then lay on opposite sides of the bed and received reinfusions of a half liter of blood each while defendant Bruyneel sat in a chair watching and commented on how well the two were going to race the following day in the time trial." Bruyneel didn't respond to requests for comment. In a May 2010 press conference, after Landis's allegations became public, Bruyneel said, "I absolutely deny everything he said."

Philippe Maire: *The Secret Race*, T. Hamilton and D. Coyle. In 2012, Maire called the allegations against him "bullshit."

USPS Bike Sales for Cash: "The Case of the Missing Bikes," WSJ, 7/3/10.

Idyllwild: Interview with Landis in his cabin.

Landis's drinking: "Where is Floyd?" VN, 8/21/09.

CHAPTER TWO

Amateur Bicycle League of America registrations, 1973: Dzierak, *The Evolution of American Bicycle Racing*.

Borysewicz's cycling career in Poland: Interviews with Borysewicz and Mike Fraysse.

Borysewicz's training methods: Interviews with Borysewicz and Mike Fraysse.

LeMond and the Olympic boycott: Interviews with Greg LeMond.

The Russian doping effort: The belief that the Russians were doping before the 1980 Olympics and preparing with those methods for the 1984 Olympics was a widely held view among Americans involved in Olympic cycling. However, there are those who argue the Russian doping effort was overplayed.

Soviet cycling equipment: Interview with Fraysse and Borysewicz.

The early days of the 7-Eleven team: Interviews with Jim Ochowicz and Eric Heiden.

The Eddie B–Och rivalry: Though the 7-Eleven team was professional, amateur Olympic riders were allowed to join so long as their compensation stayed low enough that they did not have to declare themselves professionals.

Ed Burke's blood-boosting memo: The note, dated 9/30/83, says, "RE: Blood boosting; Olympic Games." Burke wrote: "Is it doping or illegal; my personal opinion and interpretation is no."

Brent Emery allegation of East German doping: Interview with Emery.

Leonard Harvey Nitz 1984 Olympics: In "Cyclist Says Blood Doping Recommended," 2/26/85, *The Bulletin*, Nitz said: "I did ride strong for five days. I usually ride strong for just three days."

The *Rolling Stone* leak: In interviews, Borysewicz and Fraysse said they suspect Sheila Young Ochowicz was behind the leak to *Rolling Stone*. But according to articles in *The Milwaukee Journal*—"Politics Play Part in Cycling Story," 2/20/85, and "Blood-Boosting Investigation Satisfies Nobody," 2/22/85—many at the time blamed Rob Lea, then president of the US Cycling Federation's executive board. *Milwaukee Journal* reporter Gary Van Sickle wrote, for instance, that "critics" of Jim and Sheila Ochowicz "say Lea was merely doing their bidding and that they are trying to take control of the federation and get top positions for themselves and Roger Young, Sheila's brother and the trainer for 7-Eleven," one of the stories noted. Jim told the newspaper that the allegation was "ridiculous," and Lea denied he was working with Jim or Sheila. Sheila at the time served on the competition committee of the cycling federation board. Van Sickle mentioned the friction between Jim Ochowicz and Borysewicz, describing them as "enemies."

Thom Weisel approaching Eddie B in 1985: Interviews with Fraysse, Borysewicz, and Weisel.

Thom Weisel's childhood and speed skating career: Interviews with Weisel; *Capital Instincts*, R. Brandt and T. Weisel.

CHAPTER THREE

Lance Armstrong competing in IronKids National Championship: "Iron Kids Can Run, Swim, Bike to Prizes," HC, 8/22/85.

Terry Armstrong bet with another father: *Lance*, J. Wilcockson.

Lance's relationships with Terry and Linda: Interviews with Scott Eder, Rick Crawford, John Boggan, Adam Wilk; *No Mountain High Enough*, L. Armstrong Kelly.

Linda Mooneyham's alcoholic father: *No Mountain High Enough*, L. Armstrong Kelly.

Terry hit Lance with a paddle: *Lance*, J.: Wilcockson; *No Mountain High Enough*, L. Armstrong Kelly; *It's Not About the Bike*, L. Armstrong.

Terry love notes to another woman: *It's Not About the Bike*, L. Armstrong.

Linda doctored birth certificate: Interview with Jim Woodman and one other triathlon promoter who also remembers the doctored document; *No Mountain High Enough*, L. Armstrong Kelly.

Rick Crawford meeting: Interview with Crawford and Scott Eder.

Lance lost his sponsorship deal with Kestrel: Interview with Eder, who recalls that the footage was shown on an ESPN program featuring highlights from the race.

Oakley sponsorship: Oakley provided him with a dozen pair of shades every quarter, and about $2,500 a year, according to our interview with former Oakley CEO Michael Parnell.

Crawford heard Lance callously teasing competitors: Interview with Crawford.

Lance's angry response to Terry: Woodman, Eder, Crawford, Wilk, Boggan interviews.

Lance thought Terry was emotionally abusive: Interview with a person familiar with Lance.

Lance's VO$_2$ test: Interview with Eder.

Bending Oaks High School's heroin and suicide problem: *It's Not About the Bike*, L. Armstrong.

High speed chase in Camaro: Boggan, Wilk interviews; *Lance*, J. Wilcockson.

Eddie B discovers Lance: Interviews with Borysewicz and Fraysse.

Weisel's explosive temper: Interview with Paul Willerton.

Lance refused to work on Reiss's behalf: *Lance*, J. Wilcockson; *It's Not About the Bike*, L. Armstrong.

CHAPTER FOUR
_____

Ochowicz's Motorola team signing: Interviews with Ochowicz and Sheila Griffin.

The South Club Inc. Ochowicz set up the South Club Inc. as a nonstock corporation, according to articles of incorporation and other documents obtained from the Wisconsin Department of Financial Institutions. The South Club Inc. filed its first annual report in 1986, the documents show, and the state agency also has annual reports from 1987 to 1989, from 1994 to 2001, and from 2003. The records show a notice of administrative dissolution.

Armstrong's conversation with Weisel: *Capital Instincts*, R. Brandt and T. Weisel; interviews with Weisel.

Triple Crown payoff: Testimony of Stephen Swart during the SCA arbitration and his signed affidavit in the USADA report. An interview with Frankie Andreu. One other person directly involved in the transaction who did not want his name used confirmed that the payoff did, indeed, occur.

The pizza restaurant incident: Interview with Betsy Andreu.

Armstrong's jealousy of Hampsten: Interview with Paul Sherwen, 2013.

Linda Armstrong's visit to Minnesota with the LeMonds: Interview with Greg and Kathy LeMond.

Lance's relationship with Sonni and Danielle: Interviews with Sonni Evans and Danielle Overgaag.

Lance's offer to rent the LeMonds' house in Belgium: Interview with Greg and Kathy LeMond.

Armstrong urging team to dope in 1995: Affidavits of George Hincapie and Frankie Andreu for the USADA report. Interview with Stephen Swart.

EPO as "Edgar Allan Poe": Interviews with riders and the USADA report.

Massimo Testa's hematocrit testing during the 1995 Tour: Interview with Swart.

Ferrari's bank records: USADA report.

Ferrari's training regimen: Explained by Ferrari on his website and on Velo-News diaries he wrote for the cycling website. These were backed up by testimony from riders in the USADA report and in interviews with *The Wall Street Journal.*

CHAPTER FIVE

Mark Gorski's financial career: "He's Back in Business: Careers: Cycling Gold Medalist Mark Gorski Switches Gears and Starts a New Career," LAT, 6/24/90.

Gorski organizing meet with the Soviets: "A Chance This Time: For Berryman, the Races with the Soviets Are Critical," LAT, 8/3/87.

Gorski hiring at USA Cycling: "Gorski Knows He Made the Right Move," HC, 2/11/93; R. Brandt and T. Weisel; *Capital Instincts,* interview with Weisel.

Steve Disson's cycling and sports marketing business: Interviews with Steve Disson.

Meeting between Loren Smith, Weisel, and Gorski: Interviews with Smith.

Gorski's deal with LeMond: Based on extensive and detailed interviews with Greg LeMond. Gorski said the deal was never final and LeMond was paid appropriately.

Postal Service's international marketing efforts: Interviews with Loren Smith.

The Tour de France had an "open slot" for an American team: "Postal Team Director Eyes '97 Tour de France," *Worcester Telegram & Gazette,* 7/7/96.

"Hamilton's Success Has Gone in Cycles. He's Hoping to Ride High in Tour de France," *The Boston Globe*, 6/5/97.

Weisel hearing from Ochowicz about Armstrong's attitude on Motorola: Interview with Weisel, 2008.

Tension between Gorski and Eddie B: Interviews with Borysewicz, Weisel, and former Motorola riders.

Armstrong's early cancer symptoms: *It's Not About the Bike,* L. Armstrong.

Lance's cancer treatments: *It's Not About the Bike,* L. Armstrong; *No Mountain High Enough,* L. Armstrong Kelly.

Hospital room scene: Interviews with Betsy and Frankie Andreu, their sworn affidavits from the USADA report, and their testimony from the SCA arbitration.

Armstrong's 1996 discussion of doping with Jim Woodman: Interview with Woodman in 2012.

Early days of the Lance Armstrong Foundation: Interviews with Chris Brewer, John Korioth, Greg LeMond, Steve Whisnant.

Eddie B's ideas about Gorski, the USPS team, and capitalism: Interviews with Borysewicz.

Gorski's hiring of Pedro Celaya: Interview with Scott Mercier. In an interview, Eddie B remembered Gorski hiring Celaya.

Steve Whisnant's conversation with Jeff Garvey: Interview with Whisnant.

Eddie B's comment about Armstrong's health: In interviews, Eddie was vague about his knowledge of Armstrong's performance-enhancing drugs. His son, Eddie Borysewicz Jr., told us that his father was concerned about performance-enhancing drugs causing Armstrong's cancer to come back.

Armstrong's hematocrit tests and levels after his comeback from cancer: We reviewed a spreadsheet that became part of the evidence in Michele Ferrari's doping trial in 2001. Ferrari accidentally sent an un-redacted spreadsheet containing the names of riders and dates of their hematocrit tests to another doctor. The purpose of the spreadsheet was to show the effects of EPO on training and hematocrit.

CHAPTER SIX

Armstrong's manager pulling him off women as a teenager: A former handler who wishes to remain anonymous.

Lance's FedEx moniker: *It's Not About the Bike*, L. Armstrong.

The 1998 Paris-Nice debacle: "Armstrong Leaves European Racing Circuit," AP, 3/18/98; "Armstrong Weary of Life on the Road," AP, 3/20/98; "Armstrong Dispels Retirement Fears—Cycling," *The Times* of London, 3/24/98. According to the *Times* article, Armstrong denied a dispute with the team over tactics, but was quoted second-guessing the team's tactics.

Heated e-mail exchange between Frankie Andreu and Lance Armstrong: USADA report.

Emma O'Reilly's encounter with customs agents; USPS reaction to Festina affair: Affidavits of Emma O'Reilly and George Hincapie in the USADA Report.

Willy Voet saga and the Festina affair: "Tour Slowdown/Riders Protest Over Scandal," *Daily Telegraph*, 7/25/98; "Drugs Scandal Whittles Down Tour de France," Agence France-Presse, 7/30/98.

Pepe Martí and Garcia del Moral's EPO deliveries: Affidavits of Hamilton, Vaughters, Vande Velde, in the USADA case. Garcia del Moral gave Frankie Andreu EPO injections, according to Andreu and Hincapie, and injections of Actovegin and cortisone to Vande Velde, according to Vande Velde. In a June 2012 interview with *The Wall Street Journal*, del Moral denied providing banned drugs or performing illegal procedures on athletes. Del Moral did not contest USADA's changes. Pepe Martí is fighting USADA's doping case.

John visibly drunk at Lance's rehearsal dinner: In her book, *No Mountain High Enough*, Linda Armstrong Kelly describes the evening. John Walling was her husband at the time of Lance's wedding. He didn't return messages seeking comment.

The butter code name for EPO: Affidavit of Jonathan Vaughters in the USADA report.

The 50 percent rule: In a 1/12/13 interview with *Vrij Nederland* magazine, Verbruggen said that some team directors wanted a stricter approach and preferred 47 percent. But UCI lawyers and other experts advised against that approach, because a section of the population has a naturally higher hematocrit level.

Advanced warnings of drug tests: Several former riders on the USPS said they would often be told by the team when surprise drug tests were about to happen. Sometimes, the warnings came a day or so in advance. Other times, the warnings gave the team just 15 or 20 minutes to prepare.

Vaughters run-in with Armstrong during the 1998 Vuelta a España: Vaughters affidavit to USADA.

Armstrong and Bruyneel meeting at 1998 Vuelta: *We Might As Well Win*, J. Bruyneel.

Ferrari's magic wattage number: Ferrari gave numerous interviews and wrote blog entries for Cycling News during the period he was training Armstrong. He explained his wattage per kilogram methodology, as well "vertical ascent per minute." These measurements became common terms in the hard-core cycling community.

Early training in the mountains with Bruyneel: *We Might As Well Win*, J. Bruyneel.

The plan to use EPO in the 1999 Tour de France: The Tyler Hamilton affidavit to USADA; interviews with Frankie and Betsy Andreu.

Celaya's stinginess with drugs: Jonathan Vaughters affidavit to USADA.

Celaya's experimentation with drugs: Several interviews with former USPS riders, and affidavits in the USADA report.

LeMond's point of view of the 1999 Tour de France: Interviews with LeMond.

Betsy Andreu's concern after the Sestriere stage: Interview with Betsy.

Giving up EPO in the last week of the 1999 Tour de France: Tyler Hamilton affidavit to USADA.

The UCI's pressure to test for corticosteroids: Interview with David Howman of the World Anti-Doping Agency.

The plan to come up with a backdated prescription for saddle sore cream: Sworn testimony of Emma O'Reilly in SCA case 1/31/06. "Will Thomas Weisel, Who Owns Lance Armstrong's U.S. Postal Team, Get Charged with Fraud?" *Bloomberg Businessweek*, 1/15/13. Weisel had "no contemporaneous knowledge" that Armstrong was doping, Weisel's lawyer said.

Samuel Abt: Shortly after Armstrong was stripped of his titles by USADA, Abt wrote that he didn't pursue the doping story because he didn't view that as his job as a sports writer. "Rip Lance Time," NYT, 8/26/13.

CHAPTER SEVEN

The post-Tour party in 1999: This scene was pieced together from several articles, videos of the event, and interviews with people in attendance.

The "Just Do It" commercial: The commercial, which featured Armstrong dispelling rumors that he used performance-enhancing drugs, would come back to bite him—and Nike—after his admission to doping.

Individual deals, list and value: "Armstrong Rolls to Market Gold," *USA Today*, 5/4/00.

Steve Disson's departure: Interview with Disson.

The creation of Tailwind Sports: According to the government's amended complaint in the Landis whistle-blower suit, the life of Tailwind lasted from June 25, 2002, until December 31, 2007, when it filed a certificate of dissolution with the secretary of state of Delaware. The lawsuit notes, "Delaware law provides for the continuation of corporations for a period of three years after their dissolution, however, for the purpose of prosecuting and defending lawsuits."

The perks of being a Tailwind investor: Interviews with Harvey Schiller, Richard Cashin, and other investors.

The value of the USPS sponsorship deal: According to the government's amended complaint in the whistle-blower lawsuit, Tailwind collected around $40 million from 1998 to 20004.

Tiger Williams and his investment: Tailwind Sports, board meeting presentation, 2/1/02; people familiar with his thinking.

Details of Ochowicz's management of Verbruggen's money: Interviews with Ochowicz and a former UCI employee with knowledge of the matter; "New Twist in Armstrong Saga," WSJ, 1/17/13. Ochowicz, who was hired by Thomas Weisel Partners in 2001, confirmed in an interview that Weisel's firm managed the Verbruggen brokerage account. "There was no hanky-panky," he said, adding that Weisel didn't have "direct access" to Verbruggen's account. He declined to say how much money was in Verbruggen's account. He added: "I have no recollection of talking about Hein's accounts with Thom Weisel." Ochowicz said he traveled to UCI's Aigle, Switzerland, headquarters "three times in my life." Verbruggen and Ochowicz often talked about the investments with Weisel's firm, according to a person familiar with the meetings. In interviews with us, as well as Dutch magazine *Vrij Nederland*, Verbruggen said he didn't personally know Weisel.

USADA view that the financial relationship was a conflict of interest: Interview in January 2013 with Tygart, who said: "To have the head of the sport, who's responsible for enforcing anti-doping rules, in business with the owner of the team that won seven straight Tours de France in violation of those rules—it certainly stinks to high heaven, particularly now, given what's been exposed that happened under [Verbruggen's] watch."

CHAPTER EIGHT

Hiring of Viatcheslav Ekimov: Ekimov was a star in cycling circles when Gorski was competing in the 1980s and had been a major competitor of Armstrong's during the Tour DuPont in the 1990s. Armstrong needed veterans like Ekimov around to show the Americans—even him—how the professional circuit worked. Despite Armstrong's success, he was still very much a guest in a foreign sport.

The development of the EPO test in 2000: Affidavit of Jonathan Vaughters; interviews with Floyd Landis. Landis explains in his second amended complaint in the whistle-blower lawsuit that "Armstrong also explained to Mr. Landis the evolution of EPO testing and how transfusions were now necessary due to the new test, *i.e.*, EPO could no longer be used during races in large quantities."

Kristin's complicity in the doping: Jonathan Vaughters swore under oath that she knew and even participated in the program. In Landis's second amended complaint in his whistle-blower suit, the complaint says Lance "gave him a package of 2.5 ml testosterone patches in front of Mr. Armstrong's wife at the time, Kirsten Armstrong [*sic*]." Later, the lawsuit says that in September 2003, Landis ran into Lance, Kristin, and their three children in Girona. "Armstrong then handed Mr. Landis a box of EPO in full view of his wife and three children."

Encounters with drug testers: *Every Second Counts*, L. Armstrong. Dialogue according to Armstrong.

The 2000 blood transfusion: Affidavit of Tyler Hamilton to USADA.

The 2000 Tour de France: Pieced together from CN live blogs, video of the races, and news articles.

LeMond's reaction to the Actovegin controversy: Interview with LeMond. Julien de Vriese has denied having any knowledge of doping on the U.S. Postal team.

The 2001 EPO test: A person with direct knowledge of the test and an interview with Travis Tygart. Since 2001, the practice of drug testing has changed. Now, every time an athlete tests positive on a laboratory test, the World Anti-Doping Agency is notified independently. In theory, WADA is supposed to keep track of the number of positive tests announced by each signatory, and make sure they match with the numbers reported by the laboratories.

Steve Whisnant and the Lance Armstrong Foundation: Interviews with Whisnant.

Mark Gorski's conversation with Jonathan Vaughters about Actovegin and mad cow disease: Interview with Vaughters. Gorski says he does not remember the phone call.

E-mails between Haven Hamilton and Betsy Andreu: Andreu mailed her old, broken laptop to us in 2011. In exchange for extracting the data from the hard drive, she allowed us to use information in her e-mail inbox for our reporting.

Lance's relationship with John Korioth: Interviews with Korioth.

Landis's introduction to the US Postal team: Interviews with Landis.

The Yellow Rose: Landis described the scene at the Yellow Rose and party at Stapleton's office in detail, and his account was corroborated by other riders who were there. "Armstrong had no contact with strippers or cocaine," his lawyer, Tim Herman, told us in July 2010. "Blood Brothers," WSJ, 7/2/10.

CHAPTER NINE

Landis's VO$_2$ max test: Interview with Landis.

Landis training with Armstrong in St. Moritz in summer 2002: Interview with Landis.

Landis as the chief domestique at the 2002 Dauphiné: Interview with Landis.

Bruyneel's role in Landis's first doping experience. Landis's second amended complaint in his whistle-blower lawsuit against Lance, Bruyneel, et al. "Mr. Landis was approached by Mr. Bruyneel in his hotel room in Grenoble, France. . . . Armstrong would give him some testosterone patches. . . . 'Dr. Ferrari' would help him extract a half liter of blood to be reinfused during the Tour de France."

Description of the 2002 Tour de France: CN live blogs and other news stories.

Floyd Landis: Much of this chapter, at least where it concerns Landis, came from extensive interviews with him in the spring and summer of 2010. Where the facts were contentious, we made efforts to corroborate them with other sources.

Lance's suspicious test in the 2001 Tour de Suisse: In an interview, Verbruggen described the test finding as "suspicious." In his federal whistle-blower lawsuit and USADA affidavit, and an interview, Landis said Armstrong told him the test result was positive. Armstrong and Verbruggen both deny that there was ever a payoff or a cover-up of a positive test. In a 1/12/13 interview with *Vrij Nederland* magazine, Verbruggen said UCI doctor Mario Zorzoli and Lon Schattenberg, a member of the UCI anti-doping committee, contacted Lance, who immediately tried to bluff his way out. "He said that the test was faulty. He didn't use doping. The test was shit," Verbruggen said.

Lance's relationships with his mother and J.T. Neal: Interviews with several friends and ex-girlfriends of Armstrong's and a person familiar with Neal's thinking; some aspects of Armstrong's relationship with Neal were covered in *Images of a Champion*, Armstrong's book with Graham Watson. In *No Mountain High Enough*, Armstrong's mother describes her conversations with Neal about Armstrong.

Mike Anderson's relationship with Armstrong: Interview with Anderson.

Landis's bike crash: Interview with Landis; *Positively False*, F. Landis.

Landis's surgery: Interview with Landis.

Blood transfusions in Girona, Spain: Interviews with Landis and the affidavit of George Hincapie to USADA.

David Walsh's book: Interviews with Swart, Betsy and Frankie Andreu, O'Reilly, Walsh; and *Seven Deadly Sins*, D. Walsh.

E-mails between Andreu and Armstrong in the 2003 Tour de France: Provided by Betsy Andreu, cited in the USADA report.

The 2003 Tour de France: CN live blog, news clips, and videos.

CHAPTER TEN
———————

Armstrong's meeting with equipment sponsors at the Standard Hotel in 2004: Interview in 2009 with Toshi Corbet.

Walsh's call to Andreu: Interviews with the Andreus and e-mails between the Andreus and Armstrong at the time; interview with Walsh.

Andreu-Armstrong e-mails about the David Walsh book: E-mails were provided to us by the Andreus and later included in the USADA report.

Emma O'Reilly's arrangement with David Walsh: Walsh asked O'Reilly to fact-check a 47,000-word transcript and parts of his manuscript. After she spent a considerable amount of time fact-checking, Walsh and his coauthor, Pierre Ballester, agreed to pay O'Reilly a percentage of proceeds from the book, which came out to 5,000 British pounds for the work. In addition, Walsh explained to O'Reilly that if she were sued, she would be provided with legal protection from the publisher.

The Daniel Coyle book: According to Landis, Coyle eventually fell out of favor with Armstrong, who instructed Landis to stop providing access to Coyle. Landis, however, ignored Armstrong's prohibition. During his reporting, Coyle became friends with Tyler Hamilton, whose autobiography he would later coauthor.

Landis's outburst and subsequent conflict with Bruyneel and Duffy over the bike parts: Interview with Landis and another person who witnessed many of the events. Trek confirmed that it had become concerned about the underground bike sales in Europe. A spokesman for Trek says it was unaware of doping on the team. Its concern about the bike sales pertained to its belief that the sales undermined Trek's business in Belgium by taking sales away from bike dealerships.

The Andreu tape recording of Stapleton and Knaggs during the 2004 Tour: A transcript of the audio tape was included in the USADA report.

Crow's flight to Belgium for the blood transfusion: A person familiar with the matter.

Simeoni's conflict with Armstrong: Simeoni's affidavit in the USADA report.

Simeoni's final-day attack: Live blog on CN.

Floyd's conversation with Tiger Williams after the 2004 Tour: Interview with Landis; a person familiar with the matter.

Landis's contract negotiations with Lance, Stapleton, and Ochowicz's involvement with his Phonak negotiation: Interview with Landis in 2010.

Landis's magic pill at the 2004 Vuelta: Interview with a rider familiar with the matter and later confirmed by Landis.

Hamilton's positive test in 2004: Interviews with people close to Hamilton; *The Secret Race*, T. Hamilton and D. Coyle.

SCA and Bob Hamman's inquiry into doping: Interviews with Bob Hamman and Jeff Tillotson.

Trek's response to LeMond and efforts to purchase Merckx bikes: Internal Trek documents made public in the Trek-LeMond lawsuit.

CHAPTER ELEVEN

American riders and their falling-out with Armstrong: Tyler Hamilton's tension with Armstrong was more personal than professional. Hamilton told people he thought Armstrong was hitting on his wife. Armstrong would later go on a date with Haven after their divorce. Leipheimer and Zabriskie both left US Postal for largely contractual reasons, but Armstrong viewed anyone who left the team as a traitor. Kevin Livingston fell into that category, but had retired.

Armstrong's taunt of Landis at the Tour de Georgia: CN and an interview with Landis.

Zabriskie's initiation into the doping culture: USADA report.

Zabriskie's crash and Armstrong's refusal to wear yellow: CN live blog, video of the race.

Hincapie's stage win: Video of the race, CN live blog.

Betsy's relationship with Hamman and the involvement of Stephanie McIlvain: Interview with Andreu in 2013.

Tillotson's mind-set during his deposition of Armstrong: Interview with Tillotson, 2013.

The SCA arbitration and hearings, Betsy's deposition: Transcripts of the testimony and interviews with Tillotson.

Vrijman's relationship with Verbruggen: Verbruggen denies he was friends with Vrijman and says they were merely acquaintances. Paul Scholten, another lawyer who worked with Vrijman on the report, said Verbruggen and Vrijman were friends.

The *Penthouse* model at the football game: Interview with Tillotson.

Andy Rihs's involvement in the Phonak team's doping program: Interviews with Landis. In 2010, Rihs denied any knowledge of doping on the team through a spokesman. Rihs said in a July 2011 interview with *The Australian*: "I still try not to think about it anymore. It is a very sad story. Nobody wanted to believe what happened with Landis."

The 2006 Tour de France: Videos of the race, CN live blogs, interviews with Landis.

Armstrong's offer of $20,000 to work against Landis: Landis told us this in an interview, and one of Landis's teammates confirmed that Landis had mentioned it during the 2006 race. However, the riders who Landis says approached him said they did not remember any such offer.

Armstrong's call with advice to Landis: Interview with Landis.

Vaughters early conversations with Landis: Interviews with Landis and Vaughters.

Landis's meeting with Ochowicz and the threats of extortion: Interview with Landis in 2010. Landis's second amended complaint also describes the scene. "The two met at Sheryl Crow's house in California. . . . Landis openly referenced the doping program of the US Postal Service team. . . . Mr. Ocho-wicz did not express any surprise regarding Mr. Landis' references to doping on the USPS team, implicitly indicating he already was aware of the fact."

The help from Armstrong's wealthy backers: Interviews with Landis and several of the backers who helped out. Landis claims that many of the backers knew there was rampant doping on the Postal team, but the backers deny any direct knowledge of doping.

CHAPTER TWELVE

Lance's attempt to purchase the Tour de France: "Lance's Plan for France," WSJ, 3/27/09.

Amaury's feud with the UCI: Interview with people directly involved in the feud.

Trek-LeMond lawsuit: "Feud Sends Cycling World Spinning," WSJ, 6/10/09.

Armstrong enlisting public strategies: Public Strategies was listed as the creator of a Trek slide show shown to bike dealers that attempted to discredit LeMond. Later, Trek hired Public Strategies to conduct PR work.

Armstrong's work with Don Catlin: We attended the announcement of this testing program at the Clinton Global Initiative in New York City in 2008.

The plasticizer plot: Two people familiar with the plan; "Officials Pursued Armstrong for Years," WSJ, 8/25/12.

CHAPTER THIRTEEN

Floyd's admissions to some of his wealthy backers: Interviews with Landis and other people familiar with the matter.

Landis's conversation with Steve Johnson in 2008: Interview with Landis. Steve Johnson has said he had no knowledge of doping in the sport prior to Landis's admission.

Baker's alleged hacking: Baker said that he received the documents from an anonymous source. Instead of officially releasing the documents to the media, Baker says he sent the e-mails from an anonymous account he created. The e-mail was easily traced back to his IP address. Baker and Landis were both convicted of hacking in France and handed down a suspended prison sentence.

Smashing the Tour de France trophy: Interview with Landis and Will Geoghegan.

Falling-out between Williams and Armstrong: "For Cycling's Backers, Joyride Ends in Grief," WSJ, 12/18/10.

Armstrong's accusation of extortion: Interviews with Landis, Will Geoghegan, and members of the Bahati team management, as well as e-mails between Arnie Baker and Armstrong about their conversations.

Encounter between Tygart and Vaughters on the chairlift: Interviews with Vaughters and Tygart.

Tygart's missed warning signs: Interview with Tygart. In addition, Betsy Andreu recalls that after Frankie Andreu admitted to his own doping, Tygart contacted him, but didn't ask him for information about Armstrong. Instead, Tygart asked about Landis. Betsy was annoyed. Why was Tygart so myopically focused on Landis, she wondered.

Jeff Novitzky and BALCO: *Game of Shadows*, Fainaru-Wada and Williams.

CHAPTER FOURTEEN

Floyd's preparation to wear a wire: Interview with Landis.

The case against Michael Ball: Two people familiar with the matter.

Zabriskie's testimony on May 25: A person familiar with the matter.

Novitzky's subpoenas in the spring and summer of 2010: In some cases, people familiar with the matter told us under condition of anonymity, either because they were afraid of retribution for talking with us, or because it could jeopardize their careers. In other cases, such as that of Tyler Hamilton, riders themselves were open about their subpoenas and testimony.

Doping itself is not a crime in the United States: The Food, Drug, and Cosmetic Act does criminalize certain things related to doping. Transporting misbranded drugs, or drugs that have adulterated substances in them, can be violations of the act.

Major sponsor contracts included clauses that prohibited the team from doping: These contracts didn't include any language spelling out to the athletes that if they had doped, they could be prosecuted for fraud.

LeMond's subpoena: Interview with Greg LeMond.

Michael Barry's allegation of witness tampering: Barry's 2012 USADA affidavit; interview with Barry in 2013.

Rick Crawford's reaction to the investigation and interaction with Armstrong: Interview with Crawford.

Novitzky and the prosecutors on the closing of the investigation: People familiar with their thinking. "US Probe of Armstrong Dropped in Rare Fashion," *Daily Journal*, 2/6/12. Doug Miller told the reporter: "More so than ever in my career, I would like to comment. However, I cannot."

Zabriskie's interview with USADA: Interview with Bill Bock. According to Bock, USADA had been planning on moving forward with its investigation, regardless of the outcome of the criminal investigation. USADA wanted to bring a case against Armstrong while at least some of his Tour de France victories were still within the eight year statute of limitations.

CHAPTER FIFTEEN

The whistle-blower subpoena: Court documents; people familiar with the matter.

Bock's phone call to Levinstein: People familiar with the matter.

Armstrong's point of view on USADA's allegations: A person close to Armstrong.

The views of Armstrong's legal team: In their lawsuit against USADA on July 9, 2012, Herman, Levinstein, and Luskin wrote that Tygart and No-vitzky share an "obsession" with nailing Armstrong, simply because he's a "big fish." They pointed to Armstrong's "500–600" passed drug tests. "In its mul-timillion dollar zeal to 'get' Armstrong, USADA has been unable to turn up a single positive drug test from Mr. Armstrong," they wrote. They called USADA's arbitration process a "kangaroo court" and said that if Armstrong were given a fair proceeding, the allegations "against Mr. Armstrong would be revealed as unfounded."

Armstrong's point of view in fighting USADA and filing the lawsuit: A person familiar with Armstrong's thinking.

Livestrong's lobbying effort: "Livestrong Lobbyist's Agenda Is Questioned," WSJ, 7/16/13.

Lance's personal benefits at Livestrong events: "The Line Between Cause and Cult: Inside Livestrong," Roopstigo, 11/21/2012.

Clark Calvin Griffith's case: "Ex-Law Professor, 70, Sentenced for Indecent Exposure; Claims Student, 24, Victimized Him," *St. Paul Pioneer Press*, 7/26/12.

Paul Willerton's reaction to Armstrong: Interview with Willerton.

CHAPTER SIXTEEN

Nike dropped Armstrong: Nike wouldn't comment on the circumstances of the firing.

Armstrong and his attorneys' point of view on the SCA suit and the whistle-blower case: Armstrong's attorneys have been outspoken in public about their views on the Landis whistle-blower suit. Specifically, they say that the USPS was not harmed, and therefore any alleged false claims committed by the managers of the USPS team are null and void.

Lance's meeting with USADA: Former Colorado governor Bill Ritter confirmed the meeting, which took place at his office, and several others with direct and detailed knowledge about the meeting told us what took place.

USADA's agreement to write a letter to DOJ on the whistle-blower suit: This was discussed at the meeting in Colorado. One person with knowledge of the inner workings of USADA told us Tygart had been prepared to send such a letter.

Adam Wilk and the Nike swag: Interview with Wilk.

Armstrong's legal team's response to the Oprah interview idea: Two people who know Lance Armstrong explained that his legal team had issues with the Oprah interview. Two other people, who had direct dealings with some of Armstrong's attorneys, also corroborated this fact.

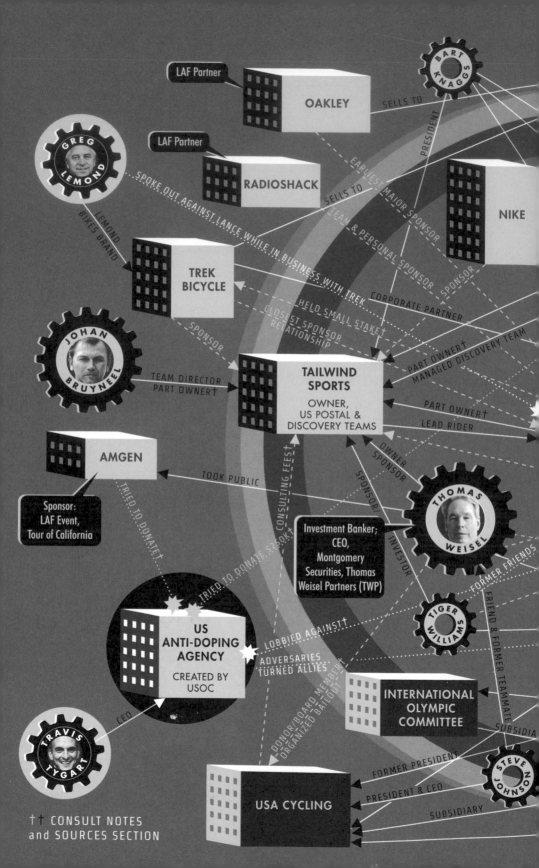